BARRIOS and
BORDERLANDS

BARRIOS and BORDERLANDS

Cultures of Latinos and Latinas in the United States

DENIS LYNN DALY HEYCK

ROUTLEDGE
New York • London

Published in 1994 by
Routledge
29 West 35th Street
New York, NY 10001

Published in Great Britain by
Routledge
11 New Fetter Lane
London EC4P 4EE

Library of Congress Cataloging-in-Publication Data

Barrios and borderlands : cultures of Latinos & Latinas in the United States /
    [edited by] Denis Lynn Daly Heyck.
        p. cm.
    Includes bibliographical references (p.) and index.
    ISBN 0-415-90394-7
    ISBN 0-415-90395-5 (pbk.)
    1. American literature—Hispanic American authors.   2. Hispanic Americans
—Literary collections.   3. Hispanic Americans—civilization.   I. Heyck, Denis
Lynn Daly.   II. Title: Barrios and borderlands.
PS508.H57B37   1994
810.8′0868—dc30   94-4773
                                                               CIP

British Library Cataloging-in-Publication also available.

Contents

Preface

The purpose of this anthology is to paint a portrait of the rich, complex, and fascinating mixture of Latino cultures in the United States today. It departs from the standard literary or political anthologies, and from those that treat only one Latino ethnic population, by being broadly inclusive in terms of genre, discipline, and ethnicity. Thus this book is intended for readers interested in any or all of the major aspects of Latino cultures—literature, cultural anthropology, ethnography, religion, the arts, community studies, and (im)migration studies. I hope that any reader can learn from the book, if only by dipping and sampling. However, I have prepared it very much with the teacher in mind, in hope that it will stimulate lively class discussions.

Barrios and Borderlands is organized around six central cultural themes: family, religion, community, the arts, (im)migration and exile, and cultural identity. My judgment is simply that if readers understand these themes, they will have a good sense of the Latino cultures in all their richness and fluidity. Each chapter contains diverse types of readings that shed light on its theme from a variety of different angles. Hence the readings include short stories, poems, essays, excerpts from novels, a play, photographs, and even a few songs and recipes. A special feature of this anthology is the inclusion of interviews and oral histories of Latinos from diverse walks of life and geographical areas. A migrant worker from the orange groves of Florida; an ethnomusicologist from northern New Mexico; a community organizer in the *maquiladoras*, or foreign-owned assembly plants, that line the border; a refugee from Central America; a muralist from Los Angeles; a museum director from Chicago; and a Spanish-language television executive from Chile are some of those whose stories enrich this anthology.

The title *Barrios and Borderlands* is intended to suggest not only the historical grounding and broad scope of the anthologized materials, but also the extensive presence of the Latino populations in urban and rural areas throughout the United States today. The term "borders" implies more than geographical boundaries between countries; it also implies a critique of arbitrary barriers erected to separate cultures, language groups, races, sexes, and economic and political groups. Explicitly and implicitly, the chapter readings question the functions and effects of borders in both the limited and broader meanings of the word.

This work both highlights the diversity of Latino cultural expressions and points out the distinctive features of the three major Latino populations—Mexican, Puerto Rican, and Cuban. Each of the main groups has

developed along very particular lines, so that what is true for Puerto Ricans, for example, may not be at all true for Cubans. Given their very different histories, not all Latinos fit comfortably under the umbrella term "Latino." "Hispanic" is the term of choice of the United States government, non-Hispanics, and some Hispanics. Despite the "official" usage, I have chosen "Latino" because it is more inclusive —incorporating Brazilians, for example—and because more people refer to themselves as "Latinos" than refer to themselves as "Hispanics." However, much more appropriate than either "Hispanic" or "Latino" would be *mexicanos, puertorriqueños,* or *cubanos,* for this is how people are most apt to describe themselves. A recent survey, for example, indicates that 86 percent of Mexican, 85 percent of Puerto Rican, and 83 percent of Cuban immigrants polled prefer to be called *mexicano, puertorriqueño,* or *cubano,* respectively. That is not surprising. What is remarkable are the high percentages of those who were born in the United States but who *still* wish to be called *mexicano, puertorriqueño,* or *cubano*— 62 percent of Mexican Americans, 57 percent of Puerto Ricans, and 41 percent of Cuban Americans.[1]

However, in order to communicate, we must be able to generalize, or we run the risk of becoming like the famous Argentine writer Jorge Luis Borges's character Funes in the story "Funes el memorioso," who could describe precisely and completely each leaf on the tree outside his window, but who was unable to conceptualize the tree as a whole. To Borges, because

Funes was incapable of generalizing, he was incapable of thinking. Hence, our "tree" will be "Latino," but we will not forget the special qualities of each individual "leaf" (or at least each "branch"); for our "tree" term is not intended to suggest that all trees in the Latino forest are the same, nor that they share a single identity, or even an emotional or political solidarity. Members of different Latino ethnic groups are often either ignorant or suspicious of members of the other Latino groups. Hence "Latino" serves as an enabler: on a practical level, it enables us to communicate more clearly and to avoid cumbersome prose; on a conceptual level, it enables us to make comparisons and contrasts, and to gain cultural insights.

Because the stories of Latino cultures have been neglected until very recently, it is no more likely that Latinos will know their cultural histories than it is that non-Latinos will. Thus, *Barrios and Borderlands* is intended for both publics, so that all may learn the fascinating cultural heritages of the Latino peoples, valuable in themselves, but also for the myriad ways in which they have enriched the United States cultural mosaic.

The more different pieces there are, the more brilliant the mosaic, but also the greater the need for wisdom and tolerance. The aim of *Barrios and Borderlands* is to celebrate the brilliance of the Latino pluralistic mosaic by providing essential information from a variety of perspectives, and by assisting the reader in developing a cultural understanding infused with receptivity and sensitivity.

Acknowledgements

Barrios and Borderlands is a collective endeavor. I am deeply grateful to many people throughout the United States who unstintingly gave of their time and expertise to help with this project. I owe a tremendous dept of gratitude to my good friends Sr. Paula Schwendinger, PBVM, Sr. Mary DeCock, BVM, Sr. Carol Frances Jegen, BVM, and Sr. Mary Martens, BVM, who extended themselves especially.

I am very grateful to all those whose interviews, essays, and creative pieces appear in the chapters that follow. Warmest thanks also to José Ríos, Dolores Huerta, Tika Boley, Viviana Carballo, Alicia and Tony Tremols, Sr. Carmel Purcell, BVM, Sr. Theresa Gleeson, BVM, Ed Krueger, Phil Wingerer, Sr. Therese Corkery, PBVM, Ms. Cathy Judge, Lilia Rubio and her mother, and Anna Marie Reynes and her mother, for facilitating introductions to wonderful people and for making valuable experiences possible; to Otto López for showing me some of his favorite places in Los Angeles; to Arsenio Córdova for his generosity; and to Sr. Catherine O'Dwyer and other kind hearted souls for allowing me to stay in their homes, apartments, and trailers while I was doing research on a modest budget.

Librarians Sr. Frances Loretta Berger, BVM, of the former Mundelein College, Ms. María Otero-Boisvert of Loyola University, and Mr. Charlie Fineman of Northwestern University tracked down the most obscure references without batting an eye. I am grateful for the early interest shown by Carment Navarrete, Esther Nieves, Miriam Torrado, Anna Montt, Iris Maldonado, and Vincenta Padilla, for the valuable observations offered by Helen Valdez, and for the encouragement provided by my dear friend and colleague Kateri O'Shea. I am particularly thankful for the enthusiasm, energy, and freshness of my students at Loyola University and Mundelein College. They have been a never-ending source of renewal for me, and they are, in fact, the inspiration for this work. Many thanks to Loyola University for the leave of absence, Fall 1992, that enabled me to make great strides in the research, and to Loyola University Research Services for providing much-needed travel funds. I appreciate especially the support of my department chairs, Ann Bugliani and Andrew McKenna, and of my Dean, Kathleen McCourt.

I am indebted to my editor at Routledge, Cecelia Cancellaro for her prompt interest in the project, and to Stewart Cauley for his excellent work and friendly manner. Thanks also to Maura Burnett, Esther Kaplan, Mary Neal Meador, and Michael Esposito for their thorough and conscientious care of the manuscript at all stages, and to Claudia Gorelick for her assistance at the end of the process.

My son Hunter and my daughter Shannon helped in more ways than they can imagine, and to them I am always grateful for their love and support. The deepest thanks go, however, to Bill Heyck who pushed, prodded, praised, cajoled, read, and reread, and who was in every way possible the most enthusiastic and constant supporter, as well as the most valued critic, of *Barrios and Borderlands*.

The inevitable errors, including those in translation, are my own.

A Chronology of Latino Events

BC
10,500
Humans inhabit Americas from Alaska to the tip of South America.

900
Olmec people create first great civilization of Central America.

AD
120
Puerto Rico settled, probably from Florida, by Igneri people, makers of beautiful pottery.

500
Maya civilization at its height in present-day Mexico, Guatemala, Honduras.

1325
Aztecs, successors to the Maya, found great city of Tenochtitlán; they trade macaw feathers and other goods with tribes to the north, in present-day U.S.

1400
Height of Inca civilization in Peru.

1420
Europeans begin voyages of exploration in the Atlantic Ocean.

1491
Ciboney, Arawak, and Carib peoples inhabit present-day Cuba, Puerto Rico, Dominican Republic, and other islands of Caribbean.

1492–93
Columbus visits present-day Haiti, Cuba, Puerto Rico.

1502
Montezuma becomes ruler of the Aztecs.

1510
Spanish colonize Puerto Rico.

1513
Ponce de León arrives in Florida from Puerto Rico.

1515
Spanish build colony at Havana, Cuba.

1519
Cortéz conquers Montezuma and Tenochtitlán.

1522
First Africans brought to Cuba as slaves.

1527
Cabeza de Vaca shipwrecked on Texas coast; begins his journey through Southwest.

1533
Pizarro conquers the Incas.

1535
Viceroyalty of New Spain establishes Spanish empire throughout the Americas; system of forced labor for Native Americans codified.

1538
Hernando de Soto explores area between Florida and Louisiana.

1540
Coronado searches Oklahoma and Kansas for cities of gold described by de Vaca; finds only poor villages.

1565
San Augustine founded in Florida; first city in North America.

1598
Juan de Oñante colonizes New Mexico.

1650
A poor frontier colony, New Mexico becomes haven for Jews, Arabs, and others unwelcome in Spain.

1690
Perhaps the first novel written in the New World is *The Misfortunes of Alonso Ramírez,* by Sigüenza y Góngora.

1725
Missions are being established across Texas.

1789
First play in Spanish performed in San Francisco.

1800
California mission system well on the way to being built—twenty-one missions, each a day's walk apart.

1803–15
Napoleonic Wars in Europe loosen Spain's control of American colonies; they begin to trade with the U.S.

1821
Mexico wins its independence from Spain.

1822
Growing Cuban population
in Tampa elects
Joseph M. Hernández
the first Hispanic member
of U.S. Congress.

1836
Tejanos (Texas Mexicans)
lose control of their region to Anglo
settlers, despite the fact that some
fought at the Alamo for an
independent Texas Republic.

1846
War with Mexico sends
first U.S. military throughout the
Southwest.

1848
Treaty of Guadalupe-Hidalgo cedes
huge territory to the U.S.;
former Mexican citizens in this area
suffer sweeping loss of rights.

1849
Anglos pouring in during the
California Gold Rush displace
Mexican residents;
El Jíbaro, novel of Puerto Rican
peasant life by Manuel Alonso,
published in Mexico.

1868
Birth of José Dolores López,
great folk sculptor of New Mexico.

1882
Cuban José Martí moves to New
York seeking intellectual freedom;
Chinese Exclusion Act
creates demand for Mexican
labor in Southwest.

1892
Martí organizes Cuban
independence movement
from New York; his writings gain
worldwide influence.

1898
Spanish-American War
makes Cuba and Puerto Rico
U.S. possessions.

1899
La Patria, Cuban paper
in New York, organizes a benefit
to raise money for Martí's tomb.

1902
Cuba granted independence
by the U.S.;
English made second official
language of Puerto Rico.

1903
Panama Canal Treaty increases U.S.
contacts with Central America.

1909
Free trade with U.S. causes
sugar boom in Puerto Rico;
population begins to increase.

1910
Turmoil of revolution in Mexico
and growth of labor-intensive
agriculture in U.S. increase Mexican
immigration to Southwest.

1912
First U.S. Marine incursion in Nicaragua; Cuban baseball great Adolfo Luque begins 23-year career in U.S. big leagues.

1914
Birth of Puerto Rican poet Julia de Burgos

1917
Puerto Rican residents acquire U.S. citizenship and begin first wave of immigration; deportation of Mexican Americans begins with striking copper miners.

1920
Majority of Mexican Americans now employed in industry, not farming.

1929
League of United Latin American Citizens formed in U.S.

1932
Collapse of sugar boom combined with population explosion sends massive wave of Puerto Rican immigration to U.S.; deportation of Mexicans during the Depression includes U.S. citizens.

1935
New Mexico makes Dennis Chávez first Latino in U.S. Senate.

1940
Machito forms the *Afro-Cubans* in New York; band will influence all of U.S. popular music.

1941
World War II brings thousands of Mexican and Puerto Rican Americans into U.S. armed forces.

1942
Wartime labor needs cause U.S. to begin "bracero" program with Mexican government; program imports 5 million workers by 1964.

1943
Anti-Mexican "Zoot-Suit Riots" begun by U.S. military personnel in Los Angeles; first Pro-Independence Congress held in Puerto Rico; poet Pedro Pietri born there.

1945
Largest wave of Puerto Rican migration begins, aided by expanded air travel; U.S. tourism to Cuba is aided as well, as is contact with all Central and South America.

1948
American GI Forum founded to protect rights of Mexican American veterans.

1954
Operation Wetback begins forced removal of 1 million people from U.S. to Mexico (including U.S. citizens), even as "bracero" program continues.

1955
Cuban Revolution begins.

1959
Castro takes power in Cuba; wave of immigration to U.S. begins.

1960
Aspira founded to aid education of Puerto Rican Americans.

1961
Castro embraces Communism; U.S. military and Cuban exiles stage Bay of Pigs invasion; *A Puerto Rican in New York* published by Jesús Colón.

1962
Number of Cuban refugees to U.S. reaches a quarter million.

1963
Puerto Rican Family Institute founded.

1965
César Chávez founds United Farm Workers in California and begins grape boycott.

1967
Puerto Rico votes to maintain Commonwealth relationship with U.S.; rejects independence.

1968
Mexican American Legal Defense Fund and "La Raza" founded as Chicano Movement begins.

1970
High unemployment in Puerto Rico continues to encourage travel to U.S. for work.

1971
Family Unification Program brings 300,000 more Cubans to U.S.

1972
Puerto Rican Legal Defense and Education Fund founded; Chicano mural art movement in full swing.

1973
First publication of *The Valley* by Rolando Hinojosa; Roberto Clemente elected to Baseball Hall of Fame.

1975
Chávez and UFW achieve passage of California Agricultural Labor Relations Act; first "Nuyorican Poets" anthology published in New York.

1976
Economic crisis in Mexico causes new wave of immigration to U.S.

1979
Political turmoil in Nicaragua, Honduras, Guatemala, and El Salvador increases U.S. population from those countries; earnings of Cuban American households equal the national average.

1980
Castro allows 120,000 *"marielitos"* to flee to US.

1988
Lauro Cavazos named Secretary of Education—first Latin American named to the Cabinet; Gloria Estefan and Miami Sound Machine win Grammy for songs in Spanish and English.

1989
Manuel Luján named Secretary of the Interior.

1990
Latinos become second-fastest growing segment of U.S. population. Spanish named official language of Puerto Rico.

1993
Henry Cisneros named Secretary of Housing and Urban Development; English reinstated as second official language of Puerto Rico.

2010
Latinos make up 13% of U.S. population.

2030
Latino population of the US reaches 50 million.

Introduction: Latinos, Past and Present

The way to begin understanding Latino cultures in the United States is to remember five essential points: (1) that there are a great *many* Latinos in the United States; (2) that there is not *one*, but rather, there are *many* Latino cultures in the United States; (3) that Latinos have lived in the territory now occupied by the United States for a *long* time; (4) that Latinos have often been *discriminated against* and *victimized* by Anglos; and (5) that Latinos are often seen as an American "problem," when, in fact, they are a great cultural *treasure.*

Who Are the Latinos?

The Latino peoples of the United States comprise one of the largest and fastest growing minority groups in the country. They currently number about 24 million, making up 9 percent of the overall United States population of 255 million, and are expected to reach 12.9 percent of the United States population by 2010.[1] Latinos will account for more than 40 percent of all United States population growth over the next sixty years. According to the Census Bureau's revised estimates, their numbers will reach 49 million in 2020 and 81 million in 2050. The overall U. S. population is expected to attain 383 million by 2050, a 50 percent increase in six decades, but the

expected percentage growth rate of the Latino population from 1992 to 2050 is 237.5 percent, second only to that of Asians and Pacific Islanders, whose estimated rate is 412.5 percent.[2]

Not only is the Latino population growing rapidly, it is also very young. More than 50 percent of Latinos are under twenty-six years of age, and more than 33 percent are under the age of eighteen. Within the Mexican-origin population of 14 million, nearly 33 percent are younger than sixteen years of age.[3] For purposes of comparison, the median age of the United States population is thirty-three, the highest in its history.[4] Over 70 percent of the Latino population are clustered in the states of California, Texas, New York, and Florida, in that order.[5] More than 88 percent of United States Latinos live in cities, while three cities, New York, Miami, and Los Angeles, hold over 40 percent of those who responded as "Hispanic" to the 1990 census.[6]

With regard to educational attainment, figures show that of Latino high school graduates between eighteen and twenty-four years of age, 29 percent were attending college in 1990, up from 26.1 percent in 1985. By comparison, of African American high school graduates in the same age group, 33 percent were attending college in 1990,

also up from 26.1 percent in 1985. Among white high school graduates in the same age group, 39.4 percent were attending college in 1990, up from 34.4 percent in 1985. Though the college attendance levels for Latinos are on the rise, the proportion of Latinos who graduate from high school is declining, dropping from 62.9 percent in 1985 to 54.5 percent in 1990. During that same period the high school graduation rate for whites dipped only slightly, from 83.6 percent to 82.5 percent, while that for African Americans rose slightly, from 75.6 percent to 77 percent. One problem that Latinos face is the tiny number of Latino teachers in the public schools. For example, in the Houston Independent School District, where Latinos comprise 42.6 percent of the student population, only 10.4 percent of elementary school teachers, 5.2 percent of middle school teachers, and 6.4 percent of high school teachers are Latinos.[7]

Statistics on language show that usage of English by Latinos is increasing markedly. Indeed, the larger the proportion of United States–born Latinos in a given population, the stronger the move to English usage. Only 20 percent of United States–born Mexicans, Puerto Ricans, and Cubans report use of Spanish as their preferred, but not exclusive, language.[8] Further, children show a decided preference for English over Spanish, with United States–born children of Spanish-speaking parents overwhelmingly choosing English as their principal or only language.[9]

Thus we see that there are a great many Latinos in the United States, that their numbers are increasing dramatically, and that they are predominantly urban. The Latino population has tended to cluster in the borderland states of the Southwest, in New York, and in Florida, though it is more and more mobile all the time. While Latinos are struggling to participate more fully in the educational and economic benefits of the American system, they show a strong preference for the English language, the single most important tool for "making it" in the United States. Most United States Latinos are of Mexican origin, for that population is more than twice as large as all other Latino groups combined. However, the Latino population contains within it *highly* diverse cultures, as exemplified by the markedly different histories of the three main Latino ethnic groups, Mexicans, Puerto Ricans, and Cubans, whose stories we will return to later.

History

Figures are very useful in creating a profile of the Latino presence in the United States, but they are unable to give us a feel for the long, rich, and fascinating human history behind the numbers.

The eastern part of the United States and the borderlands of the southwest have historically belonged to two different worlds. Usually, we think only of the east when considering early American history. Occasionally, we remember that the Spanish and Indian heritages have predominated in the southwest, but we are largely unaware of the fact that "geographically, the Southwest is one with Mexico," not with the rest of the United States.[10] Further, as historian and journalist Carey McWilliams reminds us, the Mexican-origin peoples

of the southwest "are not interlopers or immigrants but an indigenous people."[11] We need to know the story of this "indigenous people" in order gain a more complete and accurate understanding of United States cultural history.

The story begins at least as early as 1513, when Juan Ponce de León first arrived in Florida and named his discovery La Gran Pascua Florida, meaning Easter season, or Easter celebration, in the Spanish language. The city of St. Augustine, the oldest permanent settlement in the United States, was founded in 1565 by Pedro Méndez de Aviles, roughly fifty-five years before the pilgrims set out from Plymouth, England, in the *Mayflower*. In 1538, Hernando de Soto explored Tampa Bay, the Carolinas, Georgia, Alabama, and Louisiana. In 1696, Pensacola was established as the second permanent Spanish colony in Florida.

Meanwhile, an amazing series of events that culminated in the exploration of the Southwest was already underway. In 1527, a Spanish expedition of 600 led by the intrepid Panfilo de Narváez explored the Gulf coast and was shipwrecked on Galveston Island where the Spaniards were enslaved by Indians. Those who escaped included Alvar Núñez Cabeza de Vaca, Alonso del Castillo Maldonado, Andrés Dorantes, and el negro Estévan, or black Estévan, as he is known. These survivors *walk*ed across Texas, New Mexico, and Arizona, and in 1536 somehow arrived in Mexico to relate their adventures to their astonished brethren. The stories they recounted were of constant danger and hardship, and of on-the-spot improvisation, such as Cabeza de Vaca's claiming to

be a shaman in order to ingratiate himself and his group with the different tribes they encountered.[12]

Cabeza de Vaca and his men also told tales of riches to be found in the fabled seven cities of Cíbola. In 1540 Francisco Vásquez de Coronado explored Arizona, New Mexico, Oklahoma, and Kansas in search of treasure, but he only came upon poor Indian villages. In 1542, Rodríguez Cabrillo explored the coast of California, which he declared to be "peopled by black women," and "very close to the Terrestrial Paradise."[13] In 1598, Juan de Oñate began the colonization of New Mexico, just about the time William Shakespeare was writing *Henry V*. Oñate founded the city of Santa Fe in 1609, making it the oldest capital city in the United States.

Spanish exploration in the sixteenth century ranged from St. Augustine to San Diego, but the sojourners found no gold or other wealth. The more inaccessible areas, such as California, remained neglected for well over one hundred and fifty years. Missions in Texas, such as Goliad, Nacogdoches, and San Antonio, were founded early in the 1700s, well before those in California, but Texas too was ignored by Spanish authorities for over one hundred years. It was remote from Spanish authority in New Spain (Mexico) and supplies could take years to arrive, if they arrived at all. Further, the fierce Apache and Comanche Indians, having developed a horse culture with the descendants of the horses first introduced by the Spanish, presented a constant threat to settlements in Texas, as well as to those in New Mexico and Arizona. The California missions were founded later in the

eighteenth century by Father Junípero Serra. There were twenty-one in all, and none was more than a day's walk from the previous one. When Father Serra established the San Francisco mission in 1776, the eastern part of the United States was declaring its independence from England.

These Spanish borderland settlements were intended to bring new territories, wealth, and souls to the Catholic crown. But the colonies were poor and isolated from one another, from Mexico, from the United States, and, most of all, from Spain. Life was difficult and dangerous. Harsh conditions in the borderlands slowed Anglo settlement and allowed plenty of time for Spanish ways to become thoroughly ingrained. Though the Spanish settlers faced great peril at the hands of the Indians, ultimately, the Indians faced even greater peril at the hands of the Spanish. Even so, the two cultures needed each other. For example, the Spaniards would never have survived in the borderlands had it not been for the expert assistance of the Indians as guides and interpreters in a hostile environment. They took the settlers to watering holes, protected them from the elements, gave them food in their villages, and taught them how to survive in the isolation of an unforgiving land. The Spanish, for their part, brought the first cattle, horses, goats, and pigs; a variety of fruits, including peaches, figs, oranges, apples, and grapes; grains such as wheat and alfalfa; and agricultural tools such as hoes, grinding stones, plows, and wheels. From the Spaniards, the Indians learned the arts of hammering silver and copper, working iron, and

carding and weaving wool.[14] Relations were determined by mutual need, but carried out in a climate of mutual distrust.

Borderlands culture developed in relative isolation until the 1830s, when North American settlers in Texas revolted against Mexico, which had itself won independence from Spain in 1821. In 1836, with cries of "Remember the Alamo and Goliad!," Texans under Sam Houston, including some *tejanos*, or Mexicans living in Texas, defeated Santa Anna's army at San Jacinto. Texas became an independent republic and was later (1845) admitted as a state, opening the floodgates to North American settlers.

Much more drastic changes were soon to intrude upon the tranquility of borderlands life. The Treaty of Guadalupe-Hidalgo ended the United States–Mexican War (1846–48) and cost Mexico one half of its national territory: California, Arizona, New Mexico, and other lands. Overnight, Mexicans in the borderlands became United States citizens, like it or not.

The effect of the war on the borderlands people was devastating. It reduced the entire population to poverty and passivity, instilling in them a deep mistrust of the political process. Mexicans were promised civil rights and property titles by the treaty. But discrimination, beatings, and even lynchings were the heavy price they paid when they sought to exercise those rights in the borderlands. Violence against the Mexican-origin population was exacerbated by the Gold Rush of 1848 in California, where unrestrained lawlessness resulted in a net loss of Mexican population from that

state as Mexicans fled and gold-hungry Anglos took over. Institutional violence also played a major role throughout the borderlands: squatters who seized Mexicans' land were not prosecuted; Mexicans could not testify in court because they were not white; real estate taxes were raised until Mexicans lost their properties, and, most importantly, crimes against Mexicans, including murder, were not punished.[15]

By the 1880s Mexican Americans, who were not seen to be desirable as landowners or as United States citizens, were avidly sought as cheap labor in agriculture, mining, and railroad construction. Mexican nationals were also eagerly solicited, so great was the demand for labor, especially since Chinese laborers had just been banned by the Chinese Exclusion Act of 1882. Mexican nationals were regarded as docile, hardworking, and easy to send packing on short notice.[16]

Thus we see that the foundations of Anglo American society in the borderlands were laid by the Spaniards and Mexicans centuries before the Anglos arrived in Texas, California, New Mexico, Arizona, and Colorado. When the borderlands were forceably annexed, Anglo culture was officially imposed, but Mexican patterns of culture remained deeply embedded throughout the Southwest.

Mexican Americans

It is difficult to determine the defining characteristics of the Mexican American people because they are a numerous and widespread population; because they maintain close ties to Mexico (they are ambivalent about the Mexican immigrants and cynical about the Mexican government); and because, since World War II, they have come to occupy a variety of professions. Nevertheless, of the three main Latino groups in the United States, the Mexican Americans stand out for their stoicism, religious faith, and devotion to traditional values, most especially the sanctity of the family. These traits have enabled Mexican Americans to survive, first as an annexed people, and later as a people who have suffered segregation and discrimination in their long struggle for civil rights.

By the early twentieth century, the Mexican American population began to be established outside of the Southwest, with enclaves in the Midwest and New York. As in previous decades, Mexican nationals were recruited to come to *el norte* and work on railroads and in the developing industries of the Midwest and the East. The widespread use of irrigation techniques brought about a tremendous expansion in fruit and vegetable farming in the Southwest and the rapid growth of the sugar beet industry in states such as California, Colorado, Montana, Michigan, and Minnesota. Such developments required still more workers. These factors, plus the dislocation and general uprooting of large populations occasioned by the Mexican Revolution of 1910 to 1917, meant more Mexican immigrants for the United States workforce. Yet the main growth sector was not agriculture, but industry. By 1928, 80 percent of the Burlington Railroad's workers were Mexican or Mexican American.[17] Still others worked in meat-packing houses, steel mills, tanneries, and cement plants in a number of United States cities.

It helped that jobs were plentiful in the cities, because, by the late 1920s they were disappearing in agriculture due to drought, the Depression, and mechanization. During the 1930s, Mexican Americans became a predominantly *urban* ethnic group. This tendency was accelerated by World War II, during which the thousands of Mexican Americans and Puerto Ricans who served in the armed forces learned new skills, came to speak better English, and saw a broader slice of the world than any of them would have dreamed possible even a few years before. However, neither Mexican Americans nor Mexican nationals were welcomed warmly by the communities that, from about 1900 to 1930, had sought their strong arms and backs. Instead, when Mexicans ventured outside their ethnic enclaves, they were met with open discrimination in restaurants, barbershops, churches, and in their search for housing and employment.[18]

Social, economic, and political discrimination continued to dog the Mexican and the Mexican American. Many Mexicans, legal and illegal, were summarily deported during the thirties because of the Depression. In June 1943, the infamous "zoot suit" riots occurred in Los Angeles, so called because of the style of baggy, high-waisted pegged pants and long coats in fashion at the time among some Mexican youths. Such attire, during a period of wartime jingoism, was, to many Angelenos, servicemen, and police, like waving a red flag in front of a bull. If one wore a zoot suit (or sometimes, if one was merely of Mexican descent), that was, in the highly charged atmosphere of the time, proof enough of unpatriotic, or even subversive character. Tensions mounted until finally several thousand United States servicemen and civilians, angry because eleven sailors had been beaten, allegedly by a Mexican-origin gang, rioted through the streets of Los Angeles. They assaulted hundreds of Mexicans—youths, adults, men, women, children—while police stood by and then moved in afterward to club the victims. These disturbances would have been more appropriately termed the "police-inspired" riots, because it was later learned that some members of the Los Angeles Police Department had deliberately provoked the violence in order to demonstrate to the public the need for harsh police methods, hoping that the jury would acquit one of their number who was coming to trial accused of having kicked a prisoner to death.[19]

The need for labor in the United States during World War II was insatiable. The United States and Mexican governments entered into various visiting worker agreements, such as the bracero program. (The term bracero comes from the Spanish word *brazo*, meaning arm.) The program lasted from 1942 to 1964 and brought five million Mexican workers to this country.[20] The bracero program allowed controlled numbers of Mexican nationals to enter the country for seasonal agricultural work at low pay, after which they were to return to Mexico. During the tenure of the agreement, various religious and community groups became outraged at the appalling and unsanitary conditions in which workers were kept, and at the

abuses by growers, some of whom even charged rent for the trees under which the migrants slept. The Mexican government complained repeatedly about the treatment of Mexican nationals in the States, and after 1962 made no attempt to reinstate or to extend the expiration date of the agreement. The United States recession in 1953 and fears of overwhelming immigration led to Operation Wetback in 1954, during which one million Mexicans were returned to Mexico, including some United States citizens caught in the indiscriminate roundup, with many other abuses committed in the process.[21]

A milestone for the Mexican American worker was the creation of the United Farm Workers Union in 1965 by César Chávez (1927–1993), a remarkable achievement when one considers that unionizing efforts among other Latino workers had been put down. For example, in 1917 when Mexican workers in Arizona struck the copper mines over the issue of unequal pay, they were shipped off to Mexico. In 1938, when San Antonio pecan shellers struck, they were beaten and jailed by the police. The UFW (founded first as the National Farm Workers' Association by Chávez in 1962) was the first and is the most successful agricultural workers' union in the United States. Chávez's work has led to the promulgation of labor laws, such as the California Agricultural Labor Relations Act in 1975, and to major improvements in wages and working conditions for agricultural workers. Chávez's nonviolent movement, which has been the victim of brutal treatment by growers and authorities, is motivated by the spirituality of nonviolence of Jesus, St. Francis of Assisi, and Martin Luther King. Its major tactic has been the boycott. The first was the grape boycott 1965 to 1970, followed by the boycott and picketing of the lettuce and grape industry in the 1970s, and by Chávez's third series of grape boycotts from 1984 to 1988 to protest the use of pesticides. Toward the end of this third strike, in the summer of 1988, Chávez fasted for thirty-six days in an effort to bring national attention to the cause.[22] The farm workers' movement, which continues to use the boycott tactic today, has enjoyed widespread popular support and credibility because of its nonviolent principles; its religious symbolism, including the ubiquitous banner of the Virgen de Guadalupe, and the model of personal sacrifice provided by Chávez himself, whose stipend of five dollars a week set a standard for frugality.[23] During their marches and pickets in the turbulent 1960s, union members were encouraged and entertained by Luis Valdez's famous Teatro Campesino, a traveling rural theater that provided one act sketches called *actos* that usually parodied the union's opponents and portrayed the eventual victory of the simple, but virtuous, farm worker.[24]

The farm workers' cause also galvanized into action existing groups such as the American G.I. Forum (founded in 1948); LULAC (the League of United Latin American Citizens, founded in 1929); and CSO (Community Service Organization), founded in 1947 by Fred Ross, disciple of the Chicago organizer Saul Alinsky. These groups and others began to work more assidu-

ously for school desegregation and for civil rights for Mexican Americans. Later organizations came to life during the Chicano movement of the 1960s and 1970s. These include groups such as MACC (the Mexican American Cultural Center, founded in 1971); COPS (Communities Organized for Public Service, founded in 1973); PADRES (Priests Associated for Religious, Educational and Social Rights, founded in 1969); Las Hermanas (founded in 1970); La Raza (founded in 1968), and MALDEF (the Mexican-American Legal Defense Fund, founded in 1968).[25]

These organizations were part of a broader Chicano movement, which had as its goal obtaining civil rights and respect for Mexican Americans and their culture. The movement resulted in a heightened political awareness, affirmative action support, and an interest in Chicano history and origins, as in the popularity of the concept of Aztlán as the mythical southwestern homeland of the Aztecs.[26] The Chicano movement produced programs in Chicano Studies, provided a great stimulus to Chicano art and writing, and had the effect of encouraging feminist studies among Latinas. Unlike the farm workers' movement, which had a religious inspiration and included many clergy among its numbers, the Chicano movement was secular and counted among its key figures Mexican American veterans of World War II who had become professionals and student leaders at the university level. During the 1980s and 1990s, Mexican Americans have continued to give expression to a positive sense of identity and self-worth while pursuing educational and economic

integration with the United States mainstream.

Mexican Americans have historically been the victims of hardship, discrimination, injustice, and violence. They have been at the mercy of capricious United States economic cycles, ardently desired as workers in field and factory during times of labor shortage and rudely dismissed, or worse, when the crises are over. The crowning irony is that so many Mexican Americans have been treated as foreigners in what is, after all, their native land. Throughout, the Mexican American people have shown a stoic strength, a deep religious faith, and a quiet dignity as they have respectfully, but insistently, pushed at the edges of American society seeking acceptance while simultaneously holding fast to their most treasured values and traditions.

Puerto Ricans

The Puerto Rican's story is very different from that of the Mexican, except for the common experience of discrimination and isolation from the mainstream. Puerto Rico was first visited by Christopher Columbus in 1493, and remained a Spanish colony until it was ceded to the United States in 1898 after the Spanish American War. Until the middle of the twentieth century, Puerto Rico was a predominantly rural and agricultural island. Between, roughly, 1900 and the 1930s, Puerto Ricans began moving to eastern cities of the mainland and to agricultural jobs in the East. At first, the movement was slow: between 1900 and 1909, only 2,000 Puerto Ricans had come to the mainland. But beginning in 1917, when

Puerto Ricans gained United States citizenship, many began to come, and they did not return to the island after World War I. Most Puerto Rican military veterans settled in New York. By 1940, there were 70,000 Puerto Ricans living in New York City. By far the greatest exodus from the island began after World War II, and has continued more or less steadily since then. From 1950 to 1960, the mainland Puerto Rican population nearly doubled, soaring from 300,000 to 887,000. By 1970, it had reached 1.4 million.[27]

Puerto Ricans are the first "airborne" migrant group of Spanish-speaking United States citizens. Their massive departure from Puerto Rico occurred because of the decline of agriculture on the island, where real unemployment in 1970 was 30 percent.[28] However, the Puerto Rican migrants' main problem has been neither unemployment on the island, nor adjusting to life on the mainland. Rather, it is the awesome task of creating a national cultural identity, of knowing what it means to be Puerto Rican. This is the great challenge for Puerto Rican migrants, because they arrive here *already* suffering from serious economic and psychological dislocation, and from cultural confusion.

A recent example of cultural confusion is the repeal in 1993 by the Puerto Rican Senate of the 1991 law that set Spanish as the only official language on the island of 3.5 million people. From 1902 to 1991 both English and Spanish were official languages. Then Governor Rafael Hernández Colón (1985–1993) supported the Spanish-only law as a way to reaffirm Puerto Rico's cultural identity in the face of its increasing absorption by the United States. However, his successor, Governor Pedro Rosselló, who took office in January 1993, and his New Progressive Party, favor statehood; thus he pushed for repeal of the Spanish-only law.[29] English is again required in primary and secondary schools in Puerto Rico, though there are many ways to get around the law. For example, while textbooks may be written in English, classes are often conducted in Spanish.

The identity problem is likewise embedded in Puerto Rico's unique relationship with the United States: Puerto Ricans are United States citizens, receive federal benefits such as Social Security and food stamps, and are eligible for United States military service and the draft. But they do not pay United States taxes and cannot vote in federal elections, though Puerto Rico sends a nonvoting delegate to the United States Congress.[30] Thus, the island culture is a melange of United States and native traditions and institutions: from the open-air *mercado*, or market, to the enclosed shopping mall; from the rhythms and lyrics of the Afro–Puerto Rican plena to United States–style rock music—that is, from the drum to the boom box.

Puerto Rico's political and educational structures, its musical and linguistic habits, are not the only indicators of cultural flux. There is a religious barometer as well. More than one hundred years of earnest missionary activity have had the effect of retarding the development of a native clergy that might have acted to preserve traditional Puerto Rican cultural values and identity, and that might

have helped cushion the psychological effects of the economic blows that the island has suffered. Further, the rampant industrialization of the island as a result of projects like Operation Bootstrap, initiated in the 1950s by Governor Luis Muñoz Marín (1947–1964) to industrialize and modernize the island, has run roughshod over traditional rural values. As a result, disrupted families and displaced farmers have been forced to migrate to cities like San Juan in search of work. Along the way, they have had to adapt to a new way of life.

Puerto Ricans arrive in the mainland already having experienced serious loss, not so much economic loss like the Mexicans, or political like the Cubans, but rather severe cultural deprivation and loss of community and family coping mechanisms. Though Puerto Ricans, unlike Cubans, can always go back if things do not work out here, this fact has hindered the creation of identity and community among Puerto Ricans. It has given rise to a situation of perpetual movement, of migration to the mainland and of return migration to the island. Ease of movement has made it difficult for Puerto Ricans to develop a sense of belonging either to the island or to the mainland Nuyorican culture.

This feeling of impermanence has meant that Puerto Ricans in the States have been slow to organize, whether on the neighborhood or the national level. Further, unlike previous immigrants, Catholic Puerto Ricans brought no native clergy with them. This means that they have had to deal with integrated, not ethnic, parishes. To a large extent, the popularity of the Pentecostal Church among Puerto Ricans is due to the Pentecostals' ability to

offer a warm, emotional welcome to a people in search of community. The dispersed pattern of settlement in New York City has also militated against the creation of strong cultural ties among Puerto Ricans. Further, as United States citizens, Puerto Ricans are eligible for public housing, where no attempt is made to cluster residents along ethnic or national-origin lines.

The impermanence and dispersal of the mainland United States Puerto Rican population has meant that persons who do put down deep roots are likely to experience the heartache of being uprooted again when the factory closes or the next layoff comes. But things on the island are no better. When one moves back, it is often to face bitter disappointment, for unemployment is chronic. In 1978, when the food stamp program was extended to Puerto Rico, *two thirds* of the island's families qualified.[31] Moreover, returnees experience the additional shock of finding that the island has changed so drastically that it hardly seems like home any more. The Puerto Rican Family Institute, established in New York in 1963, found it necessary to open an office on the island to help Puerto Ricans with return migration adjustment problems, including sometimes traumatic school placements for mainland children and discrimination by islanders once the Nuyoricans arrived "back home."[32] Return migration is especially hard on children who have adopted the American way of life and whose identification with the island is tenuous at best.

Curiously, it is in New York, not on the island, that certain typical features of Puerto Rican culture are being preserved. A wonderful example are the casitas—small, brightly-painted wood-

en shacks with a pointed roof that serve as cultural centers. The casitas replicate structures on the island that date from the turn of the century and which were built from shipments of wood sent to Puerto Rico by the Americans after the invasion in 1898. The difference is that on the island the casitas are disappearing, while in the city they are bringing life, music, and a sense of belonging to people surrounded by burned-out buildings and drug-infested barrios. These tiny shacks, some with vegetable gardens and chickens, are a bit of rural life that has been successfully transplanted to the concrete of the city. They serve as repositories of traditional Puerto Rican musical culture, such as the African-inspired bomba and plena, and Puerto Rico's guajiro or country, "hillbilly" music.[33]

An additional factor that complicates the question of identity for the Puerto Rican is the issue of race. Most Puerto Ricans are of mixed ancestry (Spanish, Amerindian, and African), and many are of African heritage. While Puerto Ricans may call themselves *trigueño*, or wheat-colored, to many North Americans they are black. Culturally, however, they are Latinos, and while they do have much in common with African Americans, they do not belong to that community either. Nor do Puerto Ricans feel that they belong to other Latino immigrant groups in New York City. In fact, the growing numbers of Dominicans, Colombians, and Ecuadorians only make the Puerto Rican stand out more, for while these immigrant groups regard themselves and each other as Latin Americans, they view the Puerto Rican, even the second or third generation Nuyorican, as a citizen of an American possession, not as part of

the Latino family.[34] In spite of the fact that one third of all Puerto Ricans now live in the United States, and nearly half of them have been born here, they are still foreigners, both to other Latin Americans and to other United States citizens.[35]

Education levels are improving for second and third generation Puerto Ricans; nevertheless, the New York City public high school dropout rate for Puerto Ricans is alarming. It falls somewhere between 60 and 80 percent. These startlingly high figures mean that the youth unemployment rate will only increase, though for New York African American and Latino youths it is already the highest in the nation.[36] In terms of education and occupation, Puerto Ricans are the poorest of all groups in New York city.[37] Nearly 40 percent of Puerto Rican families in New York City are receiving public welfare, and in 1980, 49.8 percent of Puerto Rican families were headed by single women.[38] It should be pointed out that to some extent these statistics reflect the economic independence of Puerto Rican women, who are overwhelmingly employed; the lack of employment for Puerto Rican males (unemployment for young Puerto Rican men is about 40 percent); and the availability of welfare, which means that women do not have to remain in unhappy or abusive marriages.[39]

For all these reasons, Puerto Rican community organizations were both desperately needed and late in getting off the ground. The Puerto Rican Forum was founded in the mid-1950s to promote youth and the importance of education. Then came Aspira, or "aspire," in 1961, the most sucessful of all the grass roots organizations,

which has done a superhuman job in places like New York, Puerto Rico, and Chicago of keeping Puerto Rican youths from dropping out of school. Aspira was followed in New York by the PRCDP (the Puerto Rican Community Development Project), which provided valuable community services, but whose leader Ramón Vélez was accused of mismanagement and corruption by then Mayor Koch, among others, resulting in the agency being reorganized.[40] Much later, PROGRESO (the Puerto Rican Organization for Growth, Research, Education and Self-Sufficiency, founded in 1981) was established to continue some of the tutoring, job training, and drug prevention programs of the PRCDP, but also to provide technical assistance to neighborhood organizations and to assist them in managing their programs. The Puerto Rican Family Institute, like Aspira, is a grass roots social service organization. It was founded by social workers who wanted to create a support system for newly arrived families to help ease the period of adjustment. The Institute tries to recreate on the mainland the ritual kinship system of *compadrazgo* typical of Latin American cultures, by matching settled families with those who are recently arrived. The Institute also provides counseling and mental health services on both the island and the mainland. Another important community agency is the Puerto Rican Legal Defense and Education Fund, created in 1972 and patterned on the NAACP Legal Defense Fund.[41]

The remarkable thing about Puerto Rican culture on the mainland is not that it is embattled, but that it continues to insist on being recognized, and

stubbornly to resist being eroded or otherwise absorbed. The above-mentioned organizations as well as cultural institutions ranging from Miriam Colón's famous Puerto Rican Traveling Theater, to Hunter College's (City University of New York) Instituto de Estudios Puertorriqueños, and the lively jam sessions at the casitas attest to the resilience, vitality, and uniqueness of Puerto Rican culture.

Cubans

The Cuban story is unique in yet another way, for it expresses the experience of the political exile. Further, since most Cubans came fleeing the communist government of Fidel Castro, they were welcomed and granted asylum by the anti-communist United States government. This was a highly unusual and favorable situation for the immigrants, for it meant not only that Cubans did not have to worry about their immigration status, but also that they were eligible for federal (and charitable) assistance, which was made available to the first anti-Castro Cuban groups in the form of food, clothing, shelter, job training, small business loans, and English classes. There was also a Cuban community already in Florida that dated back one hundred years: the cigar-making industries of Tampa and Ybor City, which were ready to extend a hand. (Ironically, the United States embargo on the Castro regime destroyed the "Havana" cigar industry of Florida.) Waves of Cubans began emigrating from the island as soon as Fidel Castro came to power in 1959. Between 1959 and 1960, 64,000 Cubans arrived on United States shores. By the Cuban missile crisis of 1962, 181,000 more

had sought refuge here. From 1959 to 1962, 14,048 unaccompanied children came to Miami because parents in Cuba feared that their children would be taken away from them by the state. From 1962 to 1965, 55,916 more Cubans came ashore. By 1971, under a program of family reunification, 297,318 more arrived. There followed a lull, which ended in 1980 when 120,000 emigrants left from the Cuban port of Mariel. This last wave, known collectively as *marielitos,* was treated with both scorn and sympathy by those Cubans of the first wave, from 1959 to 1962. This was because the *marielitos* were largely unskilled and uneducated, racially mixed, and socially "questionable" (65 percent were black, 10 percent were criminals, and 12 percent were homosexuals), as compared to the first group, which was composed of overwhelmingly white, highly educated professionals. The second wave, which ended in 1973, was still educated and predominantly white, but more heterogeneous in terms of race and occupation.[42] By the end of 1980, 875,000 Cubans of all colors, educational levels, and occupations had come to Florida, most of them to Miami.[43]

It is common knowledge that Cubans in the United States, generally speaking, have very strong political views, usually ranging from the merely anti-Castro to the extreme right wing. A case in point is the Cuban American National Foundation, comprised of wealthy exile businessmen such as the well-known Jorge Más Canosa, the major promoter of Radio Martí, a vehicle for anti-Castro propaganda. The Foundation's political branch, the Coalition for a Free Cuba, supports anti-communist activities, the most notable recent example being the contra war to overturn the Sandinista government in Nicaragua.[44] Cuban Americans tend to vote Republican, and they were strong supporters of Presidents Nixon, Reagan, and Bush. Many Cuban Americans have never forgiven either the Kennedys or the Democrats for the Bay of Pigs fiasco of 1961, in which many Cubans exiles fought and died. The Little Havana section of Miami is peopled with old men who are veterans of the Bay of Pigs invasion and who spend their time drinking coffee, playing dominoes, and talking politics. They also share the fantasy they have created of Cuba, its memories and myths. Young *cubanos,* however, are not much interested in the failed dreams of their elders. They dream instead of a move to the suburbs, expecially now that so many Nicaraguans and Salvadorans are moving in.[45]

Cubans are known among other Latinos not only for their politics, but also for their pride and their sense of humor, both of which shine through in a widely told fable of the early years of exile. One day, a thin, small, scraggly Cuban dog was walking down the street in Miami. It came across a group of large, sleek, healthy American dogs that made fun of the little thing. After enduring their insults, the little Cuban dog said, "Go ahead and laugh. You see me as I am now, but in Cuba I was a German shepherd."[46]

Cubans see themselves as "invited guests" of the United States and have never felt apologetic about anything.[47] "We Cubans are aggressive, progressive. We make the opportunity; it is not given to us," says Andrea

Camps, a member of the social elite in Houston, when asked to describe the Cuban experience here.[48] Sociologist Lisandro Pérez of Florida International University elaborates: "There is an absence of minority-group orientation. Cubans have a very high self-concept—at times there is a certain arrogance—that's very different from the self-concept of Mexican-Americans and Puerto Ricans."[49] The older Cubans certainly were aggressive. During the 1970s, Cubans naturalized at higher rates than immigrants from any other country.[50] They created a stable ethnic economy such that by 1979 the Cuban household earnings were on a par with the national median. This community absorbed an amazing number of the 1980 Mariel refugees, employing them in businesses owned by Cuban nationals. Close to 20 percent of those so employed became self-employed after six years in the United States.[51]

Cubans have energetically embraced the free-market system. Cuban-owned firms in Little Havana increased rapidly, from 919 in 1967 to 8,000 in 1976, to 28,000 in 1990. Most businesses are small, averaging about eight employees, but these numbers also include substantial factories.[52] According to immigration scholar Alejandro Portes, ethnic enclaves such as Little Havana develop because immigrants arrive already possessing business expertise, and because they have access both to capital and to labor.[53] Thus, when one thinks of Cubans, one thinks not only of politics and humor but also of business success.

Some Cubans, such as social scientist Omar Betancourt, stress the im-

portance of bilingual skills in making it possible for Cubans not only to develop their businesses, but also to make Miami "the capital of Latin America."[54] Betancourt declares bilingualism to be "the most powerful difference between success and failure for our kids."[55] He criticizes those American-born Cubans who don't know Spanish and have forgotten "how to be Cubans," though he says that they are not to blame, for culture conflict is inevitable when young people "come home to an antiquated set of values, a culture trapped in a mud hole living in the past, stuck in 1959, the official Cuban 'end of time.'"[56]

Through their use of English, their bilingualism, their good humor, their relative acceptance of and by Americans, their entrepreneurship, and the assistance of the United States government, Cuban immigrants have come to realize their dream of belonging to a society made up of free people. This shared aspiration is the strongest bond uniting Cubans to each other and to United States culture.[57] For Cubans, unlike Mexicans or Puerto Ricans, the "search for political and social equality started with American citizenship" and an embrace of the political process as the way to achieve institutional equality.[58]

Cultural Themes

Given the separate histories and diverse experiences of each major group of Latinos in the United States—Mexican, Cuban, and Puerto Rican—it is not surprising to find that each represents a quite distinct Latino culture. Moreover, these three are not the only

cultures; for, while these are the largest groups, the smaller ones, like Dominicans, Colombians, and Salvadorans, also each form a separate Latino culture. However, commonalities do exist, and they are instructive. Thus, Allan Figueroa Deck's definition of culture as "the meanings, values, thoughts, and feelings mutually shared by a people" provides a sensible description and a useful starting point.[59] It allows us to highlight distinctive cultural themes that can be analyzed according to several categories: (1) family, (2) religion, (3) community, (4) the arts, (5) the experience of (im)migration and exile, and (6) the question of cultural identity. Of course, these categories overlap and interweave with one another, and they are set apart for analytical purposes here. What this book attempts to do is show what T. S. Eliot called "the whole way of life of a people." A person embedded in a culture, after all, experiences every aspect simultaneously, but what we are doing is reading our way into it.

As North Americans enter the twenty-first century, the myths of the melting pot and of total assimilation appear both naive and arrogant. At any rate, they have faded into the background, for they have not always worked and they are no longer generally held to be particularly desirable. Industrialization, urbanization, modernization, and secularization have by no means replaced the desire for cul-

tural autonomy of Latino ethnic groups in the United States; in fact, what we have witnessed over the past thirty or forty years is a resurgence of ethnicity. Americans live in a pluralistic society, but we have not yet determined whether it will be a brilliant mosaic of cultural pluralism that emphasizes sharing, borrowing, bi- and even multilingualism, or one that separates groups along social, economic, ethnic, and racial lines. Indeed, the decision we face is how Mexican Americans, Cuban Americans, Puerto Ricans, African Americans, Native Americans, Italian Americans, Greek Americans, can live together respectfully and productively as part of the same national society.

In this regard, the function of an anthology such as this is to enable us to understand better the Latino cultural experience, and, in so doing, to come to understand ourselves better.[60] The more we learn about Latino expressions of family, religion, community, arts, the experience of (im)migration and exile, and the search for cultural identity, the more knowledge we have of our own experiences and values, that is, of who we are. One hopes that knowledge brings wisdom, that the more we understand others, the more capable we will become of resolving conflict, of tolerating difference, and of celebrating unity in difference; for, as theologian Virgil Elizondo proclaims, "the future is *mestizo*," and it belongs to all of us.[61]

Part I
The Ties That Bind:
La Familia

Street Festival, San Antonio, Texas

Day Care Center, PUENTE Community Center, Los Angeles

Church Picnic, Wahneta, Florida

*Holy Family, Los Pastores,
Taos, New Mexico*

The Ties That Bind: La Familia

The family is the basic unit in Latino cultures. The Latino world is comprised of a web of intimate personal relationships, at the center of which is the family. Here the Latino, whatever his or her national heritage, develops a sense of individuality, identity, and a worldview. One's most important responsibilities are to family first and then to friends, not to abstract principles or to institutions. Children, from the beginning, are taught to behave with respect and deference toward their parents and elders.

The mother is indisputably the principal care giver in most Latino families; however, a child's development involves the whole family, not just parent and child. For example, child rearing and courtship in Latino cultures are family affairs. Often, older siblings, aunts, uncles, and grandparents all share in child care responsibilities, while for a marriage, both the groom's and the bride's families are actively involved in all stages of planning. Likewise, the entire family is involved in the celebration of the *quinceañera*, a girl's fifteenth birthday. Parents, extended kin, and friends may prepare for this event months in advance, since it can require not only a large party, complete with dinner,

but also a church service, including a weddinglike gown for the honoree and a rented tux for the father. Expenses may be considerable in the more lavish *quinceañera* extravaganzas, and they are usually borne by family members and friends. In ceremonial events such as this, the institution of *compadrazgo*, a network of kinshiplike relationships among very close friends, plays an important role, for it is really a mutual assistance and support group that, through moral and financial aid, extends the family and reinforces a personalistic rather than an institutional or bureaucratic view of the world.

The Latino family is a hierarchical institution, with the patriarch as the unchallenged head, and women exercising power behind the scenes. Authority is passed down from father to son, with the oldest son playing an important leadership role. In a traditional Latino family, the male expects to be obeyed and does not necessarily feel obliged to consult with family members before making family decisions. A double standard of sexual morality often prevails, with the wife expected to be absolutely faithful and the daughter to be "pure" until her wedding night The father and sons, on the other hand, are often encouraged to exercise their freedom through sexual affairs, a sign of machismo. This sexual double standard conflicts with the prevailing North American morality and has come under attack in households where children have grown up in this country more influenced by the attitudes of their peers than of their elders.

Perhaps the biggest source of conflict in the Latino family today is over the authority of the father. It is especially hard for youngsters to square such absolute authority with the emphasis on individual rights and personal freedom that they see all around them. The traditional Latino father, after any time in the United States sees his authority being progressively diminished by American society and culture. Many fathers are absent from home because they are holding down two or more jobs in order to support their families. This has its effect simply because the father may not be home enough to back up his authority with his presence. Further, the type of jobs the father holds are not likely to be ones in which he enjoys much autonomy or power. As more wives and daughters work out of the home, and as more children grow up with American ways, the role of the father as authority and provider is inevitably eroded. This change is often very difficult for fathers and other family members to accept. Sometimes nerves fray and domestic tensions can erupt into violence.

Latino fathers, mothers, and children have a very difficult time of it today, for they see the wreckage of American society strewn all about them—disobedient and disrespectful

children, drugs, teenage pregnancy, AIDS, gangs. They are caught between traditional and modern values as, increasingly, both parents and teenage children must work in order to secure for themselves and their children even a small slice of the American dream pie. For example, nearly 80 percent of the Mexican-origin population are in blue collar jobs.[1] As many family members as possible must work in order to stay out of poverty, which already claims over 23 percent of all Latino families, and which threatens many more.[2]

Further, if Latino families are to "make it" in the United States, they must, to some extent at least, substitute impersonal and institutional norms of behavior for personal and family ones in order to secure employment and advancement, which in this country, more often than not, depend on merit more than on personal or family ties. Though the Latino family is under great pressure today—generational, cultural, and economic—still it represents the most basic source of cultural values for Latinos in the United States and their major source of strength. [3]

The selected readings in this chapter highlight these distinctive qualities: the sanctity of the mother; respect for the father; deference to elders; the patriarchal structure, including machismo and a double standard of morality; the strength of the single mother; the importance of the extended family, particularly the *abuela*, or grandmother; the prevalence of the system of *compadrazgo*; the centrality of ritualistic family occasions, such as the *quinceañera* and the tradition of *noviazgo,* or courtship; and the primacy of family responsibilities over individual aspirations.

These qualities make for highly complex family dynamics and, to a considerable degree, account for the stresses and strains as well as the joys and strengths of the Latino family. Life in the United States sharpens points of conflict and convergence between traditional and changing family and gender roles and expectations.

Victor Villaseñor

Victor Villaseñor is the author of the novel *Macho!* (Houston: Arte Público Press, 1991); a nonfiction work, *Jury: The People vs. Juan Corona* (Boston: Little, Brown, 1977); a screenplay, "The Ballad of Gregorio Cortez" (1982), and the novel *Rain of Gold* (Houston: Arte Público Press, 1991). The last, from which the following reading is taken, tells the story of Villaseñor's own family over several generations, beginning in 1911 in revolutionary Mexico and ending in California. It is a moving and humorous saga of idiosyncratic and cunning family members, of crafty schemes to make a buck, of survival as immigrants, and, above all, of romantic "true love."

Our reading combines two brief excerpts, both concerning courtship rituals. In the first, the mother, Doña Guadalupe, and her *comadre*, Doña Manza, mercilessly grill the young suitor, Salvador Villaseñor, who has come to seek the hand of the lovely Lupe, while the father, Don Victor, watches bemusedly on the sidelines. The other excerpt describes the joyous wedding that follows.

from *Rain of Gold*

"*Querida*," said Don Victor, opening the front flap of the tent, "come outside. I'd like you to meet our champion, Salvador Villaseñor!"

"*A sus órdenes*," said Salvador, taking off his hat and bowing with a flair.

"*Con mucho gusto*," said Doña Guadalupe, coming outside. "Guadalupe Gomez." Salvador took her hand.

"Well, sit down, make yourself at home," she said, making room for Salvador to sit on one of the crates that they'd gotten from the orchard across the road. "Or would you prefer to go inside?" she asked.

"Whatever you wish, *señora*," said Salvador, looking at the short, plump old lady very carefully. She had beautiful white hair and large, wonderful, hazel-green eyes that sparkled with mischief and contrasted with her dark, serious Indian features.

"Well, then, come in," she said, deciding that she could best handle this innocent, girl-stealing coyote inside.

On going into the long tent, Salvador felt like he'd entered the web of a spider, the old woman was eyeing him so deliberately.

"So, where are you from?" she asked, sitting down on a crate that Don Victor had brought in for her.

"Los Altos de Jalisco," said Salvador, sitting on a crate.

"I see, and are your parents living?"

"Thank God, my mother is," he said, smiling grandly. "She's the love of my life!"

The old lady raised up her left eyebrow, smoothing out the apron on her lap. Either this man was too good to be true or he was the worst kind of coyote, a man capable of stealing a woman's heart and soul.

"And where does your mother live?" she asked.

"In Corona, just north of here."

"I see. And may I ask, how do you manage to do so well here in this country?" she said, eyeing his fine clothes.

Salvador was taken by surprise. He hadn't expected such direct questioning. Especially before he'd even made his intentions known regarding Lupe. He looked at the old lady, choosing his words carefully, staring straight back at her as she studied his eyes. After all, he wasn't a professional gambler for nothing.

"I move fertilizer," he said, lying to her, staring at her, eye-to-eye, giving absolutely nothing away. "I have trucks and contracts with several ranches."

"Oh," she said, noticing that neither of his eyes had moved. "And this pays well, he?" she added.

He laughed. She'd accepted his words. Duel had, indeed, taught him well. "Yes, very well, if you got enough manure," he said.

Watching the whole exchange, Don Victor burst out laughing, thinking of all the times that his wife had outwitted him. Doña Guadalupe gave him a dirty look. Getting to his feet, Don Victor returned his wife's dirty look and went outside to smoke. He could see that his crafty, old wife had her hands full.

For the next ten minutes, Doña Guadalupe pounded Salvador with question after question, but Salvador only smiled, answering whatever she asked.

The sun was going down and it was getting late. Salvador still hadn't seen or heard Lupe. He began to feel trapped. Yes, of course, he remembered that his mother had told him that he had to get to know Lupe's mother, but this was ridiculous.

Then Doña Manza came through the front flap. She, too, had fixed her hair and changed her dress.

"You've come just in time, Doña Manza," said Doña Guadalupe to her old friend. "I'd like you to meet Salvador Villaseñor."

Standing up, Salvador pulled at his collar nervously. He'd seen this before, back home when the she-boars got together, going after the lion that had gotten in to their den.

"Glad to meet you, *señora*," said Salvador, taking Doña Manza's hand. Salvador could hear Don Victor laughing outside, truly enjoying his predicament.

Out back, Lupe was done rewashing the dishes. She was watching the little children play in the sewage water that ran down the line between the tents. She couldn't figure out what was going on. Her mother was behaving as badly as Carlota.

Manuelita came running up. She'd changed clothes and fixed her hair, too.

"But what is going on?" asked Lupe. "First, Carlota doesn't like Salvador and then my mother fixes herself up to meet him, and now you come all dressed up like we're going to a dance."

"Oh, Lupe, don't you really know what's going on?"

"No, I guess not," said Lupe.

"Well, remember back in La Lluvia when the Colonel decided to stay at your house above all other houses in the village?"

"Well, yes, but that was only because he didn't want his wife near the plaza where the soldiers stayed."

"But then why didn't he stay at someone else's house?" she asked, watching Lupe's eyes. "Oh, Lupe, you really don't see it, do you? This is why Rose-Mary hated you so much and still does. No matter how many private finishing schools Don Manuel sends his daughters to, they will never have the dignity that you acquired from your own home.

"Lupe, that's why our mothers are best friends. They have a sense of values that cannot be taught. They are *el eje* of their *casas*, the inspiration of our lives. And now this man who slayed the dragon out in the fields has come to court you with the force of the heavens! Every girl in the camp is excited with envy!"

"Of me?"

"Yes, of you!" said Manuelita.

Lupe looked her friend in the eyes and she knew deep down inside that Manuelita spoke the truth. This man, Salvador, did cause excitement, just as her Colonel had done.

Doña Guadalupe was just beginning to continue her questioning when Victoriano and Carlota drove up in Salvador's grand automobile.

"Mama!" said Carlota, rushing inside the tent, "come outside and see his car; it's beautiful!"

"Here," said Victoriano, giving the keys back to Salvador, "that's the most powerful car I've ever driven! It's even more powerful than your Dodge!"

"Yes," said Salvador, taking the keys. "It is nice, isn't it?" he added, hoping that the interrogation had ended. But he was wrong.

"All right," said Doña Guadalupe, "enough about cars."

"But don't you want to see it?" asked Victoriano.

"No," said the old woman, "I know nothing about them. Now, please keep still while Doña Manza and I continue talking with Salvador. And you, Carlota, go to the back and help your sister make some tea for us."

"Maybe I can help," said Salvador, jumping to his feet, hoping he might get away from this old lady and see Lupe before it became too late.

"Certainly no," said Doña Guadalupe, "you sit down. They'll bring us the tea." Salvador sat back down.

"Well," said Victoriano, giving Salvador a look of sympathy, "you three talk; I'm going outside to look at the car some more."

Salvador tossed him the keys. Victoriano caught them.

"Well," said the old woman, smoothing out her apron once more, "as we were saying, Doña Manza and I saw the Revolution ruin many *familias*. But, still, we both think that the greatest threat to a marriage is alcohol and cards. Don't you agree?"

"Well, yes, in a way," said Salvador.

"Good, I'm glad you agree with us," said Doña Guadalupe, "because speaking quite frankly, I want you to know that we will never permit one of our daughters to marry a man who drinks alcohol. In fact, we've both instructed our daughters since they were small of the terrible vices of liquor and cards.

"I worked hard, Salvador," said the old woman, tears suddenly coming to her eyes, "to keep my family together through the war, and I will protect my flesh until my last breath! Do you hear me?"

"Well, yes, I do," said Salvador, taken aback by her sudden outburst. Hell, he hadn't even asked for the hand of any of her daughters. So why were these two old ladies saying all these things to him? Was his love for Lupe so obvious that everyone already knew his true intentions?

He glanced away, trying to gather his thoughts. This old woman was incredible. But, on the other hand, maybe his own mother would have done the same thing if she'd had the chance.

"No, *señora*, I don't drink or gamble; I'm a businessman," said Salvador.

"Well, we're very glad to hear that," said Doña Guadalupe as the girls came in with the tea.

Seeing Lupe, Salvador leaped to his feet. But he hit the hanging lantern with his head, almost knocking himself back down.

Putting down the teapot, Lupe rushed to his side. "Are you all right?" she asked.

"I don't know," he said. He then got an idea and gripped Lupe's arm. "I'm pretty dizzy. Maybe you better get me a wet towel. Here, I'll go with you."

Salvador quickly started toward the rear of the tent with Lupe before anyone could say anything. Doña Guadalupe and Doña Manza glanced at each other.

"Well, he is quick," said Doña Manza.

"Yes, I noticed," said Doña Guadalupe. "And don't take too long!" she shouted after Lupe and Salvador.

"My God," said Salvador, once they were outside, "I thought I'd never get to see you."

Lupe laughed. "I just don't know why my mother is behaving like this." She took a clean rag, wringing it out. "Does it hurt?"

"Yes," he said, "but standing here with you, I can never feel pain again."

They eyes met, the world stopped again—just as it had out in the fields—and it was paradise. Lupe blushed, becoming self-conscious, and put the wet rag to Salvador's head.

"There," she said, "I hope it will help."

"How can it not," he said, "coming from you?"

And he wanted to say more, much more, all he had locked up inside his heart and soul, but he couldn't. It was just too much. He now knew why it felt so good being with this woman. It was as if he'd known her from another lifetime; as if every move, every expression she made, reminded him of another great love that he'd had before. Oh, he was swimming with good feelings, bursting with love!

"Well," said Lupe, "I think we better go back inside before the tea gets cold."

"Of course," he said.

When Lupe and the girls came out with the tray of tea and sweet breads, they were told to go back inside. Then, Lupe's mother came after him, wanting blood.

"Well," she said, "now, getting back to our conversation of the other night, I want to ask you what you think of the Mexican tradition that says that money should only be handled by men."

Salvador almost spilled his tea. "Well, to tell the truth," he said, putting his cup down, "I've never thought too much of it."

Lupe's mother glanced at Doña Manza. "Well, to be perfectly frank," she continued, "my *comadre* and I have spoken of this topic at great length and we think that this custom of ours that says money should never be put in the hands of women and children isn't just wrong, but actually destructive for the very survival of the family."

"Oh, I see," he said. "I never thought of that."

"Of course not," she said, going right on without hesitation, "because tradition tells you that men are free to do with the money as they please and the church agrees with them, making our tradition sound as if it came straight from God. And so no one ever questions it. But my *comadre* and I, who raised our children alone half of the time, were forced to think of this," she continued, "and so we can't possibly agree with this very Mexican belief that men alone were made superior by God to handle money. In fact, personally, I'll go so far as to say that I believe that some women are more capable of handling money than men."

And saying this, she stopped and stared at Salvador straight in the eyes, daring him to contradict her.

But Salvador gave her nothing, then taking a deep breath he glanced at Don Victor, who must have known what was in store for him this night, because he winked at Salvador.

"Yes, of course, I can see what you mean," said Salvador calmly. But inside his soul, he was raging. He'd never heard such talk in all his life. The first time, this old woman had said that cards and liquor were worse than war for marriage, and now she was saying that women were more capable of handling money than men. This was blasphemy! Why, the Pope, himself, was a man! And Jesus Christ had put him in charge of mankind's destiny on earth!

But before Salvador could say anything, the old lady went right on. "And to go further," she said, "I'll tell you this: I believe that women, with their instincts of a mother protecting her young, have the obligation for the survival of the family to handle the money that their husbands make. And I don't say this lightly or with malice or with ignorance. No, I say this from what I've seen again and again all my life. And if a man is a man, he, too, can open his eyes and see this very important fact. Money must be used for the good of the entire family and not just for man's arrogant need of cards and liquor!"

Salvador put down his sweet bread. Why, next she'd be saying that a son-in-law's obligation was to turn his paycheck over to his mother-in-law.

"And now, Salvador," she said, sitting back, "what do you think?" she asked, smiling. "And be perfectly frank. Because, after all, what I've just said is far removed from the common ideas of our people. So, of course, it would be unfair of me to not understand a young man being disturbed with these ideas of mine." And there she stopped, smiling such a sweet, innocent little smile that Salvador almost laughed. Why, she was as cunning as his own mother.

He took a deep breath and glanced at Doña Manza. She, too, was smiling sweetly. He glanced down at his shoes, trying to gain time and think of how his own mother would handle this situation. But looking down, he saw that his beautiful black and white shoes were covered with flies. The bacon grease that he'd taken from Kenny's kitchen to shine his shoes with had melted and attracted all these flies. And one big horsefly was stuck on the tip of his right shoe, crawling around in a circle, making desperate sounds as it tried to get free. His mind went blank. He could think of nothing. And yet, he fully realized that this was the most important test of his life, if he ever hoped to marry Lupe.

Glancing up, he saw that both women were also staring at his shoes. He turned crimson with embarrassment and reached own, pinching the fly off his shoe, then brought out his red silk handkerchief, wiping off his hand.

"Well," he said, wishing that he had a pint bottle of whiskey so he could take a good swig. "What can I say?" he continued, brushing the crumbs off his pant legs from the sweet bread he'd eaten. "Except that you're right, *señora,* absolutely right." He figured that he'd lie straight out, but that he wouldn't stray too far from the truth, in case he had to eat his own lies some day. Oh, it was a good thing that his mother had prepared him or he'd be feeling pretty helpless right now.

"And my dear mother would be in complete agreement with you," he added, not quite knowing where he was going, but hoping to wing it. "For I remember my parents' arguments when I was small and, most of the time, they were about money. My father was a hard worker—the hardest—and excellent with horses and cattle, too, but he just wasn't good with money."

He glanced into the well-lit tent and he saw Lupe and the other young women. Carlota was giggling and pointing at his shoes. He breathed deeply, brushing the rest of the crumbs off his pants, and stomped his feet, getting rid of the flies, then coughed, clearing his voice.

"And so, as I was saying," he said, "my father was big, handsome man with a huge, red two-handled moustache and he had tremendous power for fighting and working. But, still, even as a child, I somehow knew that my mother knew more about money matters than he did. Once, I'll never forget, we were up on the slopes and he got so mad at our goats that he began to yell and scream. A shrewd businessman happened to come by on horseback.

"'Don Juan,' he said to my father, 'I'll take those troublesome goats off your hands right now. Here's a twenty peso gold piece.' And before my older brother Jose could say a word, my father said 'All right. Give me the money, you got a deal!'

"And so, angrily, my father took the money, sent my brother and me home, and went to town to drink. When he got home that night, my poor mother—who, in the meantime, had borrowed and scraped together all the money she could from friends and relatives—said to my father, 'Look, Don Juan, you must go back to that man you sold our goats to and buy them back. Here is twenty-five pesos gold. Let him make a five-peso profit, but get our goats back. We need them to live.'

"But my father said, 'I can't do that, woman! I made a deal with that man and my word is my honor!' 'But Juan,' pleaded my mother, 'those goats are our life. The cattle and horses don't give us the money we need to buy our staples. It's the cheese that we make from the goat milk that buys our supplies in town. Please, I beg of you, take this money and go back to that man. Tell him you were angry this morning and you weren't in your best frame of mine and he'll understand.'

"You would have thought my mother had insulted my father, for he turned on her with such a rage, yelling at her, 'Woman, are you crazy? No Villaseñor has gone back on his word in five hundred years!'

"'But, Don Juan,' begged my mother, 'that man tricked you. He knows about your famous temper, so he took advantage of you.'

"Well, I'm embarrassed to tell you, *señora*, but my father—a gigantic man, whose family had come from northern Spain—then grabbed my poor little mother and shouted into her face like a wild man, 'No man takes advantage of a Villaseñor and lives!' he bellowed.

"And so he got his gun to go kill the man and my mother had to turn around and plead with him that everything was all right and maybe it hadn't been such a bad deal. But still, since she'd already raised the money, could he please go back to that man and talk reasonably to him and get their goats back."

"And your father?" said Doña Guadalupe, looking very concerned, "was he also one of these men that hit women?"

Instantly, Salvador could see where the old woman was headed with this one. "No," he said breathing deeply. "My father had many faults, but that wasn't one of them." And he wasn't lying; it was true.

"I'm glad to hear that," said Doña Guadalupe. "Go on." She glanced toward the tent, hoping that the girls were listening. And, of course, they were. Especially Lupe and Manuelita who were catching every single word.

"And so that night my poor mother begged my father as no wife should ever have to beg," continued Salvador. "'*Querido,*' she said 'please understand me, I'm not complaining that you spent part of the money. Please, believe me, I'm only saying that we need those goats back.'

"But my father never heard my mother's words. No, he just flew into another rage, saying if she wasn't complaining, then why in the devil was she bringing it all up! And then he shouted that he was a Villaseñor and that he came from kings and no little . . . " But here, Salvador stopped, tears coming to his eyes, remembering how his father had next called his mother *una india pendeja,* a stupid, backward, ignorant Indian. And that night, his brother Jose, the great, left their home never to set foot in it again while his father was there. Oh, Jose's eyes had burned like fire, wanting to kill their father.

"And so, well, to make it short," said Salvador, never having meant to go this far, "I can truly say that I sympathize with you, *señora*. For that shrewd businessman robbed my father, and we went hungry that year." Salvador tried to stop, but he just couldn't. He was hot, wishing that he'd been big enough to knock his own father down!

"So, yes, *señora,* to answer your question, I can honestly say with all my heart that I agree with you one thousand times one thousand! That a man is not necessarily superior to a woman in handling money!" He wanted to stop, he truly did, but he just couldn't. "In fact, it has been my experience to find almost the opposite to be true!" he yelled. "I have found that women—with their instincts of the mother pig protecting her young—are often more capable of handling the family finances than men!

"My mother, I swear it," he said, standing up and pounding the air with his huge fists, "if she'd handled our money, we would have never come to ruin, even in the middle of the Revolution!" His hands were fists and he didn't want to, but he couldn't help himself, and he struck the heavy crate that he'd been sitting on with such force that it shattered into pieces. "We went hungry after my father sold those goats!" he bellowed, the cords of his neck coming up like ropes. "Hungry! And I'd never seen this, *señora,* until now! But that was the beginning of our destruction! And my poor mother, what could she do? Nothing! Even when she turned to Jose, my older brother, and tried to get him to come back home and talk things over, my father was against it, and gave the reins of our family to Alejo, who was blue-eyed like himself!"

When Salvador finally stopped, he could see that everyone was staring at him. He tried to apologize, to say that he was sorry, but he was still so upset that he could do nothing but tremble like a leaf.

Getting to her feet, Doña Guadalupe took each of his big hands in hers. "It's a heartwarming experience to find a young man as strong and capable as you who can also see the predicament of women. Your mother must be a great, great woman to have raised such a son!"

"She is," said Salvador, wiping his eyes, "she really is, thank you."

"The pleasure is all mine," said Doña Guadalupe. "Would you like to come and join us for dinner tomorrow?" she asked.

"Why, yes, I'd like that," he said.

"Good, and please come early so we can continue our conversation."

"I will," he said.

And just then, as they were talking, a cat came up and started licking Salvador's shoes. Salvador didn't move, hoping to God that the cat would go away.

"Well," laughed Lupe's mother, "at least you didn't frighten the animals," she said.

"How could he?" said Carlota, coming out of the tent with the other girls, "wearing shoes that smell like *chicarrones!*" Carlota laughed, and she would've gone on ridiculing Salvador if Don Victor hadn't chased the animal away.

"Enough!" he said to Carlota. "I, too, have put bacon grease on my shoes many times. It preserves the leather and makes it waterproof." He stuck out his hand to Salvador. "I salute you!" he said. "I don't know of any man who could've stood up better than you have under the fire of these women!"

"The pleasure was mine," said Salvador, taking his hand. "And I'm sorry about the crate. I just got so mad, thinking of our goats and the hunger we went through, that, well, I just . . . "

"There's no need to explain yourself. It was a terrible Revolution for all of us," said the old man. "I respect you; you are a real *macho!*"

• • •

In the rear of the church, Doña Guadalupe hugged her daughter one last time, then hurried up the side aisle to the front, where she was supposed to be with her family, across from Salvador's people. She could hear something going on up front, but she didn't think too much of it. All week she'd been cooking and working and sewing so much that she was exhausted. She was so tired that she almost felt like going against all her principles and having herself a good shot of tequila.

Don Victor was dressed in a dark brown suit. When Lupe came out of the little side room full of giggling women, he took her arm, and they started up the long aisle. Lupe was dressed all in white and Maria's little daughter, Isabel, was holding the long white peacock train of her magnificent dress.

The commotion was still going on up at the front of the church, but Lupe ignored it and came up the aisle with her father, taking long, slow, deliberate steps, trying to look as calm and serene as she possibly could.

But, oh, she was going crazy inside. This was, indeed, the most important step of her entire life. This was the man that she was going to marry; this was the man that was going to be the father of her children; this was the person that she was going to share all the dreams and joys and sorrows with for the rest of her life.

The noise at the front of the church subsided. Lupe continued down the aisle on her father's arm, concentrating with all her being, all her heart and soul, trying to keep calm, passing all these people who were smiling at her . . . people she knew but couldn't recognize at the moment because she was so frightened.

It felt like the longest journey of Lupe's life, traveling step by step, towards the distant altar. She breathed deeply and recalled the day they'd come out of their beloved box canyon and that dangerous walk that they'd had along the cliffs called El Diablo. She realized how far they'd come since that day that they'd walked those cliffs and crossed that mighty river. She suddenly saw very clearly that she was once more walking on the cliffs of fate, ready to cross yet another mighty river on her journey of womanhood. She wondered if, indeed, she would ever get to see her beloved canyon again before she died.

Oh, those great towering cathedral rocks, they were the altar at which she'd always thought that she would marry one day. But those great rocks of her youth were gone, gone just like her Colonel. Then they stopped, and her father drew her close, kissed her on the cheek, and turned her about, giving her arm to . . . to . . . to, oh, my God, Salvador, a total stranger.

"All right," she heard her father say as in a faraway dream, "she's yours now . . . take good care of our angel."

"With all my heart and soul," said Salvador, coming out of the pew and taking her arm.

Lupe felt like adding the words, "you better!" but she didn't. She felt Salvador turn her about, and together they approached the altar, hand in hand, all alone and far, far away from their parents. Oh, she was dreaming, dreaming, gliding over the towering cliffs back home, sweeping over the high country of her youth, and this was beautiful. For this was the sacred dream of all her years of yearning;

this was the reality of all her childhood fantasies that she'd had of her Colonel. This was it; this was, indeed, life—*la vida.*

Then, Lupe saw the priest standing before them on the steps of the dark, blood-red carpet. He smiled at them and opened his black book. He began to read, and time stood still. She stood mesmerized, not quite able to comprehend the words that he recited.

But then, she saw the priest turn to Salvador, and she heard him say, "Juan Salvador Villaseñor, do you take Maria de Guadalupe Gomez to be your wife? Do you promise to be true to her in good times and in bad, in sickness and in health, to love and honor her all the days of your life?"

As in a dream, Lupe turned and she saw the moustache on Salvador's upper lip move like a long, fat worm as he said, "Yes, I do."

Then the priest spoke to her. "Maria de Guadalupe Gomez, do you take Juan Salvador Villaseñor to be your husband? Do you promise to be true to him in good times and in bad, in sickness and in health, to love him and honor him all the days of your life?"

Lupe considered the words, especially the ones, "in bad times" and wondered if this was wise. Why would any woman in her right mind agree to this?

Leaning in close, the man of God whispered, "Say, 'I do,' my child."

"What?" said Lupe, trying her hardest to stop thinking of all these things that came flashing to her mind. "Oh, yes, I do, of course, Father."

Looking relieved, the priest continued, and the next set of words Salvador repeated, word by word.

Then it was Lupe's turn to repeat the holy words of acceptance. And, when she came to the passage, "To have and to hold from this day forward, for better for worse, for richer, for poorer, in sickness and in health, until death do us part," tears came to her eyes. For she now understood for the first time in her life what these words truly meant.

The words were, indeed the secret; these words were the power, these were the words that had given her mother—and her mother's mother—the strength to endure the years. The words, "until death do us part," were the foundation of every marriage. They were what gave a woman the vision with which to raise up like a mighty star and join God's graces, just like Doña Margarita had told her.

This, then, was the true secret with which every ordinary woman became extraordinary and gained the power within herself to resurrect her family from the dead, again and again, and give her family the conviction of heart to go on, no matter what.

And these sacred words were now hers, too, "until death do us part."

Tears streamed down her face; and in her mind's eye, Lupe now saw the gates of Eden open, and there lay paradise just beyond her at arm's length—golden, serene, and as beautiful as La Lluvia de Oro right after a summer rain, with all the flowers and plants and trees breathing, breathing, and all the birds and bees and deer and possums playing; and, high above, there were the towering cathedral cliffs, raining down in a waterfall of glistening gold, and an eagle circling overhead, screeching to the heavens.

She'd done it, she really had. Here in her heart of hearts, she'd gotten married in the true spirit of the beloved canyon of her youth.

Salvador saw the tears of joy streaming down Lupe's gorgeous face and he was filled with such joy that he just knew that they'd passed through the gates of Eden. This was his new true love and yes, one thousand times yes, his mother had been right; only with a clean soul can a man enter into the paradise of marriage.

Lupe and Salvador exchanged their rings and she promised to love, cherish, and obey and she noticed that Salvador only had to love and cherish; he hadn't needed to say that he'd obey. They kissed, and the worm on his upper lip tickled her. She tried not to laugh, but giggled anyway.

The bells rang, the people applauded, and then the priest raised up his hands, silencing everyone once again.

"Lupe, Salvador," he said grandly, "from now on, you two are of one body, one soul; and it is your duty to take care of each other, so that your union of marriage will transcend even over death itself, and together you will enter the Kingdom of God for all eternity."

Lupe's whole body was filled with rapture, and her feet never touched the ground as they turned and started back down the aisle, she and her husband—this man, this stranger, her true love—who was now and forever closer to her than her own brother or sisters, or even her own mother.

She could feel his hand pulsating in her palm, and she could hear his breathing, coming and going in rhythm with her own. These, then, would now be the sounds of her new home. This man's warmth would now be the one that she'd reach across the warm-smelling bed for each morning.

As they came out of the church into the bright sunlight, Salvador hugged Lupe close and two photographers took their photos, and everyone threw rice and confetti at them. The kids set off firecrackers, and everyone cheered.

Salvador then took Lupe's left hand in both of his two huge hands, and he looked down at her diamond ring pensively. The two photographers snapped this picture, too. And it was a lovely moment—Lupe looking at his thick mane of curly black hair as he gazed at her huge diamond, a stone so fantastic that most of the people in the crowd had never even seen one until now.

Oh, they'd done it, they really had. They were so happy, and everyone was so proud of them. Even Luisa. And Carlota, who'd been green with envy of Lupe all these years, was now heard to say, "Yes, that's right, she's my, well, older sister, and yes, it's a real diamond . . . of the highest quality!"

Salvador walked Lupe to the Moon, opened her door for her, and felt so light-headed, so much in love with love itself, that he gave a shout of *gusto*, feeling wonderful.

Rolando Hinojosa Smith

One of the most prolific of Latino writers, Hinojosa is famous for his Klail City Death Trip series, the multigenerational story of small-town folk in a fictional county in the lower Rio Grande Valley. His acclaimed *Estampas del Valle* (1973; published in English by Arte Público Press as *The Valley,* 1983) is part of this series, characterized by its picaresque satire and acute observation of local customs and language.

The following brief essay shows Hinojosa's interest in local customs, for it describes the time-honored family tradition of the *quince-añera* and wryly remarks on the importance of having *padrinos* and *madrinas,* part of the extended support network of family and friends, to help foot the bill for these extravaganzas in which "overspending is the rule." Tradition for Latino families is important not least for the plea-sure it gives the family, considerations of afford-ability and practicality aside.

Sweet Fifteen

I was thirteen years old and much too short to be dancing with a fifteen-year-old, but the occasion was her debut, she was fifteen (*Tenía quince años*), and it was her *quinceañera* party. This was the midforties, in Mercedes in the Rio Grande Valley, where *quinceañera* parties were not to be missed. I was a *chambelán* (attendant), and my date and I were one of the fourteen couples in the *quinceañera's* court of honor. The *quinceañera* and her escort made the fifteenth pair—one couple for every year.

Unknown to many Anglos, *quinceañera* parties are the coming-out balls of Mexico and Spanish-speaking Texas, seemingly composed of equal parts wedding, debutante party, and bas mitzvah. The demure fifteen-year old honoree wears a gown and veil like a bride, family and friends throw a big bash, and the festivities commence with mass at the Catholic church. A *quinceañera* party signals a girl's coming of age.

Two years after that party, doing my social duty, I traveled to Brownsville for my second go-around. That affair, like the first, was *muy mexicano*, but since Brownsville was a bigger town, the party was bigger and showier. Lines of *damas* (female attendants) and *chambelanes* formed, with the *quinceañera* and her escort leading them. The band struck up some pomp-and-circumstance march, and we all promenaded around El Jardín hotel ballroom. The room was decked out in crepe paper and bouquets of flowers, and a special spotlight shone on the *quinceañera*. After the promenade she danced with her father as everyone else watched. Then the lights dimmed, and the dance opened for the rest of us.

On the drive back home to Mercedes, my father explained that *quinceañera* parties were a Mexican export. They were held in parts of South America too, he said, and he thought that they must have originated in Spain. In the Valley, though, only those families he called "very *mexicanos*" held *quinceañera* parties, referring to Mexicans who had been in this country one, perhaps two, generations but who still clung to old Mexican traditions.

Today *quinceañera* parties are major undertakings that begin with a morning mass, followed by a formal reception, a sit-down dinner, and a dance. Instead of just a trio, two bands may play, each with a contract for the number and type of songs to be performed. And instead of donning a homemade dress, the honoree wears a formal white gown that is as elaborate as the family can afford. As many as one thousand guests might attend, and in the Valley the newspapers report all the fashion details and list the out-of-town guests.

The increase in expenses has made the role of the sponsors—the *padrinos* and the *madrinas*—much more important. Rather than the parents bearing all the cost, the *quinceañera* party has become more of a collaborative effort. And it had to be. Considering that many Valley families earn $8,000 to $10,000 annually, the *padrino-madrina* collective is imperative for a party that can cost as much as $5,000. There are *padrinos* and *madrinas* for just about everything: The dress, hat, gloves, ring, shoes, veil, cake, cake knife, and bouquets, plus the bands, photographers, church services, and myriad other functions. True, this is a once-in-a-life-time affair, but if there are three girls in the family, what then?

Some businesses and caterers specialize in *quinceañera* parties, and loans may be arranged to pay for them. The expense can be traced back to an old custom, *echar la casa por la ventana*—literally "throw the house out the window"—which means to go all out, no stinting on food or drink, and if the band tries to quit, pay it double. Hang the expense, and see if the next set of parents can top *this*.

In my present home of Austin, the Mexican professional community, dispersed though it is, maintains a hold on its South Texas-Valley roots and has added twists to the *quinceañera* parties. The professional community and the family may share a genteel and sedate early breakfast with the parish priest. The weekend party is usually small but posh, and depending on the family's cash flow, an out-of-town trip for the *quinceañera* and some of her friends might be arranged. In Houston and Dallas the celebrations are much the same; many Valley people and many "very *mexicanos*" live there too. And then there's San Antonio, where all four La Feria department stores carry *quinceañera* dresses. In El Paso many Texans buy the festive dresses in Juárez, which stocks a cornucopia of *quinceañera* gear. Across the *río* it is no different. After all, Mexico exported the *quinceañera* parties, and just like here, the more money a family has, the more it spends on these events. Social pressure is such that whatever the family income, overspending is the rule, and the practice cuts across all social lines.

Just how long has this been going on? I have an elaborate 1979 invitation that includes a 1929 picture of a *quinceañera* (now the grandmother), a 1951 photo of the honoree's mother, and a picture of the 1979 *quinceañera*. It has a family tree and pictures of the honoree at birth, baptism, and First Communion and in various ballet and dancing outfits. It also includes the names of the *chambelanes* and *damas*; the announcement that an invitation is required for admission to the reception, dinner, and dance; and a verse written for the *quinceañera* by a friend of her grandfather's.

When will the spending stop? Who knows, and why should it? As we say in the Valley, it gives pleasure to many. And with the dresses looking more and more like bridal gowns, perhaps another future expense may be out of the way.

¿Bailamos? "Want to dance?"

Chris Baca

Chris Baca is director of the Youth Development Corporation in Albuquerque, which sponsors a large and varied number of social service programs for area youths and families.

To Baca, family is everything. He was brought up in a poor, rural, close-knit, patriarchal family in which responsibility, self-sufficiency, and the contributions of each member were highly valued. Baca's stable and supportive family environment is deeply rooted in the traditions and history of New Mexico, where families have tended to live in the same community for hundreds of years. Because his own positive family experiences have been crucial to his development, and because changing times are placing great stresses on families everywhere, Baca feels a special commitment to help those young people who have not had the kind of family experience that he has enjoyed. His organization is, in effect, serving some of the functions of families in a time when economic and social change is eroding traditional Latino families.

Interview

My family goes back to about 1598 here in New Mexico, when the first European settlers arrived. They came here with the expedition of Juan de Oñate to explore the area that had been seen by Cabeza de Vaca, who was one of the first Europeans to explore the interior of North America. They were shipwrecked off the coast of Texas, at Galveston, and there were just three survivors, Cabeza de Vaca, *el moro* Esteban (Esteban the Moor), and another. They wandered around the interior for seven years, going from one Indian tribe to another. They would be enslaved and eventually set free because they had some knowledge of medicine, which they learned from the Indians. They managed through their own wiles and skills to stay alive. They went all the way through Nuevo Mexico, up into the plains of Kansas. They were wandering off their course, but they were able to see many areas of previously unexplored territory. They finally figured out that if they went south they would hit Mexico City. On the way, they encountered another Spanish exploration group, who took them back to Mexico City.

There, everybody wanted to make a name for himself and to claim something for Spain. They asked Cabeza de Vaca if he would lead an expedition north, but he said, "No, are you crazy? I've been up there seven years, I just came back, I don't want to go anyplace." So he stayed in Mexico City, and that expedition was led by Esteban. This is all leading up to Juan de Oñate finally coming to Nuevo Mexico. The Spaniards were looking for the seven cities of gold. But anyway, there was also great curiousity about what it was like up north, and that's when the expedition of Oñate came. With him came a Capitán Cristobal Baca, my namesake, along with others, most prominently the Bacas and the Chaveses, to settle the area. That's the beginning of my family in New Mexico. We're from a little town south of Belén, called Veguita; it's also called Las Nutrias. It lies at the end of the Chihuahua Trail and the beginning of the Old Santa Fe Trail. That's where my parents grew up, and my family has been in that town forever.

In between Juan de Oñate and my folks, my research has taken me to about 1740, when the family was still there. But then the records become very scarce even though the Catholic missionaries kept very fine records. Unless you have exactly the right names and the right times, you really bounce around. But in 1740 they were still there in this little place.

My ancestors became farmers. They farmed everything it took to survive, which was all their crops, corn, chiles. They raised all their own animals, cattle, sheep, horses, alfalfa fields. It was communal; in order to survive you had to pool what resources you had, because you have to understand that during those times the

Spanish were very few in number, the land was vast, and the settlers were constantly subject to raids by the Comanches and Apaches. It wasn't always the other way around, where people say that the Spanish went in there and subjugated the Indians. It wasn't quite that way. The Indians didn't give up anything easily. Only one side of that story has been told. But at any rate, in order for them to survive, they had to pool their resources, because they were essentially cut off from Mexico City, and forget about Spain. They were just some little outpost with no gold. The only ones who were interested were the missionaries who were looking for converts. The Church played a very big role.

On my father's side, some of the women were Indian. What I've been able to find in my genealogical search is that one grandmother was actually listed on the rolls as Indian. Her name was Guadalupe Griego, but that was the name of the family that she was a servant to. No others are mentioned as being Indian, but there undoubtedly were some. That's the kind of rich history that I identify with.

We have never been and have never felt like the minority in this state. The fact of the matter is we have set the form of government, and we have elected senators and governors and congressmen, not just recently, but way into the past. That's why we feel very much part of this land. Basically because we've had the experience of having to coexist with others, share the meager resources, we can get along. It wasn't always peaceful. We're also different from other Hispanics who live places where there are recent immigrants who come in with little or no power, who feel disenfranchised, who don't know how to access anything. That's not New Mexico. We get some immigrants, but mostly they go to the larger cities where there's more work: to Los Angeles, Washington, D.C.; New York; Chicago; or Miami. We have bilingual programs for the new immigrants, but we don't have many immigrants who stay. I like bilingual education because it recognizes the contributions of our culture here.

I became interested in family history when my family would talk about *"los tiempos de antes,"* the times of old, and I was fascinated by their stories. They had their own *ganados*, livestock, and fields, and you began to wonder what made us such survivors. When you hit the midlife crisis, which I hit at forty, you start to think about these things—where are you going? Before you figure out where you're going, it would be nice to find out where you've been. The root search is part of my search for self, and part of what I want to pass on to my kids.

Half of my family was born in Las Nutrias, like my parents. There are eleven of us and the first five or six were born in Las Nutrias. After World War II they moved to Albuquerque. As you know, that's when things really began to revolutionize here. That's when the military-industrial complex began to take root. Jobs were created here and the little communities began to dry up. They could no longer continue to live in the traditional ways. You couldn't rely on barter anymore, which is what my folks had done when they were growing up. They traded. For example, when my dad needed a car, he would trade animals that he had raised for that car. My mom used to call my dad "Let's Make a Deal" when Monty Hall was on—in the sixties, right? The Manhattan Project to destroy the world was birthed here, and a few miles away my father was still bartering in the traditional style. It's very anachronistic. I still remember chopping wood and pumping water and not having an indoor toilet. I was born in 1949, and that was in the fifties and sixties that I'm remembering. I was the product of a very rural and traditional lifestyle.

My family was a very strong patriarchy. My father was the ruler, and not only the ruler until you were eighteen, but beyond that. I can recall some of my older brothers who are now close to sixty having marital difficulties. Their wives would come to my father and tell him what the problems were. Then he would yank my brothers in and dress them down, and say, "You're married now, you're supposed to be responsible for your wife and your children." All of that. Whenever one of the families went down, lost their job or something, he would go out and collect money from everybody else, saying, "Your brother is having a hard time here." He was always the head of the family.

It never came up whether they considered themselves Spanish, or Mexican, or New Mexican or what. I think our culture was more Mexican, and there were *mexicanos* who would come up for trade, and I can remember hearing their accents. I think this tie with Spain is recent in New Mexico. It comes as a result of the Anglo influence, when there was a battle for control of this area between the Anglos and those that were here. It was very ugly, with much fighting and killing. At that time the Anglos called us Mexicans, and they used the term in a very derogatory way, and it stuck. Mexican had such a bad connotation that, later on, we tried to find another name for our identity. You see that among the blacks too; they say they're African or African American. They do that because we're trying to live down the negative attitude that has been imposed on us by that name. I think more up north in the state there is a stronger identification with Spain. The reason not to be identified with Mexicans is that derogatory use when we were growing up.

It's also true that if you take a good look at Mexican culture and our culture, you will see that they're different. I mean, there are similarities, but it's very different. I was in Mexico a month ago, in Oaxaca, and I found it very beautiful, but it's not my culture. Neither is Mexico City, or Monterrey, or Tijuana. Nuevo Mexicano is what I am. My oldest son asked me, "Dad, what are we, Chicano, Mexican, Hispanic, or Latino?" I had to tell him, "I don't know, I think we are still under that search for identity." That's one of the reasons why I did this root search, to know for myself and to be able to tell my kids who we are. Where is the Mexican, the Indian, the Spanish in us? We New Mexicans have a longer history than the Mexicans. You would consider somebody a Mexican who just arrived here three generations ago; that's recent for us, when you're talking about four hundred years. I think that what I am is a New Mexican American. If I could claim Mexico's proud history I would, but I can't claim something that isn't mine. I have to claim what is mine, which is being a Nuevo Mexicano, whatever that means!

Part of our identity involves a strong sense of place, families staying not only in the same part of the state, but even in the same town or village for hundreds of years. People always ask me why I don't move and go somewhere else. I'm not interested. If you cut me right now, you'd probably get the dust from the Southwest coming out. We're so much attached to our land, and that's why the land grant movement was so strong in New Mexico. This is where Reies Tijerina—he's Texan—chose to come, here rather than Texas, because the movement was so strong. Right now, people my age and younger, you ask them what they want, and they say, "I want to have my horse and some cows and do my own garden." Everybody aspires to that. Nobody wants a condo. You have to have at least an acre, and they're all aiming for that. They don't want to go to New York or L.A. If you pull the rug out from under me and some company doesn't want to pay me, here I can grow my own food. It's security and a survival instinct; it's not just love for the land. Think about right now, what is happening across America right now when everybody is in economic danger. No matter how much money you make, you are just several payments away from being homeless. If you haven't paid for your house, and you miss three payments on it, see what happens. Out you go, and then what do you do? Out here, people say, "I can make it on my own." By and large people own their own land because they have had it for so long. Of my eleven brothers and sisters, almost every single one owns their own house. I'm the only one who has a mortgage on mine, the others own theirs outright. They bought the land and built their houses. My dad would help them build, and we would all pitch in. The one who lives farthest away is my brother Ben, who lives in Los Chaves, which is even closer to Las Nutrias than any of us. All of us are in public service of one kind or another, either policemen or social work. Our ancestors were involved in military or civil service, and that's basically what we're doing here. My oldest brother is the undersheriff of Sandoval County. He's retired twice now. He was once the chief deputy for the sheriff's department, then he retired, and now they hired him over at the Pueblos to come and set up their police department. He retired from there, and six days later the sheriff from Sandoval County called him, so he's in another job still. My other brother was basically in public service even when the very first economic opportunity projects came along. Remember the War on Poverty? He was very involved in that here. He's done many, many things.

My sisters are very traditional. They did not work, but stayed home and raised their families. Only recently have they gone out to work, but my oldest sister still has never worked. My wife does not work either, she tends to be very traditional in that the women have held very traditional roles, which has made our families very strong. Eleven brothers and sisters and, in this day and age, no divorces. Out of about fifty nieces and nephews, maybe three divorces. The statistics should be about fifty percent. The family is the strongest institution, that strong patriarchy, with the man being the breadwinner and the woman running the home, which is as complex as anything else. That kind of teamwork and division of labor has kept the family together. The economic need for both husband and wife to work is growing. But what ends up happening is that the wife has to do two jobs. In all cultures across the country this is happening. It is very stressful on everybody. The number one cause of divorce is economic, with spouses fighting over this and that. To some extent that has not been the problem here, because we are in a relatively poor state. We rank forty-fifth in the nation in terms of per capita income.

But making money isn't everything. People ask me why don't I make more money going somewhere else, and I say, what's money got to do with it? I know what I want, and it's family. My wife was working when we got married, and she thought that after a while she might like to go back to work. She has that option if she wants to do that. When we talk about our role, what is the legacy we leave behind? How big our house is, or how many cars we have, or is it our children? I see so many people right now mortgaging their children's future because they want to keep up with the Joneses, move to a better neighborhood, a bigger house. What does that have to do with the quality of life you are providing your children? That doesn't make a home. I live right across from a housing project. Some people have told me that I should move, that I am an executive and can afford another house. They say there are gangs there and drug dealing, but as far as I'm concerned, that's everywhere. I'm working in a field where I'm trying to change all that, and I'm going to change things by moving out?

I went to school right down the street from where I grew up in the south valley. First of all, I was delivered at home by a *curandera*, a midwife and healer. They paid the *curandera* a sack of flour for delivering me. I went to an elementary school called Kit Carson, really, and Ernie Pyle Middle School, then Río Grande High School, all public schools. Private schools? Forget it, we couldn't afford that. Even right now, if you were to look at the schools and identify those most at risk in the district, they would say the three that I have mentioned, because they are low-income barrio schools. But then I was lucky enough to get into a program called Upward Bound, a beautiful program, which reaches out into "disadvantaged communities," in quotation marks because it is only economically disadvantaged, and so rich in other ways.

They identified me as a student who had "potential," as they called it. I was a good student, I liked school. I went to the university here, which was then St. Joseph's College, a Catholic college, and has since gone under. They had the nurturing spirit. It's too bad, because right now if you go to the universities here, the freshman English class, you have what, five hundred students? When you need it the most, you don't get any individual attention. You need it more the first couple of years, not the last ones. It's backwards. If you're coming from high school, you're making a big transition, and you don't know how to cope. Anyway, St. Joseph's College later on became the University of Albuquerque, still Catholic. Because I was an Upward Bound student, the director of the program at the University of Albuquerque told me I could work for him as a tutor. My work-study program as I worked my way through college was as a tutor for the Upward Bound program.

I was the first in my family to graduate from college, fewer than half of my brothers and sisters graduated from high school. The others went back later to get their high school equivalency degree. In those days, the ninth grade was considered, at least by my parents, to be pretty well educated. My father got a third grade education, and my mom got a fifth grade one. By ninth grade you were fourteen years old, and, hey, it's time to work! Besides, you had to contribute that to the family. With thirteen people, you needed to add to the income.

My dad worked in construction, when I was growing up he was always a supervisor because he was good at managing people. I think that trait is in my family genes because everybody is a supervisor, very organized. My dad also learned politics because you had to be involved, like it or not, especially if you worked for the state. Even in the sixties, I remember if you weren't affiliated with the party that was in, then you were gone. Depending on the outcome of the election, my dad was sometimes out of a job. The patronage system is still strong here, although with the merit system it's not as bad now.

My parents were very anxious for me to pursue my education. By then, they understood how important education was. My first semester I thought seriously of dropping out of school. I could handle the work; I just wasn't disciplined. For most kids, it's not a problem of being intelligent enough to handle the subject matter; it's having the discipline to do it. Even with my kids, I tell him that the discipline is important; that's why they go to Catholic schools. But they encouraged me, and, after four years, I made it. People don't realize how really poor you are when you are a student. I remember, having been brought up the way I was, bills were not something you wanted to have. You did not want to owe anybody anything. In a barter system, you're paid off. The student loans at that time had a 3 percent interest rate, which is very low, but I couldn't afford them. I told the university, I don't want any more loans; I'm going to pay as I go. Every month, I would pay my student loan, and I would have ten dollars left for the month. It was tough but I had been raised that way. I worked hard and did well; by the end of my senior year in college I had a 4.02 average. I majored in economics, and worked twenty hours a week for Upward Bound, recruiting for them. I was there in the summers, too, because we had a summer program. I worked all summer and I lived on campus. When I graduated, I felt confident, like I had accomplished a great deal.

Then I started applying to graduate schools for a master's degree. I got several offers, but I wanted to go here to the University of New Mexico. By that time my father had died, my mother was alone, my brother and my mom were the only ones at home, and I felt that I couldn't leave. So I went to graduate school at University of New Mexico in public administration. It was much easier than being an undergraduate, but by then I was sick of school. Besides, I wanted to make some money to help my family and myself too. I interned in graduate school—I was both a state government intern, and an intern for the state Department of Economic Development, since I had a degree in economics. That's how I worked my way through graduate school, plus I had a planning fellowship. At that time, the federal government wanted more minorities with planning background, so I did that.

That was enough school for me. I was about to graduate and the position came up for director of the Youth Development Project. It was a small program with about eight employees—this was in 1973. They were looking for somebody who knew the area, had an advanced degree, and youth services background. I was from the south valley, had an advanced degree, and I had just done Upward Bound for four years. It was perfect. I was only twenty-four years old, and I didn't know anything. I still wonder why they took such a risk on me. All of a sudden I had a staff, a budget, and I didn't know anything, nothing. They handed me a manila folder and said, "Okay, you're hired." And then they left. On-the-job training consisted of an envelope with nothing in it and a demoralized staff. I had to confront that right away, the nonperformance of staff. They were very suspicious of me. These were older people with their own agendas. Some thought they should be director. It was not easy for a green kid—I mean, at some staff meetings, people wanted to challenge me, and what they meant by that was to go outside and fight! "I'll show you who's director," they would say. But they backed down. About then I said, "Gee, I should've stayed in school."

At that time, we were in a little shack on Dead Man's Corner. After years of gradually gaining people's confidence, bringing in new people, expanding the vision, getting people to trust you—it's never smooth sailing—but by being fair and consistent and human, people came to respect what I was doing. I tell people, "We are a *human* human services organization," because there are some human service organizations that are not very human. My concept is respect for the individual, their beliefs, their abilities, everything has to be based on that. I have a staff of about one hundred and fifty now, a fifteenfold increase. We had a budget of about $125,000 when I began; now, it's about $4 million. We have three corporations, not just the one. We have Youth Development, Youth Enterprises System, and Foundation for Youth. They each have a little different mission. Locations, we have about ten.

Our programs include First Offenders, GED Preparation, Substance Abuse, Youth Motivation Outreach Counseling, Transitional Living—kids who are transitioning from group homes to independent living on their own. Many of our kids are homeless and don't have parents. Homelessness among teenagers is a big problem because of the disintegration of families. We have many very dysfunctional families. The problem is, what happens to the kids? I mean, the kids can't live in a situation of such instability and conflict that it is unhealthy for them. The best option for many of these kids, as bad as it is, is to be on the street. We have shelters that handle those kinds of cases; we've had them for twenty years. We serve in the neighborhood of 17,000 youths and families per year.

We have Youth Enterprises now, we have our own restaurant, our own desktop publishing, our own painting and affordable housing businesses. Teatro Consejo is a brilliant project, it's about getting young people involved in different artistic forms. It's a theater of counsel, advice, taking young people and letting them express themselves through the outlet of drama and art. We believe in a very holistic approach to mental health, to dealing with families, to everything. Some organizations do counseling only, or shelter only. We do the gamut, whatever it takes.

Measuring our success is very difficult. Say you have a kid who doesn't go to school at all, but you get him to go to school two times a week, but he's still missing three. Is that success? Well, yes, for us that's success, because we're getting him to go to school at least twice a week. But the school might say, he's got too many absences, we want to throw him out. We're saying, "He's making progress." Or take a family that would respond to every crisis by slapping their kid around.

Now they no longer slap the kid around, maybe they just yell at him, but it's still abuse. You can only measure success by what was happening before to that individual. But people want percentages, 95 percent of our kids this or that. We realize, however, that you measure by tiny increments.

We are brought up in an era of instant success, and people give up too easily. Well, they were on welfare last year, so this year they have to be off. It doesn't work that way. Many people believe that we are wasting money on social service agencies trying to help these people, because if they wanted to work they could. Basically, I say, welfare is a significant problem for many reasons. From the viewpoint of the taxpayer, because it's their tax dollars; from my viewpoint, because it's wasted human resources. If you had a tumor on your arm right here and you said, the rest of my body is okay, it's just this part is not cooperating with me, should I treat it or ignore it? What happens in that case? And this is a health issue, because it involves the health of our nation; you can choose to ignore it, not to treat it, but the long-term implications are extremely serious. That's the way I explain it.

In 1990–91, I did the Harvard University State and Local Executives Program at the John F. Kennedy School. It was about learning how to manage states and communities and nations. It's a yearlong program, but you only have to do summers there and the rest is here. It was a great program. Then I participated in the Kellogg National Fellows program. What it's about is giving new and emerging leaders for the nation new ways to learn from other people. It's not academia-based, most of the people are already Ph.D.s or M.D.s or whatever. They're already established leaders in their field, but what Kellogg provides is the opportunity to learn from people all over the world. They select about forty to fifty people as fellows.

I have been very fortunate in these opportunities. Sometimes people tell me that I should move on to bigger things, to a job of more importance or status. But I'm happy here. I'm doing what I believe in, working for youth and families in our community. I mean, after twenty years, I see very clearly that I belong here. I think that God prepares you for something, some challenge in life, and this is it for me.

Sandra Cisneros

Sandra Cisneros grew up in Chicago and currently resides in San Antonio. Her works include the widely praised collection of stories *Woman Hollering Creek* (New York: Random House, 1991) and an imaginative book of childhood vignettes, *The House on Mango Street* (©1985, New York: Vintage Books, 1991). Sandra Cisneros has a highly personal and intimate style of writing that is extremely sensitive and rich in its suggestive power.

The following excerpts from *The House on Mango Street* are intensely evocative portraits of family life in the city: of a loving, hardworking father; the duties of the oldest child; and a young woman who dreams of the university rather than the "factory" and the "rolling pin." Cisneros excels at capturing the small moments of tenderness and sadness in family relationships.

from *The House on Mango Street*

Papa Who Wakes Up Tired in the Dark

Your *abuelito* is dead, Papa says early one morning in my room. *Esta muerto*, and then, as if he just heard the news himself, crumples like a coat and cries, my brave Papa cries. I have never seen my Papa cry and don't know what to do.

I know he will have to go away, that he will take a plane to Mexico, all the uncles and aunts will be there, and they will have a black and white photo taken in front of the tomb with flowers shaped like spears in a white vase because this is how they send the dead away in that country.

Because I am the oldest, my father has told me first, and now it is my turn to tell the others. I will have to explain why we can't play. I will have to tell them to be quiet today.

My Papa, his thick hands and thick shoes, who wakes up tired in the dark, who combs his hair with water, drinks his coffee, and is gone before we wake, today is sitting on my bed.

And I think if my own Papa died what would I do. I hold Papa in my arms. I hold him and hold him.

Alicia Who Sees Mice

Close your eyes and they'll go away, her father says, or, you're just imagining. And anyway, a woman's place is sleeping so she can wake up early with the tortilla star, the one that appears early just in time to rise and catch the hind legs hidden behind the sink, beneath the four-clawed tub, under the swollen floorboards nobody fixes, in the corner of your eyes.

Alicia, whose mama died, is sorry there is no one older to rise and make the lunchbox tortillas. Alicia, who inherited her mama's rolling pin and sleepiness, is young and smart and studies for the first time at the university. Two trains and a bus, because she doesn't want to spend her whole life in a factory or behind a rolling pin. Is a good girl, my friend, studies all night and sees the mice, the ones her father says do not exist. Is afraid of nothing except four-legged fur and fathers.

Carmen Velázquez

Carmen Velázquez's story is one of struggle and courage in the face of personal and financial limitations. It is also the story of many single mothers on welfare who do what they can to provide for their children. Both in Puerto Rico and in New York, the going was rough for Velázquez, who recently moved to Florida in hopes of offering her family a life free of crime, gangs, and drugs.

Interview

I was born in Puerto Rico in 1956 in a small town about fifteen minutes from San Juan. When I was ten my mama took me to the U.S., to Brooklyn. When I was twelve my mama died and I had to take care of my six brothers and sisters. Four were younger and two were older, but when she died the two oldest left, leaving me with the younger children and my papa. Since I had no mother, and my father didn't work, we lived on welfare.

New York was a huge change from Puerto Rico—the cold, the other kids always wanting to beat us up because we were *hispanos*—but it wasn't that bad, because when we were little we adjusted just fine. I never attended school in Puerto Rico. It was in New York that I went to school for the first time. I went for one year only. Everything was in English; it was horrible, a complete disaster for me. That was about the time my mama died, and I had to take care of the other children, so I quit school. What English I know I have learned *a fuerza*, as they say, by having to go to the doctor or deal with some agency. I learned it *en la calle*, on the street. I was never able to work: they always fired me from my jobs, plus it was just too difficult because I was also caring for the younger kids and my father.

That is, until I was seventeen, when I got married and I went back to Puerto Rico. I married a Puerto Rican who was living in New York also. We were together for seven years, after which we divorced and I returned to New York with the four kids because in Puerto Rico *la vida es más fuerte*—life is even harder and salaries are low.

So I went back to my papa and my brothers and sisters who were still in Brooklyn and things were better there, but still difficult. We were very poor, but the church helped us a lot. English was again a problem for me, after spending seven years in Puerto Rico. I never went out to look for work. My earlier experiences were that I couldn't keep a job, plus the children were young. The shopkeeper at the neighborhood *bodega* gave me food on credit for the children until I could get food coupons. He owned the store below our apartment, he was a *dominicano*. They're like Puerto Ricans, like brothers. I spent more time with the Dominicans than with the Puerto Ricans actually, there were so many in our *barrio*.

What I liked most about New York was the ease with which I could get from one place to another, not like here in Florida where you have to have a car to go anywhere. I can't go to church, go shopping, I always have to wait for someone to take me. I've spent almost twelve years by myself, and I've gotten used to going out and doing things by myself, so it is a big adjustment. However, it's not so easy in New York now either. Before, I could take the bus and go to the Bronx, Brooklyn, wherever, and if I got lost I could ask a policeman or a fireman and they would take me back home. But now, there are too many people, and if you ask someone in the street, they're just as likely to push you down or hit you as to answer your question. They have no heart. I'm talking especially about the Puerto Ricans. I think they are the rudest now, and it's dangerous because sometimes they would intentionally tell me to get on the wrong train. It got to the point where I would only ask information of black Americans because they would always help me. But, even if I wasn't safe, at least in New York I could get around places.

In New York, in spite of the fact that I did not work, I had a pretty apartment. I had everything I needed and so did my kids. There were six people, four bedrooms, a living room, a kitchen and a bath. I filled out the form for low-income city-sponsored housing and I've never had a landlord, I've always lived in a city-owned apartment. The rent was between twelve and fifteen hundred a month, but the city paid it. I paid between two and three hundred. It was great. You really had to fight to get one of those apartments. You had not only to fill out the forms, but to keep calling every day, because there were so many people who wanted one of these places. You had to keep pushing and I did.

The church has always helped us as well. The priest was American but he spoke Spanish. I first met the father when I was ten and had just come from Puerto Rico. He would give us many things, such as presents at Christmas. We continued going to mass there after mama died. I made my first communion, my brothers and sisters too, and later I joined the Daughters of Mary, for about seven years. We all went to church except for my papa. He was an alcoholic, and I had many problems with him. If he would get up after a drunken binge and find that I wasn't there, even if I was at church with the Daughters of Mary, he would have a fit. He made life difficult for me. Once, just for spite, he refused to buy me a white dress for the ceremony for the Daughters of Mary, but the father and the church bought the material and made the dress for me so that I could participate in the coronation of the Virgin.

In New York the Catholic Church is different from that in Puerto Rico and from that here in Florida. The Daughters of Mary for example, always had a special day in the church year that was for the Virgin Mary, and they crowned her and brought her flowers, some twenty or thirty girls all dressed in white. They would put the blue on the Virgin too. For this ceremony the church would be packed. I was amazed that here in Florida they don't seem to celebrate the Virgin; there's nothing.

In time, I will adjust to our new life here. We simply had to get out of New York. It seems to me to be about to collapse. You can't trust anyone now. I was afraid to go outside my door because of the violence. I decided to come here so that my children could get away from the violence in the streets and in their schools, and from the drug addicts in our neighborhood. The violence surrounds you there, you can't escape it. I stayed for ten years because I didn't think that I could make it in Puerto Rico with five children, because by then I was taking care of an additional child. I also have three handicapped children who the government gives me money to support. In Puerto Rico I wouldn't receive this aid. Here in Florida I receive the same benefits as in New York, so I decided to come here. I was afraid every day that my kids would go off to school and I would get a phone call during the day that they were victims of the violence. It finally got so bad that I was afraid to go out at all; I feared that some drug addict would get me.

We've been here for eight months now, and my five kids are definitely better off. Nancy is sixteen years old. When we left New York she was going to be in the tenth grade, but they put her back to the eighth grade here. She misses her friends at school in New York, but they were almost all guys, and they were in gangs. This was in junior high, and when she would get into fights with other girls, she would call on her "friends" to help her out. They were black like the other kids at her school but they liked Puerto Ricans, and they protected her.

My younger daughter always had to get out one period early from her school so she wouldn't have any trouble going home. But even so, there were some guys who would wait outside to beat her up. One of them punched her boyfriend and broke his jaw. The cops arrested him for drugs and for having a gun. Those boys said they were going to get my daughter next. By then I was already so afraid that I said, let's get out of here!

Despite all that, my daughters miss New York and the oldest wants to move back. The youngest likes it here better, though she has found different things to be afraid of. She had to walk through a field of cows the other day, and she said that it was scarier than walking down the streets of New York! She thought they were going to attack her.

It's better here. The doctor told me that the fear I felt in New York was making me ill. I was nervous and jumpy all the time. The boys are happier here because they can go outside—they don't have to worry about gangs or drugs or the elevator, they just open the door and go outside.

Edward Rivera

Edward Rivera was born in Puerto Rico and grew up in Spanish Harlem. Memories of Puerto Rico and experiences in New York City provide the inspiration for Rivera's prose, including his autobiographical *Family Installments* (New York: Penguin, 1982), the humorous, lively, and poignant recreation of the Puerto Rican migration experience.

In this excerpt from *Family Installments,* the son, Santos, paints an affectionate portrait of his father, Papi. Rivera communicates vividly and engagingly both the comic and sad moments of revelation of this close-knit family living on the edge of poverty.

from Family Installments

In spite of his poor eyesight, Papi was a farsighted man. He was also thoughtful, responsible, and concerned for the future of his two sons. "Too late for mine," he would say. He wanted us to do well, without specifying what we should do. Instead of telling me and Tego, "I want you two boys to become airplane pilots or army generals," he would say, "You're both going to finish school," by which he meant high school. He thought college was only for geniuses, men like this Einstein he had heard about, and Tego and I just didn't have that kind of brains. There were plenty of good jobs open to high school graduates.

The time Tego hinted that he wouldn't mind getting a summer job at the American Combining Company, ("Just so I won't have to be asking you and Mami for movie money all the time."), Papi cut him short: "The ACC is my problem, Tego. I don't want you to go near that place. Just study. I'll give you the money for the movies."

Tego hated print. The sports pages of the *New York Post* were okay (he read them slowly, as if he were just learning to read), but anything else was boring. So instead of books he studied gambling. He owned about five packs of cards; he carried a pack of Tally-Hos in his pocket at all times, and practiced winning pennies, nickels and dimes from his friends on stoops, in basements, on rooftops, wherever the cops weren't likely to show up. Papi couldn't have known about this "vice." If he had, Tego would have been put under house arrest for at least a week and his packs of cards confiscated, his movie money (with which he gambled) cut off, his smallest move surveyed. Keeping track of his moves would have been hard, though short of locking him up in our bedroom. He was very secretive about his vice (he wouldn't even tell me about it; I was too young for that, he said), and he had private ways of disguising his scent.

Mami may have known about the gambling, but if so, she must have figured that boys have to have hobbies. What she didn't know was that this hobby was turning into a passion, an addiction and a vocation that would eventually take Tego, along with his wife and their baby son and daughter back to the island. "Back where we started," Papi was to say, not too thrilled, when it was too late.

He had done what he could, though he would have been the last to admit it. He was strict about our choice of friends. He didn't want us to bring home any "hoodlums," or his idea of hoodlums. Almost any boy who didn't go to a parochial school was a hoodlum. Better yet, any boy who didn't go to Saint Misericordia's parochial school. There was another parochial in the neighborhood, a dingy-looking version of Saint Misericordia's, named after an Irish-American airman or seaman who had been killed in the Second World War. It was situated in a block that Papi called "a street of vices," and he was against our making friends among its students. A graduate of that school had been written up in *El Diario* and the *News,* front page of *El Diario,* page forty-something on the *News.* He had been caught burglarizing the Park Avenue apartment of a famous Italian-American nightclub tenor, sent to the Tombs before sentencing, and found hanged in his cell, with his own belt, the morning after they put him away.

"Even a Catholic education," Papi told me and Tego (in the preachy way we disliked), "is no guarantee that a man won't hang himself. With his own belt, too! Why don't they remove their belts when they lock them up?"

"They do," said Mami. "Maybe they forgot this time. You never know."

Tego and I excused ourselves before this turned into a sermon on the evils of breaking and entering. We had our own cynicism going for us on the side. Sometimes we overdid it. We also kept most of our friends a secret. The more interesting ones went to public school, and we never brought any of them home. The way they talked and acted would have given them away as students of P.S. something or other, and Papi might embarrass us with stares and frowns, until our friends got the message and left.

One of his regrets was that he couldn't go with us to the nine o'clock Mass every weekday morning. If his job had been a good one, he told me, he would have the time to go with us to church. If only for that reason, we were glad he didn't have a better job. The other students would have laughed at us—except for those students whose own parents went to church with them, the ones everyone avoided.

It wasn't always easy to get on with a man who didn't want his two sons to make what he called his "mistakes" (I never knew what he meant by this word when he applied it to himself.) But we respected him from a distance. It was hard not to. For one thing, he wasn't the kind of parent who believed in smacking his children around. He couldn't stand violence. He couldn't understand, he said, how the Old Testament tolerated it, why it "glorified" it. An eye for an eye was a disgrace, he used to say.

What didn't occur to him, though, was that his tongue compensated for his hand. So did his disapproving looks whenever Tego or I got out of hand. With his stares and frowns, he didn't need slaps or kicks or his belt to get the message across. That was the way his mother's father had brought up him and his brothers—or had been bringing them up before he died—and it was the way he was going to bring up his own two sons.

He took after his grandfather in other ways. He kept our supply of rice and beans going no matter what. He was making fifty-something a week at the ACC, a cheap outfit that was always threatening to move down South if the union acted up. No problem. This union Papi belonged to was a corrupt local, he told us. Some of its officials, if not all, were members of organized crime. "They are in the cahoots with the bosses," he said.

To supplement his fifty-something, he had to enroll us on Home Relief one year (pronounced by most of us as "real-if"). "This disgrace may have to go on," he said, bunching his mouth, "until Tego finishes school." (He didn't suspect that

Tego might never finish school.) This real-if enrollment was an example of what he called a little *"maroma,"* a caper, an acrobatic stunt, walking the tightrope, saving oneself from drowning.

A lot of people on our block were enrolled in this real-if, but no one was shameless enough to admit it—only certain men when they got drunk and became suddenly confidential and indiscreet. "Lend me your ear a second, Tito. I am one of those elements who is on the home real-if. Don't tell anyone about this, above all your wife." Tito would promise not to, and then go on to tell his drinking partner that he too was one of those "elements." And the next day everyone on the block would know about it. It was like a small village in that sense.

On the long-awaited morning when real-if checks were due, all kinds of "clients" (mostly women, old people and unemployed men) gathered on the stoops to discuss the weather and the unfeeling landlord (most of the buildings on our block were owned by an anonymous syndicate whose name ended in Associates, Inc.), certain news items they had heard over the radio or read about in the omniscient *El Diario,* and Americans in general (the "enemy"). There was also a great deal of talk about the day when I and You, We and Us were going to save up some money and go back to the island, because this New York experiment was a mistake. But most of that was just talk. The majority of us knew we weren't going back. Maybe to the Bronx or Brooklyn, but not much farther than that. And then, if one had the luck, and the money, one could get decently buried in the city sized cemetery out in Queens, on the way to the airport: close to the airplanes, but close didn't count.

This grab bag gab on the stoops would go on until the mailman arrived, his shoulder pouch stuffed with perforated green checks, Department of Welfare, State of New York, which he refused to hand out to the clients out there on the stoop.

"You'll just have to wait till I put 'em inside the mailboxes, he'd tell them firmly. "That's the law. You want me to lose my job?" He had passed a tough civil service test for that job, he explained; he was working his way up the ranks to a sitting position; he had his dependents to consider, his self-respect to uphold. At least half the mailboxes in our building had no locks; some had no doors, but that made no difference to him—rules were rules, the law was the law, no special favors. So the clients would just have to wait. "Line up," he'd say. "The line starts here." And he'd point to the spot where he wanted the clients to position themselves single file. "No sneaking up."

Papi, always self-conscious, disapproved of those twice-a-month stoop conventions. "This is supposed to be a private disgrace," he told Mami. "An embarrassing necessity, a humiliation I'll never live down. Not a public spectacle. Don't you agree, Lilia?"

Yes, she did, though not necessarily in the same words. She used fewer words than he did. "Your father," she used to tell me, "uses more words than he has to. I think he likes to hear himself talk too much."

She was the one who pulled our real-if checks out of the mailbox, as if they were dead mice. She held them by one corner, between two fingers, like a mouse's tail. And then she would go and wash her hands. Her method of approaching the mailbox for those checks was also peculiar. She'd wait for the other clients to disperse (she could see them from the front-bedroom window), and then sneak downstairs with the mailbox key. She was so ashamed of those checks that she couldn't bring herself to open the envelope. Papi had to do it. That was a man's *maroma* as far as she was concerned. So was cashing the thing at Matamorros's *bodega,* La Flor de Mi Patria, or Al Arentsky's semi-kosher establishment (a holdout from the old days).

"Here, let me have the check, Lilia," he'd say, putting on the self-confidence. "This isn't exactly my idea of a *maroma,* by the way."

"Whatever you call it,"she'd tell him back, "I want no part of it." She was always afraid we'd be found out, someone might stool on us, and we'd be arrested for defrauding the government. So was he, although he pretended there was no way they could catch him at that *maroma,* "as long as we keep our mouths shut."

If "they" found out he was putting in forty to fifty hours a week at the factory, Tego and I thought, they'd send him up the river. At the least, they'd sue him for stealing public funds; he'd have to pay interest on that debt. Or they might deport all four of us, and we'd end up depending on Mami's father to survive. If that happened, Papagante would never let us live it down.

"Don't worry," Papi said. "We'll pay it all back. Every penny. The boys will help when they finish school." A lot depended on our finishing school.

"Is this something we should confess to the priest?" Mami once asked him.

"It's up to you," Papi said, "but be careful which priest you tell it to. Some of them look like informers to me. The secret of the confessional doesn't mean a thing." And he gave her the names of those priests he thought were potential stool pigeons. "We don't want one of those announcing it from the pulpit one Sunday, Lilia. God may approve of what we're doing, but priests don't always see eye to eye with Him." But she wasn't all that sure God approved.

Most of his *maromas* were a mystery to her (and to me and Tego), and she wanted to keep it that way. Some of those stunts, though, were too obvious to conceal: things like borrowing simultaneously from banks and loan-shark agencies in order to replace the floral-pattern carpet in our living room, or the last-legs sofa left behind by the previous tenants, whom he was still paying back, via airmail, in interminable installments.

"Don't wear your shoes in the house," he told me and Tego. "It uses up the leather and scuffs the carpet. Wear your sneakers. or better yet, walk barefoot in here. It's good for your feet." It also saved money on shoes and sneakers.

He had to buy most things on easy payments, the notorious layaway plan, which sounded to him, he said, like an ad for the funeral director, Don Gonzaga of Madison, one of the most thriving entrepreneurs in the neighborhood. So, for that matter, was the tacos and enchiladas vendor, a bona fide Mexican, who sold his homemade products to mourners coming and going out of Gonzaga's establishment. Two smart businessmen. Maybe they, too, were in cahoots. Many obvious jokes made the rounds concerning the source of the Mexican's taco meat. "He gets it on the layaway plan," Tego used to say, convinced by now that the only way to keep from drowning was to manipulate this layaway plan racket. And for that you didn't need a high school diploma, just smarts, connections, angles.

Tego was already set on dropping out of Chelsea Vocational and finding a job "somewheres." "To help Papi pay the interest," he once told me.

"Are you going to break the bank of Montesinos, or something?" I said.

"What Montesinos, Santos? Where's that at? I never heard of this Montesinos."

"That Gambling joint somewheres in France or Italy."

"That's Monte*carlos*. In Spain. *Carlos*. You read too much, Santos. You get things all confused."

I'd been reading *Gone With The Wind* for two straight weeks, and it was making him nervous. He had flipped through it. "Trash, Santos. Waste of time." More than one book a year, as he saw it, was too much, self-indulgence, a sign that one wasn't practical. At Chelsea, he said, they stuck to reading manuals with more diagrams than print. He was good with his hands. His ability to shuffle his decks of Tally-Hos always amazed me. When I tried it, at his suggestion, "just to see what it's like, Santos." I littered the floor with the pack. "I guess it takes a special aptitude," he said. "You read; I deal. It all comes out to the same thing in the end, I guess."

Once I caught him reading Mickey Spillane. The cover, depicting a half-stripped blonde with tits the size of beachballs, must have been responsible for that purchase. He didn't finish it, though. He had dog-eared it on page 30 and left it inside our bureau. When I asked him why he hadn't finished it, he said, "The sex sucks, Santos. That's not the way it is. Don't waste your time."

I tried to give him a short lecture on the difference between life and literature. After all, anyone who had read every word of *Gone with the Wind* should know. But he wasn't interested. "And another thing, Santos. You shouldn't be wasting Papi's money on them paperbacks. Use the library. That's what its for. Papi's working his ass off paying for them Third Avenue crooks, and you're wasting his dough on cheap books. They got him by the balls. You know how I'd like to get them?" He didn't have to tell me. We had that much in common.

Every merchant on Third was out to suck one's blood, like Gonzaga with his corpses. No exceptions, as far as we were concerned. Some of these crooks were members of our church, the aristocracy of our parish. They sat in the balcony, counting their beads. "So they won't have to catch our bad breath," Tego used to say. A few were good friends of the pastor. More cahoots. *Sindicatos*. But most of them lived in other parishes and other boroughs.

It was Tego who came up with a name for what Papi brought home from their establishments. "*Fakerías*, Santos." Fake furniture, cardboard shoes, synthetic clothes, warped carpets, shoddy curtains, imitation bedspreads. You name the shit, Third Avenue had it. The furniture, always "antique," came with names like Colonial, Provincial, Imperial, Baroque, Rococo, Revival, Quattrocento, Victorian, Edwardian, Renaissance, and others. A style for every epoch, "custom-made" period stuff, Pine or plastic, pine and plastic, pine, plastic, Formica, inlaid *junkerías,* cedars of Lebanon, mahoganies of Shangri-la, Duramicas of Arcadia, marbles of Ancient Greece, evergreens of Utopia. Crap of Third. You had to be careful how you sat down on the armchair or the Colonial sofa (Papi's choice, after much window-shopping and showroom testing): one of the springs might pop up and stab you, just as you were about to relax over some TV, or shut your eyes to go over tomorrow morning's homework.

"*Fakerías,*" Tego and I used to chant every time something broke down, usually before it was paid. "*Todo* is fake." We kept these remarks to ourselves. Papi and Mami would have been hurt if they'd heard. They would have lectured us. "They wouldn't understand," Tego told me. I wasn't so sure of that. But they would have pretended they didn't. It was either that or sticking their heads out the window and howling, baying at the moon over Central Park.

Over our Colonial sofa was a big blank space; the wall was warped and cracked. Old plumbing and the seasons had done that to it. "Unleavened plaster," Papi once termed some white flakes on his head, droppings from that wall, as if trying to bring the New and Old Testaments up to date. He laid fresh plaster and paint on it in thick coats, but he couldn't keep the cracks from coming through. They were out to get him; they began reproducing as soon as he turned his back on them. This was a humid, stubborn wall; it broke out in year-round sweats: cold sweats in the winter, steaming sweats in summer, and lukewarm sweats in the spring and fall. No matter what the season, the paint went on peeling and the plaster went on splitting. We could always rely on that. And Papi, always patient with a hopeless situation, felt obliged to conceal the cracks for a while, as if not doing so would amount to a sin. The reason he gave us, though, was that these cracks were an embarrassment to the eye, anybody's eye, ours and the occasional visitor's; and all visitors, as he and Mami saw it, were potential critics, even his own brother, who liked to keep his criticism to himself.

So this wall became an obsession with him, as if his self-respect depended on how well he dealt with it. Maybe his life, too, he seemed that desperate. He used to curse it when he thought we weren't listening.

"He's talking to the wall again, Santos," Tego would tell me, while shuffling a deck of cards.

"I hear him, Tego. Is it talking back?"

"Not yet. Give it time. He just called its mother the great whore. He'll have to confess that one."

"Lay off," I'd say. "That's Calumny."

"Calumny, shit. Your head's still in parochial school."

Papi discussed it with our janitor, Don Bartolo, a man who liked to nip a little *vino* once in a while. Nobody condemned him for it; it helped him get through the day. "I never think about the week," he used to say, not to mention the day. Now what about this wall, Don Gerán? What's wrong with it?

"You can see for yourself, Don Bartolo."

"Those little cracks? Don't let that keep you up at night, Don Gerán. Every wall in this building—but if you can't stand the sight of it, let me suggest a little solution . . . "

Papi tipped him for the suggestion. "An inspiration," he called it, and attributed it to Don Bartolo's sips of wine.

The inspiration was a large mirror. Don Bartolo had seen it in a Third Avenue window, on sale. A clearing-out sale, one of those Everything Must Go temptations. And if he were Papi, Don Bartolo said, he'd get his coat on right away and go take a look before someone else took it away. He put his mouth up close to Papi's ear and told him the name of the dealer who was selling it. "One of a kind, Don Gerán."

By this time Papi's obsession with the wall had gotten out of hand, and almost any suggestion would have sounded like a solution, as long as it wasn't made by someone in his own family. Mami had told him many times to forget it, it would go away by itself, or not at all, it wasn't important. But he told her she was too close to the problem to see it as an insult to all four of us, and he had drawn the line. So she told him to go ahead and do whatever he thought he had to do, but not to look at her afterward.

He went ahead and bought the mirror, on installments. Household Finance chipped in. Fifty bucks, twenty five down from the original price. There were no other mirrors like this in existence, the dealer told him. A collector's item. On purpose the manufacturer had broken the only mold. Someday it would be worth something. An investment, an instant heirloom. Easy payments.

When Mami asked him how much, he said he'd tell her if she promised not to panic, and he told me and Tego to go inside our bedroom for a few minutes. But Mami insisted we stay. "If they go," she said, "I go. How else are they going to avoid our mistakes?"

"Don't pass judgement before you look, Lilia."

In front of me and Tego, he told her he paid fifty dollars for it, cash. HFC's cash. Interest on the loan, he said, would double the value of the mirror. It was an illustrated mirror, one flamingo on the left and one on the right, facing each other, one leg in the water, the other bent at the knee, or what the artist tried to pass off as a knee, a long stem with a joint and something like claws at the end.

"Those things don't look like flamingos to me," Mami said, after he had hung it up. It covered most of the walls cracks.

"What do you mean, not flamingos, Lilia?"

"That's my opinion, Gerán. Ask the boys."

We said we didn't want to take sides, but he insisted. So we told him. Tego thought they looked more like a pair of big pink chickens, and I picked condors, just to pick something.

"You're all ignorant," Papi said, feeling betrayed. "No eyes to see."

"I wouldn't talk if I were you," Mami told him.

Later, in our room, while their dialogue continued in the living room and then in the kitchen, Tego, shuffling a deck of Tally Hos desperately, said, "He got carried away with that wall. Some *maroma*."

"You couldn't have done any better," I said, "so shut up."

"I'll play you a game of knuckles, Santos."

"Get out of here with your cards. Go play with your friends."

He did. He didn't get back till close to midnight. They didn't tell him anything. "Goddamn flamingos," he said under the blanket. "Pink chickens, vultures."

We had to live with those pink chickens, or whatever they were, for a couple of months. Then, before Papi was finished with the installments, the mirror's frame came apart at the joints. Papi tried prolonging its life with Elmer's Glue, but he might as well have tried prayers, for all the good that solution did. And he refused to admit his expensive mistake. At least he wouldn't admit it openly. Mami suggested he give it to the super, who she thought deserved it for misleading him into making one of the worst mistakes of his life, maybe *the* worst.

"That's your opinion, Lilia," he told her. "And I'm not giving it to Don Bartolo. It stays where it is."

She didn't want to waste time arguing with him—his self-respect was on the line again—so she left him alone with what she began calling his "illusion," his high-priced *maroma.*

He finally did take it down, when he thought none of us was looking, but only after the home real-if investigator embarrassed him over those flamingos. She came around on a routine inspection, to see how our standard of living was coming along, and immediately wanted to know where Papi had gotten the mirror. He was ready for her. "I won it in a church raffle. It's the first time I ever won anything in a raffle."

She didn't look convinced. "What kind of birds are those? What species?"

"Flamingos," he said. "Florida's full of them. The pink species."

"Aren't they all pink, Mr. Malánguez?"

"I don't think so." His eyes were giving him away, cornered. "I hear there are black ones, too."

"Black flamingos? You must mean swans." She was enjoying this. "I've never heard of black flamingos."

"I don't think it's important," he said, offended. This woman, this impersonal private eye, was trying to embarrass him in front of his wife and sons, and she had succeeded.

"Well, whatever they are, Mr. Malánguez, maybe the church raffle should have given you cash instead of a mirror."

"They don't give cash," he said.

"Why not?"

"I don't know, I'm not a priest. They don't have any money. It's a poor parish."

"Well, who paid for the mirror?"

"I don't know, I didn't ask."

"I think it was a donation, Señora." Mami said.

"Maybe you can sell it. Do you really need a mirror like that on your living-room wall?"

"It hides the cracks," he said.

"Cracks?"

"The cracks on the wall," Mami said.

"Isn't that what plaster's for?"

"It's supposed to be, but it doesn't work on this wall."

"Why not?"

"It's damp, it sweats. The plaster won't hold. This is not an ordinary wall." And he went on to tell her the whole story of this wall, inventing details here and there to make his point: that this raffle mirror was a necessity, and not, as she suspected, a luxury. I don't think she was convinced by his explanation, but by the time he got finished, she looked too tired to continue the cross-examination. Either this man was a liar, she must have concluded, or a nut, and she left in a hurry, shaking her head.

Next day he took down the mirror—carefully, so it wouldn't collapse on him—and left it at the entrance to Don Bartolo's basement apartment. "Let him live with it," he said, "for deceiving me."

Mami was furious. "I don't think he's the only one who deceived you."

"Just what do you mean by that, Lilia?"

"Nothing. I don't want to talk about it." And she found a quick excuse to visit the drugstore.

Next week he took us off the home real-if. "No more hand-outs," he said. "Let's try starving. It may help." What wouldn't? Eating?

"I think I'm going to get a job soon." Tego told me privately. He was a junior at Chelsea, and the thought of spending another year in that school, "in any school, Santos," was "messing with my sleep."

Papi had insured himself for a thousand dollars, "just in case anything happens to me," he explained to us the day he signed the contract. This had been another illegal *maroma*, but also justified as far as he was concerned. "For one thing," he said, "we may have to fly back home someday. And this policy will pay for the plane tickets and a few other things."

"Another illusion," Mami said, but not to him. "What does he think we'll do when we get there? Raise chickens? They'll laugh us back to here."

He tried talking the insurance collector into giving us an advance on the premium. "I have to pay off some debts," he said.

The collector said he sympathized—maybe he did—but that there was nothing he could do. "There's no such thing as an advance on a premium, Mr. Malánguez. I'm sorry."

So Papi would just have to wait until the policy matured; that wouldn't be for a long time. "In other words, Lilia," he said, "we'll just have to rob a bank."

"Anytime you're ready," she said, and nobody laughed.

So he continued pulling his *maroma* stunts whenever he had no choice, which was most of the time, and justifying them on the grounds that someone in his situation had to do something dishonest from time to time. "Otherwise I'll have to answer for it someday." He believed in divine retribution.

One of my favorite of his *maromas* was something he called *El Pícaro*. This was a thick, short black wire that stole electricity from the light meter, an antique gray box between the kitchen and the bathroom. He attached *El Pícaro* to the meter in such a way that the current wouldn't register. He hooked up this thieving wire for a couple of hours every day after sunset. Someone at work, another *maromero,* had shown him how to do it. "It's a sin," he said, "but what's another sin?"

"Show me how to work this *Pícaro*, Papi," Tego asked him once. "Maybe I can sell this stunt and make a killing for us."

But Papi would have none of that. "You're asking your own father to show you how to steal?"

"From those buzzards? Why not? It's them or us. You said yourself God doesn't mind."

"I said for me He doesn't mind."

"How come you're so special?"

"I'll tell you why, Tego. Because I don't have a HIGHSCHOOLDIPLOMA! That is why."

Tego, unconvinced, reminded him of the quickie diploma offer he'd seen in the subway. "Easy payments, Papi. Why don't you get one of those if they mean so much?"

"I don't want to buy a diploma, Tego. That's one reason. You're supposed to work for it."

"I understand," Tego said. "I think I do anyway." And I could tell from where I sat in the bedroom, studying history, that he didn't mean a word of it. "Let me go do some studying," he said. Then he came inside the room, looked over my shoulder, and asked how I was coming along with "them books."

"Not bad," I said. "Some of it's boring."

"Don't go blind, Santos." He pulled an old pack of cards out of our bureau.

"Don't let him catch you." I said.

"No problem. His eyes ain't so good no more. That's all he needs now, blindness."

"He'll ship you back to the island."

"I ain't going back to no island."

"To the Tombs, then."

"Don't be funny. See you later."

And he was gone again, to some gambling den in a basement. I was asleep when he got back. On the way to school next morning, I found two quarters in my coat pocket. Part of his winnings the night before. I wished he'd given them to Papi instead, but that would have led to questions, and lies, and might have given his gambling hobby away.

"There has to be a way," Mami said, daydreaming. but there wasn't. So she stopped talking like that.

Then Don Baldomero, one of Papi's fellow workers, offered himself as a solution. He had a legitimate *maroma* in mind, he told Papi. It was called the Tenement Syndicate. He had come from a village called Las Piedras, which immediately put Papi on his guard: Anyone born and raised in a place called The Rocks should be suspected on sight.

Don Baldo had been "kind" to Papi at work ("He talks to me."), and Papi, in a gesture rare for him, once invited him to dinner. Mami went to the *bodega* and came home with a bag full of food, all of it on credit. She cooked two kinds of plantains, green and ripe. She cut them into thin wedges and fried them carefully, in oil instead of lard. And there were pork chops instead of chicken, long-grain rice cooked slowly in saffron; chick peas *and* bean sauce, instead of one or the other. Black bean sauce, because Papi had told her this Don Baldo was crazy about black beans. Some Cuban at work had turned him on to them. She had bought them raw and soaked them overnight, and first thing next morning, throwing in spices, she put them on a low burner. And there was beer, a six pack, and homemade egg custard, and all the demitasse Don Baldo could drink. She had put a lot of hours into this meal, and the grocer had put a lot of arithmetic into the price of it.

The invitation had been a crazy impulse, Papi told us afterwards. "For a special guest. A man who knows how to enjoy a good meal, too. He's the one who showed me how to hook up *El Pícaro*. He's a clever man, but he also has some crazy ideas sometimes." Just the same, Don Baldo's *Pícaro* scheme had been saving Papi as much as five dollars a week on light bills, and the least we could do for the man was treat him to a well-cooked meal.

"Let him come and eat his five dollars' worth, then," Mami said, and went to work.

Before he arrived, Papi told us that he was a father of five or six in his fifties, that he was one of the senior workers at the factory, but that his boss had never considered promoting him because he was too outspoken on wages and working conditions, and that he was hard at work saving what he could in order to buy a run-down tenement on St. Ann's Avenue, the Bronx, and fix it up to show the American landlords how to run a decent tenement. The janitor of the building in question was, he said, a man with a good business head. The only problem was that, like too many janitors nowadays, he drank a little more than was good for his health. He drank something called Vino Bravo, which was the same thing as taking poison, as Don Baldo saw it.

"Wasting his time and talent, Don Gerán." Don Baldo told Papi at his dinner table. "And that's why he has to live in the basement. No rent, you see. Free utilities. His wife and children ran out on him. And now he lives down there with a dog that catches rats and mice for him. He uses linoleum and cardboard to fire the boiler. It saves on oil.

This man, whose name was Pipa something, was a cousin of Don Baldo's wife, and he had put Don Baldo onto this five story tenement that was up for sale cheap. "I think we should own this building," Don Baldo told Papi. "But unfortunately I don't have all the cash on hand." So he was organizing a syndicate of men like himself to take it out of the landlord's hands. "And what I'm proposing to you, Don Gerán, is that you join us. We need one more partner, someone intelligent and progressive . . . one of our own kind." And he went on to talk to us about integrity, doing what one could for one's own people, trustworthiness, and the courage to take risks, even though this tenement scheme wouldn't be much of a gamble. There was not way it could fail, once they had the money to buy. "And I don't hesitate to say, Don Gerán, that you are a perfect candidate for this syndicate. To be honest with you, I think you're the best candidate for it." What kind of snowjob was this?

"Maybe I fit your description," Papi said, "and maybe I don't." The rest of us were too embarrassed to look up. Tego finally excused himself and left the table. He must have had a card game that couldn't wait. And Papi, looking inspired, went on with his reply to Don Baldo's scheme. "But I can tell you in all honesty that I don't have the capital—or cash, as you put it. I still owe our grocer twelve dollars for last month's bill, and this month is almost over. In the second place, I don't have a head for business like your wife's cousin Vino Bravo."

"Pipa," Don Baldo corrected.

"All right, Pipa. Whoever he is, he's a brave man. I also don't share your interest in tenements. It's bad enough we have to live in one. I don't think I'd enjoy being the boss of that super who keeps sticking pieces of carpet in the boiler to save money on real fuel. The smoke poisons people."

And so on for a few more minutes. He had spoken. All Don Baldo could do was stare at him while he was improvising his speech; he was getting a close-up look at a side of Papi that had been in hiding all these years. At least at work it had. And from the look on Don Baldo's face, he didn't want to get another look at this side again. We couldn't blame him. He went back to his meal and the tall glasses of cold beer that Mami kept pouring for him. He ate in silence, squinting at his plate like someone who wasn't used to this kind of food, until Papi tried to open up a conversation on something safe: old folksongs.

"Have you heard that old rendition of 'Lamento Jibaro' over *La Voz Hispana*?" he asked Don Baldo.

"Sure I have," said Don Baldo very seriously, almost grimly. "How can I help it? It comes on at least six times a week. I think they should try something different once in a while."

"Not for my money," Papi said.

"Your money? What money?"

"That's just a way of speaking, Don Baldo. I forget what it's called."

"It can't be important, Don Gerán. May I have another glass of cold beer, Doña Lilia?"

So much for the old folksongs. I wanted to join Tego, wherever he was, but it was the wrong time to run out on Papi, and Mami, who was doing her best to save face for all three of us. The beer helped.

Afterward, Papi brought out his guitar ("If there's nothing to talk about," he used to say," try music.") and played some old tunes. Don Baldo, buzzed from the six pack, only pretended to listen, until it was time to give us a polite goodnight. He didn't want us to think he was just a common, crude, eat-and-run type, so he put up with Papi's singing and playing for a while, then got up, thanked Mami for the meal ("The best cooking I've had in years, Doña Lilia." She smiled, pretending to believe him.) belched a couple of times, and left. I went back to my room, to work on a crude translation of *El Gibaro*, partly to keep up my dying Spanish. But I had trouble concentrating. He and Mami were having a little disagreement in the living room.

"Did you have to give him a speech?" she was asking.

"Yes," he said. "Yes, I did." His voice was cracking. "This wasn't the first time he pulled that *sindicato* proposal, Lilia. It started months ago at work. Maybe he was trying to humiliate me in front of my own family. Where's Tego?"

"He escaped." she said. "He couldn't take any more."

"I'll talk to him later. Where's Santos?"

"He's in their room. I guess he's trying to avoid our mistakes. Maybe he's just hiding, I don't know. Why couldn't you just say no to this Don Baldo? You're good at saying no when you want to."

"No, I'm not. And besides, I tried the straight approach already. At least thirty-six times. But in my house I draw the line, even if the walls are cracking. Did you notice the way he was looking at that wall? I'm sure if he were our landlord, he wouldn't put up with it."

"Now they'll laugh at you at the factory," she said. "He looks like a man of gossip to me."

"So let them laugh, Lilia. It won't be the first time. That's their problem."

"You win," she said. Then she went back to their bedroom. She was reading Volume I of the *Wonderland of Wisdom.* He went straight to the dining room, to work on his new hobby, leather tooling.

In a little while I went back there to see how he was coming along. He didn't notice me looking at him. "Your *maroma* paid off that time," I said.

He looked up. He was wearing his thick lenses. "What *maroma*?"

"The way you told Don Baldo off. Put him in his place."

"That's not a *maroma*. Maybe you don't know what a *maroma* is. That was more like a disaster. And if you don't believe me, ask your mother. She'll tell you what it was."

"Maybe she misunderstood what you were up to."

"No, she didn't misunderstand. She understood it perfectly. Maybe she understood it better than I did."

"Well, it's a matter of opinion, then. He put that six-pack of beer away pretty good."

"I guess he needed a six-pack after my speech. Some speech."

"It was a good speech, Papi. Don't knock it. It was honest."

"I could have done better, but he caught me by surprise. My fault. I should have been expecting it. *Sindicato!* Schemers . . . "

I fixed us each a cup of coffee and sat there with him for a while. He worked away on the leather and hummed to himself. Old folksongs were coming out of his nose. He was cutting the leather with an X-Acto knife as if one mistake might get him hanged. His cutting hand was shaking and he had to go easy or ruin the leather. I had to look away. Those pieces of cured calfskin might start bleeding any second. Then I couldn't take any more and left with my cup of coffee. I don't think he noticed.

Carmen Arceo

This coal miner's daughter has always regarded work as a basic family value. Not only did her father work double shifts at the mine, but he also ran a meat market and general store, owned property, and raised vegetables in order to provide for his family. For Arceo, these various enterprises meant that she and her siblings shared significant work responsibilities from a very early age. These and other memories of the unique culture of a New Mexico mining camp, including the spectacular Christmas and Easter celebrations sponsored by the mine owner, are fondly and vividly recalled in the following interview.

Interview

My dad came from Zacatecas, Mexico, when he was about twenty-five years old. My mother was born in Las Vegas, New Mexico. My dad, when he came from Mexico, went straight to Morley, Colorado, a coal mining camp, which is where my brother Cleto and I were born. That was a long time ago because they used to pull the coal cars out with mules back then. In Mexico, my grandfather had a store and my dad had always helped out there. He opened up a store here, too; he always did both, worked in the mines and had a little general store. He was a hard-working man, I remember that above all, that his biggest concern was to provide for my mother and us.

Anyway, those mines closed, must've been about 1934, because I was born in 1930, my brother was born in 1928—we're the only ones who were born in Colorado. After Morley, we moved to Terrero, New Mexico. It's a national park now, but those used to be mines, not coal mines, but some kind of mineral. The place is still there. At that time, my daddy set up a store for himself; I remember very clearly going to his store. And they used to pay the miners with paper money, like coupons—I remember walking across a swinging bridge with my brother to go buy candy at the general store, and we paid with coupons. The miners used to be lowered in buckets into the mines. We were not there long; I guess it was about '35 when the mines in Terrero closed too.

Then my daddy came to Madrid, they may say Madríd today, but we knew it as Mádrid. There was no place to live there; the camp was full of people who had migrated from other camps, Italians, Mexicans, Lebanese. The Albuquerque and Cerrillos Coal Company policy was that, if you worked in Madrid, you had to live there. When we came here it was owned by Oscar Huber. Now my dad never liked to pay rent, so he told Joe Huber, the son, that he wasn't going to work there anymore. He said that the mines were dangerous, a lot of people got killed in those mines, and if he got killed, who was going to take care of his children and where would they live? He wanted his own house for the security it would give us. By then we were already four kids, Cleto, myself, Orti (Hortensia), and Martha. My dad was a good worker, and they didn't want to lose him. In those days, they needed a high volume of production and good workers because they were using a lot of coal for trains as well as at Los Alamos. So Oscar Huber told him he could live in Cerrillos and work in Madrid if he wanted; he just waived the rules.

We had a real nice house, but a flood came and carried it away. My dad worked so hard so he could buy a little land and put up a house, but then the San Marcos River took it away. Just like that. But he went back and started again. He was not one to give up. After the flood, we moved to a ranch across the river where we had

✺✺ ✺✺ ✺✺ ✺✺ ✺✺ ✺✺ ✺✺ ✺✺

to haul water and everything else. We didn't have any lights or running water until about 1950 when they brought electricity from Santa Fe to Cerrillos. Before then it was just coal lamps; we did our homework by coal oil lamps. Mama was always home with us, taking care of us. After a while, dad saved enough to buy some land in Cerrillos. We were able to raise most of our own food that way. He was a very smart man.

During the war there was a big demand for coal, and I remember my dad getting up at 5:30 in the morning and my mama would make him fresh tortillas. She would make him burritos and fill his lunch bucket with two lunches because he worked a double shift whenever possible. When he came home, it was to rest, eat supper, and go to bed. By then, Oscar Huber had let more people live in Cerrillos, about three miles from Madrid, and I remember my dad putting on his mining helmet and car-bide lamp and big thick coveralls, leaving the house with his lunch bucket, and then he and his coworkers would walk across the hill to Madrid to save on gasoline.

When he would finish one shift, he would go to the Lamp Hotel there in Madrid, rest for an hour or two, take a shower, eat his second lunch, and then go back into the mine again for a second shift. He would come home every single day, we would see him every day. He would come home in the morning, sleep awhile, and then he would go again. When he was doing double shifts he also worked on Saturday and Sunday. He didn't like working on Sunday, but he would say, God knows that I always pray to him, he knows that I have a family and I have to support them. But he made sure we went to church on Sundays; if we didn't, we got in trouble.

By the time my dad retired he had black lung. Mama got a black lung pension. He worked in the mines for about thirty years. He used pick and dynamite. He suf-fered a lot from lumbago in his back because many times the mines were very low, and they had to work on their knees. And the workers were paid per ton of coal, so the more they dug, the more they got paid, so daddy dug and dug. Dad was paid well, he became a foreman, and he always managed to double his money because he had the little store on the side.

He set up the store and was there mostly in the evenings, but my brother and I ran it after school. He taught us to work very hard from the time we were very lit-tle. We never had time to play because we planted that ranch, acres and acres of corn, beans, carrots, peanuts, potatoes, everything. And we watered from the Gal-isteo River. He had a pump and we watered from there, we irrigated the whole land, we weeded and everything. When we finished that, then my dad would give us a little vacation and a little money. We would take the train to Trinidad, Col-orado, the train that was running on the steam from the coal that my dad dug, and on the water from Cerrillos.

I forgot one important thing about Madrid that I must tell you. I'm going to backtrack in time because you need this for your book; everybody will tell you that. When we were children, the happiest moments of our lives were the famous Christ-mas and Easter celebrations in Madrid. All the miners had a club, and the fathers would help build a kind of miniature Disney Land, all sponsored by the Hubers. They had Santa Claus, reindeer, Cinderella, Little Boy Blue, the Easter Bunny right there on the playground and on the mountainside, all illuminated. You could see it for miles around. Some of the displays were a hundred feet long and thirty or forty feet high. The giant Christmas tree consisted of about twenty or thirty large trees wired to a pole and lighted by electric lights and mirrors, so that it looked like a river of light. A huge star was placed above the Bethlehem display, which even had an adobe wall built around it. They were fantastic, beautiful spectacles that brought thousands of people to Madrid, and Trans World Airlines even changed its route so that they could point the Chrismas lights out to their passengers.

As a child I especially loved the toyland, with Peter the Pumpkin Eater, Jack and Jill, the Three Little Pigs, Jack and the Bean Stalk, Little Red Riding Hood, Mickey Mouse, you name it. Just imagine, all of this was illuminated, with power from the town's generator. They had a little train too, and during the holidays my dad would take a roll of tickets and at least two or three times a week at night he would take us to Madrid. I mean, people came from everywhere to see the Madrid lights, from all over the world! The Bethlehem display was especially wonderful because it was up in the hills and the way they made the lights go on and off it looked like the angel was going back and forth to Bethlehem. They had a real donkey, a real cow, St. Joseph, the Blessed Mother, everything.

On Christmas morning you would get a ticket and it would say Girl 4, or whatever, your sex and your age. And you would take this ticket and go see Santa, I knew he was the real one because there were reindeer on the roof, and you would give Santa the ticket. He would then give you a package that said Girl 4 and a huge stocking with candy, popcorn, peanuts, everything. The miners had this club and they each contributed a little, but mostly it was the company that did this. It was a good company. Of course, now the town is closed; when the Hubers sold out that was the end. Now, there's nobody in Madrid who is originally from there, not one single family.

Easter was another wonderful holiday there. Now, this, the company sponsored themselves. They used to boil thousands of dozens of eggs and they would color them. This was for Madrid and Cerrillos, not just for the kids whose parents worked there; there were at least five hundred families. We lived in a garage for awhile in Madrid before we moved to Cerrillos, and I remember that the company would send trucks around for us kids and they would take us up to the mountains where they would hide the eggs. They always had a special golden egg, wrapped in gold foil, and if you found it you would get a silver dollar. I never found one, but my brother did, and he gave the silver dollar to my grandmother in Trinidad; that's who we would go see every summer after we had finished planting. Years later, after my grandmother died and I was going through her things, I came across that same silver dollar, and I gave it back to my brother.

Another special day was the Fourth of July. The men from Cerrillos and from Madrid had a baseball team made up of the miners' sons mostly, but some team members were also miners because kids started working there very young. But they had this baseball game, and they would give out free popcorn, and they had a free fireworks display. The Hubers were very good to the people.

They had what they called scrip, like a token; it had an M engraved in the middle. If the miners needed money between pay periods, they would go to the pay office and say they needed thirty or forty dollars in scrip, and the office would give it to them. That scrip wasn't good outside the mining camp either, they had to use it there. Fortunately, we produced what we needed ourselves, vegetables, chickens, and even a few pigs and cows. He would butcher them, and mama would dry the meat and make jerky.

When the union came into being, my daddy became a union man; he believed strongly in the union, the United Mine Workers of America. Mama got a check from the union after he died. The ones that did not belong to the union they used to call *esclavos,* slaves. My dad believed in the union because it gave the workers more rights, better pay, and better hours.

Anyway, the mines in Madrid closed about, let's see, by '54. I know because by then I was working at the employment office, and I see this pile of claims for unemployment, and I see my dad's name, and my uncle's, and my cousin's. That's how I found out that the mine had closed. My dad got a contract and he kept operating one mine on his own until my brother made him stop. It was too hard, and he was already coughing black coal, coughing, coughing, and all this black stuff, coal dust, would come up, and they would even get chunks of coal from their ears. There were no protective laws; they didn't even wear anything to cover their mouths. Luckily they passed that black lung pension, which mama got until she passed away. All the miners from Madrid that I've heard of so far have died from black lung. I mean it was *black.*

But I remember growing up in Madrid as being very happy. It was a good life; there was a strong sense of community. We had a little car and my dad cut it down and made it into a little truck. We used to go to every house in Madrid selling meat and corn and anything else he could get his hands on. There were a lot of poor families there. My dad was a very sociable man; he would talk with everyone in his broken English as we made the rounds.

I started working in the income tax department in '54, and I retired in '82 from the same department. I loved my job. The reason I stopped was that my mother went blind—she was a diabetic—and I wanted to spend time with her. To me my mother was everything in the world. So I retired at the age of fifty-two. I'm glad I did, because I enjoyed my mother for one whole year, and then she died in her sleep.

After mama died, I started working in the Goldfield mines in Dolores, way up there in the Ortiz mountains, there in Cerrillos. It was a working gold mine for about seven years. I had already worked for twenty-eight years in an office with computers, so I said, My body needs to move, not my brain, so I pushed a broom. I did janitorial work, cleaning the offices for the miners and for the employees. Once in a while, I helped correct and edit errors in the computers, but I had enough of that: I wanted to do a job where at the end of the day I knew it was finished. I worked at the Goldfield mines until they closed down, from '84 until they closed in '88.

At the same time, I was also working in a gift shop in Madrid during the day. I would work until about four o'clock and then I would go up to the mine and clean until about eleven or so. After they closed the mine, I continued working at the gift shop in Madrid. I finally quit my job in Madrid because they came to make that movie *Young Guns*. Most of the movie was filmed in Cerrillos, and they used my house for the film. I couldn't work in Madrid and take care of my house, and I couldn't just leave my house because they were using it as the *Young Guns* director's office and also as the sheriff's office. I had Lou Diamond Phillips in there, I had Emilio Estevez there, all those stars that the teenagers like, and I had teenagers in and out of my house constantly, so I had to be there. We had a lot of fun. After the filming was finished I was going to open my own gift shop, but that's when my sister-in-law became very sick and that's the reason I'm back here in Albuquerque, to help take care of her.

I think I covered most of what I wanted to tell you. My life reminds me of that song "Coal Miner's Daughter" by Loretta Lynn. In the summer my mother would get the Montgomery Ward or Sears catalogue and she would order material and thread. My grandmother had a pedal sewing machine, and she would come from Trinidad every summer and sew dresses for us. Then my mother would buy us two dresses each from the Montgomery Ward catalogue. And that's what we had, plus a pair of everyday shoes. My dad used to take them to Juan Montoya, and he'd put new soles on them, and again, and again. All year around it was the same pair of shoes, plus one that we set aside to wear only on Sunday. Once someone gave my grandmother a coat, a beige coat with a great big fur collar. It was a ladies' coat, but she cut it down for me, and it was beautiful. All that reminds me of Loretta Lynn. I love that song because it reminds me of my whole life. And that other one, "Sixteen Tons," that reminds me so much of my dad. We were a very close family and my childhood was very happy, even though we all worked very hard.

Danny Santiago

In *Famous All Over Town* (New York: Simon & Schuster, 1983), Danny Santiago portrays with humor and direct street language the daily life of a troubled Mexican family in Los Angeles, as seen through the eyes of the four-teen-year-old son. The freshness of the narrator's perspective provides comic relief from serious themes, such as the father's abuse of the mother, the rebelliousness of the daughter Lena, the violent *machismo* of the father, and the possible perpetuation of *machista* values in the son himself.

Though Danny Santiago (pen name for Daniel James) is not a Latino himself, he has lived and worked in Latino communities in Los Angeles for so long and he writes with such an intimate understanding of Latino culture, that his work belongs in this anthology.

from Famous All Over Town

"Hey hey, look who's all dressed up like a princess," I told my baby sister. She kicked her tiny arms and legs at me and nearly smiled. It was that same Sunday night, and I noted an open Sears box on the bed. "Don't tell me you're gonna baptize her in Mexico?" I asked for a joke, but what else could such a dress be meant for, all ribbons and lace?

"Why not?" my mother answered.

I was shocked. "You mean all by yourself? Without my father or none of us?"

"My mother will be there." She stripped the little dress off Dolores and hid it in the bottom of her suitcase. "Now get out," she said. "I'm sleepy. Quick! *Pa' fuera,* Out!" And shut the door on me.

Whenever my mother mentioned my father, her voice got edgy. I wondered why. I never remembered them what you might call lovey-dovey, but in the old days they weren't like this. Maybe even at that age married people had their little secrets. There were too many secrets in this house of ours, and I didn't care for it at all.

Dr. Kildare cured his patient of the week on the TV, and I was on my way to bed when my father came charging up the steps. "Where's your sister at?" he yelled at me.

"How should I know?"

He grabbed my arm.

"A brother guards his sister, that's how. In Mexico, even the lowest knows that, but up here you don't know nothing."

He turned me loose and yanked open the bedroom door. "Where's my daughter:" he yelled into the dark. My mother groaned herself awake.

"In the crib." she said. My father swore at her and shook the bed. She came out pulling on her robe. Her eyes were still asleep and her mouth and hair.

"Maybe she's over Aurora's house, I think," my mother yawned.

"Liar!"

"What's this big noise all about?"

"Public scandal's what," my father shouted, "and with one of those *bracero* devils, those no-good son of a bitch rapers."

"Who says?"

"Never mind who, it's all over town. But what do you care? Do you know where your daughter goes at night? No, not you. Just turn her loose on the town!"

"Calm yourself. Drink coffee."

They were in the kitchen now. I heard a slap and a coffee mug went rolling, but from my mother not a sound. She was too proud to scream like most. And now she came on real strong.

"You bore me," she said. "All you damn men. Think you're king over us because you got that ugly thing that dangles down your pants. A bull's got bigger, or a burro."

SLAP.

"Hey, cut it out," I called. What else? If I went in there it only made things worse. I felt sympathy for my mother, but tonight, in another way, I was on my father's side. This so-called romance of my sister should have been stomped before it got started, and I had a feeling my mother knew more than she admitted. Lately there had been a lot of *misterioso* whispering between those two women and our house was split down the middle, where back in the old days Lena was always Papa's little girl and used to sit at his feet and trim his rocky toenails.

"What you want in there?" my mother called.

My father was in the bedroom now, racketing through the closet. For the .45? I wondered.

"You'll never find it," my mother promised him.

My father knew better than to try to beat it out of her. He would have to kill her first, she was that kind of Indian. I heard the closet shelf come crashing down. Dolores woke up and yelled. My father's face was wild, wild red, and his teeth were grinding. His fists looked like battle-axes. My mother tried to stop him.

"You'll only make a scandal."

He brushed her off his sleeve and banged out the door. I ran after, but already he was in the Buick and gone. I shook all over. My father's voice set me on fire. I couldn't sit home doing nothing. I had to find them and save my sister even if I had to kill the guy. But that Armando was twenty-four years old, his papers said. I went for my baseball bat. And what about the cops? Which always show up when you need them least? And what about their smart remarks? "Well, well, if it isn't the home-run king," they no doubt might say. "Climb in and we'll drive you to the ball park." No. A knife was more private. I grabbed the chicken-killer from the kitchen drawer and slided it inside my pants where the belt would hold the handle. My mother sat at the table, eyes shut, touching her bruised face here and there with her finger tips.

"Are you okay?" I asked.

She didn't say she wasn't, so I went running down Shamrock and up Main to Huxley Street. Lots of apartments there rent to *braceros*, and junky old hotels. Behind any one of these closed doors that rat could have my sister. Possibly he got her drunk or gave her some kind of pill. I could see him riding her with his pants shoved down over those checkered shoes. Raging all the way, I cut into yards and listened outside suspicious windows, but all I heard was televisions and snoring. I kept tight hold of my knife so it wouldn't slip down my pants. This would be my first time to stab into flesh. "Don't stab high," everybody always told me."Drive in for the belly." I needed practice. Lucky for me, it was garbage night. I stabbed paper sacks and plastic bags and ripped them from the navel up. I left a fine trail of garbage up Huxley Street and people might hate me in the morning, but by the time I hit Broadway I was quite expert with that blade.

From Webster & Ponce's Funeral Home on the corner I cruised down toward Bailey Street, but they would never risk all the bright lights of Broadway, no they would be locked into some dark bedroom, which there were hundreds of in Eastside, if not thousands.

I was just going to turn back when by some miracle I saw them at the Mexicatessen. It's the least dark place in town. Neons shoot red and blue arrows and bulbs wink on and off till your eyes can't stand it.

They were sitting outside at one of those cement tables where you bring your food from the service window, the only ones out there. It was wet from today's rain and a cold wind was blowing but they didn't seem to notice. They didn't even notice when I walked up to them. My hand was folded round the knife handle ready for anything, and under my pants the blade froze my skin.

"My father wants you," I told my sister, very rugged.

That *bracero* jumped up like electrocuted, not Lena.

"This here's my brother," she told the guy as calm as if she'd been expecting me. He held out his hand. Automatic, my own hand reached out like an idiot. I pulled it back too late. The knife slid down my pants leg and rattled on the cement. We all inspected it. I made a grab but Lena's foot got there first.

"Jees Christ," she yelled. "Do you want to kill somebody?"

"Why not?" I said.

She whipped the knife into her bag and started scolding, but to my surprise the guy took my side.

"If it was my sister, I would do the same," he said. "What does your brother know of my intentions? Rodolfo," he seemed to know my name, "I swear to you by my mother that I am honest and sincere with your sister. Never once did I touch her the wrong way, or even suggest it."

"Sit down, little brother," Lena told me. She yanked my wrist. My knees seemed watery and there I was on the bench facing them.

"Permit me to buy you a hamburger," Armando begged, "or even a steak sandwich."

To sit at the same table was bad enough. To eat was going too far.

"Rodolfo," he sang in that decorated Spanish they use down there, "I am not like those others from my country who come up here to take advantage. Pure brutes they are, for the major part, and lacking in *cultura* and *educación*." Where he himself had gone one year to the *politécnico* and his family was highly respected, to hear him tell it, with a *licenciado* for a cousin and a far uncle that was a priest. But his mother was a widow and life was hard down there so every week he sent his money home. Oh yes, I knew all about his "money home" from that lady's letters. But I didn't mention it at the time.

I knew it was my place to hate the guy, but he was so polite, what could I do? Especially since I'd lost my blade. While he talked I inspected him closely. He was light color, as light as Lena and more the Latin type than Indian. His pearly teeth were the first thing you noticed. They were on view all the time, a whole mouthful of them. He had narrow eyebrows that met over his nose which was thin and straight and even looked okay from the side, and not like mine. Girls would no doubt call him very handsome. And his hands were like a woman's. You knew he wore gloves to work.

"Rodolfo," how he loved that name, "I confess I am here illegal. I wanted to come the right way but the list was too long. My Mexican papers are all in order." He pulled out a letter which stated he had a good character and had never been in jail. It was from his chief of police, as if that might make a hit with me.

"What else can I say?" he said, "except that I have fallen honorably in love with your sister, not only for the beauty of her face, but for the beauty of her soul and for her gentle quiet ways."

Quiet ways? Lena?

I looked at her and she winked. Wait till the guy heard her banging around the kitchen. So anyway he respected my sister and my mother and my father and me. He didn't mention the baby, but no doubt he respected her too.

"Shall I show him something?" Lena asked the guy in Spanish, then held out her wedding finger and there was a ring on it with a tiny sparkle that could be a diamond.

"We're gonna get married by church," Lena told me, "just like Espie's wedding only I've decided on yellow for the bridesmaids because it's cheerfuller, and we're gonna have twelve instead of eight."

"*¿Qué dices?*" Armando asked her.

My sister had slipped out of her Spanish. It seems she was giving him English lessons, but if so he hadn't gotten very far. So then I had to sit back and listen to them rave in both languages, how the chamberlains would wear those new King Edward–style tuxedos and they would hire a Cadillac convertible to drive to church and have *mariachis* at their reception and a rock band for their dance, and of course, Mexican style, Armando would pay for everything.

"What's he do?" I asked my sister. "Rob banks?"

It seemed that temporarily Armando was making the potato salad over at X-Cell Packing which he did in a cement mixer, feeding in the potatoes and hard-boiled eggs by shovel and the mayonnaise by hose.

"But my true career is *artista,*" Armando said.

He had only five lessons more to go on his draw-by-mail course and would soon earn up to $200 a week in his spare time. To prove it he opened up his sketch pad which he always carried with him. The first page was a big head of Lena. I have to admit it was very pretty, but you would hardly know it for my sister, the way he had tamed down that fighting nose of hers. He showed me other pictures too, all dollies in bikinis with left legs crossed over for stylish. They were quite sexy too, except no hands or feet because that would be covered in the next lesson. Till finally I got bored of pictures and threw him the one big question.

"What about my father?"

"I will pay him a formal visit," Armando promised, "to ask for your sister's hand."

"And he'll give you both fists."

"If I treat your father with respect," Armando thought, "he will respect me too. I would let him set the wedding day. We could wait six months, one year even, and both save money till the happy day when I stand beside the altar and your father leads your sister down the aisle with a carnation in his buttonhole."

I seriously doubted any of us would live to see that day.

"He's looking for you right now," I told Lena. "He could drive by any minute." That stopped the conversation.

"I am not afraid of him," Armando boasted. "I am a master of Kung Fu," but Lena dragged him off in the shadows to say goodnight. She tried to kiss the guy but he didn't let her, possibly out of respect for me.

"Now shake hands with your future brother-in-law," she ordered me.

I hated to, but to please her finally I did, keeping fingers crossed behind my back. So then Armando went his way and we went ours down Huxley street.

"How come all this garbage?" Lena asked after stepping on a grapefruit skin. "Did Jack the Ripper pass by here?"

I changed the subject.

"My father's gonna murder you."

"Oh well," she said, "you only live once."

Lena hung lovey-dovey on my arm like I might be her boyfriend, but all she could talk about was Armando and what a fine dancer he was and how he talked like poems, besides being so polite and well-dressed.

"Oh sure," I said. "The guy's a prince and no doubt his little wife in Mexico thinks the same."

Lena threw my arm away.

"There's no little wife!" she yelled. "I asked him. And besides he's very Catholic-minded."

"He's only marrying you to get immigrated."

"Thanks a lot, little brother. You make me feel real charming."

"There's plenty of guys from up here, and you've known them all your life," I pointed out.

"Fat Manuel? Your friend Gorilla?"

I named various others.

"A lot you know," she said. "All they ever want is just one thing. 'Come on, honeee, let's make out, huh?' And 'Ooooo,' and 'Aaaaah,' and, 'Eeeeee,' like some dirty kind of animal. My toes get sore from kicking shins. Where with Armando, holding hands is good enough for him, and he talks to me so fine, 'My little green-eye orchid of the jungle,' he calls me in Spanish."

"What do you call *him*? My potato salad?"

Lena blazed and slapped. There was no room beside her on the sidewalk after that. Single file we passed the brewery and the Aztecs' club. On Shamrock my sister's feet started dragging and I didn't blame them. "Maybe I won't tell the whole truth exactly just yet," she said.

The Buick wasn't home yet. Still the lights were on in the house and possibly he could be waiting.

"I'll go first just in case," I said.

My mother was alone, at the kitchen table. Her left eye was turning black.

"Mama, look at your face!" Lena screamed, then turned on me. "And I suppose you just stood around as usual!"

I ignored her and went outside to watch for my father. I turned off the porch light and sat in the shadows and their voices came rattling through the screen door.

"But I gotta face him sometime!"

"Not tonight. Tomorrow he'll be grumpy, but mornings he doesn't slap. Or better, wait till the afternoon. He'll cool down at work. Go spend the night at Virgie's."

Lena groaned. "Why not Aurora's?"

"Because he'll bust in her door, which he wouldn't dare with my *comadre*. And after work tomorrow I'll phone you what mood he's in. And I'll make him *chile verde* which he loves and hand over Dolores for him to play with . . . "

On and on they went like that. What politicians! My dumb innocent little mother had my father figured to his slightest sneeze. They may claim *mexicanas* are slaves to their husbands, but sitting out there on the porch and listening to those two, I wondered if I myself would ever dare to marry with any member of that tribe.

Carlos Cumpián

Carlos Cumpián is editor and publisher of MARCH/Abrazo Press and author of *Coyote Sun* (Chicago: MARCH/Abrazo, 1990), a collection of Chicano poetry. His poetry has been published in *Spoon River Quarterly, Exquisite Corpse, Literati Internationale,* and in numerous anthologies. Originally from San Antonio, Cumpián resides in Chicago where he is an active promoter of poetry and founder of the La Palabra reading series at Randolph Street Gallery.

In "After Calling," from *Coyote Sun,* grandmother and grandson keep in close touch by telephone, though one can still feel the loneliness across the miles.

After Calling

Sola mi
abuela
has my ear
at home
under a San Antonio
año nuevo
moon

In Chicago I hear
her complaints
and promise
the pain will go away
before we need to
hang up
alone.

Roberto Fernández

This Cuban-born writer is best known for his satiric treatment of the Cuban community in Miami, whose language, both English and Spanish, idiosyncrasies, and extreme political views he treats with sharp wit. Fernández's best-known works are *La vida es un special* (Miami: Universal, 1982 [Life is a Special]), *La montaña rusa* (Houston: Arte Público Press, 1985 [The Roller Coaster]), and *Raining Backwards* (Houston: Arte Público Press, 1988), from which collection our story is taken.

The reading tells of young Miqui who helps his eccentric Cuban grandmother fulfill her last wish, though it seems a very odd request at the time. Years later, when Miqui himself is a grandfather, things become clearer. The story "Raining Backwards" reminds us of the special role that grandparents play in the family.

Raining Backwards

"Michael, Miqui, Miguel. Come here!"

"Yes, *abuela.*"

"Your *abuela* is no waiting for the paramedics, no waiting for the ambulance. You hear that siren? The next one is for me, but they won't catch me!"

"Slowly, *abuela.* Slowly. Come again."

"I need your help. You help your *abuela,* okay? You love your *abuela,* right?"

"Okay, Okay *abuela,* make it quick."

"The rescue, Miqui, the rescue, the paramedics, Miqui. Once they get you, they plug you in and you just cannot die. Besides, I no want to be bury in this country. I will be the first one here and who knows where the next one will be, dead and all alone! The whole world gets scatter in America, even dead people. When I am gone I want to be right next to my sister, Hilda, in Havana. I owe it to her. Me bury in Havana, okay? No here."

"*Abuela,* don't call me Miqui. You know I don't like it. What's your problem?"

"I am dying."

"C'mon. You aren't dying."

"Anytime now. I already have . . . let me think how many years I have. Mari, Mari, Mari-Clara, child, you remember how many years I have?"

"Please, mother! I'm trying to concentrate on this last posture. Don't bother me now."

"I know I have many. Anytime now. It was raining backwards yesterday. When my father died it was raining backwards also."

"There you go again, *abuela.* It can't rain backwards! What a silly idea."

"Why you can no believe me? You think your *abuela* would trick you?"

"You had too much coffee, *abuela.* Coffee makes you high. *Mucho café!*"

"Why you can no believe me? I believe you when you told me many years ago that a man went to sleep for twenty years and when he woke up his beard reach his feet. I remember, I told it to Barbarita and Mirta. They were very impressed. I even told it to that woman that use to rent her daughter dressed as a flag for parties and political rallies. What was her name? You remember, Miqui?"

"*Abuela,* please. My name is Michael."

"Mari, Mari, Mari-Clara, you remember the name of that woman that use to rent her daughter for social events dressed as a flag?"

"Mother, please, you made me lose my concentration."

"Anyway, *abuela* is no staying here, okay. Hilda is too alone without me and she needs me so much. I go accompany her!"

"But Hilda is dead. You told me so. Hilda is dead, Grandma!"

"Dead people feel alone too, they have feelings, you know. So you are going to help me, yes or no?"

"Okay, okay. What do you want me to do? But make it quick. I gotta be at the tryouts in half an hour. It's football season, *abuela*."

"Mother, you're eighty-three. Her name was Emelina and her daughter's Linda Lucia."

The following morning, *abuela* gave me the details of her flight, and I had to swear never to reveal her plan. After the swearing in ceremony was over, I lent her a hand and we were on our way to the woods a few miles from the house. We went looking for a sturdy tree. In the midst of the thicket *abuela* sniffed at a tall mahogany and said, "What you waiting for?" She placed a sharp ax in my hands, and, like a mad cheerleader, started shouting, "Miqui, Miqui, cut it, cut it, rah-rah-rah." It was then that my eye caught a black seagull's nest perched on the mahogany's canopy. I knew that it was the sturdiest tree, but the black seagulls were on my Boy Scouts list of endangered species. I thought for a few minutes and told her that the mahogany was a sick tree. "You choose, now," said *abuela*. I looked around, selecting an old perforated oak. She smiled when I was able to bring it down with just a few blows.

"You cut good, Miqui. I like that!"

From then on, I followed her orders like a robot. She was so determined that I couldn't question her. She instructed me to start carving a hole right in the center of the tree.

"Come on. Take the arms off! Get the arms off the tree first!"

I didn't quite understand what she meant, and *abuela*, losing her patience, grabbed the ax, dismembering the unsuspecting vegetable. That afternoon the oak had the appearance of an old board being consumed by human termites. Then *abuela* fell asleep for a couple of hours, while I continued laboring. She awoke, inspected the work, and patted me on my back. I grinned while thinking that I had surely saved the black seagulls from an impetuous old lady who I didn't quite understand.

For the next two months, we returned faithfully to our secret enterprise, where, camouflaged under a heavy cover of pine straw, the ark was being built. It had two compartments, one for sitting up and one to keep the canned goods and water pail. It had no self-propulsion, but a fake wheel and a hole in which to place a white flag. She had patiently covered the exterior with rhinestones and pictures of Julio Iglesias and German Garcia all pasted to the surface with Superglue.

One afternoon, the admiral, while inspecting the day's work, asked me a few questions to determine my nautical knowledge. Somewhat ashamed, I told her that I could doggie paddle. Very calmly, *abuela* ordered me to go to the library and to obtain, using any means at my disposal, a navigational chart.

"Miqui, when you learn the chart, we are going to go to steal the pickup truck of your father and put the canoe in the bed, then we go to the Key Biscayne Marina and we rent motor boat, understand you?"

"I guess so . . ."

"Then we go to tow the vessel to where the Gulf Stream flows. You know the Gulf Stream is very, very close. I heard it in a radio program. Then I go from the motor boat to the canoe and you cut the rope, understand you?"

"But why?"

"I am going South. I'm going away, Miqui, and I come back no more."

"But you will die on the way!"

"No worry. I will be there in two days. I get off the boat. I wave my white flag. I drink a cup of coffee. I take a taxi and head for where Hilda rests and then it will begin to rain backwards . . ."

So there I was in the library stealing a navigational chart from an old dilapidated *National Geographic.* I remember I put it inside my underwear to avoid detection by the electronic sensor. When I got home, I opened it. Puzzled by its contents, I stored it in my bottom drawer. Learning that chart would take me almost three weeks. When I told her I had everything down pat, she went to her room, changed to her Sunday best and headed to catch a bus for Dadeland Mall with Mom's gold American Express. When *abuela* returned, she had bought two evening gowns, a flowery parasol and seven tape players, which would have been the envy of any kid. She showed me her purchases, while repeating several times that she just couldn't arrive empty handed.

"The purple dress is for Hilda. Is low cut, she had nice breasts."

The big day came and *abuela* was wearing a red sequined dress and carrying her parasol like an authentic tropical toreador. I led her to the pickup, and with great reverence, à la Walter Raleigh, took her by the hand while opening the door. I was euphoric! For the first time in my life I was driving my father's truck. He was completely unaware of what we were doing, because he was partying with Mom. During the night, *abuela* had managed to steal the keys from my father's drawer.

After a couple of jerky starts, we drove towards the woods. We got out of the truck and, after struggling for a while, with the help of three pulleys, we managed to place the canoe inside. It was around three in the morning. I was going to have my first solo drive along U.S.1. I was so happy and *abuela* was beaming. I pulled into the parking lot like a pro and went straight to the office. We rented the motor boat using Mom's credit card. Once we were inside the boat, *abuela* opened a bottle of cognac that she had hidden under her gown. I almost choked with the first sip. She asked me to drink the rest after returning to port. *Abuela* drank hers in a single gulp.

We headed southeast in search of the Gulf Stream. Our boat was moving slowly. It wasn't easy to tow the refurbished tree trunk. *Abuela* was really bubbly, talking incessantly, telling me of everything from the day she caught her finger grinding coffee beans to the first kiss my grandfather gave her through the iron gates that covered the living room window. We were getting closer to the point where I thought the current would take her directly to her destination. The waters were turning deep blue. I slowed down, and *abuela*, sensing that we were closing in on the Gulf Stream, turned very thoughtful and, losing her previous effervescence, said, "You know why I have to accompany Hilda? Well, I am going to tell you. The kiss your grandfather gave me was no for me, I knew that afternoon he was going to pass by to see her because he had been enamoring her for almost a year, and then I covered my face with a silk veil and he kissed me through it, thoughting I was Hilda. Then I took the cover off my face and he was bewitched by me. Hilda died a lonely old maid throwing up stars."

"Stars?" I said.

"Yes, stars. It was God's way to reward her sufferings on earth. No believe me?"

"You can't throw up stars!"

"What if I tell you that she ate a can of chicken and stars soup before she died, you believe me now?"

"Well, it makes more sense . . . not a whole lot, but it makes more sense since she had the soup."

Abuela was in a trance for a few minutes, rewinding her mind. Then her voice was trembling when she added, "I have something more to tell you. It is no all. I cheated on your grandfather once in my life. Kirby was in love with me!"

"Kirby, the black bean soup maker?"

"No, Michael. No be ignorant. They teach you nothing in school? The poet. He was learning Spanish to talk to me because at that time I knew very little English. I remember he used to tell me in the factory, whispering in my ear, 'My poems are palest green and flaming scarlet, a wounded deer that searches for a refuge in the forest.' Pretty, eh? I memorized the lines, but I left him because he loved to say bad words and I no like ordinary people. We both worked for the Libby factory, it still makes peaches in heavy syrup. He was the foreman, but he disillusioned me because every day at five o'clock when the whistle sound he used to tell me, 'Nelia, *cojon*, no more work, enough for today, *cojon*.' That is why I left him and we never became nothing. I never like ordinary people that say bad words."

"*Abuela*, he probably was saying 'go home,' not '*cojon*.'"

"Well, it is too late now. But I think I loved your grandfather the most."

After our last dialogue, *abuela* stepped across a plank from the tow boat to the canoe as I was pulling the rope free from the tow. Her vessel was moving now in all directions. She smiled, threw me a kiss, and said, "You be good, Miqui, okay? Make sure your mother drinks her warm milk, your father has the paper at breakfast and your brothers' tennis shoes are always clean, and you no worry for me. If I'll have problems I buy them with the tape players. That is why I carry them with me. You be good Miqui, okay?"

I didn't look back. I started the motor and kept my eyes fixed on the horizon, heading for port.

The tides have come and gone thousands of times, and I have come to the same marina as many times just to gaze South and have a shot of cognac. A week ago, for the first time, I noticed that my shoes were soaked and my head was dry. It was raining backwards! Then I realized that rabbits can't lay eggs and that my time was coming. I told my grandson and he said, "Grandpa Mike, you had too much coffee." I went straight to the old chest and found the yellowish chart we had used. I studied it for a while. I was determined to land where she had. Suddenly I realized the arrows indicating the direction of the current were pointing northeast, not south like I had thought. I had read it upside down, or maybe backwards. I pictured *abuela*'s frozen figure in her sequined dress, holding her parasol inside some floating iceberg off the coast of Norway, having died alone like an old tropical Viking. Somehow I felt the iceberg's chill. Then the ambulance's siren brought me back from what I thought was simply a deep slumber and someone was shouting, "Mouth to mouth! Give him mouth to mouth. Get some air in his lungs. Hook him up to the machine!"

Part 2
Buenos Días, Mi Dios:
La Religión

Good Friday in Pilsen Neighborhood, Chicago

Milagros at Chimayó

Horacio Valdéz and Santos, New Mexico

Shrine at Chimayó, New Mexico

El Santo Niño de
Atocha, Chimayó

Buenos Días, Mi Dios: La Religión

Religion for Latinos is very much associated with family traditions, practices, and ritual events. It, too, is a family affair and is at the heart of nearly every family celebration, from baptisms to *quinceañeras*. Religion is thus an intensely personal matter, involving a close relationship between the individual and God, Jesus, and the saints if one is Catholic; and the African *orixás*, or gods, if one practices some form of *santería*, a syncretic mixture of Catholicism and African religions. Relationships between Latinos and the deity (or deities) are intimate and consist of long conversations, cajoling, bargaining, scolding, or giving thanks and offerings for favors received and tragedies avoided. Many Catholic Latinos pray to their favorite saints to intercede for them, reserving to the saints the function of spiritual *compadre*, or special friend.[1] More evangelical Latinos, such as the Pentecostals, sing their praises in emotional services that offer hope and solidarity in times of need. Latino religious practices highlight ritual, *romerías* (pilgrimages), thanksgiving, and praise. Partly because of its locus in the family, religion for the Latino tends to be more popular than official, and much more emotionally than theologically based. Thus, Latino religious practices reflect the character of the practitioners more than that of the rule-makers.

Being religious, for a Latino, does not necessarily involve going to church or being active in an organized religion; rather, it means belonging to a religious people.[2] The very personal relationship that Latinos have with their religion most often takes place outside the organized church. Because they are often closer to their own popular beliefs than they are to the institutional church, Latinos can be anticlerical without being antireligious. The respected scholar of Puerto Rican culture, Father Joseph Fitzpatrick, tells the story of the soldiers during the Spanish Civil War who "would risk their lives to rescue their santos from the Catholic churches they had just set on fire."[3]

Many religious Latinos, whether they are Catholic, Protestant, followers of the seven African deities, or members of some new sect, believe in spiritualism. They accept the existence of the spirit world, and they trust that the medium can exert influence on that world, either to change events or to affect behavior. Often, when people are troubled they will seek the help of a spiritualist who will say prayers with them and prescribe some natural potion to rid their client of the evil spirits that have inhabited him or her. Many individuals who would never go to a psychiatrist, either because they do not want people to think that they are mentally ill, or because they can't afford it, will consult a spiritualist and become cured of the problem, or bad spirit, that was troubling them.[4]

In virtually every Latino barrio—Cuban, Dominican, Puerto Rican, Mexican—in every major city from New York to Miami to Chicago to Los Angeles—one can enter the local *botánica*, a kind of pharmacy that sells herbs, prayers, folk remedies and other nontraditional medicines, and find just what the "doctor" ordered for, say, the *mal de ojo*, or evil eye. The "doctor" is sometimes a spiritualist, but more often a *curandero/a*, or healer, who prays over the afflicted one, but who in addition possesses some knowledge of folk medicine. People who consult *curanderos* and spiritualists are most often Latinos who believe that spiritual and physical health are interrelated, but adherents also include well-educated Anglos in search of a more holistic, nontraditional medicine.

Thus, while most Latinos are Catholic, Latino religious practices are by no means homogeneous; rather, they express the great diversity of the Latino peoples. Readings in this chapter reflect that diversity as they present historic religious traditions, such as the miracle plays brought from Spain in the sixteenth century; popular religious symbols, such as the *altarcitos*, or altars in the home for personal devotion; and key themes such as resignation, alienation, *machismo*, anticlericalism, spiritualism, pentecostalism, and the often-problematic relationship between Latinos and established churches. Above all, what stands out in these readings is the deep faith of the Latino peoples.

Roberta Fernández

Roberta Fernández's short stories treat the aesthetic and spiritual qualities of women's lives and work, especially as these are expressed through handicrafts, the domestic arts, and traditional religious rituals. Fernández, a native of Laredo, Texas, is particularly interested in the contributions of Latinas to the culture of the Southwest.

Our story, "Filomena," comes from Fernández's award-winning collection of six portraits of southwestern women, *Intaglio: A Novel in Six Stories* (Houston: Arte Público Press, 1990). Moving back and forth between Mexico and Texas, "Filomena" treats three deeply rooted traditions in Mexican and Mexican American spirituality: the *altarcitos; romerías,* or pilgrimages; and the Day of the Dead celebrations. Central to the maintenance of popular religious traditions and observances is the figure of the woman, in this case Filomena, whose cultural significance and wisdom the young narrator comes to appreciate fully over time.

Filomena

I

Every year, in early November, the life of the dead assumed primary importance for Filomena and me, and in preparation for our commemoration, we were making our purchases at the *mercado*. All around us, pails of flowers—mostly *zempoalxochitles,* the color of the sun—were displayed, as one vendor after another tried to entice us with the same statement: *"!Flores para los muertos! !Flores para los muertos!"* As we walked around, my arms formed a circle around the sweet-smelling clusters of flowers that Filomena had already picked out.

To get a little relief from the scent of the flowers, I turned my head upwards and saw that from the second floor of the *mercado,* sheets with large bold letters announced *"El 2 de noviembre—Día de los Muertos."* All over the signs, painted skeletons danced around a central figure who was draped over a chair with a scythe in his right hand. Years before, Filomena had hold me his name—Mictlantecuhtli, the Lord of the Dead. *"Pobrecito Mictlantecuhtli,"* I thought to myself, "no one in school ever talks about you. Maybe they're all hiding from you." Looking at his bony figure, I whispered, "Ah, Mictlantecuhtli," you certainly are no stranger to Filomena and me."

I turned to Filomena to point out the skeletons on the sheets, then skipped the gesture. It was obvious she was through with her purchases and we were ready to go past the throng of celebrants choosing their offerings for the holiday. Awed with the beauty of the scene we would soon be leaving behind, I now took in one deep breath after another until I became intoxicated with the smell of the flowers. Like me, Filomena was holding the bouquets to her nose. Not wanting to break the spell of the moment, we walked in silence, content simply to be together.

Her house was only a few blocks from the marketplace, and as we approached it, I began to measure my steps by hers, giving her quick side glances. Today, as on most days, she had gathered her long dark hair at the nape of her neck with a black barrette. Her face was free of any make-up and she was wearing a gray rayon dress which came to her midcalf. No doubt it was this simplicity of manner that gave her a certain agelessness and enigmatic wisdom. My mother, who had just turned forty, had once told me that she and Filomena were about the same age. This I found hard to comprehend, for they seemed so different from each other. My mother had a certain quickness of manner, while Filomena moved in slow steady paces—one, a volatile, unpredictable spirit, the other, deeply rooted and steadfast.

As we walked along, I kept thinking of the three people we'd soon be honoring: Alejandro, Nalberto, and Martín. In the four years I had been helping Filomena with the commemoration, I had picked up a lot of disjointed details about Nalberto, her father, who had been killed in a battle at Zacatecas, a few months before she had been born. Even though I knew an assortment of facts about his life, my sense of Nalberto was vague, no doubt because of Filomena's own sense of her father. Perhaps more confusing for me was the fact that Filomena was already fifteen years older than her father had been when a *federal* had pierced his heart with a bullet. He looked so young in the only photograph she had of him that I kept imagining her as Nalberto's mother rather than his daughter.

In contrast to the indefiniteness that surrounded Nalberto, Martín had continued to maintain a presence in Filomena's life. They had been married in 1932, the year they settled in our area, and although she was always reticent about expressing her feelings verbally, she still had given me a sense of the undying love she felt for Martín. Often she described his fiery Pedro Armendáriz smile and his brawny body which heavy physical labor had made more sinewy. A deep sadness overtook her whenever she remembered the day he had been called to serve in the war, leaving her behind with the three children.

Every day she had gathered them in her little bedroom where she had set up an altar in honor of the *Virgen de San Juan de los Lagos*. Her *altarcito* had consisted only of a table with a small statue of the lovely dark-haired Virgin surrounded by her father's photograph and several snapshots of Martín. The altar had expanded, however, since she had added a small offering for every month Martín was gone. Then one day a young Marine had knocked on her door telling her that her husband had been wounded in Iwo Jima. A few days after that visit, she had quietly joined the legion of other women who mourned their loved ones with small black crosses on their windows.

Almost immediately she had enlarged her altar with a picture of the Sacred Heart of Mary. Her neighbors, knowing she found consolation through her sacred articles, had added two new pieces to her collection: a statue of the Virgen de Guadalupe and a tin *retablo* of the Holy Trinity, which she nailed to the wall, next to the images of the Virgin. In the evenings, after the children went to bed, she would spend hours kneeling in front of her altar, lighting and relighting candles, ridding herself of any accusations she might have made against God and the Virgin in the moments of initial grief. During the day as she cleaned houses she whispered away her sorrow: "and pray for us sinners, now and at the hour of our death. *Amén.*"

Slowly she began to realize that she could not take care of the children by herself, for the work she was able to do never yielded a sufficient income. Bureaucratic stipulations overwhelmed her and she was unable to handle the required paperwork for her widow's pension. So, on the day she finally came to terms with what she perceived as her only solution, she gently informed the children about her decision. Alejandro would be boarded in a Catholic school and Lucila and Mateo would be sent for a short while to live with relatives in Michoacán. As soon as she resolved her finances, she'd send for the younger two.

From then on she worked at various chores at once but her primary job consisted of helping my mother take care of me. Needing to activate her quiescent maternal feelings, Filomena showered me with affection and I, sensing her deep love,

began to view her as my second mother. By the time I was five I knew all about the various saints she admired, and on many occasions I attended novenas with her. On the day she was initiated into the Marian Sodality, I too became one of the *Hijitas* with the long white dresses and blue scapulars. Feeling that I was now connected to all the saints and martyrs who had ever lived and to the hundreds still to come, I began to listen with fascination to Filomena's endless references to an ever expanding pantheon of saints. I particularly enjoyed her descriptions of the religious festivals in which she participated every year when she and Alejandro went back to Michoacán to visit the other children.

Lucila and Mateo never came to visit Filomena, telling her they felt no need to leave the land of their ancestors where they were both quite happy. So Alejandro, Filomena and I spent more and more time together. During the summers and on holidays, Alejandro took a break from his tasks at boarding school and accompanied us to so many parish celebrations I soon began to feel like his littlest sister. I admired his gentle ways and considered him a good substitute for the brother I did not have.

When I was seven, Alejandro graduated from high school. Right away he got a job, hoping to reunite his brother and sister with his mother. By then, however, the seventeen-year-old Lucila had a *novio* she did not want to leave behind; and Mateo, at fifteen, had clearly accepted his role as the youngest son in his aunt's family. Alejandro was truly disappointed at their decision, for it was unlikely he could join them in Uruapan, a place that had never been home for him. Filomena consoled Alejandro for the way things had turned out and affirmed that their lives were now to be spent in our city. Alejandro then wrote a long letter to his brother encouraging him to prepare himself scholastically so he could attend the university in Morelia. Then he dedicated himself to his role as breadwinner for his divided family. At that time he begged Filomena to take a rest while he provided for their needs. She agreed to remain at home, but continued to take in ironing.

One afternoon while I was helping Filomena with her work, Alejandro walked in with three white wrought iron birdcages. We both admired their unusual workmanship, following him to the tiny screened-in porch in the back of the house where he hung them next to the geraniums. They remained empty for several weeks and finally Filomena suggested using them as planters for more flowers. As soon as she said this, Alejandro told her that within a week he would make sure she would never again be alone during his absence. Much to my pleasant surprise, in exactly two days he filled the cages with a variety of finches, canaries and orange-breasted lovebirds which added a joyful twittering to the house. Filomena gave a name to each of the birds and began to note the unique characteristics she found in each one. I had never seen her so enthusiastic before and she admitted that Alejandro had given her the best present she had ever received.

"I'll have to give you an even better present," he had remarked.

Alejandro was true to his word, and on a bright September morning when Filomena and I had just returned from Mass, he asked us to step out to the porch. There in a huge domed cage was a radiant green macaw with a crimson breast and a yellow poll. When she saw us she squawked, "*¡Loro! ¡Loro! ¡Loro!*" Then, as she walked along the dome of the cage gripping the roof with her large claws, she told us her name in a throaty voice: "*¡Kika! ¡Kika!*"

"Do you like her?" Alejandro asked with a glowing smile. "If you like her, she's yours."

"*Mira, nomás,*" Filomena shook her head as if she could not take it all in.

"*Es tuya, Mamá.* She's yours," he repeated once again.

For a moment I was afraid Filomena was not going to accept Kika as she stood there with her arms crossed, shaking her head yet smiling as she inspected the parrot.

"Kika's an Amazona parrot from either the Yucatán or Central America," Alejandro explained. "I bought her from Mrs. Arzuela on the condition that I could take her back if you didn't like her."

Much to my relief, Filomena accepted Kika and since the *guacamaya* had been well trained by Mrs. Arzuela, the bird was allowed free rein of the house. During the day, Kika flew from room to room but she always returned to her favorite perch, a swing Alejandro had hitched onto a corner of the ceiling in the living-room. At night, on her own she walked into her cage. Then Filomena would cover it with dark towels, letting Kika know it was time to go to sleep. In the mornings when Filomena removed the towels from all four cages, she was immediately greeted by the happy trills of the finches and canaries and Kika would add to the rituals with her own rasping sounds. Occasionally she also let out two or three whistles. The house which had been quiet for so many years had suddenly come alive again, thanks to Alejandro.

Unfortunately, Alejandro did not have enough time to enjoy the melodic pleasures he had brought to his home. Within six months after his graduation he was inducted into the service to fight the atheistic communists who, we were constantly reminded in school, wanted to take over the entire free world.

"Don't worry," Alejandro had said to his mother. "I'll be back. In the meantime you have Kika and the other birds to remind you of me. Every time you hear their singing, remember that my spirit will always speak to you through their songs."

And so Alejandro went away once again. Almost as soon as he left, Filomena taped a large map of Asia to the wall. In front of the map she placed a small statue of the *Santo Niño de Atocha.* The patron saint of travelers, she explained to me. And every night when she recited her prayers, she would look at the names of the strange-sounding places she heard pronounced on the radio and console herself with the thought that at least Alejandro might be fighting the heathens in some of those towns and villages whose names she herself did not try to articulate. In school we heard about the Yellow Peril that Alejandro had gone to fight, an enemy I tended to imagine as John Wayne riding over the eastern horizon with hordes of barbarians behind him, just as I had seen him do in "The Conquerer." As Filomena and I prayed for Alejandro, I would envision him as St. George slaying the dragon of the Mongolians. "Come home, Alejandro. Come home," I would repeat over and over after every prayer, hoping that when I opened my eyes, Alejandro would appear in the room with us.

Alejandro did not come back to us alive. Within a year of his departure he was sent home from Korea in a casket. I was so grief-stricken with his death and the denial of my supplications that for days I wept without stopping. All around me the neighbors shook their heads and said that fairness had betrayed herself when she had dealt with Filomena. Hearing this, I cried all the more, forcing my mother to keep me away from Filomena so that my lamentations would not add to her sorrow.

So, I only saw Filomena at the funeral where I was surprised that unlike the neighbors' strong reactions and my own uncontrollable sobbing, she seemed to respond to Alejandro's death with equanimity, for she only cried a little, both before and after the funeral, and then during the sounding of the taps. After that, she retired to her little room where once again she sat in front of her altar for long hours, praying for the souls of the three men in her family whose lives had been prematurely snuffed out in distant wars. This time Filomena's mourning period lasted through a month of solitary prayer and silent meditation.

At home, my mother recited stories to me about her own losses as a child and Tía Griselda told me about the way she had coped when her father had died when she was ten. "Every time I'd shut my eyes," she'd say, "I would see my father behind a bright streak of light. So I would sit for hours with my eyes closed, trying to get a glimpse of his face behind the light." Even as she spoke, Alejandro's young face would appear before me, covered by a golden aura, which in my mind I would try to push up, away from his face. Little Adriana would touch my shoulder, then whisper in her little baby's voice, "He is up there. You can't see him but he sees everything you do. Don't cry anymore. He's going to be with you again." The matter-of-fact tone in which she made her prediction consoled me immensely and I resolved to keep the memory of Alejandro alive.

When my mother thought it was proper for me to resume my old habit of spending the late afternoons with Filomena, I found that she had completely reassembled and expanded her altar. The table had been replaced with a wooden pedestal on which she had crowded in her various statues. Green votive glasses with perpetually lit candles were interspersed between the photographs, and on the wall above the altar she had hung a large tin mirror on which the flickering of the candles was repeated in soothing rhythms. Zacarías, her neighbor, had attached thick hooks into the ceiling above the altar. There she had hung her bird cages, seemingly to include the birds' warbles and the parrot's noisy voice as part of her offering. Moved by the beatific spirit of Filomena's simple heart, I took off my gold chain with the tiny medallion of the Virgen de Guadalupe, then placed it on the altar in front of Alejandro's picture. After that I joined her in prayer every afternoon while the birds chirped softly above us. As I knelt there I began to realize that my prayers were no longer murmurs of petition; instead, they had become statements of resolution: "Thy will be done on earth as it is in heaven."

II

As the end of October approached, Filomena was planning a trip to Michoacán to participate in the traditional Tarascan rituals of the Day of the Dead. Part of her pilgrimage would include the observances on the island of Janitzio and she wanted me to benefit from them also. My parents, who had never allowed me to travel with any of my friends even to nearby places, surprised me by being open to Filomena's suggestion. The experience might be a good spiritual cleansing for me, they reasoned, as they discussed the trip with the rest of the family. As a result of the conversations, Griselda finally agreed to go with us. So, on the 28th of October, Griselda, Filomena and I set out to Morelia on the all night express offered by Tres Estrellos de Oro.

In Morelia we made connections to Uruapan, where Mateo, Lucila, and her *novio* Mauricio met us. At first I felt a bit uncomfortable with Filomena's real children, knowing that in the last several years I had spent more time with her than they had. Both were very amiable, however, trying their best to put me at ease. "Lucila and I speak Spanish and English," Mateo had let me know. "So you can speak to us in either language."

"Let's speak in both," I suggested. "Sometimes in English and sometimes in Spanish. We can also use Tex-Mex." With that, we all laughed and settled down to the business of preparing the offerings we would be taking with us to Janitzio.

Rosa—Filomena's sister—and her husband had already taken care of the preliminary details. They proudly pointed to a five-foot cross made out of chicken-wire which was ready to have the chrysanthemums mounted on it. Two days later, all the young people, including Rosa's and Arturo's three children, spent the morning in the adjoining field gathering the yellow flowers; later, we hooked them onto the cross with tiny wires. While we were busy with the cross, Filomena, Rosa and Griselda prepared the dishes we would be taking with us to the island. By mid-afternoon we were ready to set out in Arturo's truck to Pátzcuaro where we would be taking a small boat to the island.

Filomena and Griselda rode with Arturo while Lucila, Mateo, and I sat in the bed of the truck holding on to the cross and the other offerings. Along the way we took turns sprinkling water from a large bucket on the flowers. We also waved now and then to other families on the road who were as loaded down as we were.

"Alejandro would love all this," Lucila sighed. "He relished ceremonies. From the time we were very small, Mamá passed on to us a sense of ritual. Alejandro picked it up even more than I did. He loved getting dressed up in white during the month of May when he and all the other kids in the neighborhood would go to offer flowers to the virgin." She looked into the distance, then repeated, "Alejandro loved ceremony."

Mateo must have noticed that I had gotten very quiet, for he suddenly asked me what single memory of his brother stood out the most for me. After a pause I described the day when Alejandro had brought Kika home to complete the household of birds. "The birds have now multiplied," I explained, "so that every time there's a new batch I realize that Alejandro's music will be with us forever. He gave your mother the perfect gift."

After a while, Mateo said he was tired of only good memories. "Let's face it," he said, "Alejandro was mother's favorite and that's why she kept him with her."

"I used to get very jealous about that too," Lucila admitted, "but sometime in

the last three years I realized that she really did want us all together. She just didn't have the slightest notion of how to go about supporting us. I think Mamá assumed we would all come together again at some point. But it just didn't work out that way. Or at least you and I ended up messing up her plan."

"*No. No. No.* We really should have all come back here together." Mateo insisted.

"Once Papi died, Mamá would not have left him back there all alone. Now, you know she'll stay there forever. She's got to take care of both Papi's and Alejandro's graves."

"At least we're all here now, Nenita," he patted my cheek just as Arturo knocked on the back window to let us know we had arrived in Pátzcuaro.

Before heading for the lake he whirled us through the town, stopping at the *zócalo* where I was amazed at the size of the colonial plaza and the activity already underway for the big festivities. When we finally got to the lake, many small boats were setting out, just as a dozen or so Tarascan fishermen with their huge butter-fly nets were riding in with the tide. Already I was beginning to feel more at peace than I had ever felt before.

"You're staying with our friends in Pátzcuaro tonight," Arturo told Griselda and me. "And tomorrow you're being taken across the lake to Janitzio." Then he turned to Filomena, "Tomorrow you'll have to leave by three o'clock. The lake will be full of boats by dusk."

The next day we were at the shores of Lake Pátzcuaro by two thirty, loaded down with all the offerings we were taking. The boatman, an experienced navi-gator of the lake, was not at all surprised at our cargo. Compared to other loads he had carried to Janitzio in other years, he thought ours was rather light. His small boat was built in such a way that the cross could easily go in an upright position in the middle section. Filomena, Griselda and I rode in the prow and the others in the stern. By three o'clock we were on our way, gliding on the tranquil waters of the lake. Already by then, other small craft like ours dotted the view clear to the horizon.

"I'm really on a pilgrimage," I thought to myself, and with the waters lapping the side of the boat, I gently closed my eyes, promising myself I would accept what-ever happened. Opening them a few seconds later, I saw slightly ahead of us a small crew of fishermen with giant butterfly nets gracefully dipping in the placid water for the white fish that had made the lake famous. Watching the fishermen line up their boats in a row while they dipped to the right, then to the left, I felt I was entering a state of blissful surrender. My parents had been right; I was defi-nitely undergoing a spiritual cleansing. While in this peaceful state I glanced first at Filomena, then at Griselda, and I realized that they too were in a sublime mood.

As we got closer to Janitzio we saw hundreds of pilgrims already milling around at the highest point of the island, where the cemetery was located. Griselda point-ed to the terraced slopes we'd have to climb to reach the top, then sighed, looking at the steep stairway. "Don't worry," Filomena reassured her. It would be worth the effort. She promised that in the morning, after we finished with the ceremo-ny, we could continue farther up the steps to the balcony where we would have a spectacular view. In the meantime we followed her as she made her way through the multitude of people heading towards the cemetery with their offerings.

Inching our way through the crowds, we finally located the spot where Arturo's father was buried, knowing it was the only grave we could rightfully claim. First Mateo dug a small hole at the head of the grave, where we immediately buried the stem of the cross. Upright on the grave we placed about a dozen tall candles while Lucila arranged vases full of chrysanthemums here and there along the edges of the grave. The rest of us scattered yellow petals on the mound itself, where we then placed our photographs. When we were finished, Griselda rolled out a long cloth alongside the grave and Filomena gave each of us a small cushion.

As the evening wore on we took turns praying the rosary together, then relaxing, watching the people closest to us. All around us, crosses sheathed in golden blossoms let out a gentle fragrance and the glow of the candles added a sense of splendor against the darkness. Then, as the night emerged, the dewy wetness in the air became saturated with the pungent aroma of the flowers and the candles, and a sense of peace seemed to envelop the entire place.

After a while Filomena began to express the doubts we had each secretly started to feel. "None of them is buried here," she whispered. What if their spirits could not make their way back here as we believed they would? In the end, however, the joyous scene aroused our faith and we set aside our doubts, opening our baskets, and placing the food on top of the grave. Lucila poured water into glasses and hot chocolate into ceramic cups for our guests. Out of another basket we took out our own food and ate, keeping conversation to a minimum, and, although I was sure the others were as tired as I was, none of us lay down to sleep.

As the first light of day streaked the sky, the Indian flutes began to sound here and there throughout the cemetery. Their high monotones calling the spirits home dissipated any misgivings we ever had about our loved ones. I shut my eyes tightly, envisioning Alejandro smiling at me, with Kika perched on his shoulder. Then, just as quickly as he had appeared, his face was covered by a blaze of light. In the distance I could hear the chirping of the birds getting louder as he and Kika were suddenly absorbed by the sun. "I saw him," I whispered to Filomena as she gently nodded her head. Griselda, too, had an expression of bliss, and even Mateo was very quiet, staring out into the distance.

Lucila got up to embrace her mother, and Filomena extended her hand to Mateo. "*Hijitos,* now more than ever, I know I have to return to my little home up North. Why don't you come back with me?"

Lucila put her head against her mother's shoulder, whispering that just as her mother felt she belonged in *el norte,* so she and Mateo now had their home in this beautiful land of perpetual springtime.

"Don't worry, Mamá. Everything is okay," Mateo murmured.

I kept looking at Filomena as we began to gather our things. This is the happiest I've ever seen her, I thought. Then she smiled at me, "Here we all find what we are looking for."

The island of Janitzio

III

For the next three years, in contrast to the public communal festivities in Janitzio, Filomena held a private observance of the Day of the Dead; as her assistant I was her only witness. We tried to keep our ceremonies as close as possible to those in Janitzio, even though we did not go into the elaborate preparations that had taken place there. Here we simply gathered the *zempoalxochitles* and other flowers at the market on the eve of the holiday. Lucila, who was now coming for yearly visits, was bringing us decorated beeswax candles which Filomena stored in the refrigerator until we needed them. This was the one night she would leave the bird room lit up so that Kika's screeches and the other nocturnal sounds could also form part of the offerings. I loved our private ceremony, but up to then, I had not been able to recapture the spirit of the Indian celebration on the island nor the strong connection I had felt to Alejandro as the sun broke out on that special morning of personal transcendence. Filomena reassured me that I would have that experience again whenever I opened up to the gift of faith as I had done in Janitzio.

Over the last three years, Filomena's birds had multiplied many times over and her small house had become a music box of magnificent proportions, especially in the early morning and at sunset. The daily concerts could be heard blocks away but no one ever complained about Filomena's happy birds. In fact, the other children from the neighborhood had started to flock to the house they were now calling "la Pajarera Blanca, the white home of the birds." At first, five or six children had gathered on the sidewalk at dusk as the birds warbled away. Then more youngsters began to huddle together. One day Filomena discovered close to twenty children mingling outside, delightedly listening to her birds. "If you promise to be quiet, I'll let you come in," she had cautioned the children who then tiptoed into her house in hushed whispers.

In her cage, Kika squeaked with excitement at the visitors. As if they could sense the pleasure the children were getting from their song, the birds twittered ceaselessly in splendid sycnhronism. From then on, Filomena routinely invited the little friends into her home. Once inside the house, the children became enthralled with the incandescent lights and incense beckoning them to Filomena's altar. First, one or two youngsters were invited to pray with us; then, five or six joined in. Pretty soon, as many children as could be accommodated in the little room could be heard reciting Filomena's litanies in soft, repetitive sounds.

For the celebration we would be observing in a few hours Filomena had invited everyone who had been in her house within the last month. Who would come would depend upon the neighbors' willingness to give parental permission. As far as I knew, most of the children observed the occasion strictly as All Souls Day, as I had done in the past, and their main ritual would consist of visiting the cemetery with their parents, who would lay a wreath on the grave of their own dear ones. Most of them had never participated in celebrations as joyous and elaborate as the one Filomena and I had been sharing for so long.

As we neared the house, we heard the sweet trills of the canaries and finches which now took up the entire back porch. Their harmonizing seemed to rise a tone or two as soon as we stepped into the house, and while we placed the flowers in the different containers already prearranged around the altar, Kika flew above us in anticipation of what was to follow.

By sundown we finished with the basic assembling; next, we distributed the bread onto plates nestled here and there around the altar and then as darkness set in, we lit the candles, which made the room take on a bright glow. In the back porch we lit the only lights in the house. Tonight we would not use any towels on the cages, for we hoped that as we pronounced our benediction our feathered friends would accompany us with their song.

Before long the children started to arrive.

First Rosita and Laura from next door appeared, bringing four white sugar skulls with our names written across the foreheads. Next, Pepe and his four brothers showed up, each bearing candleholders shaped like a tree of life, which immediately went upon the altar. Zacarías's son brought his flute made of bamboo and Micaela's daughters each carried a tambourine. My best friend Aura and her brothers gave Filomena miniatures of skeleton-musicians made of gesso and gayly painted in vivid colors. Patricia and Adriana brought a surprise especially for me: a small wooden cross which they had decorated with chrysanthemums to look like the crosses in Mexico I had described to them. Even Verónica joined us bringing exquisitely embroidered napkins to cover the bread. Before long, eighteen children were gathered in front of Filomena's shining altar.

With Kika perched on her shoulder, Filomena invited everyone to kneel. As she recited the prayers for the dead, Marcos began to play on his flute and the Miranda girls gently sounded the tambourines which elicited the birds into song. Pretty soon we were enveloped into one voice, as the incense of the candles and the perfumes of the *zempoalxochitles* floated around the room. As the different timbres and vapors merged above my head, I became entranced with the joyous reverence around me, and slowly, slowly, a dreamlike image of Alejandro began to take shape in front of me. At that instant I thought the birds' song had reached perfection. Accompanying them, the flute resounded higher and higher, filling the room; then the sounds and scents seemed to swirl their way out the window, taking the birds' trills with them up, up, up, into the night. Suddenly Kika left Filomena's shoulder and perched herself on the altar. I looked at her red lores and her blue cheeks while she positioned herself for a night's sleep, and I knew that just a few seconds before, Alejandro had finally come home once again. Rejoicing I prayed, "Amen! Amen! Amen!"

IV

By coincidence, ten years later I was home on the day that Kika died of a sudden attack of pneumonia.

"*Se murió la Kika anoche,*" Filomena told me when I came by unexpectedly in the late morning.

"How can that be? What happened?" Aware of how long Amazona parrots are supposed to live, I had assumed that Kika would be around for years and years. In shock, I let Filomena guide me into the kitchen where Kika was laid out in a bright lacquered wooden chest from Olinalá. Filomena had lined the box with Kika's grains, then laid her sideways on top of her food.

My eyes filled with tears as I listened to the silence in the house and marveled at how the other birds must be sensing the passing of their companion. The only sounds came from Filomena as she described her surprise at finding Kika on her back, her claws gripping the heavy air above her. Her first reaction had been to cradle Kika in her arms, and when she had finally accepted that her pet was dead, she called a taxidermist in the hopes of giving her a new life. Now, quite resolutely she stated that her memories of her parrot would suffice. Kika's great bird nature had consisted precisely in her moving about from room to room, letting out her rasping screeches. "*Fue una buena compañera.* A wonderful present from my Alejandro."

We took Kika's box to the back yard and buried her under a pecan tree. Then, as we were down on our knees patting down the mound, we began to hear the cooing of the finches. One by one the birds picked up the sounds. Suddenly they burst out into their usual song.

"How lovely! They're saying good-bye to their friend," Filomena commented very matter-of-factly. Then, she traced the sign of the cross on the loose dirt. "*Requiescat in pacem,*" she murmured.

V

For many hours Filomena and I conversed, reminiscing over the many memories we shared of Kika and of Alejandro. As we went over the old days, I felt somewhat reaffirmed in what I subconsciously had come to seek. Lately I had been feeling very uncomfortable in one of my first graduate classes at the university. A middle-aged professor-poet, already on his way to becoming one of the major voices in American letters, taught his literature class with a degree of cynicism that made me uncomfortable. His total rejection of spiritual epiphanies bothered other members of the class, as well, and so we had started to meet on our own to comment more freely on some of the writers we were reading. Even with our more open discussions in the small group, I still felt I was losing my old sense of identity. At times I even felt that many new images were being imprinted on me and that I had not even had the chance to approve or reject what was happening.

A few days before coming home I had paid a visit to the campus chapel, where I had sat by myself in the front pew for a long time, staring at the statues on the strangely austere altar, unable to draw out the familiar consolation I sought. "Maybe I'm becoming a nonbeliever," I had thought to myself as I gathered my things, then headed down the lonely, narrow aisle, never to come back. Outside, the bright afternoon light only emphasized my sadness, which I tried to overcome by recalling the many happy hours I had spent with Filomena and Kika and the neighborhood children who had come to our novenas. The contrast between the past and the present was so immense that I began to question whether things had really been the way I was remembering them. I knew then that I needed to go home.

Now, even Kika was gone. As I faced Filomena I suddenly began to have an uneasy feeling, which soon seemed to take control of me. Perhaps the visit was not doing me much good after all.

"She's too accepting of everything that happens to her," I complained to my mother. "'*Así lo quiere Dios*' is always on her lips."

"That's true. But Filomena is truly one of the happiest people I know, in spite of all the blows life has given her," was my mother's response, adding to my emerging dissatisfaction with what I perceived as their lack of critical thinking.

When I left that weekend I was even more confused than when I had come. Kika's death saddened me tremendously, for she had been my direct link to the memory of Alejandro and to the saddest and the happiest moments of my childhood. I was also very disturbed with Filomena's resignation at the death of so many of her loved ones. How easily she seemed to have given up Kika. Perhaps she hadn't really cared deeply about her, after all. Nor about any of the people in her life. This might be the reason why she had been willing to part with her children so many years ago. Would she react the same way if I went away for good?

As a defense against my new confusion, I began to give myself full-heartedly to the ideas of writers I admired for asking the right questions about being and about giving meaning to one's life through action: Sartre, Camus, Sábato, Beckett. Still, I sensed that in the end their philosophical conclusion about the essence of life seemed so meaningless and absurd. How long could one really appreciate their principles? "At bottom, it's a decadent philosophy isn't it? Their ideas strike me as the perspective of a world in agony," I commented to one of my favorite professors.

"You do need to question the position of those writers," she advised. "Here, I think you'll enjoy reading this little story. From what you've told me about yourself, I think you'll relate to it." She smiled as she handed me a copy of *Trois contes*. "Read 'Un coeur simple.' 'A Simple Heart.' It's Flaubert's masterpiece. As you read it you'll see why I'm suggesting it to you."

"This story is about Filomena," I said to myself as I mulled over every word about the simple-hearted Félicité and the great love she bore for her parrot Loulou whom she eventually transformed into her own image of God. Always physically and psychologically isolated, Félicité lived through a state of loneliness that became more acute as she got older. Loulou then assumed a position of paramount importance in her life, leading Félicité to conclude that the bird that people usually identified with the Holy Ghost had mistakenly been seen as a dove when in reality she had actually been a parrot. Convinced that Loulou was really an extension of the deity, Félicité managed to transform her parrot into the image of God at the moment of her own death. As her spirit entered heaven in a mist of incense, Flaubert describes the parting of the clouds and the emergence of a large parrot which opened its wings to welcome and embrace the soul of Félicité. Touched, I closed the book, amazed that the cynical Flaubert had actually given such credence to the faith of a simplehearted maid.

What answer I had found I was not really sure, but for the moment I decided that I needed to put a halt to the years of abstract thinking and to involve myself more with tangible and communal action. For me these new interests became personified in community activities. I found a real sense of authenticity through new contacts in many different projects, but it was in the community arts that I found my most meaningful outlet. For a long time I participated in colorful exhibits in the parks, poetry readings in community centers, sales of folk crafts, coordination of children's folkloric dances. I felt that these actifities connected me back to the stimulating creativity of the people who had served as my mentors as I was growing up, at the same time that they satisfied my new needs to move away from an alienating individualism towards a public collectivism much more in keeping with the experiences of my youth.

For many years these activities fulfilled me. Then one day I came across a new folk art which caught me completely off-guard. There, on a table underneath a blossoming magnolia tree, I saw dozens of earrings made to resemble the folk altars that many contemporary artists were assembling and exhibiting in galleries and museums. As I approached the table, I noticed that the artist-vendor was wearing a pair. I stared at the leather-backed keychains on which she had pasted a laminated holy card of *la Virgen de Guadalupe*. Around the inch-square "altar", she had glued rhinestones, interspersed with red and green glass beads to resemble the lights around some village altars. Amazed at the creation, I listened to the artist describe how she had sold two dozen in just two hours. "But friends have been advising me never to wear these in Mexico," she laughed. "They tell me that people might get upset that I've taken their national symbol out of context."

"*Sabes*, I've never had any real objection to people wearing clothing that resembles the American flag," I quickly told her. "Somehow that seems pretty abstract to me. But I'll admit that the sight of your earrings really galls me. I find them to be very insensitive to the spiritual beliefs of the people in the *pueblos*. I have a dear friend who would probably feel pretty sad at seeing you make light of her deeply felt respect for religious icons. It's terribly personal with her."

"Oh, no! *No entiendes,*" she retorted. "This is my way of showing respect for your friend's faith. I grew up in this sprawling metropolis." She spread her arms to emphasize her point. "So I never had any direct contact with the traditional religious sentiment that you are talking about. This is my way of giving tribute to that experience."

"I'll believe you," I smiled as I opened my purse. "How much are you asking for a pair?"

With the earrings in my purse I made my way through aisles of tables filled with folkwares. As I walked around, I ran my fingers over the smoothness of the laminated cover on the icon. "Now, why did I spend my money?" I thought. "I wonder what Filomena would think if I gave them to her?" Immediately I felt ashamed for even allowing the thought to pass through my mind, then concluded, "Only someone from this centerless city could have come up with these gaudy creations!"

I paused to look around me, at one colorful table after another. Wafts of sweet-smelling grass drifted about everywhere. At the far end of the park, a combo was blaring out its electrical instruments. As I made my way through the people's artwork, I looked up to see dozens of colorful balloons which had just been released. For a long time I watched the balloons moving upwards until they disappeared into the distant air.

As I stood there, I kept wondering if I would forever go from one crisis to another. How unlike Filomena who had stood firm in the face of real calamities. Perhaps some day I would once again draw some strength from the little *altarcitos* that I had known in my childhood.

On the way home, I stopped at a dimestore to buy some crayons. For hours that evening I drew a huge image of Kika as I remembered her: thick green feathers, yellow poll, blue cheeks, and crimson breast. Satisfied, I ran my fingers over the waxen image several times, then folded up my drawing into a thick square. Cramming it into a glass jar, I was ready to put the lid on it when I remembered the earrings. "They will serve a purpose after all," I thought, as I dropped them into a jar and headed towards my car, then drove to a nearby eucalyptus grove.

The scents from the eucalyptus trees became more pungent as I drove further into the grove, looking for just the right spot. In front of me, the road curved precariously, but I drove slowly, knowing that no one was behind me. Suddenly the light of the moon filtering through the branches lit the tallest tree up ahead and I knew I had found what I had been searching for. As I stepped out of the car, in the distance I heard an owl repeating the same sound over and over. What a contrast it made with the happy chirps of the birds that had been Filomena's and Kika's companions. The owl's song was supposed to announce an impending death, I remembered. I listened to the bird, recalling other sounds I had associated with Filomena. Suddenly, whispering voices came to me from among the trees.

"¡Flores para los muertos! ¡Flores para los muertos!"

The voices continued as I made a shallow hole beneath the tallest eucalyptus, where I buried the jar. Suddenly I thought I heard a loud screech like that of the white owl of my youth. Uncertain, I listened out there in the dark for a long time. But no. It had been only the brown barn owl after all. I stood up as the wind rustled through the branches and watched a lone lizard scurry up a tree.

As I headed to the car, a faint chant sounded behind me once again. *"¡Flores para los muertos! ¡Flores para los muertos!"* I did not look back.

Carlos Cumpián

In "Coyote Sun" (*Coyote Sun* [Chicago: MARCH/Abrazo, 1990]), Cumpián expresses the connectedness that many Chicanos feel to Aztec and Native American religious traditions. Through rituals involving drums, prayers, and herbs, the poet-priestess María Sabina evokes a holistic spirituality in which earth and sky, the human and the natural world, are one.

Coyote Sun

para María Sabina
y Anne Waldman

Gathered on Oaxaca's
huarache-worn stones,
made smooth by the soles
of thousands of believers-
never resting on their *petates*,
but dancing the ceremonial *mitote*,
where inspired beats leaped from a drum
and the mushrooms of language sang
through a poet-priestess—
María Sabina, duality's sister.

We never chanted in a *temaskal*,
never bowed stripped down to a
fire in the sweatlodge as
steam rose from the
lightning bolt's navel
carrying bile and filth to
the bowels of the desert.

You read everything as you listened
to the Folkways record,
and like a bold *sinvergüenza*
you performed *nuestra santa voz*
indigena for *los otros*.

But, where were the *hongos* of vital skin,
episodes of enrapture with the
living word as prayers passed,
round the candlestar hut.

You missed the children's sweetgrass breath
that prepares the way for hot *aguardiente*
tobacco and food, humble gifts for the ritual
where old man armadillo watched
the Mazatecan sky, waiting for
his ever-young brother Coyote Sun
to come back up—
Coyote Sun who tricks the
night into chasing him.

María Sabina in a flower *huipil*
adorned with a headdress of
silver braids, aflame with the
medicinal and sacred herbs of Christ.

María Sabina, the one we
talked about so far from
your boulder,
María Sabina, who heard
the jasmine tongue of heaven,
raised her palms to the saints
then clapped and whistled
as the true fast-speaking one,
a psi-eyed woman,
the one
who knows Coyote Sun.

Arsenio Córdova

Arsenio Córdova is a highly regarded ethnomusicologist who lives and works in northern New Mexico. He has dedicated himself to keeping alive the oral performance tradition in New Mexican folk and religious culture. To this end, he has collected and retold stories of cowboys and Indians that he first heard at his grandmother's knee; conducted painstaking research to reconstruct ritual Indian dances and celebrations from the earliest days of New Mexico; and revived the tradition of the Spanish morality plays that date from the end of the sixteenth century. Córdova is best known for his revivals of this form of religious theater, although his musical compositions, both original pieces based on his daily prayers and reconstructions of ancient church music, are sung in churches throughout the country today.

Interview

We have here in New Mexico a long and rich tradition in the *autos sacramentales,* or morality plays, some of which date back to the sixteenth century. They are essential components of our religious and cultural heritage. That is why I have spent many years trying to recover the language, the music, and here and there to modernize the plays so that they will speak to our young people, because it is crucial that they not forget their roots.

Most of the *autos sacramentales* presented here in the New World were created in Spain and brought over to Mexico by the Spanish. One of the most beautiful, however, "Las Apariciones de Guadalupe," (The Apparitions of Guadalupe), is the first that was written in the New World. In 1531 the apparition occurred, and by the end of the century, it had been written. I don't know the name of the author, or if he put his name to his work, but *fíjate, era pura poesía* (I'll tell you, it was pure poetry).

I modernized it, changed it a little bit, but not much, because it was written in such a way that people can still understand it; plus the visual elements help too. We've performed "Guadalupe," and "Los Tres Reyes Magos," about the three wise men, and also "El Niño Perdido," about the lost Christ child whose mother is looking for him, and *el niño* prophesies his death and all that will take place in his passion. We've done these three together with the "Pastorela," or shepherd's play. There are still others such as "Adam and Eve," which we haven't presented yet, but we would like to put it on this year. [Arsenio Córdova performed "Adam and Eve" later in 1992. See page 118.]

Some of the authors are known. The missionaries brought us some *autos* from Spain, but there were different missionaries here who wrote as well. They had to create many different roles for people to play, as in the "Bailes de los Matachines," (the Dances of the Matachines), which was one of the principal dances that came to us from the north of Mexico and had a religious significance. There's a lot of debate as to where the "Matachines" came from. Some say they were dances of the Indians here; the *hispanos* claim that they brought them; some say that the Aztecs were dancing these dances when the Spaniards arrived, and that the Spaniards took a group of Aztec dancers back to Spain to present the "Matachines" to the crown. I myself think that the Spaniards brought this dance, but by the time it arrived here in the north, it represented the conversion of Moctezuma to Catholicism. Here in northern New Mexico they taught the natives that Moctezuma had embraced the Catholic religion!

I know that with the five hundred years celebration there has been much debate about the role of the Spaniards, and the emphasis has been on the harm that they caused. But they also did much good, and we have to be proud of the good that they did bring, especially here in northern New Mexico. For one thing,

Adam and Eve

they protected the local Indians. The Apaches went around robbing the Pueblos and killing, kidnapping their children, and the local Indians and the Spanish helped each other. In the Pueblo Revolt of 1680, the Indians defeated the Spanish and destroyed much of what was Spanish, except the "Bailes of the Matachines." The name comes from *mataquino*, which means "masked dancer" in Italian. That's one reason I think the dance is of European origin. The dance includes the dance of the monarch, in which the dancer in the middle represents Moctezuma. He dances and then *se hinca sobre la fe católica*, he prostrates himself before the Catholic faith. There are different dances included, we also have the "Baile de la Malinche." La Malinche dances and represents the betrayal of her people. She is dressed in white, and she dances to deceive Moctezuma. This is one of the many "Dances of the Matachines." Obviously, these dances were created in Mexico before coming north to us, but with their roots in Spain.

The Spanish arrived here in the north with Juan de Oñate, who colonized this place in 1598, and "los Matachines" was known then. It is said that Oñate brought many traditions with him. He was the first *penitente*, or penitent, because he entered New Mexico during Holy Week and did penance on Holy Thursday. "The Matachines" came early in the history of New Mexico; it came with Oñate. Then

Matachín dancer

came many missionaries, Franciscans all, and they began the third order of St. Francis. They are the founders of the *hermanos penitentes*, the penitent brothers. Some give credit to the third order of Loyola, but it was the Franciscans, although both groups believe practically the same things, especially in mortifications and penitence. I'm not a brother; I've thought about it a lot, but I'm still not prepared to take that step. It's a very serious step and one has to be spiritually prepared to take it. The oldest brother—he died last year—was always coming up to me and asking me to belong, but not yet.

New Mexico is the only place in the U.S. that I know of where the brotherhood exists. They have something in Spain, but it's different. This year a group from Spain came and talked to us, but they carry heavy altars on their shoulders; they carry altars during Holy Week procession, and the music is very different and strange. There they call themselves los *Hermanos de Nuestro Padre Jesús*, the brothers of our father Jesus. They came from the medieval *cofradías*, brotherhoods. But these *señores*, the *penitentes*, were so important to the faith in New Mexico because in the early days there was no way to go to all the villages. There were very few priests and the settlements were widely scattered. The *penitentes* became the leaders of the Catholic faith here in New Mexico. We talk about lay leadership and lay ministry now, but they were carrying out leadership duties centuries before. Sixty percent of all men in northern New Mexico were *penitentes,* and from there came the leadership of the community from the beginning up until, say, the 1930s.

Historically, the focus had been on penance. There was a Dr. Udall who left some beautiful paintings of *hermanos penitentes* at the Wurlitzer Foundation. He used to treat these people after Holy Week, and, based on the descriptions that he got from them when they came for treatments, he did a series of oil paintings. This was in the 1940s. They would cut themselves with flint; flagellate themselves with yucca whips; carry crosses; some would even be put on crosses. Their thinking was that if anybody saw their face or recognized them, the penance was in vain. So they used to be hooded, because if you are making a sacrifice for everyone to see, then you have received your reward and what you have done is in vain. The penance was one that you yourself determined and inflicted. They would also cut themselves with flint because the free flow of blood would take the infection away.

The *hermandad* was not recognized officially by the church, and they became secret societies; and that's where the sensationalism comes from. They became secret when Bishop Lamy came, around 1847 or 1850, because he didn't like them, nor did succeeding bishops; so they were not recognized by the official church. By the 1940s they weren't recognized because the church said that self-inflicted injuries were against the fifth commandment. The brothers weren't recognized until Pope John XXIII, God bless him, and Vatican II. The Pope wrote letters to the brothers saying, "You are the church." Then immediately there were a lot of wonderful priests in the area who welcomed the brothers into the church. Today in many parishes, including mine, they take over during Holy Week. I'm choir director at La Santísima Trinidad, but they're the ones who do the hymns and sing the Passion. Three men in my choir are members of the *hermandad*. Maybe some *hermanos* still practice mortification, but I think it's more prayerful meditation now, although I am speculating. Nearly all *hermanos* are lay. We need more clergy to take the lead, because once a clergy member embraces the *hermandad*, it makes it acceptable for the rest of us.

I think it's very important that the *hermanos* start documenting what they're all about. It has to come from them. They should let people know what they're about so there won't be all that speculation. Some people have tried to infiltrate the brotherhood, take pictures and expose them, but they are soon found out and don't last. Their music needs to be documented. The *alabados*, or hymns of praise, are very beautiful. We learned many of them from the hermanos in our choir, especially on Holy Thursday. They sound very Arabic and also somewhat similar to the music of the *cantos* (the songs) in the *pastorelas* (the shepherds' plays). Here in the north the brotherhood is still strong and there are many areas where there are *moradas*, or houses of worship. Their *cánticos* (songs), are wonderful; it would be fabulous to sit down with them and get permission to document their music.

The music that I write is my prayers first; that is, I just put my prayers to music. I wrote "Venid niños pastores" (Come shepherd children) and "Alarru, Chiquito" (Hush, little one) for "La Pastorela." But "Buenos Días mi Dios" (Good Morning, My God) was a morning prayer of mine. It's very personal, but I also wanted to share it with others. I have about forty-eight compositions; many are at home. I've done "Los Salmos" (The Psalms), "The Lord Is My Shepherd"; I have things

Los Pastores

scattered all over. One day before I die, I'll have to write everything down, including the music to "La Pastorela." Would you believe that I haven't even had a chance to put it on paper yet?

I really must do it, because as I told you last night at the performance of "The Shepherds' Play," when we forget, everything dies. That's why we're trying to keep the tradition alive with these kids, practicing and performing these miracle plays, so they don't forget. And we try hard to be accurate. So I was gratified by what I learned from an aged *señor* who I found in San Luís, Colorado. He's ninety-two years old, and in 1909 he was a seven-year-old who participated in a performance of "Los Pastores" here in northern New Mexico. Recently, I interviewed him and asked him to sing one of the verses, and he sang it *exactly* the way we do. I was so happy.

I began to revive the tradition of *los pastores*—you can also call them shepherds' plays, or the more generic term, morality plays; here in northern New Mexico we just say *"los pastores."* In my revival, I keep the old but add here and there, as I mentioned earlier. For example, I will add a character so there's enough to go around for everyone who wants to participate. We never do voice auditions. Everybody can take part. The *pastorela* is the most musical of all the morality plays, but they all had music. The procession of the shepherds at the beginning of the play is written down, and those are the verses that were created way back when. In my research, which I do in the state archives, I found that *los pastores* was adapted to the area early and many times, but this particular version that we are using was given to me by my wife's grandfather.

I've been reviving this tradition since 1981, but I don't take ownership; that comes from those beautiful people who did it way back centuries ago. I'm just using their instrument. The plays were dying out here—some say because of the World Wars, but I don't agree. I think that a lot of it has to do with burnout, everybody depends on the same person to do it year after year, and it's not easy. I have to sit there with each individual shepherd, and go over and over it, and some of these kids don't know Spanish at all now. So I have to teach them the Spanish. It involves much more than just rehearsals. For this *pastorela* presentation that you saw last night, I started working in October—and many of these are returnees, so it takes even longer with new *pastores*. This is all after school or after work. By the way, I'm glad that we have bilingual education in the schools, but we don't need it because of immigration; we use it to teach our kids Spanish so they don't forget it.

I had a career with human services, but I retired three years ago. Now I'm working part-time with the archdiocese of Santa Fe, with lay ministry formation programs in the north, eighteen parishes. Part-time pay, but I was committed to getting more involved in the church and to bringing back the traditions, which I was already doing in addition to my work for human services. I graduated from New Mexico Highlands University in Las Vegas in 1967. I went to the College of Santa Fe and to Mount Angel, to the seminary there, but I finished up at New Mexico Highlands University. I became a social worker, and soon after that, an administrator. My work involved a combination of benefits and services for the elderly and families with dependent children. Then I became a supervisor for the state until 1985 here in Taos. They had a layoff and my position was going to be eliminated. They said I could stay on if I took a demotion, but I wanted to get out after twenty years. So I took on a position in Santa Fe as an administrator for administrative services and provided different kinds of services, doing graphics, newsletters, ID programs, supplies supervising.

But I was a musician all along. In the seminary I studied music with an emphasis on Gregorian chants, and on voice, but you didn't have a major or a minor then. The love for it was there, but music was a sideline. Then I ended up as a county office manager in Roswell. My family was here, but I was there for about a year. Finally, I was made state director of the Commodities Bureau, and that's when I retired. The Commodities Bureau was in charge of commodities for all the school systems and all the programs for distribution of commodities to the needy; it was a statewide job. I have a retirement from them, which frees me up to do all these other things. Twenty years was enough.

I come from a long line of religious, creative people deeply identified with our culture and history. My mother was a very creative teacher, and she was the one who introduced the Matachines to her students. We lived with my grandmother; the oral tradition and the faith that they gave me were exceptionally wonderful. I mean, you talk about teachers, about love of God, love of culture—it came from them. I am a sixth-generation New Mexican, and I learned from my grandmother the stories and legends of all the generations.

For example, my grandmother was born in Mora Valley between here and Las Vegas, and, in 1867 when she was born, one of her brothers was taken captive by the Apaches. He was eight years old when he disappeared. My great-grandfather had been a scout for Kit Carson and went to ask him for help, but Carson was in failing health so he declined. My great-grandmother had a nervous breakdown, and he moved her here to Taos where her parents lived, hoping that would help. She was a very sad woman. She lived to be over one hundred years old. All her life she spent in mourning. She was exploited by the gypsies who would come through the area. When they found out that she had lost a son, they would come every year and take everything she had saying, "We'll tell you where your son is." She was a very religious woman. She walked into the church after she'd moved here and took a statue of the child Jesus. Then, addressing the statue of the Blessed Mother, she said, "As long as my son is captive, your son will remain captive," and walked up into the mountains and hid the statue there. This same lady sat and told my mother stories when my mother was a little girl. My mother tried to find the statue, but she never did. And they never found the son who was taken captive either.

My mother's paternal grandmother was also a storyteller; she sat with my mother and told her many stories. My mother says that all the stories that were oral tradition she later found in the Bible and *A Thousand and One Nights*. The stories came from the oral tradition, which had a written base. My mother is eighty-five years old, and I still sit with her wanting to hear more stories. She used to read to the men who would come over on their lunch hour. She would read them Spanish poetry and stories by Lope de Vega and Quevedo. My uncle had taught her to read when she was very young, and even then the men would come to have her read their letters to them. She later became a teacher and administrator for thirty-nine years. She's a living legend here. The Historical Society honored her last year.

My grandmother died when I was fifteen years old. I have had the benefit of both my grandmother and my mother. We would pray the rosary every night with my grandmother, and she would give us candy when we would finish. There were four of us kids—my sister, who lives in Albuquerque now; myself; and my brothers. One is an engineer, and the other is the officer in charge of the National Guard here. We were all educated because that was so important to my parents.

My dad was a shepherd. He had to quit school when he was in sixth grade because he was the oldest of the family of nine. When my grandfather died, my grandmother said, "You are the man of the family now," and she sent him off to work in the fields with the sheep. My dad later married and had four kids, but his first wife died. My mother is his second wife. My father wanted so much for us to be educated and always said, "*No quiero que pasen Uds. los trabajos que yo pasé en los campos de la borrega*" (I don't want you to have to do the same kind of work that I had to do out in the sheep camps). He had a book of South American authors that he would take every time he went off to the sheep camps in Wyoming, and he used to be alone up there a lot. He'd go for six months at a time, come back for a couple of months, and then go again. We missed him so much. I remember the book very well. Rubén Darío was one of the poets he read. My dad learned to read and write from my mother. He used to write letters, and the opening was always,

"Espero que cuando esta mal escrita carta se presente en tus manos te halle bien" (I hope that when this badly written letter reaches you, that it finds you well). I remember I would read them and say, "It's not so *mal escrita.*" My dad was gone a lot, but he was a tower of strength. Later on we became best friends. My kids were very fortunate to know him. He died in 1982.

We have three children, two natural and one adopted. Willie is now a probation officer in Alamogordo, he's twenty-three and we're very proud of him. And the one who came charging in from the back in the *pastorela,* the one with the blond hair and blue eyes, he's our twenty-year-old son, we adopted him when he was eleven. He works in construction. Tessa is our daughter. She's a junior in high school; she's seventeen and very much interested in culture and tradition and is very musical. Her mother is very musical too. Kathy, my wife, sings, and she played the Virgin Mother in the *pastores.* We sing in the choir and are a very musical family; we have a lot of fun. We also have a little mariachi group that we started. We do a lot of Mexican music, and I do the history of northern New Mexican music, too.

We have a lot of typical music here, the cradle dances for example, where you have couples form cradles with their hands and dance around in circles. We also have the *"varsoviana,"* which comes from Warsaw. When Maximilian came to Mexico, he banned Spanish music, so in northern New Mexico we took Polish music and claimed it as our own. We composed songs to the melody of "Put Your Little Foot," for example. The schottishe was very popular here in the mid-1800s. It came with explorers such as Zebulon Pike. We also have the *marcha,* all kinds of marches, which were created here and are different from wedding marches. Then there are the *inditas*; this music uses the steps of the Native American and sets them to European music and violin. Of course, we also had waltzes, but waltzes written here for guitar, violin, and recorder.

I guess I am an ethnomusicologist and composer, I don't know; I study whatever I need to preserve the cultural tradition. I believe that you die three times— when you breathe your last, when you are buried, and when you are forgotten. I'm going to do everything I can to make sure that these plays are not forgotten, and that my kids know their roots.

On one occasion my daughter's social studies teacher asked me to tell a story about Indian raids and captives being incorporated into families. So I told about my great-great-great-grandfather, a mixture of Spanish and Indian and descended from Sephardic Jews, like so many New Mexicans. My ancestors who first came here were named Martínez. Of course, they had to worship in their homes secretly. In order that other Jews could know who their friends were, who they could trust, they added "ez" to their names. So, the name probably went from Martín to Martínez. I went back and looked at pictures of my great-grandfather in the album, and he looked very Jewish, with red hair too. Anyway, so I told the story about my great-great-great-grandfather, who probably married a Navajo, and who bought four Indians from the Apaches, three women and one man, and raised them as his children, as part of this family.

Well, about four years ago, I was sharing captive stories with a priest I know; he was the editor of the *Oklahoma Catholic Sooner*. Right away, he told me of a Kiowa

Abuelos

Indian whose father was taken captive by the Indians in northern New Mexico in the late 1860s. So I took off to Oklahoma and met him. His name is Parker MacKenzie. He was the son of the Indian taken captive from northern New Mexico, and he is ninety-three years old now. There is the strongest possibility that the captive was the son of my great-great-grandfather, remember the son who was kidnapped that I was telling you about? Parker said that his father had been taken by the Apaches, traded to the Comanches, and, in turn, traded to the Kiowa as a young boy. He married a Kiowa and became an elder. His name was changed to General MacKenzie, because he shot two fingers off his hand, like General MacKenzie at Fort Sill, so the Indians called him MacKenzie.

The Spanish and Indian cultures are interwoven here. We are proud of our identity and our traditions, of both the Spanish and the Indian; we are a part of both. We've always been mixed, not pure Spanish; people lied saying they had pure Spanish blood, because that's how land was granted. But here we were not persecuted by anyone, so we are not running from the past. We don't want to forget or escape it in northern New Mexico. A person who doesn't know his past is like a tree without roots. That is why I try to keep the past alive for our young people in the beautiful tradition of our music and the ancient *autos sacramentales* such as *los pastores*. It is part of our cultural and spiritual heritage.

Buenos Días, Mi Dios

ESTRIBILLO:

Bue-nos dí-as, Se-ñor, bue-nos dí-as, mi Dios, ven-go a en-tre-gar-me a Ti. Bue-nos dí-as, Se-ñor, bue-nos dí-as, mi Dios, ven-go a a-do-rar-te a Ti.

Fin

ESTROFAS:

1. Guí - a - me en el ca - mi - no, siem - pre cuí - da - me a mí._____ An - da siem-pre con - mi - go, es - to te pi-do a Ti.
2. To - ma, Se - ñor, mi vi - da, da - me to - do tu a - mor._____ Ca - mi - nan-do con - ti - go nun - ca ten-go te - mor.
3. Can - ta - ré de tu glo - ria por do - quie - ra que voy._____ Con tu a - mor y tu gra - cia, nun - ca só - lo es - toy.

al %

Alarru, Chiquito

ESTRIBILLO:

A - la - rru, Chi - qui - to; a - la - rru, mi

Dios. _____ A - la - rru, mi Ni - ño,

| 1-4 *a las Estrofas* | Final *Fin* |

Duer - me Re - den - tor. _____

ESTROFAS:

1. Na - ci - do en pe - se - bre e - res
2. E - res Pas - tor - ci - to, e - res
3. Ni - ño lin - do san - to, na - ci -
4. Bi - en - ve - ni - do se - as, ni - ño

1. un gran Rey, _____ el _____ Rey de los
2. un gran Dios, _____ na - ci - do en - tre
3. do gran Rey, _____ de _____ hu - mil - des
4. Re - den - tor, _____ a _____ sal - var al

al 𝄋

1. po - bres na - ci - do en Be - lén. _____
2. pa - jas e - res Sal - va - dor. _____
3. pa - dres, Ma - rí - a y Jo - sé. _____
4. hom - bre, ni - ño Sal - va - dor. _____

Tomás Rivera

One of the first exponents and promoters of Chicano literature, Texas-born Tomás Rivera (1935–84) is most famous for his classic novel *Y no se lo tragó la tierra . . . And the Earth Did Not Devour Him,* (bilingual edition, Houston: Arte Público Press, 1992), which tells the dramatic story of migrant workers in the forties and fifties as seen by a young narrator who is trying to understand his life and his culture. Throughout, the spiritual strength and the generosity of the migrants is apparent. Occasionally, as in the selections included here, the observant and sensitive youth points out with humorous candor the hypocrisy and venality of the Catholic Church as he sees it, especially with regard to rigid definitions of sin, as in "First Communion," and self-promotion on the part of the local parish priest, as in "Before People Left for Up North. . . ."

from Y *no se lo tragó la tierra . . .* And the Earth Did Not Devour Him

The priest always held First Communion during midspring. I'll always remember that day in my life. I remember what I was wearing and I remember my godfather and the pastries and chocolate that we had after mass, but I also remember what I saw at the cleaners that was next to the church. I think it all happened because I left so early for church. It's that I hadn't been able to sleep the night before, trying to remember all of my sins, and worse yet, trying to arrive at an exact number. Furthermore, since Mother had placed a picture of hell at the head of the bed and since the walls of the room were papered with images of the devil and since I wanted salvation from all evil, that was all I could think of.

Remember, children, very quiet, very very quiet. You have learned your prayers well, and now you know which are the mortal sins and which are the venial sins, now you know what sacrilege is, now you know that you are God's children, but you can also be children of the devil. When you go to confession you must tell all of your sins, you must try to remember all of the sins you have committed. Because if you forget one and receive Holy Communion then that would be a sacrilege and if you commit sacrilege you will go to hell. God knows all. You cannot lie to God. You can lie to me and to the priest, but God knows everything; so if your soul is not pure of sin, then you should not receive Holy Communion. That would be a sacrilege. So everyone confess all of your sins. Recall all of your sins. Wouldn't you be ashamed if you received Holy Communion and then later remembered a sin that you had forgotten to confess? Now, let's see, let us practice confessing our sins. Who would like to start off? Let us begin with the sins that we commit with our hands when we touch our bodies. Who would like to start?

The nun liked for us to talk about the sins of the flesh. The real truth was that we practiced a lot telling our sins, but the real truth was that I didn't understand a lot of things. What did scare me was the idea of going to hell because some months earlier I had fallen against a small basin filled with hot coals which we used as a heater in the little room where we slept. I had burned my calf. I could well imagine how it might be to burn in hell forever. That was all that I understood. So I spent that night, the eve of my First Communion, going over all the sins I had committed. But what was real hard was coming up with the exact number like the nun wanted us to. It must have been dawn by the time I finally satisfied my conscience. I had committed one hundred and fifty sins, but I was going to admit two-hundred.

If I say one-hundred and fifty and I've forgotten some, that would be bad. I'll just say two-hundred and that way even if I forget lots of them I won't commit any kind of sacrilege. Yes, I have committed two-hundred sins . . . Father I have come to confess my sins . . . How many? . . . Two-hundred . . . of all kinds . . . The Commandments? Against all of the Ten Commandments . . . This way there will be no sacrilege. It's better this way. By confessing more sins you'll be purer.

I remember I got up much earlier that morning than Mother had expected. My godfather would be waiting for me at the church and I didn't want to be even one second late.

"Hurry, Mother, get my pants ready, I thought you already ironed them last night."

"It's just that I couldn't see anymore last night. My eyesight is failing me now and that's why I had to leave them for this morning. But tell me, what's your hurry now? It's still very early. Confession isn't until eight o'clock and it's only six. Your *padrino* won't be there until eight."

"I know, but I couldn't sleep. Hurry, Mother, I want to leave now."

"And what are you going to do there so early?"

"Well, I want to leave because I'm afraid I'll forget the sins I have to confess to the priest. I can think better at the church."

"All right, I'll be through in just a minute. Believe me, as long as I can see I'm able to do a lot."

I headed for church repeating my sins and reciting the Holy Sacraments. The morning was already bright and clear, but there weren't many people out in the street yet. The morning was cool. When I got to the church I found that it was closed. I think the priest might have overslept or was very busy. That was why I walked around the church and passed by the cleaners that was next to the church. The sound of the loud laughter and moans surprised me because I didn't expect anybody to be in there. I thought it might be a dog, but then it sounded like people again, and that's why I peeked in through the little window in the door. They didn't see me but I saw them. They were naked and embracing each other, lying on some shirts and dresses on the floor. I don't know why, but I couldn't move away from the window. Then they saw me and tried to cover themselves, and they yelled at me to get out of there. The woman's hair looked all messed up, and she looked like she was sick. And me, to tell the truth, I got scared and ran to the church, but I couldn't get my mind off of what I had seen. I realized then that maybe those were the sins that we committed with our hands. But I couldn't forget the sight of that woman and that man lying on the floor. When my friends started arriving I was going to tell them, but then I thought it would be better to tell them after communion. More and more I was feeling like I was the one who had committed a sin of the flesh.

There's nothing I can·do now. But I can't tell the others 'cause they'll sin like me. I better not go to communion. Better that I don't go to confession. I can't, now that I know, I can't. But what will Mom and Dad say if I don't go to communion? And my *padrino,* I can't leave him there waiting. I have to confess what I saw. I feel like going back. Maybe they're still there on the floor. No choice, I'm gonna have to lie. What if I forget it between now and confession? Maybe I didn't see anything? And if I hadn't seen anything?"

I remember that when I went in to confess and the priest asked for my sins, all I told him was two hundred and of all kinds. I did not confess the sin of the flesh. On returning to the house with my godfather, everything seemed changed, like I was and yet wasn't in the same place. Everything seemed smaller and less important. When I saw my Dad and my Mother, I imagined them on the floor. I started seeing all of the grown-ups naked and their faces even looked distorted, and I could even hear them laughing and moaning, even though they weren't laughing. Then I started imagining the priest and the nun on the floor. I couldn't hardly eat any of the sweet bread or drink the chocolate. As soon as I finished, I recall running out of the house. It felt like I couldn't breathe.

"So, what's the matter with him? Such manners!"

"Ah, *compadre,* let him be. You don't have to be concerned on my account. I have my own. These young ones, all they can think about is playing. Let him have a good time, it's the day of his First Communion."

"Sure, compadre, I'm not saying they shouldn't play. But they have to learn to be more courteous. They have to show more respect toward adults, their elders and all the more for their *padrino.*"

"No, well, that's true."

I remember I headed toward the thicket. I picked up some rocks and threw them at the cactus. Then I broke some bottles. I climbed a tree and stayed there for a long time until I got tired of thinking. I kept remembering the scene at the cleaners, and there, alone, I even liked recalling it. I even forgot that I had lied to the priest. And then I felt the same as I once had when I had heard a missionary speak about the grace of God. I felt like knowing more about everything. And then it occurred to me that maybe everything was the same.

Before people left for up north the priest would bless their cars and trucks at five dollars each. One time he made enough money to make a trip to Barcelona, in Spain, to visit his parents and friends. He brought back words of gratitude from his family and some postcards of a very modern church. These he placed by the entrance of the church for the people to see, that they might desire a church such as that one. It wasn't long before words began to appear on the cards, then crosses, lines and *con safos* symbols, just as had happened to the new church pews. The priest was never able to understand the sacrilege.

Moisés Sandoval

Historian, journalist, editor of *Fronteras: A History of the Hispanic American Church in the U.S.A. Since 1513* (San Antonio: Mexican American Cultural Center, 1983), author of *On the Move: A History of the Hispanic Church in the United States* (Maryknoll, N.Y.: Orbis Books, 1990), editor of the monthly Catholic mission magazine *Maryknoll* and its Spanish-language counterpart *Revista Maryknoll,* New Mexican native Moisés Sandoval has written extensively on the relationship between Latinos and the U.S. Catholic church.

In *On the Move,* Sandoval recounts the historic neglect of Latinos by the official church and documents the slow rise of the church of the poor. In the following reading from that book, Sandoval argues for a new church model that incorporates the contributions of those who previously have been marginalized.

The Future of the Hispanic Church

The objective—and challenge—of the bishops of the United States has been to build one church out of many ethnic groups. In the main that has happened, though some groups took longer than others to become part of the melting-pot church. Hispanics, however, remain a people apart. They continue to cling to their culture and maintain at least some of their religious traditions. There is "social distance" between them and the institutional Church. For some it is a vague discomfort of not feeling at home. For others, it is the perception that the clergy are not interested in them. Moreover, Hispanics in the main have no role in ministry: episcopal, clerical, religious, or lay. They are the objects of ministry rather than its agents.

Hispanics are largely outside the Church for the same reasons they are still peripheral in society: racism and discrimination still exist. Archbishop Pio Laghi, the apostolic delegate to the United States, reminded the nation's bishops at their annual meeting in 1988 that Hispanics are still discriminated against in the Church. The bias is more subtle than in the past, when people were told bluntly that they were not welcome, but the lack of respect can still be detected.

Hispanics who most need the Church's commitment are often of a lower economic class. This group includes the nearly one-third who live below the poverty line and the refugees and immigrants fleeing war, political persecution, or hunger in Latin America. In 1988, six out of ten Hispanic families were among the two-fifths of the poorest families in the nation.[1] Hispanics also constitute three-fourths of the farm workers in the nation, one of the most deprived labor forces. Father Joseph Fitzpatrick, a Jesuit sociologist, wrote that middle-class clergy and religious face difficulties in ministering to the poor. That is because class differences touch economic and political concerns, he wrote.[2]

The Catholic Church in the United States, increasingly middle-class in its membership and in its values, has provided the kind of ministry that its class needs. But it has little to offer a people who are not only of a lower economic class, but are also a minority for which there has been only a limited place in society. Hispanics with long tenure in the United States have yet to achieve equality. They lack adequate representation in politics, government, industry, business, and education. What Hispanics have needed from the Church is a strong commitment to social justice. That kind of Hispanic ministry has been the option of individuals—bishops, clergy, religious men and women, and laity. But for the most part, ministry to the Hispanics is not the result of structural priorities. Often, bishops, superiors, or provincials provide little backing for those who have chosen to work with Hispanics. Because the work is difficult, some are unable to sustain their efforts, suffering burnout or disillusionment. The corporate response on the part of bishops as well as religious orders and congregations has been long on rhetoric but short on action. That is why little has been done to implement the national pastoral plan for Hispanic ministry approved by bishops in 1987.

A storefront model of ministry has prevailed; the Church has largely waited for the Hispanics to come for service. From time to time, successful models of an outgoing ministry have appeared, e.g. the Mission Band of California in the 1950s, but they have not been perpetuated and expanded. The attitude has been that special models of ministry for Hispanics are not needed.

This issue, however, is not one-sided; Hispanics bear some responsibility for their alienation. Though a deeply religious people, they lack a strong tradition of priesthood. Many tend to be anticlerical. That is particularly true among Mexicans because the Church in times past often sided with the rich and powerful and failed to speak for the poor. It is also due to *machismo,* which sees the practice of religion as somehow unmanly, to be left to the women and children. The result is that vocations have not been encouraged in the home.

Socially Hispanics, both citizens and immigrants, are an uprooted people. This includes not just the nearly two million Puerto Ricans who have come to the mainland in the past fifty years and the millions of documented and undocumented immigrants and refugees who have arrived from Latin America in the past three decades. In this category belong also the majority of U.S. Hispanics who early in this century were a rural people and now are the most urbanized ethnic group in the nation. This exodus, originating both externally and internally, has ruptured traditional societies and scattered and divided families not only across state lines but also across international borders. There is a great need to reunite families, reconstruct the community, and find a home.

Because these relocated people saw themselves as sojourners wherever they settled, they did not involve themselves fully in the institutions of society. They thought that they would soon be returning home. Though few can return, many still yearn for their homeland and remain aloof when they should be immersing themselves and creating a new society where they are going to spend their lives.

The most important reason why Hispanics remain a people apart is that they are different from others in the U.S. Church. Though other ethnic groups did encounter short-term discrimination, Hispanics were rejected outright. They underwent a process that left them "colonized," "conquered," "strangers in their own land." The defeatism which is the chief effect of that sad history leaves many unable to associate on an equal basis with members of the majority culture. Though much healing has taken place in recent years, it will be a long time before the process is complete.

For all these reasons, Hispanics remain a group apart in the Church, a condition almost certain to increase in the future despite the church's hope to serve them better. By the year 2000, according to projections, there will be sixty percent fewer priests than in 1989. Already, a certain triage is becoming evident; wherever parishes are closed, as in Detroit and Chicago, they tend to be the ones serving the minorities. Hispanics in the inner cities are therefore likely to be left without priests.

Yet, little is being done to prepare for that day. While pastors and bishops are interested in developing leadership among Hispanics, what they do is train readers, ministers of the Eucharist, song leaders, and the like. But Hispanics need leadership training of a different kind, as leaders and evangelizers in small ecclesial communities. They need training such as that provided by Communities Organized for Public Service (COPS), which organizes the poor to win political power in the urban barrios. In short, they need training to liberate themselves from the fate of colonized people.

From colonial times, building a Church has been the unfinished task of Hispanics. That process, just beginning in the Southwest when that territory became part of the United States, was resumed a century later when a few structures were established by the Bishop's Committee for the Spanish-Speaking: the special office, the councils, and, later, the diocesan, regional and national apostolates. Then there were the Spanish-language branches of various movements—the *Cursillo*, Marriage Encounter, and the Charismatic movement. Perhaps the most significant has been the Encuentro movement, which led to the preparation of the national pastoral plan for Hispanic ministry. There is no comparable movement for the Church as a whole, no national pastoral plan resulting from consultation at the grassroots level.

During the heady days of the *Movimiento*, the Hispanic civil rights movement of the sixties and early seventies, activist priests sometimes talked about a separate Hispanic Church, but this has never really been an option. There have never been the bishops, clergy, and religious to lead such an institution. The only recourse has been to be a leaven and, in that way, create for Hispanics a home within the larger Church. In a sense, with such movements as the *Cursillo* and Marriage Encounter, progress is being made in that direction.

Also, Central and South American refugees may have a significant contribution to make. Among them are persons who have suffered brutal torture. Some have lost mothers, fathers, brothers, or sisters to the death squads. Some have seen their entire community massacred by the armed forces. Hundreds of thousands have had to flee for their lives. These experiences have irrevocably changed the victims and their religious values.

Suffering, however, is shared by many more than those people described above. This category also includes the so-called economic immigrants, driven by increasing hunger, who enter the country illegally. It includes the hundreds of thousands of farm workers, citizens of the United States, who have been unable to command a just wage and a work environment safe from dangerous pesticides. It includes the residents of urban slums victimized by the drug lords because they cannot get adequate law enforcement. Certainly the religious value of that suffering can have a purifying effect on the entire Church.

Among the individuals to which the Hispanic Church owes its progress in recent decades are not only a few bishops, clergy, and religious men and women, but also lay persons who have made a true option for the poor and have been able to maintain their commitment in spite of many setbacks. In that long list of lay persons, not all of whom work under auspices of the Church, one has to include

Cesar Chavez, the leader of the United Farm Workers; the late Willie Velasquez, who, as head of the Southwest Voter Registration Education Project, dedicated his life to giving Hispanics a political voice; and Ernie Cortez, the organizer of Communities Organized for Public Service in San Antonio and United Neighborhoods Organization in Los Angeles. They are models of commitment not only for the official shepherds of the Church but for the laity as well.

According to demographers, Hispanics will be the majority of the nation's Catholics by the first decade of the coming century. It remains to be seen how they will respond when they are no longer a minority. That change, however will be only among the laity. Hispanic bishops, clergy, and religious will still be a tiny minority; vocations, while increasing, are not going up sufficiently to make a difference. Nevertheless, the role of the laity, in view of the diminishing numbers of priests, will be paramount. Much more of the Church's ministry will be in their hands. To fulfill that challenge, they will need to develop a strong sense of ownership of the Church, which comes with shared responsibility, That is coming but, alas, too slowly.

Nevertheless, a Hispanic Church, defined not so much by structures as by its character, is beginning to take form. It is one that is "unabashedly affective or emotive,"[3] as the popularity of the charismatic renewal among Hispanics demonstrates. It is one that is in process of developing its own theology, following the pioneering efforts of Father Virgil Elizondo. It is one that has already developed much of its own liturgy, thanks to the work of the Institute of Hispanic Liturgy. It is one where lay leadership has come forward in recent years through the Encuentro Movement, the Hispanic deacon program, and various other movements. Whether the larger Church will accept its contribution is not certain. But one thing is certain: it will endure.

Virginia Sánchez Korrol

Virginia Sánchez Korrol teaches in the Department of Puerto Rican Studies at Brooklyn College, City College of New York, and has written books and articles on the Puerto Rican community in New York. She is the author of *From Colonia to Community: The History of Puerto Ricans in New York City, 1917–1948* (Westport, Conn.: Greenwood Press, 1983), and coeditor of the *The Way It Was and Other Writings* (Houston: Arte Público Press, 1993), a collection of writings by Puerto Rican activist Jesús Colón.

The following selection, "In Search of Unconventional Women: Histories of Puerto Rican Women in Religious Vocations Before Midcentury," uses oral history to trace the lives of three religious women, a Catholic nun and two Pentecostal missionary evangelists, who heeded their unusual calling to minister to youth and to become instruments of community development for Puerto Ricans in New York City beginning in the 1920s.

In Search of Unconventional Women: Histories of Puerto Rican Women in Religious Vocations Before Midcentury

Oral history is frequently used to document the lives of people deemed typical or representative of their group or community. The three women whose stories form the core of this essay, however, can help us understand a broader history precisely because they are unconventional: at a historical juncture in the development of Puerto Rican *barrios,* when women's roles were circumscribed by social custom and occupation, they chose to break new ground. Each followed a personal calling for spiritual and humanitarian reasons, and came to play an important pastoral and religious role. Though unknown outside of their respective religious communities, their important role in the history of the Puerto Rican community is just beginning to be understood.

The life histories of these unconventional women, as recorded through oral history, illuminate the professional and, to a lesser extent, the personal life experiences of each individual, while also documenting their contributions at specific historical points in Puerto Rican community development. In this sense, the oral histories do more than add to our growing knowledge of individual Puerto Rican lives: they are especially valuable in enabling historians to begin to construct an intergenerational view of the Puerto Rican experience.[1]

Two of the women, Sister Carmelita and Reverend Leoncia Rosado, began their careers in the 1920s and 1930s, respectively. A vulnerable period in the development of the young community, it was also a time when women were expected to follow traditional roles and remain in the home as wives and mothers. The third woman, the Reverend Aimee García Cortese, is representative of the transitional second generation of Puerto Ricans, born in the U.S.A., which internalized many of the old customs while accommodating to a mainland reality.

The period between 1917 and 1950 was highly significant for Puerto Ricans in New York City. Under the leadership and influence of the earliest substantial migration from the island's rural and urban sectors, the community in New York City began to take shape as identifiably Puerto Rican. As early as 1910, over a thousand Puerto Ricans were said to reside in the United States. American citizenship, conferred in 1917, stimulated and facilitated migration, and within a decade all of the forty-eight states reported the presence of Puerto Rican–born individuals. Estimates indicate substantial population gains throughout the 1930's and 1940s, culminating in a total population of some 425,000 by mid century, 80 percent of whom lived in New York City.[2]

Women formed an integral part of the migration experience, comprising over half the migrant flow in some decades. A partial tabulation of representative Hispanic districts in the New York State Manuscript Census of 1925 provides some insights into the earlier migrant population. Of 3,496 women listed in the census, the majority were young housewives, under thirty-five years of age, who had resided in the city for less than six years. For the most part, Puerto Rican family traditions defined women's place in the early New York community. Expected to fulfill traditional roles as wives and mothers, women were conditioned to accept these roles as their primary life functions, regardless of their degree of involvement in community, career, or work-related activities.[3]

However, when confronted with the economic realities of an overwhelmingly poor community, close to 25 percent of the migrant women went to work outside the home in factories, laundries, and restaurants. This figure would rise in the coming decades, and parallel the demand for workers in the garment and other industries. Many women worked as seamstresses and domestics; others found ways to combine homemaking with gainful employment by taking in lodgers, caring for the children of working mothers, and doing piecework at home.

While the majority of the migrant women fit into the above categories, a handful—less than 4 percent—established a foothold in other areas. These were the women who were either formally educated, skilled, or bilingual, or who, by virtue of their community involvement, exercised leadership roles. Some sought and secured white-collar office employment upon their arrival in the city; the status inherent in that work was sufficient to raise them above the ordinary. Others proceeded to launch supportive community enterprises, or to form volunteer organizations in response to the special needs of the community, as they had previously done in Puerto Rico. Still others, writers, poets, essayists, and journalists, expressed themselves through their creative and artistic talents.[4] Finally, there were the women who chose the church, and in their own way contributed towards —and help us understand—Puerto Rican community development.

Carmela Zapata Bonilla Marrerro was born in Cabo Rojo, Puerto Rico, in 1907. Raised in a rural atmosphere on the western coast of the island, she belonged to a family composed predominantly of middle-class farmers and property owners. After the premature death of her mother in 1918, a move to Mayaguez, the island's third largest city, enabled her to receive a Catholic school education. During this tender period in her life Carmelita first articulated the desire to enter a convent. At sixteen, she made the decision to become a missionary nun in the Roman Catholic Church. Leaving her home and family for Georgia, the conventual center of the Trinitarian Order, in 1923, she hardly imagined that this would be the first of many trips between Puerto Rico and the U.S.

What impressions and images must have crossed the girl's mind as she made the five-day journey alone from San Juan to Brooklyn, where the ship was due to make port! She believes she left on a Thursday because the steamship lines always sailed from Thursdays to Mondays; she remembers traveling second class which offered the same menu as first, but without the dancing; and she recalls that the nuns met her ship at the Columbia Heights Promenade at Fulton Street. Carmelita spent her first night at the Brooklyn convent painfully aware that she was in strange surroundings, and anxiously anticipating her trip to Georgia, where she would enter the Convent of the Holy Trinity to begin her novitiate. Two years later, she was given her first assignment and sent to her order's Court Street Center, in Brooklyn, the first Puerto Rican nun in their community. As a young nun, she had little choice in the matter, but the assignment proved to be propitious for the Brooklyn Puerto Rican community. As she recalled, her first impressions were:

> that center was two old houses and they were put together for the purpose of having clubs—we had Boy Scouts, Girl Scouts, Brownies, sewing clubs, manual work for the children, mother's clubs, library, arts, crafts, all that. We had hundreds of children. We had no Puerto Ricans in this neighborhood then. We had lots of Polish, Irish. It was called Irishtown . . . [There were] Polish, Lithuanian, Chinese, Filipino.[5]

Although her earliest missionary work was carried out among the poor, multiethnic children of Brooklyn, it was the plight of the Puerto Rican migrants that sparked Sister Carmelita's imagination and dedication:

> During those years it was when they use to put them, you know, out—dispossess them—and it was very hard. And I thought that it was my duty to save every Puerto Rican that I found—from anything. I felt that terrible, you know. So I remember seeing them on the sidewalk, with all their children, and their beds, and all their things—dispossessed. Then we had no welfare. So then I remember a friend of mine—in 176 Sand Street—she owned that building and one day I met her. And I used to visit Puerto Ricans there. "Sister," she said, "I have this building and nobody pays rent so I'm gonna give you the key to this building. When you see a family dispossessed, you bring them to this building." That's what I did. I had that building filled with people—no heat, but anyway, they had a house for a while.[6]

Sister Carmelita remained in Brooklyn until 1949, active in numerous social welfare programs. A familiar sight in the local precincts and hospitals, she was frequently called upon to intercede on behalf of the Puerto Rican community, to translate for them and guide their general welfare. But her return to her native Puerto Rico allowed Sister Carmelita the opportunity to teach and pursue her own academic interests within the structure of her convent. She earned a bachelor's degree as well as a master's from the University of Puerto Rico, concentrating on the study of social work, an area in which she was experienced. In time, a personal desire to return to the Brooklyn community and the families she had left behind motivated Carmelita to request a transfer to the mission center where she had initiated her career.

During the fourteen years that Carmelita spent in New York, a diverse Puerto Rican community—the *Barrio Hispano*—developed. It straddled the East River with *colonias*, or neighborhoods, on both sides. Puerto Ricans predominated among the city's Spanish-speaking population. As American citizens, they were unaffected by the immigration barriers that restricted aliens from coming to the U.S. In terms of actual numbers, however, census figures varied depending on who was taking the count. Puerto Ricans could easily fit into several groupings. They could be counted as blacks or whites or racially mixed, as citizens or immigrants. To further complicate matters, as residents of a U.S. possession, Puerto Ricans did not figure into immigration counts.

A report issued by the New York Mission Society in 1927 estimated a total of between 100,000 and 150,000 Spanish-speaking inhabitants, of whom approximately 85,000 were Puerto Ricans engaged in the cigar-making industry.[7] Overwhelmingly working class, theirs was a tightly knit, introspective community whose neighborhood organizations boasted substantial audiences of one or two hundred persons at any given function, and where Spanish-language newspapers and magazines found an appreciative reading public.[8] Culturally, the Puerto Rican community identified strongly with Spanish America. The Spanish language and Roman Catholic faith served to weld close bonds. the institutionalization of common customs and traditions insured both the insulation and isolation of the nascent *colonias*. Advocacy in their interest frequently rested with the organizations that structured the community.

The work of Sister Carmelita and her Trinitarian Sisters notwithstanding, the Catholic Church was slow to respond to the needs of the growing Puerto Rican settlements, most of which were nominally Catholic. The first church to offer masses in Spanish was Nuestra Señora de la Medalla Milagrosa, founded in East Harlem in the 1920s. La Milagrosa was followed by Santa Agonia and St. Cecilia, both of which were established during the 1930's.[9]

By 1939, the Catholic Diocese initiated reforms based on the premise that all parish churches should become integrated or multinational. Previously, the Diocese had favored ethnic or nationality-oriented churches, and these had adequately provided guidance, pastoral services, and a sense of cultural identity for earlier Polish, Irish, and Italian immigrant groups. Influential and respected institutions, the nationality churches cushioned the immigration experience by fostering ties with the native land, language, and customs. Moreover, the churches functioned as brokers or mediators between the immigrant and the dominant society. However, in the case of the Puerto Ricans, the new policies that argued against differential treatment were rationalized on several counts. First, unlike other immigrant groups before them, Puerto Ricans did not bring clergy with them to the New York settlements. Indeed, the Church failed to understand the point that in the island there had never been sufficient numbers of native-born Puerto Rican priests. Non-native, Spanish-speaking clergy had been imported to Puerto Rico for decades. Second, and more significant, the Catholic Diocese in New York had weathered a decline in third-generation national church membership. It argued that the already existing clergy, as well as schools and churches, could simply be retrained and restructured to accommodate the Puerto Ricans.[10] Partly because of the failure of this policy, many of the spiritual and social welfare needs of the Puerto Ricans defaulted to

numerous community organizations. These included charitable groups such as the Catholic Settlement Association, the New York City Mission Society, Casita Maria, and the Protestant churches.

Throughout the years, Sister Carmelita utilized the organizations, as well as the church, in her work. She was one of the founders of the settlement house Casita Maria, and she is directly credited with influencing and motivating the academic growth and aspirations of numerous youngsters of that period.[11] Her recollections evoke images of a dismally poor and needy community. She was frequently called upon to advocate for the non-English speaker; to mediate between migrant parents, intent on maintaining island customs, and their rebellious U.S.-born children; and to confront the authorities on behalf of the community. Her vocation dictated expertise in teaching, counseling, and religion, and her dedication to the people she served sharpened her knowledge of the law, public health, the penal system, and housing. Her office in St. Joseph's on Pacific Street was open to everyone, and she developed a resource network rooted as much in the leadership of the Puerto Rican *barrios* as in the church. She states:

> I was a friend of the politicians. I must admit I used to ask the politicians for help, you know, especially those that sold *bolita* [numbers racket]—the bankers—and they used to help me a lot for the poor people. And then the politicians that didn't belong to the *bolita* were right there, in Borough Hall, so they were good to the Puerto Ricans. I use to visit everybody who was Spanish-speaking, no matter what it was or when it was and that's how I met all those people. I use to ask them to please help me out, like when Thanksgiving came—*el dia del pavo* (the day of the turkey)—they use to give me two or three hundred dollars. I used to spend that in food and for Christmas. It was the same for *Reyes* [Three Kings Day].[12]

Until poor health forced her retirement in the early 1970's, Sister Carmelita continued to do what she could to influence the social, cultural, and educational development of the Brooklyn Puerto Rican community. The number of Catholic institutions providing spiritual and material resources specifically for Puerto Ricans throughout the 1930s and 1940s was clearly limited.

By contrast, there were some twenty-five Puerto Rican Protestant churches, most of them Pentecostal. These were fundamentalist sects which adhered strictly to a literal interpretation of the Bible and encouraged rejection of worldly concerns among the members. The American invasion had facilitated the Protestantization of the island, accelerating a process already evident in the late nineteenth century. By the mid-1930s one observer noted that some of the Protestant churches in New York were located on the second floor of various types of buildings, and that as one approached Upper Harlem, these became more numerous. Some religious congregations met in private homes, while others rented storefronts for prayer and worship. Although the origin of the Pentecostal movement in New York remains unclear, an estimated five percent of the Puerto Ricans living in the city during this period were Protestant.[13] And within a decade, the Pentecostals had become the fastest-growing Protestant group among Puerto Ricans.

Dependent on a grass-roots tradition for their leadership, ministers often came from the ranks of the congregants. Sects were frequently self-starting and self-sustaining, supervised by ministers who were working class themselves. Small and intimate, many Pentecostal or evangelical churches provided a sense of community not found in the more traditional denominations.[14] Women played a pivotal role in this phase of church and community development, as they did within the structure of the Catholic Church. However, if conventual roles were limited under the strict, formal policies of that complex institutional structure, they were also restricted by gender. As a nun, subordinate to a male hierarchy, Sister Carmelita's professional and private life was circumscribed. By contrast, the Pentecostal faith permitted the ascendancy of a few women to the pulpit. Among these was the Reverend Leoncia Rosado Rosseau.

Born on April 11, 1912, in Toa Alta, Puerto Rico, Leoncia Rosado Rosseau believes that she was destined for the ministry from birth. The second of five children born to Señora Gumersinda Santiago Ferrer and Don Manuel Rivera Marrero, Leoncia received her religious calling in 1932 at the age of twenty. Then followed a period of evangelism in the poorest *barrios* of Puerto Rico. A small and slender young woman, she was not afraid to enter the most alien and hostile environments because she was convinced that it was all part of God's mission. Foretold in a vision that she was destined to carry God's word across the ocean, in 1935 she left the island for New York to continue her work as a missionary and evangelist. By 1937 she had received her first certificate in divinity.[15]

In New York City, life was firmly anchored in church and community. Reverend Leoncia preached on street corners and delighted in debating scripture with nonbelievers. She offered testimony to the glory of God, visited the sick, and assisted in the general organization of her church. She traveled to the Dominican Republic and other Latin countries in the service of her church. There too she continued in her dual roles as missionary and evangelist. But while her spiritual gifts and fervent dedication were acknowledged by her fellow congregants, she was limited by tradition to addressing the congregation from the floor, and not the pulpit. On the eve of the Second World War she married a church elder, Roberto Rosado, and added to her life the dimensions of wife and homemaker.

About this time, the Puerto Rican community in New York City witnessed a decline in the numbers of individuals coming from the island and a rapid dispersement of those already residing in the city into all five boroughs. Puerto Ricans continued to fill the ranks of the working class and competed for the meager unskilled employment of the Depression period. But this situation changed radically in the 1940s, when women, minorities, and foreign nationals from bordering countries were vigorously recruited for factory and farm work. The labor shortages of the Second World War precipitated the large-scale Puerto Rican migration of the period just before and after the war. But this was only part of a broader expansion: close to 400,000 foreign contract workers entered the country in response to the demands of the labor market between 1942 and the end of the war, very few of whom were Puerto Rican. Some scholars argue that despite the general postwar contraction, the departure of many of those workers after the war created a vacuum in particular sectors of the labor market to which Puerto Rican workers responded. Between 1947 and 1949, a yearly net average of 32,000 individuals migrated from Puerto Rico, many destined to work in the garment and needle-trade industries.[16] They continued to be concentrated in blue-collar, low-paying sectors, especially in light industry. By 1948, the Migration Division of the island's Department of Labor established programs to aid potential migrants and to inform them about New York City. And by the start of midcentury, the great migration from Puerto Rico was well under way.[17]

For the charismatic Reverend Leoncia, this period represented a turning point in her life. It signaled the beginning of her ministry as pastor of the Damascus Christian Church, and it brought the church directly into the social service of the community through the creation of the Christian Youth Crusade.

According to Reverend Leoncia, both events were foretold in a vision in which the Lord took her to the edge of a river where He indicated that she was to retrieve enormous quantities of carrots from the waters. She agonized over her task and exclaimed that she could not do it, but He replied, "Yes, you can. Continue. Take them out."[18]

> Finally, I got them all out of the river and when I turned around I saw that all the carrots had become people and that most were young. Then we walked in front of the multitudes which were uncountable and we were going to find Damascus. I don't know what had happened to them, but they had a small congregation. We had loudspeakers to take the message to the entire world. That's how far I went with the Lord and I wondered what this all meant.
>
> Within a short time my husband was drafted. He was already an ordained minister. My husband at that time weighed 105 pounds because he was sick with a heart condition. And he did everything possible, even writing to the president of the United States, not to go into the army. I prayed that he wouldn't have to go, but the Lord responded, "Do not pray for this—it is my will that he go, but he will return." He [Rosado] was sure that the army would not take him. When he went for his induction, weighing 105 pounds, more infirmed than ever, he was accepted. It never crossed my mind to take over for him because I had forgotten my dream, and I could not seriously think or suggest this to him, and so we spoke of Brothers Fernando Noriega and Belén Camacho as possible substitutes. And I would assist them as I had helped [my husband]. And so we went to meet with them to discuss this, but they said, "No, not us. The one who should remain here is sister Léo." And that's how I came to be pastor of the Damascus Christian Church.[19]

Even though precedents for women to act as missionaries and evangelists existed in Puerto Rico and in the New York Puerto Rican *barrios*, it was extremely rare for women to become ministers. In Puerto Rico, Juanita Garcia Peraza, or "Mita" as she was known to her followers, epitomized the role of women as evangelists and ministers.[20] There are few objective accounts of Mita's life and work, but her achievements were known on both sides of the ocean. In the early 1940s she inaugurated her own sect and Pentecostal church, which engaged in the operation of cooperatives and provided social services for its congregants. Her disciples believed that she was God's incarnation on earth and referred to her as the "Goddess."

In the daily operations of Pentecostal churches in New York, women were also indispensable. They supervised Bible study classes, succored the sick, comforted families in distress, and performed countless acts of charity. Missionaries participated in street ministries and proselytized aggressively from door to door. Yet, despite the high degree of visibility and responsibility that women undertook in church matters, their involvement, by tradition, seldom extended to the pulpit.[21]

Although the Reverend Leoncia encountered resistance and discrimination toward her calling because of her gender, it was nothing compared to the obstacles she faced in orienting her church to the social/economic problems of the community. Until that point, pentecostalism among the Puerto Ricans in New York had served as a sanctuary from the cultural and social malaise inherent in the migration experience; it basically shielded the congregants from spiritual contamination by the outside world. Leoncia Rosado's ministry opened the way for new definitions.

When the Christian Youth Crusade was initiated in 1957, Damascus Christian Church had expanded to include branches in other boroughs. One of the earliest grass-roots programs to fight drug abuse, it was sustained by funding from within the church. It provided a refuge for gangs, addicts, alcoholics and ex-convicts, and its philosophical base was strictly religious. The addict was viewed as a sinner and only repentance and acceptance of the Lord would bring about a cure. The major center for treatment was in the Damascus Christian Church in the Bronx, but there was also an upstate site, Mountaindale, to which recovering addicts would go. In spite of its success, however, the church was most reluctant to engage in such community-oriented tasks. Reverend Leoncia recalled the confrontation with the church leaders on this matter:

> Our church was a church like any other. It did not work with alcoholics, etc. Sophisticated, illuminated with the Holy Spirit, yes, but it did not work with alcoholics. I came and told them of my vision. I understand these are alcoholics and lost souls, and the lowest people in society, but God wants us to do this work. And they said, "Not here, no, no, not here," and I said to them, "Yes here! Because God mandates it of us." The church which closes its being and heart to the clamor of lost souls does not have a right to a place in the community. What do you think you're here for? Here is where the work is to be done and if you don't do it, I'll present my resignation. I was the pastor there then. My husband had returned from the army, and he was a bishop with the church council. Then they [the congregation] gave me a place that we call the Tower of Prayer, which was a long room and there I placed beds and cots which I found.
>
> Imagine a person like me, who had never even smoked a cigarette, unworldly, working with addicts, breaking their habits cold turkey, without aspirin or anything. My husband Roberto and I and the brothers and sisters

of the church who helped us there . . . legs full of sores, and then when an addict is breaking the habit, their stinking sweat, that fever, the cold, the trembling, the heat, their screams . . . it was a tremendous thing!

And that bunch of kids—about fifteen, sometimes twenty or twenty-five, and their crying "Mama"—that's where I got the name, Mama Leo—"Mama, it hurts there, rub there, or there," and when I would treat their legs and feet, oozing full of sores, I would think, I held the feet of Our Lord.

I would make them a banquet for Thanksgiving, and they would come dirty, strung-out, sick, any way at all, but before feeding them I would provide a religious service with the other youths already saved. The kids would say, "Mama, we came for the bird and you gave us the Word!"[22]

An estimated two hundred and fifty to three hundred young people, mostly Hispanic, who were rehabilitated through that program went into the ministry. Many of them are active today in youth-oriented programs. Close to eighteen programs or schools have been established by them worldwide. Reverend Leoncia considers this her greatest and most rewarding mission.

If the community-service programs begun by Mama Léo served to initiate the church's role in the streets, her example as a pastor and as a woman illustrated new directions for some of the young Puerto Rican women growing up in New York during this period. One of these was the Reverend Aimee García Cortese. Aimee García Cortese was born in 1929, raised and educated in the New York Puerto Rican *barrio* of the South Bronx. Her close-knit and religious family offered Aimee and her two brothers and sister a stable and loving environment in which to grow. At thirteen, Aimee encountered Pentecostal outreach efforts for the first time, when local church members offered prayers and services for her ailing mother. Soon afterwards, the family became active in church affairs. As New York teenagers, steeped in the world of movies and other social activities, the Garcías at first resisted the rigor, discipline, and sacrifice expected of Pentecostal youth. However, by the time Aimee was fifteen, she confided her intention to become a minister to her pastor, the Reverend Manuel López. He replied, *"las mujeres no predican"*—women do not preach! His pronouncement notwithstanding, and fortified by her personal belief that she was named after the American preacher Aimee Semple McPherson, she returned to him and proceeded to systematically badger him into letting her preach. She received permission to do so before her sixteenth birthday.[23]

He told me that the next Sunday I would be preaching. Well I was so proud that I was going to preach, I never thought that I had nothing to say, I never thought that I wasn't prepared to face a crowd but I was so proud of the fact that I was going to preach that I got down on my knees and said Lord, you know you've got to bless me. Well next Sunday came and he told me to be at church at 5:30 a.m. I said, That's a little early. When I got there, there were four other young people. One had a flag, one had a tambourine, one had a license in his hand, and he [the pastor] said to me, "Now you go out to Brook Avenue and 134th Street and you preach." Oh, I thought I was going to be in church. "Oh no, *mi hija, ahi es donde se aprende*" [no, my daughter, that is where you'll learn], and it was there on that corner that I realized the strangest thing in the world: What do I say? I only know two verses. All my friends were coming out of the holes, like cockroaches out of a wall. All of a sudden I'm surrounded by eighty, ninety kids of the neighborhood that had never seen me in this posture, and there was the crowd! I recited John 3:16, and then I went on to this other verse about God gives peace. I said this is very important that you know it. So then I went back to John 3:16, and then I went back to God is going to give you peace. I did that about five times and then I realized that I had nothing to say. And I looked at the people and said, "Something great's happened in my life, but I don't know how to say it. One of these days I'm gonna come back and tell you," and I started to cry. One young man tapped me on the shoulder and said, "*Vámonos*" [Let's go]. And they took me back to the church. When I arrived, I was still crying, and the pastor said, "*Te di'te gusto nena?*" [Did you enjoy yourself?] I had nothing to tell them. "Well," he replied, "get ready to tell them something." And that was it. And he taught me, my first year, 365 Bible verses.[24]

Aimee García Cortese went on to tell the people something. She was ordained by her Wesleyan Methodist Church in Puerto Rico in 1964, became a missionary evangelist for the Spanish Assemblies of God, Associated Minister of Thessalonica Christian Church in the South Bronx, and the first female chaplain for the New York State Department of Corrections. Reflecting on her past experience, Reverend García Cortese credits Reverend Leoncia Rosado Rosseau, as well as other ministers and missionaries, with opening the way for women in religious life and providing experiences from which to learn.

There were women in ministry, but different types of ministry. Like take *la hermana* Cartagena. She was the missionary of our church. She will be eighty years old, come 1986. Now there was a woman, deep in the Word, a woman dedicated to visitation, and dedicated to doing God's work. To watch her, to be with her . . . and as I grew in the Lord, I grew out of proportion in terms that I did not go with the young people. They didn't satisfy me. What they were doing didn't satisfy me. What satisfied me was what *la hermana* Cartegena was doing. She would visit the sick, knock on doors, give out tracts, and I thought to myself, this is God's work! I was kind of ahead of my day. I was a young girl with a "little old lady" mentality. Now I realize it wasn't a "little old lady" mentality, it was "kingdom" mentality, but I didn't know what it was then. I didn't know I wanted to reach the world for Christ. I didn't know the extent of my drive. But now as I look back, I realize.

Elisa [Alicéa] was also a tremendous role model in the sense of daring to be innovative, in music, in leadership. [She] would pick up a trumpet and wake up a whole Puerto Rican town, in Ciales, and she did with music, you know, what, later on, I did with the Word. Just stirred people, woke them up, brought them into a "Hey, here's young people and we're doing something for God."

And there was Mama Léo. I don't ever think there was a moment I wanted to be [exactly] like her. I just loved her for what she was, but it looked like her walk was a much more difficult walk than what I could do. In other words, to me, Léo was somebody to learn from, but never to want to be. Maybe because Léo was one hundred years ahead of her time. On a one-woman scale, she did what, later on, organizations like Teen Challenge did, or an organization like Odyssey House did in the secular [world]. You're talking about a little lady, all by herself, taking on the world.[25]

The congregations directed by Reverend García Cortese, from the 1960's to the present, have incorporated many of the outreach programs that were considered radical in Reverend Leoncia Rosado's period. Today, youth and community programs are naturally included in church planning. Contemporary urban music plays a major role in attracting, and encouraging, religious expression among the youth. In Spanish or English, music has become an integral part of street ministries. If Reverend García Cortese's role as minister is no longer questioned because she is a woman, neither is the direction that she foresees for her congregation challenged. She envisions her church of the future to be a religious complex, including a community center with a swimming pool, gymnasium, physical fitness space, and Bible and Sunday schools. The building of the Sanctuary would come last because a congregation's priority should be its youth and community. All of this she believes to be a legitimate part of worship.

From Sister Carmelita's period to Reverend García Cortese's, attitudinal changes toward church and community are apparent. They resulted from a combination of the external transformations of the 1960s, the maturation of the Puerto Rican community, and differing perspectives regarding women's roles. At the same time, similarities abound in the experiences of all three women. The utilization of these oral histories, in conjunction with an analysis of specific historical periods, offers a unique intergenerational perspective. They provide a significant variant of the history of Puerto Ricans in New York City, and more importantly they allow us to understand the continuity of our experience.

The task of recovering and defining women's histories in the New York Puerto Rican community before midcentury is clearly underway. From the 1920's to just after the Second World War, Puerto Ricans struggled to lay the foundations of a distinctive community with formal and informal coping structures, internal leadership, businesses, professions, common cultural interests and modes of behavior. The population movements alone, punctuated by the unique circular nature of the Puerto Rican migration, brought repeated ruptures and renewals of ties, dismantling and reconstructions of familial, individual, and communal networks. We have identified a small segment of the population that contributed to the process of community development, assumed the reins of leadership, and embraced demanding social commitments. Through their ministries and work with young people, women like Aimee García Cortese, Leoncia Rosado Rosseau, and Sister Carmelita aided in the stabilization of the Puerto Rican community at significant points in its historical development.

Eldin Villafañe

Eldin Villafañe, of the Center for Urban Ministerial Education of Gordon-Conwell Theological Seminary in Boston, is the author of *The Liberating Spirit, Toward a Hispanic American Pentecostal Social Ethic* (Lanham, Md.: University Press of America, 1992). In this work, Villafañe details the principal characteristics of Hispanic spirituality and affirms the important role played by the Latino cultural heritage. The qualities that Villafañe lists—passion, personalism, paradox of the soul, community, pilgrimage, music, celebration, family—offer an excellent review and summary of the major points of Latino religiosity.

from *The Liberating Spirit: Toward a Hispanic American Pentecostal Social Ethic*

Characteristics of Hispanic Spirituality

The ideal type or profile of "Homo Hispanicus"[1] provides us eight basic categories which summarize the cultural traits and value orientation of Hispanics. These are ultimately placed at the service or become the means, in an anthropological sense, to that particular style of approach to union with God—Hispanic spirituality! In its most authentic and significant expressions Hispanic spirituality coheres with these eight culture traits and value orientations. These are "our own wells" from which we must drink. They are our Hispanic heritage; they are our sources, they are us.

Hispanic spirituality is the expression of a complex cultural phenomenon. Hispanic spirituality, thus, must be seen as part and parcel of the creative synthesis of the Hispanic value structure and orientation that has emerged from the three root streams that inform its cultural traits and personality. Hispanic spirituality responds to the Spanish, Amerindian, and African makeup of its "soul." In certain cases the Amerindian influence predominates, in others the African, while in most cases the Spanish influence—whose culture dominance in the Conquest prevailed—is the dominant one. It is important to note that the symbiotic relationship of Hispanic culture and Roman Catholicism is of such a nature that *all* Hispanic spirituality is deeply influenced by it.

Hispanic spirituality, while manifested in many forms and through different instrumentalities, in its most *authentic and significant Hispanic expressions* is marked by the following characteristics:

1. *Passion.* While Hispanic spirituality is not anti-intellectual or irrational per se, it resonates deeply with the passionate nature of the Hispanic soul. Feelings/emotions are accepted by Hispanics as part of a holistic response to life. Passion is at the heart of their religious expressions. The emotional fervor noted in the Catholic holy week; popular religiosity's passions plays and *posadas*; the Protestant preacher or Pentecostal worship service (especially its music), all attest to this significant characteristic of Hispanic spirituality.

2. *Personalism.* Personal relations are paramount for Hispanics, above abstract principles and institutions. It explains the significant dependence on mediation (e.g., a saint) to reach God in Catholic religiosity. Fitzpatrick's comment is relevant:

In Latin America, religious practice is marked by the quality of *personalismo,* the pattern of close, intimate personal relationships which is characteristic of Spanish cultures everywhere. Thus the individual perceives his religious life as a network of personal relationships with the saints, the Blessed Virgin, or various manifestations of the Lord.[2]

It responds to the appeal of the personal *curandera* or *curandero* (traditional curer or healer) in the Hispanic communities. The significant role played as social service providers (in very personal and intimate ways) by these folk healers is noteworthy. Melvin Delgado and Denise Humn-Delgado identify five types of folk healers in the Hispanic community: (1) spiritist; (2) *santero* (literally, saint intercessor); (3) herbalist; (4) *santiguador* (literally, healer by signing with the cross); and (5) *curandero* (traditional curer).[3]

The ever-present and quasi-religious *botanica,* the stores where herbs, potions, and other remedies are sold—and personal *consultas* (counsel/ advice) are dispensed—are finding receptive ears among Hispanics, in an otherwise impersonal society. The spiritist, with the influential teaching of Allan Kardec and Joaquin Trincado, provide alternative religious structures that respond to Hispanic needs in a very personal way.[4]

Personalism also explains the lack of trust for systems or organizations to mediate religious experience. Loyalty is often placed on persons rather than religious institutions or, for that matter, theological abstract principles distinguishing the different religious confessions. Beyond the sociopolitical nature or sources of church splits, and the distinct conception of "calling" and ministry in Hispanic pentecostalism, it would be wise to look seriously at the role played by strong personalities who evoke such loyalty and following. Personalism accounts for bringing to the religious collective life and action a subjective and personal standard.

3. *Paradox of the Soul.* Realist and idealist, one can be both without confusion or confinement. The realism and idealism entwined in the soul of the Hispanic is indeed a strange paradox that defies neat classification and proves difficult for people to understand. Not infrequently a Hispanic becomes both by turns.

In Hispanic spirituality this is best seen in the paradox of *el Cristo Español* (The Spanish Christ). The Catholicism that reached Latin America and impacted Spanish cultures everywhere presents a Christ that responds to the supreme dread of death and passion for immortality of the Hispanic soul. John A. Mackay in his classic study of Spanish spirituality notes:

In Spanish religion Christ has been the center of a cult of death. And yet, paradoxically enough, it was the passion for fleshly life and immortality that created this interest in death. The dead Christ is an expiatory victim. The details of His earthly life are of slight importance and make relatively small appeal. He is regarded as a purely supernatural being, whose humanity, being only apparent, has little ethical bearing upon ours. This docetic

Christ died as the victim of human hate, and in order to bestow immortality, that is to say, a continuation of the present, earthly, fleshly existence.
The contemplation of His passion produces a sort of catharsis, as Aristotle
would say, in the soul of the worshipper, just as in the bull-fight, an analo-
gous creation of the Spanish spirit, the Spaniard sees and feels death in all its
dread reality in the fate of a victim. The total sensation intensifies his sense
of the reality and terribleness of death; it increases his passion for life, and,
in the religious realm, makes him cling desperately and tragically to the
dead Victim that died to give him immortality.[5]

While the above does not exhaust the meaning and significance of the "Spanish Christ," it does reveal the Paradox of the Soul in Hispanic spirituality. While
this interpretation can be challenged at certain points (e.g., Mackay is not as
affirming of Catholic spirituality as I am in this study), it is indicative, nevertheless, of the need for "the development of a more biblical, indigenous and engaged
Christianity"[6] for Hispanics.

4. *Community.* Hispanic spirituality has a deep appreciation for community.
The religious experience of Hispanics, particularly first generation—those recently arrived—is often traumatized in the religious ethos of North American society.
The symbiotic relationship with its cultural milieu—shot through with its collec-
tive/communal religious ethos—in Latin America is often shredded here, producing a spiritual void and often loss of faith.

This is true particularly of Catholics whose sense of identity was tied up to a
particular *pueblo* (town or people) that historically created a community. The
plaza was the center of community life, and the church the main building on the
plaza. Public worship and demonstrations and *fiestas* abounded, reinforcing the
sense of community and their sense of being *muy católico.* Joseph P. Fitzpatrick
underscores this as well:

In the United States, the *pueblo* in this sense (the community) never wor-
ships God. It guarantees to the individual the right to worship God according to his conscience. But practice of the faith in the United States is not a
community manifestation; it is a matter of personal choice or commitment.
The latin, on the other hand is "Catholic" because he belongs to a Catholic
people. This sense of identity, based on religion, which came to penetrate
the life of Latin Americans very deeply, was related to a style of Catholicism
with which they were familiar—the Catholicism of the *pueblo,* the community of which they were a part.[7]

A deep sense of community also plays no small part in the growth of the *comunidades de base* throughout the Spanish-speaking world.

One cannot fathom the growth and the depth of Hispanic pentecostalism
and its spirituality without coming to terms with the "quest for community"

that Renato Poblete and Thomas F. O'Dea posit as the key to understanding Hispanic Pentecostalism.[8]

5. *Romerías (pilgrimages) and Cursillo (retreat).* The pilgrimages of the Amerindian are manifested in Hispanic religious culture and express themselves in journeys or travels to holy shrines or holy places. In a contemporary sense "spiritual retreats" are their functional equivalents in Hispanic spirituality.

One is not surprised at the tremendous success and significance of the Catholic "*Cursillo* Movement" among Hispanics in the United States. The *cursillo*, briefly defined by Moisés Sandoval as "a once-in-a-lifetime experience, [which] consists of a three-day series of talks and other activities aimed at achieving an encounter with Christ and renewal in the church."[9] Much of the vitality of the Catholic church in the United States among Hispanics can be attributed to the *cursillo*. It has contributed much toward the Latinization (the making more Hispanic) of the Catholic church and has "laid the basis for a social apostolate contrasting with the individualistic piety in much Latin religious worship."[10]

Sandoval undelines the important role of the *cursillo* in the following:

Perhaps no other movement has done more to Latinize the Church in the U.S. than the Cursillo. The movement started in Spain in 1947. Brought to the United States in 1957, it has influenced many leaders and developed others. César Chavez and others prominent in the *Movimiento* are cursillistas. Father José Alvarez, who has long been active in the Spanish apostolate in New York, credits the Cursillo movement with saving the faith of the Hispanic people of New York at a time when they were getting little attention in the church.[11]

In mainline Protestant and Pentecostal circles the "spiritual retreats" continue to play an ever-increasing role in leadership training.

6. *Musical élan.* To speak of a musical élan and Hispanic spirituality is to speak about that particular quality permeating Hispanic culture, a gift from our African heritage, that expresses and impresses all religious experiences with an emotional depth of transcendance, joy, and liberation.

Hispanic spirituality, particularly among Pentecostals, places great value on an emotional musical expression in its liturgy. While its hymnology may not be of "aesthetic grandeur," by some standards of "high" culture, it nevertheless is increasingly an autochthonous expression of the depth of Hispanic anguish and aspirations. On close analysis it reveals both the groans of their oppressed souls and the triumph over anguish and sorrow by their religious faith.

As noted previously, music serves many other functions than to provide joy and a sense of well-being: it unites people, transmits social values, denounces injustices, influences human behavior, and puts to sleep or awakens for the struggle.[12]

In the development of Hispanic spirituality, music in one or more of these functions has also served them well.

7. *Fiesta (celebration)*. In Hispanic spirituality there is a ubiquity of and propensity for *fiestas*. It is cause and effect of a religious cultural heritage that celebrates and affirms life as a gift. From Baptismal *fiestas* to *fiestas patronales* (patron saint festivals/celebrations) the religious and social calendar of Hispanics marks these and other occasions that celebrate life and community. According to Octavio Paz, "every true fiesta is religious because every true festival is communion."[13]

Whether Catholic, Protestant, or Pentecostal, *fiesta* characterizes and expresses a deep spirituality, a yearning of the heart, and the heart's response that life is worth living. In the words of Virgilio Elizondo, "the tragedies of their history have not obliterated laughter and joy, fiesta is the mystical celebration of a complex identity, the mystical affirmation that life is a gift and is worth living."[14]

8. *Family*. The central role of the family is one of the salient characteristics of Hispanic culture. Hispanic spirituality is imbued deeply by familism. Let me comment briefly on three familistic values: (1) *compadrazgo*, (2) *machismo*, and (3) *la Virgen*.

Compadrazgo (godparentage) plays the significant role of knitting the community and formalizing informal ties of friendship.[15] The *compadrazgo* system is at heart a religious act of committing godparents to bringing up in the faith the godchild—although it plays other socioeconomic roles. It is a formal sacralization of the extended family, so dear to Hispanic culture. It also speaks prophetically of the need to sacralize human ties beyond that of blood.

Machismo is a familistic value that has impacted spirituality in an oblique, yet fundamental way. This complex of values known as *machismo* above all speaks of a family structure where authority is vested in the male head of the family, and where a particular definition of masculinity emphasizes physical and sexual prowess. While debate and controversy surround this concept (pro and con), in the final analysis all agree that it has contributed to maintaining Hispanic women in a subordinate role and status.

There are several implications of *machismo* for Hispanic spirituality. The most obvious one is the marginalization of women from leadership roles in the church (particularly in the Catholic priesthood) and the implicit, and often explicit, assumption that only males can handle, have traffic with, and mediate the "mysterium tremendum."[16]

The seeming paradox, in view of *machismo,* is the role of *la Virgen* in Catholic spirituality. *La Virgen* is critical for our understanding Catholic spirituality. Marianism or Mariology describes that movement within the Roman Catholic Church that emphasizes the special veneration of the figure of the Virgin Mary. Catholic spirituality places great emphasis on the Virgin Mother. John A. Mackay, while speaking of the Spanish Christ, speaks of *la Virgen* as becoming the "Queen of Life" and "Sovereign Lady" in Catholic spirituality:

A Christ known in life as an infant and in death as a corpse, over whose helpless childhood and tragic fate the Virgin Mother presides; a Christ who

became man in the interests of eschatology, whose permanent reality resides in a magic wafer bestowing immortality; a Virgin Mother who by not
tasting death, became the Queen of Life—that is the Christ and that the Virgin who came to America! He came as Lord of Death and of the life that is to
be; she came as Sovereign Lady of the life that now is.[17]

In Protestant and Pentecostal spirituality the "brothers" and "sisters" in the
church become a family, often the only family available to them in the *barrio.* It
not only provides the psychological and social service support needed, but in a
deep religious sense mediates (as the "body of Christ") and sacralizes their spiritual needs.

If we are to understand Hispanic spirituality, and if we are to nurture an *authentic* and *relevant* Hispanic spirituality, we must look to and "drink from our own
wells." We must see the critical role our cultural heritage plays in our spirituality
and affirm those positive characteristics that make up our cultural traits and value
orientations; ones that indeed have been hammered out on the anvil of our socio-
history and culture.

Part 3
All for One and One for All:
La Comunidad

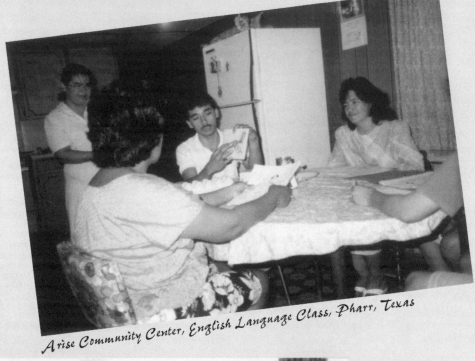

Arise Community Center, English Language Class, Pharr, Texas

Street Festival, San Antonio, Texas

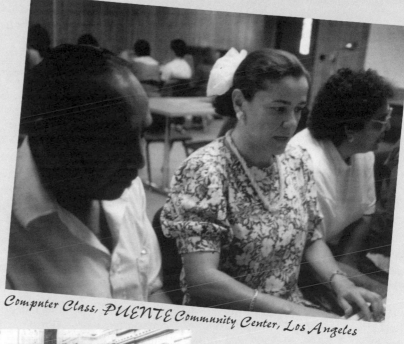

Computer Class, PUENTE Community Center, Los Angeles

Street Festival, San Antonio, Texas

Olvera Street, Los Angeles

Part 3
All for One and One for All: La Comunidad

The sociologist Daniel Bell has described commmunity as a consciousness as well as a primordial cultural link. Community, he says, "consists of individuals who feel some consciousness of kind which is not contractual, and which involves some common links through primordial cultural ties. Broadly speaking, there are four such ties: race, color, language and ethnicity."[1] As important as these ties are for the Latino, those of family and religion are even more "primordial" in creating community. In their religious beliefs and in their family practices, Latinos exhibit an organic view of life, one that sees the basic interconnectedness of the individual to the family, to God, and to the community.

Any community, including a Latino community, is made up of families sharing values and experiences and held together by popular institutions and observance of public occasions. It is not just a collection of people living in proximity, but a kind of extended family connected by self-help organizations, places of worship, neighborhood networks, community centers, business associations, educational centers, and artistic establishments, but often besieged by the social ills of the broader society, such as drugs and crime.

Yet community does not necessarily depend exclusively on tangible links and ties. Community connections, according to sociologist Benedict Anderson, can actually be mentally created where they do not already exist. They can be imagined; in other words, a sense of community can be willed into existence.[2] For example, the fantastic memories of Cuba created by some of the newly arrived exiles froze forever a 1950s idealization of Havana, Varadero Beach, and other places recalled with deep nostalgia, but they also served to unite and rally Cubans around a positive image. Similarly, displaced Chileans, Uruguayans, and Argentines who fled the brutal regimes in their countries in the 1970s often invented a mythic paradise when describing their homelands to their children born in the United States. They created a false vision, but a comforting one that bonded exiles in a common experience.

Ethnicity is both a primordial tie and a mechanism for imagining community, because for the Latino the

term "community" has little meaning without the qualifiers "Mexican," "Puerto Rican," "Cuban," or "Dominican." With these adjectives, the term "community" comes to life. It connotes pride in the *barrio* and its ethnic heritage, and solidarity in tackling community issues and problems. Parades, floats, concerts, and theatrical performances all help to strengthen ethnic identification and to promote a sense of community, of belonging. Community festivals, religious and secular, offer numerous opportunities for events in which all can participate. The solemn Good Friday procession in Chicago's predominantly Mexican Pilsen neighborhood; the boisterous Puerto Rican Day parade every June in New York City; and the raucous Calle Ocho festival every March in Miami all are public expressions of a sense of community and of identification with one's ethnic heritage.

The readings offered here explore the realm of connectedness and focus on very different types of communities: an urban *barrio* galvanized by the threat of gentrification; a rural town inspired by the leadership of a strong individual; a religious order in the throes of redefining the meaning and limits of community; political activism by public-interest coalitions; gang membership for youths desiring protection and status in the tough world of the inner city; low rider club membership for youths seeking a more positive way of belonging; and grass-roots efforts at organizing women *maquiladora* workers in Mexico.

In each case, community is a defense against disruptive change, economic deprivation, or difficult social conditions. And in each case, the value of the whole is greater than the sum of its parts.

Dolores Prida

This Cuban American playwright has been widely praised for her works such as *Beautiful Señoritas* (©1977), *Coser y Cantar* (©1981), *Savings* (©1985), *Pantallas* (©1986), and *Botánica* (©1990) (all included in *Beautiful Señoritas and Other Plays* [Houston: Arte Público Press, 1991]), which explore the themes of ethnic identity, generational and gender conflict, social class, and community through satire, music, and the incorporation of popular culture.

Savings, from which this reading is taken, is a musical comedy about a serious theme—the gentrification of a New York City neighborhood and the challenge that this unwelcome change presents to longtime residents.

Savings

Characters

LEILA ZUKOV. The bank pianist. About 50.

MRS. GLORIA DOMINGUEZ. A Puerto Rican lady, about 48.

MRS. SYLVIA CABRERA. A Cuban lady, about 45.

LEROY YOUNG. A Black man, about 30.

MRS. BORESTEIN. A frail, gentle Jewish old lady, about 80.

FRED GONZALEZ. A Hispanic yuppie (young upward mobile professional) in his late twenties. A computer consultant.

MARCELLO MOFFETTI. The bank manager, about 59.

EDDIE RODRIGUEZ. The mailman. Hispanic.

THE TELLERS. Two ladies of indeterminate age. These two actresses/singers will also play PEGGY CULPEPPER, a punk artist; MS. WONG, a neighbor; VICTORIA FRIBBLE, director of an aerobics exercise studio; JANE, her assistant; and a PARAMEDIC.

Set

The set consists of a piano, preferably a baby grand, surrounded by ten to twelve chairs with wheels. Some of these chairs will be occupied by mannequins when the action begins. The other mannequins will be placed on other chairs as the action progresses.

The backdrop should resemble the inside of a glass window at a bank. We can see part of the lettering backwards. There's a single door coming in from the street at stage right. At stage left there is the manager's office. At stage right there are the tellers' windows. The windows are half-doors, which can open completely to allow tellers to step out.

There is also a front drop which resembles the bank as seen from the street. This drop has a see-though panel (the window) through which we can see the inside of the bank. This drop is used three times during the play.

Time

OVERTURE: Sometime in the past.

ACT I covers the span of two days in the summer of 1985.

ACT II covers the next day.

Place

The lobby of a neighborhood savings bank where free piano concerts are offered every afternoon.

Musical Numbers

Act One

OVERTURE—Pianist
1. THERE GOES THE NEIGHBORHOOD—The Company
2. SUBTLETIES—Mofetti and Leila
3. TUTTI TOFUTTI—Tellers and Mailman
4. SAVINGS—Mrs. Borestein
5. IRON PUMPING WOMAN—Leroy
6. LEILA'S THEME—Leila
7. DEAR POSTMASTER GENERAL—Mailman
8. SONG TO LA VIRGEN—Mrs. Domínguez and Mrs. Cabrera

Act Two

9. GOOD AFTERNOON—Mofetti and Company
10. LEILA'S THEME (Reprise)—Leila and Company
11. GENTRIFICATION—Fred
12. LEILA AT NOONTIME—Mofetti
13. AEROBICS—Victoria Fribble and Assistant
14. MAKE ME BELIEVE—Leroy
15. ONE LAST SONG—Leila and Company
16. WE WON'T BE MOVED—Ms. Wong and Company

•

Savings was first performed at INTAR Hispanic American Theater in New York City, on 15 May 1985 with the following cast:

LEILA ZUKOV	D'Yan Forest
MARCELLO MOFETTI	Lawrence Reed
FRED GONZALEZ	Al Ferrer
SYLVIA CABRERA	Georgia Gálvez
MRS. BORESTEIN	Judith Granite
GLORIA DOMINGUEZ	Carmen Rosario
MAILMAN	Edward M. Rodríguez
LEROY YOUNG	Peter Jay Fernández
TELLER 1, PEGGY CULPEPPER, VICTORIA FRIBBLE and THE PARAMEDIC	Marilyn Schnier
TELLER 2, JANE, MS. WONG	Ricci Reyes Adán

It was directed by Max Ferrá. Music by Leon Odenz, ASCAP. Music © copyright by Leode Music Publishing, ASCAP. Lyrics by Dolores Prida. Choreography by Frank Pietri.

Overture

The front drop is down. We see the action from "outside" the bank. In the dark we hear the beginning of the overture. Slowly, a baby spot reveals LEILA *the pianist. She plays with passion and style. Immediately all the lights go up slowly and we see the bank customers sitting in various positions.* MRS. BORESTEIN *is lost in her memories;* FRED *is doing accounts on a small pocket calculator.* MRS. DOMINGUEZ *fans herself.* MRS. CABRERA *is a rapt listener.* LEROY *is distracted. The two* TELLERS *are behind their windows: one is filing her nails, the other one is reading a newspaper. As each customer speaks, he or she turns to his/her left or right and speaks to the dummy sitting there. Some of the speeches will overlap for a few lines at a time. Music plays throughout.*

FRED: . . . for example, let's say you want to know into how many slices you should cut a banana so that you have one slice for each spoonful of cornflakes, you feed the information into the computer and it tells you exactly what to do . . .

MRS. CABRERA: . . . of course, I didn't play this type of music. (*Waves toward piano.*) Señora Carrillo, my piano teacher in Havana, taught me real classy music. My best piece was "Over the Waves."

LEROY: . . . clothes make the man. You can't be too careful about the way you dress.

MRS. BORESTEIN: . . . I couldn't remember the beginning or the end of my stories . . . so finally I decided not to go to Atlantic City after all . . .

MRS. DOMINGUEZ: I used to own a *botánica* down the block . . . herbs, images, holy water, all types of utensils for the believer. People are so desperate to believe, you know . . . It was a good business. Then, they sold the building . . .

MRS. CABRERA: . . . my husband is a businessman. He owns El Malecón Chino down the block. The oldest Cuban-Chinese restaurant in this neighborhood . . . He is Dominican. I taught him Cuban cuisine. The Chinese part he learned in Chinatown.

FRED: . . . I bought it real cheap. I had my doubts about moving back to this neighborhood, but it is changing. And I am a businessman after all.

LEROY: . . . I couldn't stand wearing the same clothes day in, day out, getting all messy walking in the jungle, killing people. Wearing those clothes didn't make me a man . . .

MRS. DOMINGUEZ: . . . I now live in the Bronx. Can't afford the rent here any longer. But I still come down for the concerts. I love music.

MRS. CABRERA: . . . I haven't played the piano since I came here. The only keys I hit nowadays are those of the cash register at my husband's restaurant . . .

MRS. BORESTEIN: . . . Twenty-eight years I have been coming here. I don't come for the music. I come for the air conditioning in the summer and the heat in the winter. In the spring I go to Atlantic City . . .

At this point the musical overture should go into the beginning of the next song.

MRS. DOMINGUEZ: Back in 1946, when my mother first opened the *botánica* down the block, some people said: "There goes the neighborhood. All this voodoo hoodoo at our doorsteps!"

TELLERS begin the song stepping out of their booths. Later on everyone joins in, including MR. MOFETTI, who comes out of his office, and the MAILMAN, who enters from the street. This should have a choreography in which bank customers move the chairs around (their own and those with dummies on them).

There Goes the Neighborhood

Easy 2

Voo-doo, Hoo-doo, There goes the neigh-borhoo-doo
Voo-doo, Hoo-doo, There goes the neighborhood! (1) Bo-
(1) degas, bagel shops, bo-ta-ni-cas, sweat shops, juke boxes, record shops, ducktails and hot rods
(2) Beatles, head shops, marches at the bus stops, gurus, mantras, electric second hand shops
(3) Blacks and whites, Jews and gen- tiles, Hin- dus, Krauts, Spics and orien- tiles.
(4) Got very strange you saw diff'rent colors, heard diff'rent sounds, you smelled diff'rent odors

(1, 2, 4) It used to be so nice, it used to be so
(3) This bar- rio used to be, a dan- dy neigh-bor-

fine, But since they moved in with their voo-doo
hood,

Hoo -doo, Since they moved in There went the

Neigh- bor- hood!

(FRED AND LEROY)
Remember when the girls hung out at the candy store
Drooling over egg creams and Coca Cola

(TELLERS)
The boys they wanna marry were out in a pack
There was never any time to get them in the sack

(LEROY AND FRED)
And when the
Candy man stopped
Delivering the stuff
Then the juke box sang
Of sex and drugs
In the old candy store, yeah, yeah, yeah
At the old candy store, yeah, yeah, yeah
At the old candy . . .

Beatles, head shops,
Marches at the bus stops,
Gurus, mantras,

(FRED)
I'd rather meditate
I'd rather contemplate
I'd rather make love all night long
A girl burned her bra
A boy burned the flag
On top of the counter at the old candy store

(LEROY)
After the blast was past
And we were left alone
To pick and shovel
To riff and raff
To clean the street with our back
Again they are sayin' Hooooooooo

Everyone exits. Blackout. End of overture.

Act One

When lights come up it is another day. There are only three dummies sitting in various chairs on both sides of the piano. Only LEILA is onstage, standing by the piano arranging her sheet of music. MOFETTI opens the door of his office, sticks his head out, looks right and left, sneaks up behind LEILA.

MOFETTI: *(Smelling her ear.)* Hmmm!

LEILA: *(Startled.)* Marcello! Have you gone crazy?

MOFETTI: Long ago.

LEILA: You used to be more careful.

MOFETTI: I still am. It was just an impulse. It must be the heat.

LEILA: It is 50 degrees in here.

MOFETTI: You used to be more romantic that that.

LEILA: That was last year.

MOFETTI: What's wrong with this year?

LEILA: I don't get to see you as often.

MOFETTI: You see me every day. I see you every day.

LEILA: You know what I mean.

MOFETTI: We've been over this before, haven't we?

LEILA: Yes, we have. Still, I prefer last year. And the one before.

MOFETTI: Nothing's changed for me.

LEILA: That's easy for you to say.

MOFETTI: Leila, I never deceived you. We both have been very clear about this since the very beginning, remember?

LEILA: I remember what I said then . . . (LEILA *plays and begins the song.*)

Subtleties

LEILA:
I'm accessible
I'm obtainable
If you want me
You can have me
I am ready
I am willing
I am able
I'm available

If you want me
You can touch me
You can kiss me
I'm available

MOFETTI:
She thinks
I'm irresistible
I find she's
irrepressible
If my wife Mabel
Should find out
She'd think I'm
So contemptible

But what can I do
If she says
She's available

LEILA:
If you want to
You can touch me

MOFETTI:
I can kiss her
I can have her

LEILA:
There's no time to waste at twilight
When darkness is due to arrive

MOFETTI:
It was a convenient arrangement
Because we were hardly alive

LEILA:
I'm accessible
I'm obtainable
If you want me
I am ready
I am willing
I am able
I'm available

MOFETTI:
She thinks
I'm irresistible
I find she's
irrepressible
If my wife Mabel
Should find out
She'd think I'm
So contemptible
But what can I do
If she says
She's available

BOTH:
It's unromantic
Unacceptable

But we kept company
Early evenings
We made music
Before the rush hour
'Cause we were willing
Able
Lonely
Ready
And available

After the song FRED *enters.* MOFETTI *goes toward his office.*

FRED: Good morning, Mr. Mofetti.

MOFETTI: Good morning, Mr. González.

FRED: I wonder if you have a moment. I've been meaning to talk to you about this new line of computers I'm representing.

MOFETTI: Maybe some other time. I have a lot of work to do right now.

FRED: I'm glad you said that. Because precisely that's my point. With this computer you won't have so much work to do. It will practially manage the bank all by itself.

MOFETTI: Thanks, Fred, I like my work. Besides, don't you know what our motto is? "People to People Banking." Have a good day. (MOFETTI *goes into his office.*)

FRED: *(FRED, without missing a beat, turns to* LEILA.*)* How about you, Ms. Zukov?

LEILA: Oh, Fred, what would I do with a computer?

FRED: You mean you haven't heard about the new Japanese computer piano?

LEILA: Heaven forbid!

FRED: Ms. Zukov, you have to look ahead—into the future. You are not going to be playing the piano at this bank forever.

LEILA: Why not?

FRED: Well, for one, this bank may not be here much longer. The neighborhood is changing.

LEILA: This bank will always be here. This neighborhood has changed many times before and people always continued to save money.

FRED: The building may be sold.

LEILA: The Walenska family will never do that.

FRED: Who are they?

LEILA: The owners.

FRED: A "mom and pop" bank! That kind of business is going the way of the hula hoop. I insist you should think about that computer piano.

MRS. CABRERA: *(Entering.)* Good morning.

LEILA and FRED: Good morning, Mrs. Cabrera.

FRED: *(*MRS. CABRERA *sits down next to a dummy. She looks at it and nods hello.* FRED *sits next to her.)* Mrs. Cabrera, I was thinking . . .

MRS. CABRERA: No. *(To* LEILA.*)* Are you starting soon, Leila? I have to get back to the restaurant . . . we are short of help today.

LEILA: As soon as more people come in.

FRED: *(MRS. BORESTEIN enters from the street. She walks slowly, aided by a cane. FRED gets up and helps her to her seat.)* Mrs. Borestein, here, let me help you. How are you today?

MRS. BORESTEIN: Thank you, Leroy. I am fine. How are you? *(MRS. BORESTEIN sits on the other side of the dummy.)*

FRED: Fred. I'm Fred.

MRS. BORESTEIN: Of course you are.

FRED: Have you thought about our conversation?

MRS. BORESTEIN: I don't think I'll be going to Atlantic City this week.

FRED: No. I mean about the computer. The word processor, for your novels.

MRS. BORESTEIN: Ah, that. I gave up writing long ago. I kept forgetting the plot.

FRED: Precisely. With a computer you won't have that problem. It will remember for you . . .

MRS. BORESTEIN: Nobody reads books anymore.

FRED: Romantic novels are selling very well in the supermarkets nowadays. Now is the time for you to get back in the business. And with a computer . . .

MRS. DOMINGUEZ: *(MRS. DOMINGUEZ, entering.)* Hello, everybody. *(Sits down, exhausted.)*

MRS. CABRERA: Hi, Sylvia, you look bushed.

MRS. DOMINGUEZ: That subway was like a furnace.

FRED: In this weather you should take the bus.

MRS. DOMINGUEZ: From the Bronx? What I really would like to do is move back here. It was so easy living down the street.

FRED: Why don't you move back?

MRS. DOMINGUEZ: For the same reason I moved out. I can't afford it.

MAILMAN: *(The MAILMAN enters. In a booming voice, from the door.)* Mailman!

LEILA: Hello, Eddie, Mofetti was asking for you.

MAILMAN: I'm sure it isn't the mail he's expecting from me. *(Calling out.)* Mr. Mofetti!

MOFETTI: *(MOFETTI comes out of his office.)* Hi, Eddie, what's new?

MAILMAN: *(Handing MOFETTI a pack of letters.)* What's new? *(Gets closer to MOFETTI. Confidentially.)* If I were you, Mr. Mofetti, I'd put all my dough on Pretty Feet.

MOFETTI: That horse hasn't won a race in months! What else is new?

MAILMAN: *(Thinking.)* What else is new? . . . Hmmm . . . Oh, yes! You mean you haven't seen it?

MOFETTI: Seen what?

MAILMAN: They've just put up the sign.

MRS. CABRERA: What sign?

MAILMAN: You'll never guess what it is.

FRED: What?

MAILMAN: The new store.

MRS. DOMINGUEZ: You mean the one where my *botánica* used to be?

MAILMAN: That one. You'll never guess what it is!

FRED: An arts and crafts boutique!

LEILA: Can't be. There are already three of those on the block.

MRS. CABRERA: I hope it is a *bodega.* Since Mi Tierra closed I have to walk five blocks to the supermarket. And they don't even have yuca there.

MAILMAN: No, it's not a *bodega.* It is "Tutti-Tofutti—Health Restaurant and Salad Bar."

MRS. CABRERA: Tutti what?

FRED: Tofutti. It is a nondairy ice cream. Made from beans.

MRS. CABRERA: *(Scandalized.)* From beans! *¡Qué barbaridad!* What are they doing to *our* food!

MRS. DOMINGUEZ: And in *my* botánica!

MRS. CABRERA: Tafetta, you say?

MRS. BORESTEIN: I had a dress like that. Dark green it was . . . Dark green tafetta . . . with ruffles. It was long, a gown . . . for parties and occasions.

LEROY: *(LEROY enters eating tofutti.)* Yo! Have you seen what they just opened next to the Vade Retro Gallery?

MAILMAN: *Tofutti!*

TELLER1: *(TELLERS stick their heads out of their windows and sing in harmony.) Tofutti!*

TELLER 2: *Tofutti!*

LEROY: Yeah! and they're giving away free samples!

Music begins. TELLERS *come out of their booths and sing along with the* MAILMAN.)

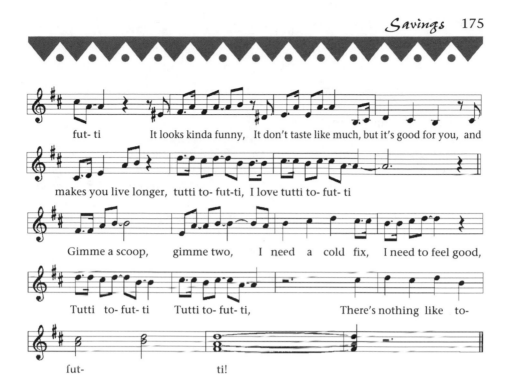

fut- ti   It looks kinda funny,   It don't taste like much, but it's good for you, and

makes you live longer, tutti to- fut-ti, I love tutti to- fut- ti

Gimme a scoop,   gimme two,   I need a cold fix, I need to feel good,

Tutti to- fut- ti   Tutti to- fut- ti,   There's nothing like to-

fut-   ti!

It costs a few pennies
It has no lactose
But it feeds you well
And makes you look better

Tutti Tofutti I love
Tutti Tofutti
There's nothing in the world
Like tofutti
Gimme a scoop
Gimme two
I need a cold fix
I need to feel good

Tutti Tofutti I love
Tutti Tofutti
There's nothing in the world
Like tofutti

The TELLERS and the MAILMAN exit through the street door, followed by FRED, MRS. CABRERA and MRS. DOMINGUEZ.

MRS. DOMINGUEZ: *(Exiting.)* Come on, let's get some!
MRS. CABRERA: *(Following MRS. DOMINGUEZ.)* I gotta try this tafetta . . .
FRED: Anything for free!

LEROY: *(After they leave,* LEROY *stands up and addresses* MOFETTI.*)* Mr. Mofetti, I wonder if I could have a word with you. Private.

MOFETTI: Sure, come into my office.

MRS. BORESTEIN: *(To herself.)* . . . I think it was blue. Blue tafetta . . . low cut . . . *(She turns to the dummy sitting next to her. Music begins.)* I wore it the first time David took me to Atlantic City . . . I have a picture right here. *(Pulls out an old perfumed soap box from her purse, opens it, and fingers some of the contents. Pulls out a photograph, shows it to dummy.)* . . . David and I used to walk for hours, up and down the boardwalk . . . under my parasol . . . *(Puts picture back. Takes out bank book, flips through the pages.)* Maybe at the end of the year I'll have enough saved to go back there . . . *(She puts bank book inside box. She sings.)*

Savings

Put a dime away
For a rainy day
Save your memories
Put it all inside
In that little box
The one he gave you
Full of perfumed soap
That Valentine's Day
In nineteen forty-eight

Put a dime away
For a rainy day
To buy a bottle of wine
With your life's savings
That fit in a box
The one he gave you
Full of perfumed soap
That Valentine's Day
In nineteen forty-eight

When you are all alone
Waiting for a check
That won't pay the bills
Piling up in that box
The one he gave you
In nineteen forty-eight

Put a dime away
For a rainy day
Hoping to make a difference
When no one will care

If you're still alive
Inside a little box
The one he gave you
That Valentine's Day
Back in nineteen forty-eight

    Mrs. Borestein *continues to look inside her box. Lights go up.* Leroy *enters from* Mofetti's *office. He looks dejected, sits next to* Mrs. Borestein. *She looks at him, returning to reality.*

Mrs. Borestein: Today is a different day, isn't it?

Leroy: Yes, it is. But tomorrow . . . tomorrow will really be more different, Mrs. B.

Mrs. Borestein: Most of the time one day is no different than the next.

Leroy: Not for me. Tomorrow I won't have a place to live in.

Mrs. Borestein: What happened, Fred?

Leroy: I'm Leroy.

Mrs. Borestein: Of course you are. What happened, son?

Leroy: I got the final notice a couple of days ago. I have to leave by tomorrow. I knew this was going to happen when the building was sold. Since then, the new owner has been harassing the tenants to get us out. I've been trying to get some money to move, but, no way . . . everything is so expensive.

Mrs. Borestein: Have you thought about Atlantic City?

Leroy: No, Mrs. B, I haven't. I like this city and I'd like to stay here. In fact, I'd like to stay in that apartment. I've lived there for eight years, I've put a lot of work in it.

Mrs. Borestein: Where are you going to sleep?

Leroy: Where to sleep is the least of my problems. There's always the subway, the streets, Grand Central Station. The problem is, where will I hang all my clothes? Shopping bags won't do.

Mrs. Borestein: Don't you have any relatives?

Leroy: Not here.

Mrs. Borestein: Atlantic City is such a nice place.

Leroy: Mrs. B, Atlantic City is not what it used to be. I've told you before. Now it's a gambling resort. It is full of casinos, chorus girls . . .

Mrs. Borestein: *(Ignoring* Leroy's *words.)* David and I used to take our constitutional along the boardwalk every evening.

Leroy: Mrs. B . . . *(To himself, giving up.)* Ah, why spoil her memories . . .

Mrs. Borestein: Here, let me show you. *(Pulls out another photograph from her box and shows it to* Leroy.) That's David. Guess who that one is? *(*Mrs. Borestein *has shown this picture to* Leroy *many times before, but he always makes believe it is the first time he sees it.* Leila *watches the action.)*

Leroy: This beautiful lady here? Who could that be? She looks like a movie star to me!

Leila: *(From the piano.)* Let me see that.

MRS. BORESTEIN: *(LEROY goes over to the piano with the photograph. MRS. BORESTEIN gets up and goes towards the piano too.)* I'm the one with the hat.
LEILA: You look beautiful, Mrs. Borestein.
LEROY: And look at Mr. Borestein! That white suit!

LEILA plays "Savings" reprise. MRS. BORESTEIN sings.

. . . Full of perfumed soap
That Valentine's Day
Back in 1948 . . .

The three remain there looking at photographs throughout the following scene. FRED enters from the street with PEGGY CULPEPPER, the punk rocker. They are both eating tofutti. They are in the middle of a conversation. They stand behind a line of dummies in front of the cashier's window.

PEGGY: . . . all this thing about beauty is a load of shit. Who said art has to be beautiful? I sing about ugliness. About everyday life ugly things. I know they are ugly. Ugly is ugly and we should learn to appreciate it . . . Oh, my God! Look at this line!
FRED: How do you describe what you do?
PEGGY: I am a minimal retro avant garde expressionist singer. That's what my boyfriend Julian says.
FRED: I see.
PEGGY: I sing Saturdays at the Scum Club. It is around the corner, you know.
FRED: Yes, I've seen it.
PEGGY: *(Impatient.)* This line is always the same! It sucks . . . and I have to cash this check. I gotta get more garbage bags.
FRED: Spring cleaning?
PEGGY: Naw, they are for a new sculpture.
FRED: Are you a sculptor, too?
PEGGY: No, Julian is. I help him at the gallery—the Vade Retro. You've seen it, next to the new Tofutti. It used to be in Soho, but he couldn't afford the rent there anymore. I think the same thing is gonna happen here—for sure . . . Are you new around here too?
FRED: Yes. And no. I live here now. I bought a house a while back. Real cheap. I just finished fixing it up. I live on the top floor. My office is on the ground floor. The rest I rent. Real expensive. But I used to live in this neighborhood a long time ago.
PEGGY: Ah. I'm from California. It was too pretty for me, ya know. I love it here. But, it's changing. I moved here because it was so different, ya know. Different people, like wow, different things. Now almost everybody looks like me. *(Impatient, looking towards TELLERS' windows.)* What are they doing in there? They are so slow!

FRED: Humans are useless for this kind of work. They should be fired and replaced with Lizzie.

PEGGY: Who's she?

FRED: It is a computer. Very efficient, very fast.

PEGGY: *(Dumb.)* Ah.

FRED: I'm a computer consultant. Here's my card. I also sell them. Could I interest you in one maybe?

PEGGY: Naw. They're not ugly enough . . . *(Looking at the line.)* This is too much! Like, ya know, I can't wait any longer. I'll come back later. *(PEGGY turns to leave. FRED follows her.)*

FRED: I'll walk you back to the gallery . . . *(Exiting.)* Vade Retro—that's a good name.

PEGGY: Julian read it somewhere, ya know, like a book or something. *(FRED and PEGGY exit.)*

LEROY: *(Holding a photograph.)* That was a nice apartment you and Mr. David had.

LEILA: *(Taking the photograph.)* Yes. They don't make them like that anymore.

MRS. BORESTEIN: I lived there before I met him. He just moved in.

LEROY: Smart move.

MRS. BORESTEIN: *(Going back to her seat.)* That's what you should do: find yourself a nice girlfriend with an apartment.

LEROY: Easier said than done. I've given up on girlfriends, Mrs. B.

MRS. BORESTEIN: Don't say that, Leroy. You never know whom you are going to meet tomorrow.

LEROY: Whom? I already met her. But it isn't working out—she's too busy working out . . . I met her at a gym where I used to hang out. The most beautiful Puerto Rican lady you ever saw. She was born in the South Bronx, but if you ask her, she always says, "I'm from Ponce." She assured me she was a direct descendant from the Taíno Indians. She showed me her teeth—shovel shaped incisors. That's the sign of the Indian, she says. She paid attention to me for a while because I was a musician. And everybody loves a serenade. I sang under her window for many a night. I fell in love with her, but she was already in love with someone else. A married someone else. She's been waiting for this guy for ten years. Can you imagine, Mrs. B? Ten years!

LEILA: I can imagine! *(Music begins.)*

MRS. BORESTEIN: How can she stand it?

LEROY: I told you. She lifts weights. *(LEROY sings:)*

Iron Pumping Woman

Iron pumping woman
With shovelshaped incisors
Double-pierced ears
And high-strung emotions
Long loving woman
With one-mouthful breasts

Honey-colored eyes
And tongue of sugar

Iron pumping woman
Running in the park
Drinking up a river
Crying up a storm

Long loving woman
Waiting by the phone
Can't hear my music
Can't hear my song

Sweet and soft woman
Pumping iron on a thought
Chasing time beating heart
Sweet tough lady how you sweat

Iron pumping woman
Trying to forget
How lonely are your nights
How cold is your bed

Long arms with big hands
Holding on to the wind
Iron pumping woman
Iron pumping woman
Pumping iron
And butterflies

Blackout.
When lights come up again it is another day. Only LEILA is onstage playing. Another two dummies occupy two more chairs.

MOFETTI: *(Entering from his office.)* Leila, I must speak to you. *(LEILA ignores him, continues playing.)*
MOFETTI: It is important.
LEILA: *(She stops playing.)* How important?
MOFETTI: Very.
LEILA: I waited for you all night.
MOFETTI: I thought so. I'm sorry. I was at a meeting with the bank's president. I couldn't get to a phone. Afterwards, I was so upset . . .
LEILA: What's going on, Marcello?
MOFETTI: Plenty, Leila. Plenty. *(He walks around the piano, sits on the stool next to LEILA.)* I don't know how to tell you. I don't know how to tell anyone.

LEILA: Try me.

MOFETTI: Leila . . . it's all over!

LEILA: What? What is over? . . . You mean . . . us . . . our . . .

MOFETTI: Yes, that. Everything. I saw it coming, but now it is final . . . The bank is closing. *(LEILA begins to play a very sad melody. MOFETTI listens for a while with head bowed.)* I know how you feel. But . . . how do you think I feel? *(Stands up.)* I've worked here all my life. It took me years to be promoted to manager. I don't know how to do anything else. At my age, where am I going to get another job? And I'm not ready for retirement yet! I'm full of vigor, you know that.

LEILA: *(LEILA stops playing. Gives him a look.)* Is the bank losing money?

MOFETTI: No.

LEILA: It doesn't have enough customers?

MOFETTI: It has enough.

LEILA: Then, why is it closing?

MOFETTI: They are selling the building. The Walenskas have been offered a deal they can't refuse. Also, they feel the bank can't compete with the giants.

LEILA: What will happen to the building?

MOFETTI: Well, the five floors above will be turned into luxury condominiums. Here, in the bank, there will be Victoria Fribble Dancercise Studio.

LEILA: Victoria Fribble! In this neighborhood?

MOFETTI: It is changing, Leila. And changing fast. Can't you tell? There's no future for this type of bank here.

LEILA: *(Pause. LEILA plays some more.)* There isn't really much to think about, is there? I mean, you are married. You have a wife, children, grandchildren, a dog, and a house in New Jersey. You are not going to commute just to see me, are you?

MOFETTI: I don't know . . . there are practical aspects to the situation . . . I have to consider . . .

LEILA: Let's not fool ourselves. We were a convenience to each other. Yet . . .

MOFETTI: *(Almost to himself.)* Yes, it was convenient . . . I mean, no, I . . . Leila, we have been seeing each other for twelve years. I hear you play every day . . . I'm going to miss you.

LEILA: I will miss you too, Marcello.

MOFETTI: *(LEILA plays. MOFETTI is thoughful.)* I remember when you started to play here. You brought happiness to this bank. We got a lot of customers because of you. What's more important: you brought *me* happiness.

MOFETTI kisses the top of LEILA's head and exits to his office. LEILA stares ahead in a daze. LEILA sings:

Leila's Theme

When I was young I wanted
To make the world laugh
When I was young I thought
I could make the world dance
When I was young I danced
And laughed and sang

I thought I was the world
Once when I was young

Life is a bowl of cherries
Life is a cabaret
Under the full moon
Rowing on the lake
Happy shooting the breeze

I paid no income taxes
I was a vaudeville star
I had a lover in every town
My hair was really blonde

Perhaps it was lack of talent
Perhaps it was lack of luck
But I don't really care
I have no regrets
I never made it to Carnegie Hall

Life is a bowl of cherries
Life is a cabaret
Over the rainbow
Playing the same songs
I'm now losing the game

I tried to be a winner
I dreamed of the heights of fame
I wanted love forever
My dreams did not come true

Perhaps it was all my fault
Perhaps it was not my doing
But I can't really say
I have no regrets
I never won the Academy Award

Life is a bowl of cherries
Life is a cabaret
Under the full moon
Rowing on the lake . . .

When I was young I thought
I could make the world laugh
When I was young I thought
I could make the world dance

*LEILA stops and cries, dabs her eyes with a tissue, then wipes the piano keys with it.
LEROY enters.*

LEROY: Miss Leila . . . ? Are you all right?

LEILA: I'm fine . . . thank you . . .

LEROY: Forgive me, Miss L, but you don't look fine to me.

LEILA: *(Trying to control herself.)* . . . It's nothing . . . nothing . . . just . . . life . . .

LEROY: *(Sitting next to LEILA on the piano stool.)* Come on, then . . . cheer up! Life is a
bowl of cherries . . . remember? You always say that.

LEILA: I do, don't I? You know what it is, Leroy, when you sing the same old songs
over and over, like I do? I guess you come to believe the words, the ideas they
express, even if they have nothing to do with reality. *(LEILA tries to smile, but
ends up crying.)*

LEROY: I've never seen you like this, Miss Leila . . . I bet it is that Mofetti.

LEILA: It isn't really his fault . . . it was an offer they couldn't refuse. *(LEILA plays her
theme. Up part. LEROY stops her.)*

LEROY: What offer? Who couldn't refuse? What are you talking about?

LEILA: I'm sure Mofetti will tell everyone later. It is the bank . . . it's going out of
business.

LEROY: *(Gets up thoroughly confused.)* Out of business? No, no, it can't be. When?

LEILA: Very soon. A few days, a few weeks . . . I don't know . . .

LEROY: *(Somewhat agitated, to himself.)* Then . . . then . . . there's no time to waste. I
gotta get moving. *(LEROY exits hurriedly.)*

MAILMAN: *(Entering from the street. He's about to announce his presence with his usual
operatic "Mailman" when LEROY runs into him, punching all the air out of the surprised MAILMAN. Catching his breath.)* He used to like me. What's wrong with
him? Did he finally go crazy?

LEILA: I think everybody is finally going crazy here today, Eddie.

MAILMAN: It can't be crazier than down at the post office.

LEILA: But at least the post office will always be there. It must be reassuring to work
in a place like that—solid, stable . . . an institution, like the Rock of Gibraltar.

MAILMAN: It is more like a rock around your neck. You can't imagine what it is like
in there, Miss Zukov. I'm fed up with the whole thing. I wrote a letter to the
postmater general. I hope to hear from him soon.

LEILA: What did you write to him about?

MAILMAN *sings:*

Dear Postmaster General

Dear postmaster general
Dear postmaster general
Your picture hangs on the wall
Next to our president
I feel I know you after all
And I want to say I'm not content
But

Down at the post
Down at the post
They just keep throwin' the mail
Down at the post
Down at the post
They just keep throwin' the mail

Dear postmaster general
Dear postmaster general
I bring the letters in a flash
I bring good news and bad news and love notes
I bring bills to pay checks to cash
Even junk mail I carefully tote
But what can you do?
Do you really care?
That
Packages get lost
Lines are too long
Stamps without glue
Zip codes are no good!
And why why oh why are the clerks
Always in such a bad mood?

Dear postmaster general
Dear postmaster general
I don't mind the dog bites
I don't mind the snow, the sleet
The rain, the fog, the gloom of night
The pain in the sole of my feet
But
Down at the post
Down at the post
They just keep throwin' the mail
Down at the post
Down at the post
They just keep throwin'
Keep throwin' the mail
Yours respectfully, Eddie Rodriguez.

MAILMAN: *(To MOFETTI entering from his office.)* Good afternoon, Mr. Mofetti. Here's
    your mail.
MOFETTI: Thank you, Eddie.
MAILMAN: Don't mention it. It is always a pleasure to deliver mail here.
MOFETTI: Don't you have any suggestions today?

MAILMAN: What's the use? The OTB parlor closed today. I hear Häagen-Dazs ice cream is moving in there. I guess we'll have to bet on the Swiss Almond Vanilla. Well, have a good day.

LEILA: Goodbye, Eddie. And good luck with your letter. (*MAILMAN tips his hat and exits.*)

MOFETTI: Leila, about what we talked about before . . .

LEILA: Yes?

MOFETTI: I'd like to ask you a favor . . . Please don't say anything to the customers about the bank closing. I . . .

LEILA: Don't say anything?!

MOFETTI: . . . Just for the moment, I . . .

LEILA: But, Marcello, why?

MOFETTI: I need some time . . . to prepare myself. To think.

LEILA: To think? About what? It is not fair to the customers. They should know what's happening.

MOFETTI: (*Edgy.*) I'll tell them tomorrow.

LEILA: Today, tomorrow . . . what's the difference?

MOFETTI: I'm making some calls, talking to some people . . .

LEILA: (*Hopeful.*) You think . . . you think there may be a chance? That something can be done?

MOFETTI: I doubt it, but . . .

LEILA: Have you talked to anybody who knows about these things?

MOFETTI: Like who?

LEILA: . . . like . . . Tina Wong?

MOFETTI: What does she know? A young attorney, just starting out.

LEILA: She's very bright. I hear she's now with the Chinatown Legal Services. Why don't you call her?

MOFETTI: What for? What can she do? Is she going to get me a few million dollars to buy the bank?

LEILA: There may be other options.

MOFETTI: I have to think about it.

LEILA: Think, think! All you do is think! You are so wishy-washy, Marcello! You just can't make a decision, face the consequences. Like that time you said you'd think about a divorce. How long ago was that? Can you remember?

MOFETTI: It's not that easy. One has to consider every angle of a situation.

MRS. CABRERA and MRS. DOMINGUEZ: (*Entering together from the street.*) Good afternoon.

LEILA and MOFETTI: Good afternoon. (*MRS. CABRERA and MRS. DOMINGUEZ sit down. MOFETTI turns to leave. LEILA follows him to his office.*)

LEILA: (*Whispering, angry.*) Well, if you don't call Tina Wong, I will.

MOFETTI: (*Breathing deep.*) Do whatever you want. It's useless, anyway. (*They both enter MOFETTI's office, arguing and whispering, closing the door behind them.*)

MRS. DOMINGUEZ: Hmmm . . . I wonder what's going . . .

MRS. CABRERA: (*Distracted.*) Where?

MRS. DOMINGUEZ: With Mr. Mofetti and Leila.

MRS. CABRERA: *(Uninterested.)* The same thing that's been going on for twelve years.

MRS. DOMINGUEZ: *(Opening her eyes in disbelief.)* You mean . . . the two of them? . . . Nooo! I can't believe it! You never told me!

MRS. CABRERA: You must be blind. I thought everyone knew.

MRS. DOMINGUEZ: I didn't know. I didn't even notice! . . . I guess I am not into *bochinche* as much as I used to . . . Ah, I think I'm getting old . . . You know . . . this morning I almost got mugged in the subway. Forty years living in New York and it had never happened to me! I was always so alert.

MRS. CABRERA: I don't know why you put up with all this. You have a house in Puerto Rico, why don't you go back?

MRS. DOMINGUEZ: I did once. After José passed away. We had struggled so hard for so many years to save money to buy that house in Guayama. It was the dream we came here with. I went back but stayed only three months. I couldn't get used to living there again. I missed New York. Isn't that crazy? *(She realizes MRS. CABRERA is not listening.)* Sylvia . . . you haven't heard a word I said! What's wrong with you today!

MRS. CABRERA: Ay, Gloria, *vieja,* I couldn't sleep a wink last night. Jacinto kept me up all night.

MRS. DOMINGUEZ: *(Laughing.)* Ho, ho . . . the old devil!

MRS. CABRERA: Not that! Jacinto is so worried. The landlord is raising the rent of the restaurant. A three hundred percent increase!

MRS. DOMINGUEZ: *Virgen del* Carmen!

MRS. CABRERA: And now he blames himself for not buying the building ten years ago. He could have bought it for a song. But he said running a restaurant was enough of a headache. He thought the price was high. But most of all, he didn't want to owe so much money to the bank. Do you know that he handles everything in cash?

MRS. DOMINGUEZ: Ay, *m'ija!* In this country unless you owe money to somebody, you are a nobody.

MRS. CABRERA: Now he's dying of regret. And I have to bite my tongue. I told him to buy that building. For the future, for our children. He said, "I don't want my children living in this lousy neighborhood." Well, look whose children are moving here now. *(Points to dummies.)* They can afford to pay $1500 a month for a closet and a bathroom.

LEILA enters from the manager's office dabbing at her eyes with a tissue. She sits at the piano and cleans the keyboard with the same tissue.

MRS. DOMINGUEZ: Maybe he can raise the price of food to make up for the difference in rent.

MRS. CABRERA: Ay, Gloria, who's going to pay $15 for a plate of rice and beans? . . . I don't know what we're going to do!

MRS. DOMINGUEZ: I'll tell you what. Take this. *(Takes out of her bag a manila envelope.)* When you pay the rent this month put some of these leaves in the envelope, together with the check.

MRS. CABRERA: Do you think that will help?

MRS. DOMINGUEZ: That, and a good prayer.

Music begins. MRS. DOMINGUEZ *and* MRS. CABRERA *turn their chairs around to face the audience. They kneel on the chairs and sing.*

MRS. DOMINGUEZ:

Virgen del Carmen . . .

MRS. CABRERA:

Virgen del Cobre . . .

They stop at the same time, look at each other.

MRS. CABRERA: *Excúsame,* Gloria, but *la Virgen del Carmen* is a Puerto Rican virgin. I'm the one with the problem, *chica.* Don't you think we should pray to a Cuban virgin?

MRS. DOMINGUEZ: Excuse me, Sylvia, but I am the one handling this. You are not even a Catholic!

MRS. CABRERA: When you are in trouble you have to be ecumenical.

MRS. DOMINGUEZ: Okay. They let's pray to both. *Por si acaso.*

Guaguancó

Song to La Virgen

Vir- gen del Cob- re

Ayu- da- nos hoy dan- os un

tech- o pa' vi- vii

mi vir- gen- ci- ta y to- dos los

san- tos yo te lo rue- go

Haz- me un fa- vor mi vir- gen-

ci- ta y to- dos los san- tos yo

te   lo   rue-   go   Haz-   me un fa-

vor.   Vir-   gen del   Car-   men

Help   us   this   day   Give   us   a

roof   a   place   to   live

O   ho-   ly   Vir-   gin   and   all   the

spir-   its   do   me   a   fa-   vor

I   beg   of   you   Mi   vir-   gen

ci-   ta y   to-   dos   los   san-   tos   yo

te   lo   rue-   go   A-   yu-   da-   nos

hoy!

Blackout. End of Act One.

Act Two

As the audience returns to their seats, part of the Overture will be played by LEILA. *Characters will be coming in one by one or in twos. Music continues playing as lights go down. In the dark we hear intro to the next song. As lights go up the characters are sitting in the same places they were in at the opening of the first act. There are more dummies now.* LEROY *is nervous and now and then looks into his shopping bag, as if to make sure something is indeed in there.* MOFETTI *enters from his office. He pauses in front of the door, breathes deeply, adjusts his tie, passes both his hands over the sides of his head and walks towards center stage.* MOFETTI *and the company sing.*

Good Afternoon

MOFETTI:
Good Afternoon
Ladies and gentlemen
Good afternoon

CHORUS:
Good afternoon
Mr. Mofetti:
Good afternoon

MAILMAN:
Good afternoon
Mr. Mofetti
Good afternoon

MOFETTI:
Good afternoon
Mr. Postman
Good afternoon

TELLERS:
Good afternoon
Mr. Mofetti

MOFETTI:
Good afternoon
My dear tellers
Good afternoon

MOFETTI:
Good afternoon
My lovely Leila
Good afternoon

LEILA:
Good afternoon
Marcello *(Spoken.)* Get on with it.

> LEILA *abruptly stops playing.* MOFETTI *addresses the group in pompous oratory.*

MOFETTI: My dear, dear customers. My most appreciated colleagues . . . today . . . today is a special day. Since this bank was established at the turn of the century in this very neighborhood, it has been more than just a bank. I feel it is indeed appropriate that I speak to you at this moment, during one of our concerts, because I think that these events are perhaps the most important characteristic of this bank. We are one of the very few banking institutions in the city still providing this service to the customers . . . These concerts have taken place through two world wars, through the Depression, when the neighborhood changed, when the customers changed, through bad times, through good times . . . And today, it is my duty to . . . today, I have to inform you that . . . today's concert marks . . . a special occasion . . . a very special occasion . . . today . . . today is . . . *Leila's birthday*!

LEILA: *(Standing up.* LEROY *jumps up from his seat.) My* birthday? Marcello?

LEROY: *Her* birthday!

MOFETTI: *(To* LEILA, *apologetic.)* I couldn't do it! *(To everybody, exiting to his office.)* I . . . I'll get the . . . champagne! *(*MOFETTI *runs to his office.* LEILA *tries to stop him. Everybody applauds.* LEILA *is surrounded by well-wishers.)*

MRS. DOMINGUEZ: I won't ask how many!

MRS. BORESTEIN: I wish I had known before . . .

FRED: Many happy returns!

TELLERS: Happy birthday, Mrs. Zukov!

MAILMAN: Enjoy your day.

LEILA: Thank you, thank you, but . . .

TELLER 2: Let's celebrate!

TELLER 1: Like in the old times!

MRS. BORESTEIN: Leila, sing us one of your old favorites.

MRS. DOMINGUEZ: Yes, yes. Remember when you used to say that you wanted to be the first female Liberace? *(Everybody laughs.)*

LEILA: But really, it is not . . .

MAILMAN: Come on, Miss Zukov. It is a special day.

LEROY: *(Mysterious.)* It sure is.

MRS. BORESTEIN: Why don't you play Mrs. Cabrera's favorite . . . what's the name of that waltz she used to play in Havana?

MRS. DOMINGUEZ: It was "Over the Waves," but Sylvia is not here today. So we don't have to listen to that again.

TELLER 2: Yes, play something else.

TELLER 1: Yes, play *your* favorite.

LEILA: That song is not what it used to be. *(*LEILA *sits at the piano. She plays and sings.)*

Leila's Theme (Reprise)

Life is a bowl of cherries
Life is a cabaret
Under the full moon
Rowing on the lake
Happy shooting the breeze

Life is a bowl of cherries
Life is a cabaret
Under the full moon
Rowing on the lake
Happy shooting the breeze
Happy shooting the breeze
Happy shooting the breeze

Everyone applauds.

MRS. BORESTEIN: Ah, that was lovely! We always have such good times.

MAILMAN: We sure do, Mrs. Borestein. I'm gonna miss this place . . . and all of you.

MRS. BORESTEIN: Are you leaving?

MRS. DOMINGUEZ: Did you win big at the horses?

LEILA: Oh, Eddie . . . It is about that letter you wrote, isn't it?

MAILMAN: Yes, Miss Zukov. I delivered a letter to myself this morning. From the postmaster general himself. I've been transferred. To the South Bronx.

FRED: Poor man. Hardship duty.

MAILMAN: It won't be harder than this neighborhood at one time. I used to be threatened to death for not delivering welfare checks on time. Not anymore, though. I hardly know the people I deliver mail to. You are the only people I know. Everybody else has moved. I don't really want to go, but I've got my orders.

LEROY: Did they give you a reason for the transfer?

MAILMAN: No.

LEROY: Maybe it's your looks, Eddie. Maybe they're getting "designer mailmen"— to go with the rest of the neighborhood, you know.

LEILA: I'm so sorry, Eddie. We'll miss you.

MRS. DOMINGUEZ: We have to give you a farewell party.

FRED: Here?

MRS. BORESTEIN: Sure. We have celebrated many occasions here.

MRS. DOMINGUEZ: When Sylvia's son Enrique, graduated from City College, Mr. Mofetti threw a party for him, right here in the bank. He did the same for Tina Wong.

FRED: Who's that?

MRS. DOMINGUEZ: The daughter of Mr. Wong, of Wong's Chinese Laundry. That was before your time. She has just passed the bar exam. That was big party! Imagine, she was the first lawyer born and bred in the neighborhood. Mr.

Wong was so happy he did everybody's laundry free for a month! *(Everybody laughs.)*

LEILA: A very bright young lady. *(Looking at MOFETTI.)* And courageous.

MRS. BORESTEIN: And when Leroy was in the hospital for a long time after coming back from the war, we used to tape Leila's concerts and send him the cassettes to the hospital.

LEROY: I sure appreciated that. It made me come back to the neighborhood. I felt I had friends here. But I had had other plans. I made all kinds of mental plans in that hospital bed.

LEILA: Yes, we are friends here. We've had good times and bad times, as Marce . . . Mr. Mofetti said.

LEROY: *(Glaring at FRED, then at the dummies.)* Too bad outsiders and newcomers can't appreciate that.

FRED: You are wrong about me. I am not an outsider. I was born here, in this neighborhood. Two blocks away, as a matter of fact. *(Everyone is surprised by the news.)*

MRS. DOMINGUEZ: You're putting us on. How come you never told us before?

LEROY: I don't believe it.

MRS. BORESTEIN: Funny, I don't remember you . . . but then, there are so many things I don't remember.

FRED: Oh yes, my mother lived in that house—the one that now has the expensive Central American arts and crafts—for many years. When the neighborhood went bad . . .

MRS. DOMINGUEZ: *(To MRS. BORESTEIN.)* He means when I opened my *botánica..*

FRED: . . . she decided she didn't want to raise her children here. She dreamed of the suburbs. Meaning Queens. So we moved there. I went to Catholic school in Elmhurst. Then that neighborhood began to change too. We moved to a small town in New Jersey. That changed too. We ended up in Connecticut . . . But I always liked this neighborhood, so when I read that this was going to be the next Soho, I bought an old house . . . I got it real cheap. It is an investment that's paying off . . . also, I feel I am helping improve the neighborhood by moving back here.

LEROY: *(To himself.)* Asshole.

MRS. BORESTEIN: You mother must be very proud of you.

FRED: I'm not so sure. She can't understand why, after she worked so hard to get me out of this neighborhood, I've come back. *(Sings.)*

Gentrification

Guaracha (in 2)

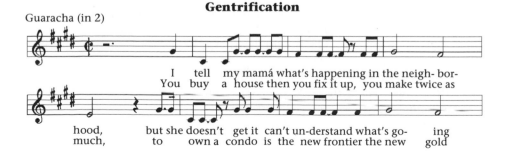

I   tell   my mamá what's happening in the neigh- bor-
You buy a house then you fix it up, you make twice as

hood,   but she doesn't get it can't un-derstand what's go-   ing
much,   to   own a condo is the new frontier the new   gold

on. I explain to her that el vie- jo barrio is not the
rush. There's the new boutique the new croissanterie and the arts and

same, Things are changing they are changing now we are playing a brand new
crafts the rents go up they keep

game! going up some people are getting the

shaft but all she says is: "O- ye m'iji- to, explain a- gain

que es lo que pasa what's going on O- ye m'iji- to, explain a- gain

no entiendo na da explíca- melo bien!"

Gen- tri- fi- ca- tion, Ma- má, gen- tri-fi-ca-

ción! "No en tien- do na- da," she says to

me. Gen- tri- fi- ca- tion, Ma- má, gen- tri-fi-ca-

ción! Los tiem- pos cam- bian We move a-

head!

I tell my *Mamá*, it's very simple to understand
This little island is turning into a wonderland
It's my Manhattan, I wanna piece of that apple pie
You'll be proud of me, I'll be proud of me

When I'm rich way before you die

I explain to her that the new ideal is to make a buck
To wear the latest, to eat the best to own some stock
The greatest thing that has ever happened in generations
The old turf, this old turf
Is going through gentrification

But all she says is
Gentrification, *qué cosa es eso*
Oye, m'ijito, explain again
Whatever happened a *toda la gente*
That lived in the *barrio*
From long ago

Gentrification, *Mamá*
Gentrificación
No entiendo nada
She says to me
Gentrification, *Mamá*
Gentrificación
Los tiempos cambian
And we move ahead
Gentrification, *Mamá*
Gentrificación

Everybody joins in the chorus, each one giving a different meaning to the word "gentrification.": MRS. CABRERA enters from the street. She's crying loudly. Music stops.

LEILA: Mrs. Cabrera!

MRS. DOMINGUEZ: Sylvia, what's the matter?

MRS. CABRERA: Ay, *chica,* that *brujería* you gave me didn't work! All the opposite.

FRED: Witchcraft? What is she talking about?

MRS. CABRERA: The landlord was going to raise my husband's rent at the restaurant 300 percent. And Gloria here gave me some leaves to put in the envelope with the rent check to make him change his mind. But it didn't work. *(She cries.)* Now he will raise the rent 400 percent!

MRS. BORESTEIN: *Gotten Nyu!*

MAILMAN: *Ay, bendito!*

MRS. DOMINGUEZ: Well, like I said, sometimes it works, sometimes it doesn't.

MRS. CABRERA: Jacinto is desperate. He says he's closing down the restaurant and going down to Miami. I know he won't be happy there. He can't retire yet. He's a workaholic. He will die before his time!

MRS. DOMINGUEZ: Nah. I thought the same thing would happen to me when I

had to close my *botánica*. And see, here I am. I keep myself busy doing part-time *trabajitos*.

MRS. BORESTEIN: It is terrible what's happening. This . . . this . . . purification . . .

FRED: Gentrification.

MRS. BORESTEIN: That. Do you know that Leroy has also lost his apartment?

LEROY: Mrs. B., please . . .

LEILA: Leroy, why didn't you tell me?

FRED: Hey man, I'm sorry to hear that. *(LEROY glares at FRED.)*

MRS. DOMINGUEZ: Oh poor Leroy! What are you going to do?

LEROY: I have plans.

MRS. BORESTEIN: I would ask him to move in with me, but you know, they don't allow men in there . . . I mean young ones.

LEROY: Thank you, Mrs. B. Thank you.

MRS. CABRERA: I don't know where we can go. Rents are even worse in other parts of the city.

FRED: There's always the river. Boat houses, like in Hong Kong. They could make Manhattan quite exotic . . . Think of it—rice and beans on the East River . . .

LEROY: *(LEROY gets up and goes for FRED's throat. MRS. CABRERA and MRS. DOMINGUEZ hold LEROY back. The MAILMAN stands in front of FRED.)* I'll kill him! I'll kill him!

FRED: But what have I done to him?

MAILMAN: *Hablas mucha mierda, mi pana!*

MOFETTI: *(MOFETTI enters from his office with a tray loaded with champagne glasses.)* Here's the champagne! *(MOFETTI puts the tray with champagne glasses on top of the piano. Everyone helps himself.)*

MRS. CABRERA: Champagne for what!

MRS. BORESTEIN: It's Leila's birthday! How wonderful! I love champagne. I haven't had a glass since my last trip to Atlantic City . . . and that must have been back in nineteen . . .

MAILMAN: *(MOFETTI offers a glass to LEILA, who is fuming.)* I propose a toast to Leila. *(Everyone lifts the glasses and freezes. Spot on the piano. MOFETTI has also raised his glass. LEILA plays. MOFETTI sings.)*

Leila at Noontime

Leila at noontime
Ivory melts under your hands
Melody drips from your fingers
Your face and your eyes are aglow
Bright stars on the piano black top

Leila at midday
Time seems to be at a standstill
The sun bends and listens to you
The days are long and brighter
Regardless of winter or fall

Leila at nighttime
I sleep in a hammock
Of musical dreams
I hold your hand in mine
And the music belongs to me
I am Bach, Chopin
Beethoven and Brahms
Just from touching your hand
Just from touching your hand

After the song, full lights come up on the whole scene. Everyone is still holding the glasses up high. Immediately VICTORIA FRIBBLE *and her assistants enter.* VICTORIA *has red hair, wears large dark glasses and is dressed in black-and-red-striped leotards and black leg warmers.*

VICTORIA: *(To* MOFETTI.*)* Ah, Mr. Mofetti! I see you were expecting me. How kind of you. This is quite a welcome! Thank you very much. *(*VICTORIA *takes the glass of champagne from* MOFETTI'*s hand. Her assistant takes a glass from someone else. They look around the bank.)*

MOFETTI: *(To* LEILA.*)* Who is she?

LEILA: That's Victoria Fribble!

MOFETTI: Victoria Fribble! . . . Ah, yes, Ms. Fribble, of course . . . why don't you . . . er . . . come into my office to discuss your . . . er . . . new account.

LEILA: *(Exasperated. Whispering.)* There you go again! This is a perfect moment to tell them!

MOFETTI: *(Whispering.)* Let me handle this.

VICTORIA: I came to check out the place. This is my assistant, Jane.

JANE: Hi!

MOFETTI: Hi.

VICTORIA: *(Looking around.)* Not bad . . . not bad at all. Of course it needs some changes . . . *(Bends down to touch the floor.)* . . . Maybe a new floor . . . Hmmm . . . I don't know . . . Jane, let's try it. *(The two lie on the floor and begin to do exercises à la Jane Fonda. They sing along.)*

Aerobics

Left right
Right left
Stretch
Stretch
Breath
Breath

And grind
Slim your waist
Flatten your tummy
Harden your ass
Don't be a fat dummy

LEROY: *(Before the number is over,* LEROY *pulls down a ski mask over his face, pulls out a gun from the shopping bag and points it at* VICTORIA *and* JANE.*)* Hold it everybody, stop this shit! Nobody moves. This is a holdup! *(To women.)* You two, in there! You are my hostages. *(Everybody screams. Women go into* TELLERS *cages.* LEROY *gives them the shopping bag.)* Here, take this. Fill it with money. Big bills. Nothing smaller than fives. And if any of you touches that alarm button, I start shooting!

VICTORIA: *(Hysterical.)* I don't even know where it is!

MRS. BORESTEIN: Leroy, what do you think you're doing?

LEROY: I'm robbing this bank, Mrs. B! That's what I'm doing! Robbing this bank!

MRS. DOMINGUEZ: But it is our money!

LEROY: Not any more!

MOFETTI: *(*LEILA *pushes* MOFETTI *forward, urging him to do something.)* Mr. Young, if I may have a word with you . . .

LEROY: Don't Mister Young me, Marcello!

LEILA: Leroy, this is crazy!

FRED: Someone should call the police!

MOFETTI: Nobody calls anybody. We'll take care of this ourselves. We are all friends here. Leroy . . .

LEROY: Shut up, Mofetti! You ain't no friend of mine. You are chicken. I have no chicken friends. When I needed you, you didn't come through!

MRS. DOMINGUEZ: Come through? With what? What?

MRS. CABRERA: What's going on here?

MOFETTI: Leroy, put that gun away and come here. Let's discuss this in a logical manner. I know you are upset about losing your apartment . . .

FRED: I wish I had my computer with me right now.

MRS. BORESTEIN: We'll help you find an apartment.

LEILA: We won't call the police.

MRS. CABRERA: Maybe my husband can get you a job in the restaurant.

MOFETTI: Leroy, I'll give you one more chance . . . *(Music begins.)*

LEROY: Sure! Tell me more! You keep us entertained with your concerts and sing-alongs while you keep *our* money, but when we need a loan to move or to buy a house, we can't get it!

MOFETTI: I don't make the rules and regulations . . . believe me, Leroy . . .

LEROY: I asked you for a loan to move and you denied it to me . . . I had no collateral! *(Sings.)*

Make Me Believe

I have to believe
I have a chance
I have to believe
My hands will come out clean
After handling the dirt
I have to believe
My mouth won't bleed
After chewing the glass

Make me believe that
I have that chance
Make me believe
And I'll run

I have to believe
I have a chance
I have to believe
I'll still enjoy the flowers
When the foul air clears
I have to believe
I'll see the light
After darkness has passed

Make me believe that
I have that chance
Make me believe
And I'll run
I can win the prize
At the end of the race
If you make me believe

I believe
I have to believe
Deep inside
I'll have a chance at peace
I'll get a crack at love
I have to believe
I have to believe

Make me believe that
I have that chance
Make me believe
And I'll run
I can win the prize
At the end of the race
If you make me believe
If you make me believe

MOFETTI: Leroy, please . . . let me explain . . .
LEROY: Explain! I don't believe a word you'd say Mofetti! You are a liar. Why don't
   you tell them! Tell them the truth! Tell them the bank is closing! Tell them it is
   going to be a Victoria Fribble Body Shop!
VICTORIA: *(Sticking her head out of a TELLER's window.)* That's me!
LEROY: Get back in there!
MRS. CABRERA: Is this true, Mr. Mofetti?

LEILA: *(To MOFETTI.)* I told you!

MRS. DOMINGUEZ: Come on, Mr. Mofetti, out with it!

MOFETTI: It is true . . . all of it.

LEILA: You forgot the condos.

MOFETTI: Yes. The apartments upstairs will be turned into luxury condominiums.

LEILA: So, dear friends, today is not my birthday. Today is really my last concert.

MRS. BORESTEIN: *(Very agitated.)* I can't believe it! I can't believe it! *(Everyone turns towards MRS. BORESTEIN.)*

MRS. DOMINGUEZ: What? What is it?

MRS. BORESTEIN: I remember everything! I remember the plots of all my novels! All of them! Even the ones I never wrote! I remember it all! Oh God . . . I remember . . . Atlantic City is full of gambling parlors! *(MRS. BORESTEIN collapses on a chair. Everyone runs towards her. FRED takes her pulse. LEROY runs to MRS. BORESTEIN. In the commotion VICTORIA FRIBBLE and her assistant escape.)*

FRED: I think she's dead. I can't feel her pulse.

LEROY: *(LEROY pushes FRED aside. Kneels down next to MRS. BORESTEIN and puts his ear to her heart.)* Don't die, old mamma! Not now. I was robbing this bank for you. To go to Atlantic City, to walk down the boardwalk, under your parasol.

FRED: You did it for her! Well, see what you've done! You've killed her! *(LEROY gets up and punches FRED who falls flat on the floor. MRS. DOMINGUEZ holds back LEROY.)*

MRS. DOMINGUEZ: Leroy, haven't you caused enough trouble? . . . Poor Mrs. Borestein. She was such a lovely lady.

MRS. CABRERA: *Una dama. Una verdadera dama.*

MOFETTI: I'll call an ambulance. *(Exits to his office.)*

MAILMAN: This is all so terrible. I don't know what to say.

    LEILA *goes to the piano and begins to play a mournful melody.* MOFETTI *returns. Front drop comes down. Now we see the action from outside.* LEILA *sings, the others join in one by one.*

One Last Song

Close the piano lid
Put away the music sheet
Turn off the lobby lights
This concert is our last

One last song just to say goodbye
One last song for the times we had
We won't sing together again
Our time is up, the ending is sad

One last song for the sake of love
One last song just because we care
We won't sing together again
Our joy is gone, vanished in the air

We sang of our pleasure
We sang of our pain
Life was so easy
Sharing it with you
Your feelings were mine
And my memory your own
Your music's my music
My song was your song
In this last concert
I wanted you to know

One last song just to say goodbye
One last song for the times we had

    After the song there's a long pause. A Paramedic *enters with a gurney.*

PARAMEDIC: Anybody called for an ambulance?

FRED: It's Mrs. Borestein there.

PARAMEDIC: *(To* Fred *and* Mailman.*)* Put her on the stretcher, please. *(To* Mrs. Borestein *while she's being moved to gurney.)* Your name, please. Address? Age? Social Security number? Medicare? Blue Cross? Blue Shield? . . .

Mrs. Cabrera: Can't you see she's dead?

PARAMEDIC: *(Taking* Mrs. Borestein's *pulse.)* No, she ain't. She just passed out.

MAILMAN: Thank God for that! *(Simultaneous exclamations of relief from the others.)*

Mrs. Dominguez: I knew the Virgin wouldn't let me down! *(A loud gong is heard. Lights go up on the audience. Everyone looks out the window.)* Ms. Wong!

FRED: Who? Where?

Mrs. Cabrera: The attorney. Mr. Wong's daughter.

Mrs. Dominguez: *(To* Fred.*)* I told you about her, remember?

Leila: Oh, I'm so glad she came!

    Leila *plays reprise of "Song to la Virgen." Front drop flies up. Actors change set. Now we are inside the bank again. While this is happening,* Ms. Wong *comes down the aisle towards the stage. When she gets to the stage, the loud gong is heard again. Music stops.*

Ms. Wong: Good afternoon.

All: Good afternoon.

Ms. Wong: I have important news. With your permission, I'd like to share it with you. There's no time to waste. I am the new executive director of the Neighborhood Tenant's Association. The tenants have decided to fight to save our neighborhood. And we need your help.

Leila: What can we do?

Ms. Wong: We'll sue!

FRED: I don't think you have a chance.

Ms. Wong: It is a better chance than sitting here, complaining about the situation. *(Murmurs of reaction.)*

Mrs. Cabrera: How about my husband's rent increase?

MS. WONG: We'll sue!

LEROY: How about my apartment?

MS. WONG: We'll march!

MAILMAN: How about my transfer?

MS. WONG: We'll lobby!

MOFETTI: How about the bank?

MS. WONG: We'll picket! But we won't be moved!

LEILA: *(Holding on to MOFETTI's arm.)* How about us?

MS. WONG: I'll get you a divorce!

FRED: That all sounds very easy, but how about the laws!

MS. WONG: We'll change them! . . . That's why I'm also running for the City Council. As you know, Chinatown has been pushed so far this way that now we are in the same district. I need your vote. Each one of you can make a difference if you vote!

FRED: But you can't stop progress! I mean, after you have the computer, you can't go back to the abacus. *(To all.)* Don't you want things to change?

MRS. CABRERA: Of course, we do. But we want to be part of the change.

LEROY: That's right. We don't want to be pushed around.

FRED: But you didn't do anything when the junkies took over the place.

LEROY: Yeah, we didn't. Maybe we've learned a lesson. Maybe now we can do something about the yuppies taking over the place.

MRS. CABRERA: And the real estate sharks.

MRS. DOMINGUEZ: But what can we do? It's too late. It's too late for me. It is much too late for Mrs. Borestein . . .

PARAMEDIC: It is too late for me. The hospital is closing down too! *(The PARAMEDIC begins to push MRS. BORESTEIN towards the street door. MRS. BORESTEIN begins to revive.)*

MS. WONG: It is not too late if you get involved, get yourselves organized. Then, we can sue, we can march, we can picket! But it will be too late if you just sit here singing old songs while the neighborhood disappears right in front of your eyes! Life is not a bowl of cherries, you know!

PARAMEDIC: I don't think any of that will really help.

MRS. BORESTEIN: *(From gurney, weakly.)* Yes, yes! We'll sue! *(Everyone rejoices at MRS. BORESTEIN's recuperation. The following lines are said almost simultaneously.)*

LEILA: Mrs. Borestein!

MRS. DOMINGUEZ: She's really alive!

MRS. CABRERA: *¡Qué alegría!*

PARAMEDIC: I knew I was good, but not that good!

MRS. BORESTEIN: We'll march!

ALL *(except FRED.)*: We'll march!

MRS. BORESTEIN: We'll picket!

ALL *(except FRED.)*: We'll picket!

MRS. BORESTEIN: But we won't be moved!

ALL *(except FRED.)*: But we won't be moved! *(FRED is to one side, away from the action. He feels isolated. He clears his throat. Everyone turns towards him, waiting. FRED clears his throat again.)*

MRS. CABRERA: Fred, I was thinking . . . maybe you can help too . . .

FRED: Me!

LEROY: That'll be the day.

MAILMAN: Yeah, man. With your computer!

LEILA: That's a wonderful idea!

FRED: *(Halfheartedly.)* Nah, nah.

MOFETTI: Fred, we need you on our side.

FRED: Well, I don't know . . . that would require designing a special program. I
don't know if I can do it.

MRS. CABRERA: I'm sure you can do it.

ALL *(Except MRS. BORESTEIN.)*: Come on, Fred! Sure, you can do it! You are a wiz! (etc.)

FRED: Maybe.

LEROY: And while you are at it, why don't you also program your heart and rent
one of your apartments to Mrs. Domínguez?

MRS. DOMINGUEZ: Oh yes, I'd love to move back here!

FRED: And have a *botánica* in *my* building? Oh, no!

MRS. DOMINGUEZ: We could negotiate that.

FRED: I'll think about it.

MRS. BORESTEIN: *(Getting up from the gurney.)* How about Atlantic City? *(Music begins.)*

MRS. BORESTEIN: We'll march! We'll picket! We'll sue!

ALL: But we won't be moved! *(They sing.)*

We Won't Be Moved

March-like

When the barrio went up in flames, when the
city was deep in trouble they shook their heads, "Oh, what a shame," and went
run- ning to the suburbs. Now their children are coming back, like an in-
va- sion of home snatchers, and the people that stayed behind find
no place to hang their hats. But we won't be moved, we won't be moved, we're
staying here, we're staying put. We won't be moved, we won't be moved, we're

going nowhere, we're holding on 'cause we be- long.

Now the city's a big boutique, and we're like window

shoppers, noses pressing on the glass to peek, at the goodies we can't af-

ford. No city can be an island, just a piece of real es-

tate, it needs a soul it's got to smile on all its

people to be great. But we won't be moved, we

won't be moved, we're staying here, we're staying put. We won't be moved,

out to the river, we won't be moved, up to the Bronx. We won't be moved, we're

staying here, we're gonna sue, our homes are here, we

won't be moved!

During the song everyone will participate in a choreography in which the chairs will again be rolled around the stage, and the dummies moved from chair to chair and some of them placed elsewhere on the stage. Extra chairs may be brought in so that there's room for everyone. With the last lines, the company will move its chairs downstage, facing the audience, and sit on them with determination, crossing arms across chests.

Blackout.

Carlos Fernández

Carlos Fernández's story tells of one man's sustained efforts to create community where none had existed before. It reveals the centrality of this community to the well-being of area migrant workers, describes the evolution of ethnic relations in central Florida over the past four decades, and serves as a powerful reminder of the role of individual commitment in community-building.

Interview

I was born in 1938 and raised in Chihuahua City, which is about five hours from the border with Ciudad Juárez. In 1949, when I was eleven years old, I came to the U.S. for the first time. We were very young, my brother and I, just us two. The first time I came, I worked picking cotton, which was very difficult. Later, I worked in nearly every type of agricultural job there was: beets, tomatoes, lettuce, pecans, apples, pears.

I also worked on shrimp boats in Port Isabel, Texas; also in Aransas Pass, Freeport, and around Houston. We shrimped in Mexican territorial waters—the American captain would just pay off the Mexican officials and we would fish the Bay of Tampico for shrimp. Once we were caught in a terrible storm. It came up suddenly and our boat capsized and sank. When that happened it created some kind of vacuum that sucked off our clothes. We were freezing, there were three of us together in the water, and one guy said, "Don't panic, and don't work against each other. Let's either die together or be saved together." Then he started telling jokes to keep our spirits up while we waited three hours in the 80 mile per hour wind for the coast guard to pick up us. They said it was a miracle that we had survived in that wind.

When I was eighteen, I came to Florida looking to work on a boat, but didn't have any luck. Then I started to work picking oranges because I was broke. I stayed on for a long time because I didn't have enough money to enable me to leave! I came here at a bad time, in April, when the early oranges are through, and you have to wait a while before the Valencias are ready to pick. While I waited I didn't have anything to eat.

From here I went to Connecticut, where I worked for the Sumatra Tobacco Company. I worked in Springfield, Massachusetts, also. In those days, as I was very young, I went from job to job. I found out about the different jobs through the Puerto Ricans who were contracted to come from Puerto Rico to New Jersey or Pennsylvania. Many would then get out of their contracts and try to find another job. Since I didn't have any papers and I looked Puerto Rican because of my curly hair, I had no problem getting jobs. I learned to speak like they did, and I never had any trouble with the *migra*. I even went to Puerto Rico twice later; it's very beautiful.

Later I met my wife, who came to Florida from Michigan. She didn't know that I was Mexican; no one knew it. There was a great deal of discrimination against illegal Mexicans then. One afternoon when we arrived home from work, I saw her for the first time. She was very young, barely fourteen years old, and I didn't take any notice of her until two years later. I picked for many years; she used to pick, too. My children have grown up out in the country. When my wife was expecting

our first child, I went to get the doctor, but no one would come because at that time they did not see *hispanos*. All we had was the public county hospital. I've never liked public assistance because when one depends on someone else, hope runs out; desire for independence runs out. We had to pay in advance for the hospital and the doctor when my first son was born. Our daughter was born in Pennsylvania, in the migrant camp there. But we had to leave when she was two days old. My daughter wasn't forty-eight hours old when she had traveled through Virginia, Maryland, North Carolina, South Carolina, and Georgia. Times were very difficult for us then.

People who complain about things now have no idea how good they have it. Look, when I arrived here, three days later the police showed up and said that we couldn't live here because we were Mexican and this was a place for Americans. Then, we went to live in a Negro neighborhood, and there they told us that we couldn't stay either, that it was exclusively for Negroes. We couldn't live with the whites, we couldn't live with the blacks, we couldn't form a neighborhood of our own because there were so few of us. So we came here, to this tiny rural settlement. Before, there were no places for recreation either, the only cantinas or recreation centers were for the Negroes. When I came here there were only five *tejano,* or Texas-Mexican, families in the whole county, but at least they could speak English.

I remember one night—this happened in 1957—some of us had gotten together at a friend's house to play poker, and the game lasted very late, so we stayed there to sleep. Early the next morning I was about to leave for work, and we heard loud voices coming from outside. We looked out to see about fifty men with kerosene cans gathered in front of the house. They said that if we didn't move out, they would burn our houses down with all our families inside. My friend told them that if they burned his house down that he would do the same to them, and burn down their kids' school. And from there the case went to court. The courts at that time, in the 50s—the judges, the police, the mayor, the *cherife,* or sheriff— were all hired or put in office by the white element, the Americans, so they each defended the other. There was no way that they were going to rule in our favor and lose the elections the next year, and we were very few people anyway. We presented our case, but it was filed and postponed, and we went to make our appearance and to give our deposition, but, in reality, they didn't do anything. There was never any sentence, verdict, or anything. It was just quietly forgotten.

Later, by the 60s, more Mexican families had arrived, and there were certain restaurants where we were allowed to eat. But that didn't happen without a lot of trouble during that period. I remember there were two couples from Illinois, from Aurora, a Mexican and a Puerto Rican guy who were each living with an American woman. They weren't married, but they were living together. They lived here with us until they could get settled. Soon after they arrived, they went to Winter Haven to buy food, and they were taken to jail just for walking down the street with Americans. That's the way it was then, but that's all changed now.

We Mexicans are very independent. Even though we have been in the United States for centuries and centuries, still we have not assimilated, we have not stopped

being Mexicans. Partly it's because of discrimination, but partly it's because we don't want to mix. The Hungarians who came after Budapest in '56 and the Italians and other groups have all assimilated, the Irish, too, but not us. Our ego will not permit us to mix in like the other groups. Father Fernández from Bartow tried to do this in the church, tried to get the Anglo community to go to Wahneta to mass, but they didn't want to and we didn't want to either. I would sit down in the pew in church and some Americans would come up, but they would not sit in my pew, they would sit at another one, even though it was not crowded, and the Mexicans did the same.

I think that American society could benefit from some things about Mexican culture, especially with regard to the family. The family is the highest value in the Mexican community. For our family we would go to the end of the world. We respect our old. When our elderly are sick, we don't put them in a nursing home, we take care of them at home. We take care of our daughters, also. I want my daughter to have a boyfriend, but I want to know him, and I want her to be pure until the day she marries. Another of our values is that we work and play together. At our dances you see babies seven months old, all the *viejitos,* or elderly, the young people, everyone comes. And if a man is at a party with his own wife, how can he become interested in another woman? My wife and I have had our problems. But we know the value of our children, and we know that divorce is out of the question because that would do away with our family, and it's very important not to sacrifice our family for whatever problem we may have.

The ambitious young Mexican comes here and sees the opportunity to earn money, so he works hard and does well. Others come and don't see beyond their nose, they live day by day, in an environment that causes them to forget little by little what their parents taught them. That's why we need healthy places for young people to have a good time. There are good youth here in our community—mostly families, but a few young single men, too. I try to get them to go to church. They're all Catholic, but not in an American way, that is, they are devoted fanatics of the Virgin of Guadalupe. I say fanatics because she is the mother of God, but she is not God.

The problem is that the great majority of Mexicans here are farm laborers, and that is synonymous with ignorance and abuse. The Mexican rural worker has been discriminated against and abused in Mexico, and here the discrimination of the peso becomes that of the dollar. And no farm worker participates in politics in Mexico because there the vote is not respected. They know that their vote will not make any difference, so it makes no sense to vote. They come here thinking that way, and they don't see any reason to become citizens. I myself have that sin of not being a citizen and not having rights, but it would be better if everyone would register and vote. Here your vote counts.

We have also had a very sad history with the church. When people started to come here, in the seventies, there was a priest named Carlos, a Spaniard, who began to say mass in Spanish. At that time the masses alternated between Bartow and Winter Haven and then somewhere else because we didn't have a church of our own. They transferred Father Carlos to Haines City and put Father Fernández

in his place. The community grew. They loaned us the social room so we could have coffee and cookies after mass. Later, we asked the bishop, the *señor obispo,* if we could collect funds to build our own church. He responded, *"Sí, cómo no?"*— "Yes, of course." Later, they said that all we *really* needed was a social hall. I'll tell you about it in minute, but the thing is they just don't understand how hard-working and how capable we Mexicans are.

For example, when I married, I had nothing, absolutely nothing, *nada, nada, nada, nada, nada.* Two weeks later, someone stole all my clothes. If you could have seen me when I started out, and look at me now, you would know that I have come a long way. My daughter graduated from one of the best schools in the U.S., Florida Southern, and my son is studying electronic engineering at the university in Orlando. If you want to measure how far I have come, you have to know where I began. No one has ever given me anything. And there are many people like myself. I'm just using myself as an example; there are others who have worked hard and gone even farther than I have. We are capable of doing so many things, but we have had great difficulty getting the church to recognize it.

For example, we all went out in the community to raise the money for the little church that we wanted to build. In just six months time we had collected enough money and had a site for our church. We put the 10 percent down payment on the land and about one hundred of us cleared it with picks and shovels; we did all the clearing ourselves. On Saturdays and Sundays we went out collecting more funds and we raised $50,000 in all. That was the total cost of the church we wanted to build, too. But, at that point, the church authorities said, "No go, no deal." The deanery said that we did not need a church, only a social hall. They wouldn't let us use the money to build a church. They thought that we would build a *porquería,* something ugly, but the *porquería* is what we have now. It was a terrible disappointment to the whole community. We still have problems in our relationship with the church.

The way I look at it, everyone is born with a vocation, some to work in a factory, others to be teachers, others to work in a shop. Well, there is also a vocation for people who like to work in the country. I had the opportunity to work in the *factoriás*—once I worked several days in Philadelphia—but I couldn't stand the eight hours that I had to be there. It was like a prison to me, I felt like I couldn't breathe. It was better for me to go out to work in the country, even if it was cold. The problem is that agricultural work is not secure. You may not work an entire week because of the weather, or because the *empacadoras,* the packing plants, are filled with fruit. Other times you have to work seven days a week.

The other problem is that they do not pay enough. Workers are paid by the field box, the *caja;* it's what one *morral,* a deep canvas shoulder bag, will hold. Minute Maid pays pretty well, ninety cents per *morral,* but there are other companies that pay sixty-five cents a *morral.* There are a few people who can pick one hundred *morrales* a day, and that would give them about eighty or one hundred dollars. But you have to remember that we leave here about 6:30 a.m. and that we return about fourteen hours later. A good worker earns seventy dollars; that's an average of about five

Church picnic, Wahneta, Florida

dollars an hour, not much. About three years ago they started where you can collect unemployment benefits, but before we didn't have any. The owner of the orchards complains when the fruit brings in less money, and he says, "We can't pay more." But when the fruit brings in a lot of money, he is silent and says nothing. The farm worker does not participate at all in the earnings; he shares the bad times with the grower, but not the good ones. You can complain, but in Florida they have "right to work," which means that if I am an owner and my workers go on strike, I have the right to fire them and to hire others. And in Florida there are many scabs.

With regard to benefits, in the past the worker had absolutely nothing, *nada*. Now he has Workmen's Compensation, which means that if he is injured or gets sick because of an insecticide or something that they will provide medical help. But a retirement plan or a health plan? Forget it, nothing. The farm worker earns money if he works, that's it. If he doesn't work, he earns nothing. When one crop is finished and the companies let the workers go, they could easily be six or eight weeks without work until other crops are ready to pick. Many go from here to Plant City to pick strawberries, for example, but during the period in between jobs there is no money.

One very bad thing here is that the companies take advantage of the crew leader, or foreman, the *contratista*, in order to obtain their workers. The crew leader is one who sells his people. The Malinche sold her race in Mexico to the Spaniards, and

Migrant workers' bus, Wahneta, Florida

the *contratista* sells his people here today. The *contratista* who makes his people pick for a low price; he is the Malinche. The *contratista* is paid well, but on condition that he make his people pick for less. The *contratista* who looks out for his people, he has no future. The company pays the crew leader to do their job for them. The company does not hire workers directly, but through the *contratista*. That is the role that I should play, to make my people pick at the lowest possible price.

But I am not guilty of being that way because my group always is paid five or ten cents more than the other groups. The company doesn't say anything because I've worked for them for a long time, and I know all the bad things about the company, and they know that I could "sing," and that would not be good for them. But they're always trying to get away with something. For example, last week, a guy comes to the orchard and gives me this paper for me to approve—it has the number of the orchard and the pay on it. I go to the orchard to see if the value of the work is what they recorded or not. Last week they put eighty-five cents, but, since I am authorized to do so, I put $1.25 because it was a fairer price, since I could see that the work there was worth more.

But, usually, the foreman who wants a future will always look out for the company's interests. It's not so bad here as it is in Wachula and places where there is much competition. There, if the foreman is not doing his job to the company's satisfaction, *zap*, just like that, they remove him and put in another. The farm worker's

pay depends on whether the foreman has a conscience or not. For example, now I have few people because I do not need many because there are not many oranges left at this time of year. I've decided not to bring in other people to finish the job quicker, but rather to make the job last for the people I have already hired. To me, it makes no sense to employ fifty people and finish the fruit in one week, and afterwards not to have any work for anyone. I earn the same regardless, but they don't.

You know, the role of the *contratista* is a very complex one. Not only do I have an important responsibility here, but also to the worker in Mexico. For example, someone will call me from Guanajato and say, "Carlos, I need a job, I want to come up there to work, but I don't have any money." Then I send them the money so they can come here and work. Once they are here, I also get phone calls like this: "Carlos, I can't pay the rent," and I pay the rent. "Carlos, I'm in jail," and I go to the jail. "Carlos, I ran out of gas at 2 a.m.," and I go pick them up. "Carlos, my wife is in labor," and I take them to the hospital. That's the only way I can be because everything that I have I owe to the people who work with me. That's payment that I owe them. Of course, there are people who you lend money to and you never see them again, but I have to have a clear conscience. Most of the time, I feel good to think that I am able to solve someone's problem.

In Mexico, I have gone to the tiniest, poorest *ranchos* where they have absolutely nothing, just shacks with dirt floors, no water, electricity, or anything. I have been called upon to perform so many functions I would never have dreamed of. For example, once when I was in Chihuahua, a baby was born in the back of my pickup. The woman went into labor and this was out in the country, there was only a burro path, so I put the husband in the front and the expectant mother and another woman who went along to help her in the back of the truck. We were hurrying to try to make it to the house of the *partera*, the midwife, but the road was bumpy and rocky, and soon I heard the sound of a baby crying. I stopped and got out and saw that the woman had given birth to a boy, and both women had passed out. So I wrapped the baby in a blanket and tried to calm his crying and also his father. I still keep in touch with that baby, who today is working in a meat-packing plant in Kansas.

The people who live in those poor *ranchos*, without knowing me personally, know who I am, they know I can help them, and they put me on a pedestal. For them, and for me also, *ser un foreman es ser algo en la vida,* to be a foreman is to be something in life. You have to be able to speak English, you have to know how to fill out forms, how to make payments, to read and write, do math—and most of the workers are illiterate. I first started working as a foreman in 1965 for Mussellman in Pennsylvania; I had been picking apples, but because I was the only one who spoke a little English they made me foreman.

The Cubans who came here have gotten ahead, some are even owners of banks now. They are educated and motivated. The problem with the Mexican is that he is uneducated and doesn't know how to motivate his children to study and get out of the cycle of poverty. They don't set a good model. A father who is illiterate can tell his kids to study, but too often these are just empty words. But if you tell

your child, "Look, I didn't have the opportunity that you have. Take advantage of it and you can be something," that's how to motivate your kids. Unfortunately, too many parents just give up; they don't know how to motivate, or they don't understand the difference it can make. When their kids are fifteen, they drop out of school to go work in the fields. This problem is something that has not changed in the more than thirty years that I have been here. *La gente que se llega ignorante se conserva igual.* People who come here ignorant, stay ignorant.

But there have been big changes in those people who come here determined to work hard, learn, and get ahead. For one thing, there has been a big change in attitudes about family planning. Most young Mexican women who marry now plan their family. Family planning and birth control are important now more than ever. The kind of *machismo* like you see on TV doesn't exist; it's just an exaggeration. Everybody knows that a family progresses economically and morally because behind that family is a woman who knows how to manage things. The mother is the true voice in the home. The Mexican woman is the *verdadera bosa,* the real boss, of everyone. The family planning change is an important one for the future. Most of us are Catholics, and you have to believe that somehow God will provide. But, nowadays, having kids just to have them, without thinking about providing for them or what they are going to do when they get older, I don't think that people believe anymore that God wants things like this.

The greatest change that I have witnessed is that people now value themselves more than before. I compare them to the Mexicans who were here when I came. If you were insulted out in the field, you were expected to keep your head down, not say anything, and just keep on working. And so many times, you'd try to find work and they'd take one look at you, see you were Mexican, and show you the door. Young people today have more rights, and the Mexican is no longer the silent Mexican of before. Now the Mexican stands up for his rights when he has to.

Mexican people recognize their worth now, they have more self-respect. It's a fundamental change. No one has to let themselves be pushed around anymore. Before, it was totally different. I remember once when immigration came to my house at 3 a.m. I opened the door, and they just barged on in without permission or a warrant and began looking under the beds and messing everything up. Now I know that I could have protested, but I didn't say anything because one was accustomed to being pushed around. This is the greatest change that I have seen in the Mexican people.

It's the environment we live in that has made us believe that we are equal. We value ourselves more because our children go to school, they see that the American believes in equal rights, and they realize that this includes them, too. This is one reason that education is so important for the future of our people. The *medio ambiente,* the environment, works on the individual, slowly but surely. It's like working a precious stone. You don't notice the work that you've done while you're doing it, but later you see the beautiful results. That's the lesson that the Mexican kid is learning in school—that he is equal to all the rest—and because of that he not only stands up for his rights, but he also respects himself.

Another important change that I see, although I wish that it were bigger, is that there are now at least a few high school graduates from our migrant community. Last year there were ten, and, of those, seven went on to some sort of college. Before, you never saw a Mexican high school graduate; there weren't any. They were like the dodo, an extinct species.

My nephews were among the first to graduate from high school. Their story is interesting. They used to live in Grand Rapids, and one day my sister-in-law called me and said that her husband no longer wanted to live with her, that he now had someone else, just out of the blue. She didn't know what she was going to do, so I told her to come on down here. She came with her kids, four boys and two girls. They lived here near us, went to catechism, made their first communion, were confirmed, graduated from high school, and got jobs. One works for Coca-Cola as a stock man; one works in the bank. They all have good jobs, and they do not work in the fields. Three years ago they went back to Grand Rapids, Michigan, and when Gilbert came back here he told me, "Uncle, I went to look for my old friends there. One is in jail, and another is in the hospital for drug abuse. I didn't find a single one of my friends doing well. I think that if I had not come here, the same would've happened to me." In our community here, we don't have problems with drugs and gangs. There are one or two guys who use marijuana or who drink too much, but that's about it.

What we have to do is all keep working hard and being responsible in order to keep our community afloat. Our comunity has a great future in that if we can motivate those who are in college now to continue living and working in the community, then we current leaders can pass the leadership on to them. Then the new leaders will not be Carlos Fernández fruit picker, but Mr. Engineer, Mr. Architect, and the young people will say, "I want to grow up and be like them." There are very few people who want to grow up and be like me. They are going to want to be professionals and have their roots here. I think that is a good combination for the future.

Father Luis Olivares

Father Luis Olivares was a Claretian priest who was actively involved in community organizing with the California farm workers and with his parish in Los Angeles. He began his clerical career as a successful, if conservative, ecclesiastical administrator. However, over the years he came to enlarge his concept of - community, to discard a "safe" view that demanded little of him, and to embrace a more controversial vision that required intense and highly visible participation in the social and political arenas. Father Olivares died on March 18, 1993.

Interview

I was born in San Antonio of Mexican immigrant parents. My father is from Parras, a little oasis just outside of Saltillo, Mexico, oasis because that whole area there, Monterrey and Saltillo, it's all a dry prairielike area, but Parras is a very rich little oasis. They grew grapes, and some of the top wineries came out of Parras. My folks came over when they were very young, my father was twelve, and my mother was fifteen. She's from another area, outside of San Luis Potosí—it's a little village that was kind of a holdout during the Revolution; they didn't get involved in the fighting.

My ancestors—my mother's great-grandmother was an Indian, in fact, she was a chief of the tribe. When the French came into Mexico, she married a French officer of Basque origin, and that's the beginning of *mestizaje*, for us anyway. The Mecas were a very peaceful tribe. My ancestor was called the Meca-Juana, and the town where my mother was born is named Miqui-Juana after her. It's kind of interesting how they got married. He was captured, and while he was in prison, she paid ransom for him, his weight in gold. They didn't know each other or anything, but she saw him, liked him, ransomed him, and married him; after all, she was a *cacica*. When my mother was fifteen, my grandmother decided to go to the U.S. because it was getting too dangerous down there. That was around 1912 or '14.

And on the other side, my father's side, my great-uncles and so forth worked for the Maderos. The Maderos had a big vineyard there in Parras, and one of my uncles was foreman of one of the ranches, but again, things were getting awfully hot there, and they decided to come to the U.S., to San Antonio.

They came to San Antonio because my grandfather had come earlier, and my grandmother's brother was a professional transporter of people, a *coyote*, and he brought them in. That's where my great-uncle used to go back and forth, between San Antonio and Mexico. My father started working as soon as he came over; he didn't go to school or anything. I think his first job was at a little foodstand in downtown San Antonio. His father, my grandfather, was a carpenter, but he was injured in a fall at work, and my grandmother was at home, so it was really the kids who had to support the family. There were three brothers and two sisters that came over and they all started working as little kids.

Neither of my parents had any education here. My mother worked —see, in San Antonio they had these *nuecerías*, pecan processing plants, and that was the equivalent of the farm workers out here in California. The immigrants were all employed in these *nuecerías*. That was also the beginning of the unionization of labor in Texas, through those pecan processing plants. It was well before 1920 that they were unionizing.

My mother died when we were very young; I was only four years old. She left seven kids. So I never really got to know my mother that well. But my dad and mom met at church, at Immaculate Heart in San Antonio.

My dad talked a lot about the history of the times. One of the things that they did both in Mexico and here in the U.S. was during the so-called persecution, under Calles in Mexico, they were like an underground railroad for the priests who would come from Mexico to San Antonio. My dad used to hide priests behind the walls, so he was involved in a kind of sanctuary movement as a young adult! That was around 1925, '26, '27.

Eventually my dad started working as a maintenance man in a hotel, first in a building downtown—the building is gone—but he actually received training as an electrician. He got his certificate as a professional electrician without an education by going to school at night. He learned English, but not that well; you know, he spoke English but he had a heavy accent. At home we spoke Spanish.

At school we were forbidden to speak Spanish, but we still did during recreation period. They wouldn't punish us, but they certainly corrected us. In Catholic school we were continually told that Spanish was forbidden on the school grounds.

In his own political interests, my dad wanted us to have all the advantages that the country could offer, so he provided for an education. It was a top priority for him, a matter of course. Two of us went to the seminary, and we got our education through the seminary formation. But he very much wanted us to have every advantage. In fact, it was always a cause of confusion that as we grew older he registered Republican, trying to identify with the people who succeed, I guess. Yet, he was still involved with Mexican things.

My grandmother raised us. She was very religious—daily mass, the whole bit. She would take us, my older brother and me, we would go with her at 6:15 in the morning every single day to Immaculate Heart. That's the origin of my vocation and my brother's too. We spent a lot of time in church. She and my aunt, my father's sister, basically raised us. The thing I remember is that even though we were poor—and my dad certainly never moved up in his social position, so we were always poor—yet the thing that I remember is that my grandmother and my dad and my uncles exercised a leadership role, not only in the church, but also in the *barrio*. People looked up to them for advice on community and personal matters, on church activities, and so forth.

My grandmother, aside from her involvement in church religious activities, also had a reputation for healing. She wasn't exactly a *curandera*, but a lot of people came to the house to be prayed over. But she didn't advertise or anything or have a trade of any sort, it just happened that she had a reputation for holiness and people would come to her and she would pray. She also used herbs in her healing. It's interesting, on my father's side, the political inclination the family was caught up in was the Revolution, the Maderos and all that. On my mother's side, they were federalists, so we have both sides in our family. I like to go back to historical vignettes because, as I said, my grandmother and my dad and my uncles were involved in some kind of underground railroad of rescuing priests, and my

great-great-great-grandmother over here on the other side is ransoming French-men! So there's some of everything. But the prayers and the herbs were part of the healing, and the different customs like a rubdown with an egg, jumping over the fire, were part of the healing.

She had one little technique for *susto*—it's very common, you know, there are a lot of conditions attributed to *susto*, including malformation, where a child is retarded and fails to grow. They would say, *"Bueno, le dieron un susto"*—"well, they gave him a bad scare." I would translate *susto* as "scare" or "shocking scare." Some-times people lose their power to speak; sometimes they are very distracted; they can't concentrate on anything; they get fevers. The cure for *susto* that she had was to shock them back into reality by taking a good swig of whisky and then catching them completely by surprise by blowing it in their face, then covering them up with a towel and drying them off. We kids used to play around with that a lot as you can imagine. She would simulate like she was not very involved in anything, but just then she would take that swig of whisky, and then the girl or the boy would be dropped through a door and she would be on the other side, and then out of nowhere she'd come out and blow this whisky in their face. It seemed to work! She treated men, women, young and old. I don't know how to account for it working. She claimed it was her faith, of course. Her prayers were Catholic prayers in Spanish.

We didn't really talk about it too much, because she wasn't called a *curandera,* but, in effect, she was because people would come to her to be healed. I guess she was afraid of the superstitious aspects and, being a deeply religious woman, want-ed to be sure that whatever healing powers would be attributed to her, that we'd be sure to know that it was because of the prayers. She knew a lot of prayers.

We were a very close family. My older brother who became a priest got a dis-pensation in due time, but we were both ordained originally, and then I have a sister who's a nun, a Benedictine. She's in San Antonio. I go back occasionally to see the family. I used to go back once or even twice a year, but I go less now.

The Hispanic communities in San Antonio and here in Los Angeles are differ-ent. There seems to be a lot more opportunity for the Hispanic in San Antonio. The Hispanic community here in L.A. is much more diverse and, therefore, not that close. They have different traditions. You know we not only have people from different areas in Mexico, but also from many different areas in Latin Amer-ica, particularly Central America, of late. There are many Central Americans in San Antonio, but not like here in L.A. It seems as though the political scene in San Antonio is better; the Mexican American is much more active there than here in L.A. If L.A. is more politicized, more *concientizado*, I would say that is due to the Central American presence here, not to the Mexican-American.

Contrast, for example, the progress of the community organizing experience in San Antonio and Los Angeles. In San Antonio there's COPS [Community Orga-nized for Public Service]; here in L.A., there's UNO [United Neighborhoods Orga-nization]. Both organizations were monitored and led by the same Industrial Areas Foundation, so there's a common origin, but a very, very different political orientation. It's much more political in San Antonio than here. They are both

mostly Mexican American. COPS is much more political, they get involved in political campaigns, in referendums, large citywide issues, which is very, very different from here. You don't hear of UNO having much of an impact on the political scene as you do with COPS. Now, political activism in the L.A. area, from my experience, is due to the Central American presence. They're much more politicized, much more organized than the Mexican Americans. Somebody was doing a survey recently and they came to me to talk about that, and that was one thing they were focusing on, why is it that Central Americans are able to mobilize so quickly and more often than the other Hispanic communities? I believe that it comes from their experiences with revolution in Central America.

In my *barrio*, growing up, we were all Mexican-American kids, but there was no experience of people differentiating or discriminating in any form that I can remember. The Benedictine sisters who took over the school, I remember them as very compassionate and understanding. They may not have had all that much experience in dealing with Mexican-American kids, but they sure did not make us feel inferior. They were all of German stock. You know people talk about their experiences in school, how they felt they were humiliated; I don't recall any of that with the Benedictine sisters.

I think in those times the difference between public school and Catholic school education was much more evident than now. So it was like a privilege to be going to Catholic school. As far as the quality of education is concerned, we may have had some difficulty in getting into high school; I was very much lacking in math for example. I had to be tutored in order to be able to pick up high school math. I think my sisters had some problems also with that transition to high school. We went to Catholic high school, too, but it was more mixed than the lower school. It was not even predominantly Hispanic. I went to the seminary at high school. But there was Central Catholic High where my other brother went. My sisters went to Providence High School. I think that the standards that we had at Immaculate Heart, the elementary school, were perhaps not up to par with other grammar schools that were feeding kids into high schools. Through it all, though, I have nothing but high regard for my teachers in grammar school; they were wonderful. They were all of German parentage, all of them, and they were all from small surrounding towns, such as Las Gallinas.

When I entered the seminary I don't even think it was accredited. I was thirteen years old, and I thought that I wanted to be a priest. It's hard for me now, in retrospect, to imagine that I knew what I was doing, but my recollection of my resolve is that I *seemed* to know what I wanted. I was a serious young person. And my dad and grandmother supported me in my decision. In those days, that's when you entered seminary, right at high school. But, as I say, I think that every vocation is a developmental process, you kind of grow into it. You may not become a priest for the same reason that you entered. And in many instances, you certainly don't remain a priest for the same reason for which you were ordained. And, also important, whether we want to admit it or not, going into the seminary meant moving up in the world, particularly for us, and those of us who were in the poor class. There was a certain pres-

tige even about being a seminarian. I think I would be dishonest if I did not admit that that had something to do with it. Aside from that, there's the example that you get from other priests. As I said before, we were at church almost all the time, and my heroes were priests.

My education at the seminary was also a productive and positive experience. I noticed the difference a little bit more in what it meant to be a minority, because in grammar school we were all Mexican Americans from the neighborhood. I can't refer to some of the practices as discriminatory necessarily, but there certainly was quite a difference. For example, there was the feeling that maybe they didn't expect as much of you because of where you came from. Not an exclusion, but lower expectations. The other thing is that you were expected nevertheless to meld in with everybody else. It's the typical approach. You felt it was imposed and you put up a resistance to it, partly by hanging around with your own. Again, the language was a problem. We were not allowed to speak Spanish in the seminary— this was 1948, '49. My teachers were all Claretians, both Spaniards and Americans, yet the Spaniards, too, insisted on English only. It was always implicit that the Mexican American was inferior to the Spaniard. I mean, they didn't come out and say it, but it was always implicit. I think in many instances it's still true among the older Spanish priests. Europe is where everything good comes from— what good can come from Latin America? That's still very prevalent.

I was at the seminary for the four years in high school, and then we went to novitiate. We had four years of college, and then four years of theology. I entered the minor seminary here in Compton just out of high school. That's when I came to California, and I've been here practically ever since. I wanted to be a Claretian, so it would've been either here or in Momence, Illinois, which is where our other seminary is in this country. I wanted to be a Claretian because my church, Immaculate Heart, was in the care of Claretians, and that was basically all I knew. Studying the philosophy of the different orders, again, that's developmental. As you live as a priest, you get to learn more about what it is to be a Claretian.

To be a Claretian means to me—well, I would say that I have had a clearer sense in the past about my Claretian identity than I do now. I think a lot of it has to do with the role you play in the community. Like right after ordination I went to the seminary as a member of the faculty and disciplinarian for the minor seminary, administrator for the seminary. I taught religion, history, and, well, they assigned things to you regardless of your expertise, I even taught English for two years. It's a good thing I didn't teach math! I was bursar for the seminary for a while; it was a position of some authority and a policy-making position within the seminary administration. At that time being a Claretian to me meant being a company man. Your identity is almost exclusively Claretian. I was ordained in 1961; then, shortly after ordination, in 1967, I was named the provincial treasurer—that's finance man for the whole western province. I was that for ten years!

We had headquarters here in Los Angeles; in fact, this building was put up as a headquarters in my tenure as treasurer. So, you had your headquarters, but you moved around the different communites to insure that proper administration

procedures were being followed; it really was a company position. You're a member of the Provincial Council; there are five people on that council, and they make all the decisions. I certainly did not have a reformist vision at that time. I was kind of a conservative cliché, as a finance man, a Claretian, and as a member of the council. You're in the middle of decision-making, so your whole life revolves around what it means to be a Claretian. That's why being a Claretian had such a clear meaning for me during those years.

There were some controversial issues that came up between '67 and '77. One of the things that has always been a conflict for us is our commitment to parish work. We were not originally founded to be in parishes, but here in the U.S. almost all our communities are in charge of parishes, so there was always a conflict over whether to keep a parish open or to close it down, that type of thing. I favored parishes because they worked, as opposed to teaching or itinerant preaching, which was our original mission. When we were first founded, we were itinerant missionaries within the country; we're not foreign missionaries. We were founded in Spain, and when we came out here to the U.S., we started preaching missions in different outlying parishes. But the bishop wanted us to be in charge of a parish, and that's how we got the cathedral in San Antonio. The fathers thought that that would be a good base to work from.

From there we developed a tradition; we, the U.S. Claretians, started a tradition of taking parish administration, and it was a controversy for the whole congregation all over the world whether we should be doing that, whether we should be administrators. Now, I've always liked to preach, and I like to think that I give a good sermon, but I never got involved in those preaching bands that we tried to establish. I'm a very strong institutional person. Even after my "conversion," I still maintain that the institution plays an extremely important role in establishing credibility and in the success of whatever project we might initiate. The institutional base to me is essential.

Unfortunately, when I was on the Provincial Council—and I think it's still true today—personnel issues are so overwhelming that you're constantly dealing with them almost as a priority, and have very little time to do any vision-setting. That's definitely the downside of the institutional emphasis, no question about it. We were plagued by that; we were constantly having to deal with personnel problems. Then the other priority, unfortunately, again, instead of vision-setting, was financial administration—where are you going to get the most for your dollar. We do very little reflection, but it should be a role of the Provincial Council to be continually setting our course, illuminating the mission that we have.

My so-called conversion experience—I actually think we go through a series of conversions and that we are given opportunities along the way to get closer to Christ by the challenges we are presented—but in 1975 I became involved with the farm workers, with the boycott in East L.A. It was almost by accident. What happened was that a seminarian applied for volunteer work with the farm workers in the East L.A. boycott. The Provincial Council gave permission on condition that there be a priest supervising him, to whom he would be accountable, and in

order to facilitate his being able to do that, I volunteered. But I thought it was just going to be checking in with him, him letting me know what he was doing, but it didn't turn out that way.

They started pulling me into their house meetings, started having me give house meetings in East L.A., and I became one of the organizers for the boycott. That's how I got to meet César, and from then my relationship with the farm workers became very close, both as priest and minister, and as organizer trying to promote the cause. We had some very exciting times with the whole organizing process.

Incidentally, the Order gave me tremendous help. Aside from my undergraduate degree, which I have from Loyola University here, I have a Business Administration degree from Notre Dame. So, it was like a career type thing, and all thanks to the Order. But, working with the farm workers, being in touch with people out in the fields, going out to their funerals and their victory marches and to their rallies and to their protest marches, I got the sense that that was where I belonged rather than in a fancy office juggling figures and managing portfolios and selling stock and buying properties. Basically, it put me back in touch with my Mexican-American roots, and with the Spanish language as well.

Really, starting with the whole seminary experience, I began to lose contact with my roots. Ideally, it would have been better had the Claretians not pushed the melting pot idea, but I don't think it would have been possible, because at that time, the whole Church, not just the Claretians, the whole Church was trying to be more American. We as Claretians were shaking off our Spanish identity, and the idea was to be more American. I have seen memos from the provincial to the vocation director saying, "You're getting too many Spanish-surnamed people into the seminary," that kind of thing. You can go through all sorts of what-ifs, but if we had followed our natural historical tendency, recognizing that as Claretians we were brought into the U.S. to serve the Hispanics, specifically, to take care of Hispanics in San Antonio, and most of our parishes began to be among Hispanics, it stands to reason that we would attract Hispanic vocations. I think that if we had followed that course, allowed that course to develop, that we as Claretians would have become an *extremely* powerful influence in the direction of the church for Hispanics. But it didn't happen, primarily because the times called for us to be American. Nor is this a viable option for the Claretians now because of the persistence among those who are in authority of the idea that we've got to be all things to all men, that we don't want to develop a specific identity as being exclusively devoted to Hispanic ministry. We're having a very hard time with that issue, because we're not getting enough vocations from the Anglo communions, and we want to maintain a strong position in Anglo parishes, but we're having a hard time. I think that if you go through the history of Spanish-speaking ministry in Texas and Arizona, you will see a strong Claretian presence, but we didn't capitalize on it. As a Hispanic, I wish we had, but, at the same time, I can understand why we didn't.

From 1975 my contact with the farm workers was very close; whenever anything happened here in L.A., I was involved. César would call me first, and we'd decide what we were going to do. But in 1967, '68, when Robert Kennedy was

here, I was doing something else—and it's the same thing, almost—when PADRES got started. PADRES is a group of Mexican-American priests who got together in San Antonio because there was a great dissatisfaction about the role that Hispanics had in the church; we were being left out. There were no Hispanic bishops at that time, and then PADRES took on the cause of having Hispanic bishops named, and very successfully accomplished that purpose. It also gave Mexican-American priests a very powerful, though controversial, voice, especially in the Southwest. Well, I wasn't involved in that either! It's really amazing, all that was completely outside the realm of my consciousness! You know, I was sitting in a fancy office, and I was very comfortable.

I don't regret those years; it would be very dishonest of me to say I didn't enjoy all that, because I did. I enjoyed the power, being treated royally, being picked up at the airport in a limousine. Definitely my family felt a great amount of pride that I was making it. But when my brother left the priesthood—he got a dispensation—I remember a comment that my dad made that has stuck in my mind because it puts a little different color on this whole situation of how my family looked at what I was doing. My dad said of my brother, "Of course he left, I don't blame him for leaving. He should've been the treasurer. He was older." It was that kind of reaction. It struck me; it kind of hurt. But it reveals very traditional Hispanic family beliefs about the older brother being responsible for everyone else. However, my brother didn't feel that way, just my dad, and that had nothing to do with why he left.

But, anyway, the farm workers is the beginning of a different twist to my ministry and to the people I run around with. I became more and more an activist. Shortly thereafter, I was elected president of PADRES, even though I hadn't been involved in the beginning. I think the Claretians had a hard time understanding what was happening. They had an image of me as a rather strict administrator, you know, no games, no nonsense, and perhaps even somewhat arrogant and power-conscious. Then suddenly I'm questioning the capitalist system, I'm questioning the excessive interest in money, I'm questioning the rather affluent lifestyle of the clergy.

Some guys kiddingly—I don't think it's true, but I guess they could make an argument—said that prior to my association with the farm workers I was "Louis," but as soon as I got involved with the farm workers and all this activism, I became "Luis." My original name is Luis on my birth certificate and my baptismal certificate. It's just that, again, in school they tell you that's your Spanish name, your *real* name is Louis. And over the years I bought into that. I accepted it in grammar school, I went with Louis to the seminary, I was Louis through those first seventeen years of my priesthood. But I was always Luis, I just used a different name for a while!

My conversion with the farm workers—well, again, it's a process, it's a developmental thing. You start by curiosity, wondering what's going on at the meetings. They tell you to come on in; they give you a bucket, go and make a collection; and then the involvement with them, little by little, deepens. That's what happened,

and never did I dream that I would be meeting César personally. Something clicked between César and me; I was very attracted to him because of everything he stood for. He's been very, very warm and appreciative. It was exciting for me, it was like there was a purpose to what I was about. I gave masses out in the field; those were the days when we could mobilize 10, 15, 20,000 people for a rally. They were exciting times. And the people's response to you was infectious; you couldn't help but get sucked into it.

I remember the funeral for Rufino Contreras, who was killed out in the fields by the son of one of the growers during the picketing. I remember arriving at midnight and having the wake, and everybody, when they see you coming, it lifts them up, as does being there through the whole funeral experience. I walked with them down the main streets of Calexico. I went to several of their funerals, and I did several of their weddings. I used to go up to La Paz for César's birthday; everybody would get together there and we would have a great time. The farm worker experience changed my life. I remained treasurer from 1975 to '77. I don't know whether the Claretians thought I was still doing a good job or not; all I know is that I wasn't elected again. But by then I was already a pastor in East L.A., a position I asked for as a result of wanting to be in closer touch with the people. La Soledad is the common name of the church, but it is officially Our Lady of Solitude.

I had a wonderful experience there. Being involved in a parish is so different from being ensconced in a fancy office. I was with people day in and day out, with Mexicans, and it certainly brought me back in touch with my past. This coincides with another important event for me, with Ernie Cortez from the Industrial Areas Foundation coming into East L.A. and talking to Bishop Arzube about the possibility of bringing a community organizing project to East L.A. The word up until then had been that it's impossible to organize the Mexican-American community. So many people had tried it, but nobody had succeeded. Here comes an outsider, and they take Arzube to San Antonio to see what happened with COPS, and he was totally sold on it, completely. He came back and got a group of us East L.A. priests and sisters together and we formed a core. So, now I was into community organizing. It was very exciting because I was in on the ground floor, and we received wonderful training in every possible detail of a campaign. We got the training through the IAF; they brought people in; that's part of their role. They also took people to New York, Chicago, and did extensive ten-day, even month-long training sessions. I never met Saul Alinsky, but I remember when he died. This IAF was around 1979, but it was already working in San Antonio. I really don't think UNO got as sophisticated in the political arena as COPS did. I think it's unfortunate, but each organization has its own identity.

The most significant project that I have been involved in with UNO was insurance red-lining. We had a long, very exciting campaign to change the stereotypes that insurance companies were operating under in determining the rates for different areas. For example, East L.A. had double the rates of Santa Monica, and all because of the stereotype that these are Mexicans and they don't care about their

cars, they drink too much, they don't have garages because they rent them out to other people, and so they leave their car on the street. For these reasons, we have to charge them more. Well, we blew that theory out of the water when we started making comparisons by zip code on the rates, how there was very little difference in the actual accident experience and claims. We did this very scientifically, and we changed things. We actually reduced the rates for East L.A. by about 42 percent. That process took a couple of years, and the community was involved with us. That's the crucial point, that's the whole difference of the community organizing process, is that you involve everyone. We used to have very, very impressive meetings on the issue, with three thousand people in attendance, and confront top insurance officials. We met in different auditoriums. During the whole insurance issue, I was the lead man on it, and that's where I got a lot of media exposure.

Strategies: We had two distinct approaches to the media. One was in preparing a press conference to make sure that all the information is delivered by hand to the different radio and TV stations, to make sure that they get it, to take a personal interest in making sure that they have all the information. Then you follow up by phone to make sure that a reporter is assigned. It's a tremendous amount of work. You can't just send out a press release and expect the media to respond; they don't. You have to coddle them into it. But aside from that, we had many meetings with editorial boards. We'd go in and explain the issue to the editorial board. The issues were clear and sharply defined. The key to successful community organization is the honing down of the issue to where it makes it exciting for them to want to deal with. We had very high level editorial board meetings with the *Los Angeles Times*, *The Herald Examiner*, *La Opinión*, the top radio stations, and TV also. We would take a team of five or six people, and each one had an aspect of the issue to deal with. We were well-versed in it, so *they* found it exciting to meet with *us* because of all the information we had. Then, because of that relationship, we were also able to garner some editorials from these major media institutions. The insurance people were lobbying hard, too, but, you know, they were so obnoxious, the whole business community was so sure that nobody could shake them, that the media didn't like them, so they favored us.

Real serious criticism of me for being a priest and being involved in "political" activity came only from the clergy, my own clergy, who were not involved, and who were primarily not wanting to be involved, and who were using that as an excuse for not becoming involved. I think that was the only serious criticism. It reflected more where they were than being a personal attack on me. But sometimes the politicians tried to tell me, "I don't tell you how to run your church, don't come here and tell me how to run my business." But you just have to let those things fly over you. You're trained not to take things personally. The core group that started UNO was religious, and it was obvious at that time that the reason they had selected these priests and nuns was because that's where the money was for the organizing. See, each religious community that was involved would contribute a certain amount of money to the project. We raised $160,000 just to get things started, mostly from religious communities, including the Claretians.

We picked the insurance red-lining because, well, the way the issues were picked at that time—I must emphasize that a lot of things have changed in the community organizing process, and, like everything else, it grows and develops into something different—but at that time what was very impressive was that the issue was determined through personal interviews. We went from house to house to house talking to people, asking, "What are the things that are bothering you? What are the things that you've got to solve in your community?" Well, this insurance thing kept coming up, that it cost more to insure the car than the car was worth. They were paying twelve and thirteen hundred dollars in insurance on an old jalopy. It had to come from the people. We couldn't go in there and tell them what we thought should be their issue. That is the main difference in successful organizing. I think lately that it's gotten a little bit heady, where the top leadership together with the organizers come up with an idea, and then they say, Let's take it to the people and see if they buy it, rather than the other way. They have been very quiet lately in terms of successes. We don't hear the same excitement. It's a natural phenomenon, too; a community organization has to be periodically disorganized to reorganize; if you don't do that, it just fizzles out.

In the eighties I continued with community organizing, but from Soledad, Our Lady of Solitude, I went to the Old Plaza Church. And there, again, we were doing community organizing at the beginning, but then the scenario changes completely. This is already 1981, and we're getting this big influx of Central Americans. I don't know if you're familiar with Our Lady Queen of Angels, Old Plaza Church, La Placita, well, it's always been like a center for Hispanics; they came from all over the county of L.A. and beyond. We used to have ten thousand people there for mass on Sunday, eleven masses every Sunday, all in Spanish, and they were all filled. We used to have two to three hundred baptisms every weekend, people coming from all over the place. I had seven priests on staff. It's changed somewhat now, but during my tenure, when I came there in 1981, that's when things were really beginning to get bad. Romero was assassinated, and waves of Central Americans, particularly Salvadorans, started to come there. It hadn't been a Mexican church, but because of the Spanish, a lot of people flocked to the place. Out of that we began responding to the need of the Central Americans; some of them were bona fide refugees and had no place to live. We had to find places for them, and it developed that we became a sanctuary church. In 1985 we declared public sanctuary. We became the first Roman Catholic church to declare public sanctuary in Los Angeles. This was a little after they were declaring sanctuary in Arizona; it was the time of the trial of the Arizona people. There were some other Protestant churches that had already declared sanctuary, but this was the first Roman Catholic one.

That's where my troubles with the diocese began. The National Conference of Catholic Bishops has never looked very kindly on sanctuary. It sees it as too political. It coincides almost to the day—our decision to declare public sanctuary, that is—coincides almost to the day with Archbishop Mahony's arrival as the new archbishop in Los Angeles. We didn't time it that way on purpose; well, yes and

no, because we had been preparing the people in the parish for a while before that as to the idea of providing refuge to Central Americans. I say in a sense yes, because I don't think we would've tried it with Cardinal Manning, because he was not attuned to anything that we were doing. But I say this is when my troubles began because when Archbishop Mahony came into town, we were one of the first people to go see him in his office, Father Mike Kennedy and I, and to present the idea to him. He was really excited, he thought it was the greatest thing, and he wanted to be part of the sanctuary movement. We were delighted! We knew he had a progressive reputation, and we thought he would say go ahead, but we didn't think that he would come out and say he wanted to be part of it.

That was in September '85, but then in November, that was the meeting of the Conference of Bishops in Washington, and when he came back, he had changed his mind. So I think somebody put pressure on him there, and, from then on, the whole situation was very ambivalent in terms of our relationship with the archbishop. We got involved in a lot of public controversy in the press. Many misunderstandings. I felt bad because, remember, I come back to the institution thing, I have a strong institutional loyalty. But I am also convinced that anything really creative that is going to make a difference as to the direction that the church takes is going to be peripheral, marginal, going to be in the minority, going to be criticized, going to be rejected. That's part of the ball game. I recognize that. Nevertheless, I felt bad. I wasn't always sure where he stood. Sometimes he was very upset, and sometimes he was very understanding.

I have to walk very carefully here. I don't want to be seen as disloyal—which is what people usually conclude when you criticize, that you're not being loyal to the institution—but I think there's a general approach to authority on the part of the Church that translates into control. Authority means control. I have a very different approach to authority, and I act accordingly. My approach is from its roots of author, that authority is initiating, encouraging, promoting, supporting, and in a sense being able at times to let go so that things can move. You don't have to be in control. Not every good idea has to come from you. Many times people have found themselves in their relationship to their bishop playing a little game, making them think that this idea is coming from them and that you're just going to play it out. I think that's very prevalent. It stifles creativity, and that's when conflicts develop.

But maybe I was getting too much publicity, too. Every time the archbishop turned around, there was Olivares on the news. He once asked me, "Do you call a press conference every time you brush your teeth?" We had a good relationship on a personal level, but there was on my part a lack of understanding that regardless of what was going on, he's the boss, and he will always be the boss, and there's no getting around that. I can't knock him out of his position as the boss. That has to sink in. But, at the same time, I wasn't going to let that stifle what I felt I had to do. He kind of understood. He told me very clearly, "I understand what you're doing, and I see that you have to do what you have to do, but don't expect me to be right there on every issue that you get involved in."

Well, from '85 the Claretian superiors felt that things had gotten out of hand at La Placita. I mean, we were having two hundred men sleeping in the basement of the hall, just street people. So, in 1989 it came out that I was going to be changed from La Placita. This was not my initiative, but I understood it. I had been there nine years, and that's a long time. Normal tenure is six years, maximum. They extended mine for an additional three because of what I was doing, so it was almost inevitable that they should want to change me. However, my concern was that what we had done there would somehow continue. That it continue to be a place of refuge for Central Americans, that it continue to reach out to the poor, that it continue to be a very strong symbol that the Church cares about the poor, which it became internationally. I wanted that to continue, but I don't think that people understand fully the concept of sanctuary as symbol. They see it in terms of its practical aspects, giving shelter, and so on. But I don't think they see the very powerful symbol that it is: in the midst of great suffering, it is a symbol that the Church cares.

I was scheduled then to go to Fort Worth, Texas, which I was okay with. It's a nice parish; I would be glad to go, a change of pace. But then I got sick. I picked up AIDS in Central America, in El Salvador, from a contaminated needle. And that took care of everything. Now I'm here just waiting it out. I don't feel angry; I feel almost like my life is already over, and I'm simply waiting for the final blow, you know. Physically I feel fine; it's a psychological problem. Sometimes I feel like I haven't really dealt with it. I'm not afraid to die; no, dying doesn't bother me; we all have to die eventually, and I know that my time will come. Motivation is the problem. It's unbelievable; I never imagined that I could ever be in this state of mind.

I was in El Salvador several times. This particular time we went to the refugee camps, and the hygienic conditions there in the clinics, and everywhere, are very bad. I have a hard time remembering the actual date, but it would have been around August 1986 or '87. I came back, and in November I got walloped with hepatitis, devastated. I was out of commission for a long time, a whole month in bed and about two or three months without going to work, recuperating. I had a stomach virus while I was there in El Salvador, then this AIDS thing popped up just since last year; it's been a year now. I was deadly sick. They didn't think I would make it, and they called my family from San Antonio. They all got together, and then I regained consciousness. I saw all my sisters and brothers, and I thought I'd already died! But I was unconscious, or semiconscious, for about a week or so, floating in and out, hallucinating. I remember some of the things that I saw, and people have told me some of the things that I said, so I know I wasn't all there. The way it manifested itself was through what they call an opportunistic infection; there's always an opportunistic infection, and that's what kills you. It might be pancreatitis, pneumonia, cancer. I got meningitis. I wasn't responding to massive doses of medication, and that's when the doctors said, "We don't think he's going to make it." But I did, and here I am. Actually, I'm feeling quite well. Every two weeks I need a blood transfusion because the AZT causes anemia, your blood count goes down very low. But aside from that, physically, I don't feel

sick at all. What I've got to deal with is what I hope to accomplish from now on. I can't get motivated to do much. It's almost like, what's the use, but I'm trying to fight that feeling.

As I look back on my life, I think that it seemed like the greatest thing that had ever happened to me was when I became pastor at Soledad; there was such closeness to an identifiable community. But as the years go by there are things that seem better, like Plaza, La Placita, such a huge place and such a myriad of activities, and so many people there that you can never get really close to many. Nevertheless, I think that what we did at Plaza—by "we" I mean Father Mike Kennedy and the other members of the team who worked with me there, and the association I had with the religious community throughout the city of Los Angeles—I got to come together with some remarkable people, both religious leaders and lay people. But what we did at Plaza was, at least for a brief period of time, to show what is possible when you want to respond to the needs of the downtrodden, the rejected. As an example, opening up the doors of the church so that people who are staying out on the street in the cold and the rain, subject to being attacked, and here's an empty church, sitting idle all night long, and how easy it was just to throw the doors open and say, "It's okay, come on in." It got to the point where we eventually had to do something because it got too big, but, nevertheless, it's so unlike all the other churches that don't see what's possible. At least we showed what's possible, that if you want to, you *can* do something. The regret I have is that it didn't outlive me, that it has changed dramatically. In a way, I think that people who establish something bear a responsibility for its continuity by making sure that enough people are on board so that after you are gone it will continue, and that's what we failed to do. We didn't build a base for it. It's ironic, but we didn't put into practice our community organizing principles—I guess because it's a lot of work, and we were so busy day to day.

I'm not disciplined enough to write, and I don't keep a journal. But these are my thoughts as I look back on my life.

Otto López

For a while, Otto López, a resident of Los Angeles and an expert auto mechanic, thought that community meant gang membership. But as his friends, one by one, became victims of gang violence, López determined to create a more positive community structure, a low riders' car club, which became an important source of unity for its members, but an irritant to the local police.

With openness, warmth, and good humor, López describes his desire to "belong" and to contribute to the broader community; in the process, he offers valuable commentary on the state of relations among various racial and ethnic communities in the city of Los Angeles.

Interview

I was four years old when I arrived here from the Yucatán with my mom and my brothers and sister. My dad had come in 1960 and started out working as a dishwasher. From there he moved up and started working at a Chevron station pumping gas. Then he moved up to salesman, to lead salesman, to manager, and then he got his own station where we are right now. We've had this station since about 1971. We recently purchased the garage next door, too. My dad has taught me certain basic values, such as what's yours is yours, and what's not yours, don't touch it; don't lie; don't steal; don't litter, and don't make fun of the Mexican national anthem. Once in a while, I'll make fun of Mexico, after I've had a few beers and they're playing the anthem. I just know a couple of bad words in Spanish from the people at work, and they use them to make fun of their national anthem. My dad gets offended when I do that. He still feels identified with Mexico.

He's still a citizen of Mexico, and I am too. I have my green card. I've lived most of my life here, but I've lived a couple of years in Mexico, too. We went back and I went to elementary school back there in the Yucatán. Out here I went to elementary, junior high, and I graduated from high school. For some years, I was involved in a gang; during that time I flunked one entire grade. One day my dad he told me—well, he didn't really tell me verbal-wise—he hit me a couple of times. I couldn't believe it. I just looked at him. The thing is that I really did deserve it, and it helped knock some sense into me.

Elementary school was good. I didn't see any racism until one day when I was in fifth grade I realized that something was wrong. I had just arrived from Mexico, my English was pretty poor, but my math was superb. I was better than the smartest student in the classroom, and I wondered why I was getting lower grades. One time we had a test, and I could answer all the questions. I was very good. Then my mom says, "You got a D in math." I couldn't believe it. "Well," she said, " you must not be studying." I knew something was wrong there. In the sixth grade I had a different teacher, and my grade went from a D to a B. He was a black teacher, and he would tell me, "Well, sometimes you really don't understand things until you're much older. It's just part of life, and it has happened to me, too." I didn't know what he was talking about until I was about twenty and I started trying to get myself together. You know, I was going back through my life and asking what I was doing and where I was going. What really hurt in the fifth grade was that I knew that I could beat everybody in that class in math. Still, I would get a D, go home, and my mom would blame me.

The junior high was very different from the elementary school. It was about 80 percent black, and most of the rest were Asians, very few Hispanics at all. Some,

not all or even most, but some of the black kids there would take the other kids' money, treat them bad, and make crude insults about Mexicans, and I was still a little kid. I didn't like the school at all. Some of the teachers were pretty good, mostly white. But I transferred to Berendo Junior High, also public, which was 60 percent Hispanic, and the rest were white, Asian, and black.

That's when I started getting close to the gangs. I mostly felt I should do it because of security. I met these friends who lived not too far from our house. We don't live in a mostly Hispanic neighborhood; it's completely mixed, white, black, Oriental, some Hispanics. We were called the 18th Street Gang. One day they approached me; they came to the house and we started talking. Then we started hanging out together. I was about fourteen when I joined them. They usually beat you up before you could become a member, but they didn't do anything to me. After that, we mostly fought other gangs. We would just see them and fight. It was always spontaneous, never planned. Thank God we didn't have very many weapons; we had some, but not like they do now. The gang thing lasted until I was about nineteen or twenty. What happened was that after my dad gave me that "lesson," I started backing away from them, and I started thinking things over for myself.

He finally hit me because of a lot of things that had built up. I had flunked a grade; I was absent for twenty-five days from one class. He was upset that I didn't care about anything, that I wasn't doing what I was supposed to be doing; hey, I wasn't doing *anything*! My attitude was terrible. When he found out that I had flunked, he wouldn't look at me or eat at the same table with me. He was trying to get me to realize that what I was doing was wrong. Gradually, I started backing away from the gang and going back to school. I started hanging around by myself, and they would come by, but they didn't put pressure on me. I was lucky because they were doing drugs by then. Some of them would do acid and drink; that was really stupid.

I remember one time at one of our parties a guy came up to us and said, "I'm gonna drop some acid, you want some?" I said, "No, thank you." So he said, "Would you just do me a favor then. Keep an eye on me because I might do something crazy." Soon after that, he started yelling, "Aaaaaahh!" I said, "Calm down, it's all right, calm down." I was scared because it was like he had gone crazy. He finally fell asleep, and later he told us that while he was high he saw a giant spider crawling up his leg. He would reach for it, but his hand kept going right through the spider, and it kept on crawling. Then another one started crawling up his leg and the same thing happened, and another one, and so on. Acid is really weird stuff.

I started with the gang for power. See, when I was in Berendo Junior High, it felt like power. Then when I went to L.A. High, it was different. There, rival gangs were always after each other. It's funny, though, how you go through life and you find some teachers, and you know some teachers really care, they really want you to make it. There was this algebra teacher, Mr. Rock, and he says to me, "Otto, this class, if you don't pass it you're not going to go to the high school." And he helped me. He stayed after school to help me; he tried to keep me away from the gang and

he gave me rides home. He was an excellent teacher and he actually cared. It's hard to find people like that. After that, I went to high school, and it was bad. I didn't find any good teachers in high school. Mostly they were at the junior high. And at high school I went through the same thing that I went through at the first junior high, that the majority—the blacks—were always after the minority—the Mexicans. One day we were hanging around—there were about six of us from our gang—and about twelve or fifteen guys came up to us and started a fight with us. There was only six of us, so we ended up running, but I tripped and fell and they all started hitting me. They beat me up so bad that I could hardly get home.

Well, we got mad and wanted to retaliate. So about thirty of us got together and we went into the school and started fighting with anybody we could find, it didn't matter who because we were just retaliating. The next day we didn't go to school, but the following day we did, and all of us got a summons to see the dean and to bring our parents. The teachers all told us how dangerous and bad we were and how we were going to get kicked out of school. My dad and I got upset because the dean, who was a black guy, started the meeting by saying, "You Mexicans always. . . ." I told the dean, "You have some nerve to tell us this, because when the black guys hit us you didn't do anything about it. You're not Mexican, and you're not going to do anything about it now either." When the dean asked my dad why I was so upset, my dad answered him, "He has good reason, because he was beat up bad." Now, I'm more mature and I see things differently. I'm good friends with a lot of black guys, and I know that good and bad come in all colors, but back then, being in a gang made the racial situation worse. I mean, gang membership and certain racial attitudes kind of went hand in hand.

Anyway, the result was that we were kicked out of L.A. High and sent to Belmont, which was mostly Hispanic. But we weren't all sent there; they split us up. Some went to Fairfax, some to Belmont, and others to Marshall High. They kicked me out of Belmont too—I don't remember for what reasons now—and I went back to L.A. High. I tried not to be scared. I just kept thinking that all you have to do is remember that if you don't bother them, they won't bother you. But since they were armed, I was armed, too. Many times I carried a gun for protection, but I never bothered anyone.

Eventually, I turned nineteen and they told me that I couldn't continue coming to day school, that I had to go to night school. So I went to night school, and I graduated from high school. After I graduated, I started a car club with six or seven other guys. A friend had told me not to do it, that they were just gangs with cars, and that the cops would stop you for no reason. But I loved cars and I was through with the gang. At first at our meetings, we would just sit there and drink. Finally, we said, look, man, we've got to do something with ourselves. It took us about two or three years to get organized. We had a 1954 Chevy, four-door, and I had been working on low riders since before I started high school. I would fix them up and put in the hydraulics, but I had given it up for a while. My first car I had when I was fifteen. It had lifts and all that, but that's when my dad found out that I wasn't going to school, so he took it away from me and sold it.

In the club we started we each owned our cars individually, and we would help each other fix their car up. Each one would contribute; we would help each other find parts, buy parts, and put them on. Little by little, we did it. One of our friends had a Monte Carlo, and I sold my Chevy and bought his Monte Carlo, and he bought a Cadillac. His Cadillac already had hydraulics, but he wanted a paint job, so he got a better paint job. Then I took my car in to get a better paint job, too. His cost about three or four thousand, and mine cost two thousand four hundred. They were candied, that's why they were so expensive. We really started fixing everybody's cars up, because the better your car looked, the more trophies you got, and the better name for your club. Our club is called the Artistics. It still exists, but most of the main guys are into other things now. We started about 1980. We would go to events and meet members of other car clubs. We would mostly find out about events through cruising, which means driving and seeing other people and other cars. You go real slow, and then you hang out at the station. You would hear that one car club was having a dance, and they would invite us, and vice versa. On our anniversary we would have dinner with a table for twenty couples. We would have baseball contests with other clubs. It was really fun; it was one of the best parts of my life. The dances were fun because you never had to worry about fighting anybody, like with a gang. We didn't want to be considered a gang, because all that does is make problems. We went cruising. I can remember, we got on really good with other car clubs and we had a big picnic where we played soccer, softball, and talked. It was really nice. I have pictures at home; I also have pictures of my car, which actually came out in a magazine.

I've sold my car now. I had a friend do an oil painting of it before I sold it, and he put my name on it. It's funny, you go cruising, you meet people, but it started getting a bad name. The police would say, "Well, look what we have here. There goes a cholo gang member." They just assumed you were a gang member if you had a low rider. They just destroyed it for me—it's terrible! I didn't want to be considered what I used to be because what I used to be wasn't good. I wanted to stay away from all that, and believe me, you want to avoid the police. Just some of the cops are bad, but still, you don't want to take any chances. Actually, three members from our car club became police officers themselves, but they don't pull low riders over because they know they're not out there to bother anybody. I was in the club for about seven years. We didn't have any girls in our car club, but we knew some girls who had cars, and they had their own club. It was fun, having a club.

You have to treat your members good for them to stay. You can't treat them like a number, but like family. You have to talk to them, hang with them, tell them what's going on, trust them, like a *compadre*. We had some good times. Once we were in a film made by Cineastes Mexicanos called *Que no me bese el mariachi*—Don't let the mariachi kiss me. It was terrible, but we had fun because we got to ride our low riders. Our club had twenty-three members. I wish I could keep it up; I put more than one hundred percent into it. But when we started getting a bad rap, it wasn't fun anymore. Maybe a few car clubs had gang members, but the rest of us didn't. I don't go cruising anymore either, because you have to

Otto López's low rider

have the car to do it. When you get a little older you start to change. For example, I have a friend who does spray paintings. I really like dolphins, and I think it would look great to have him spray paint a dolphin mural on the door here at the garage. But then I decided not to do it because my dad might not like it. After all, I'm trying to move up more in the business here.

I hate it that in the rap songs and in the movies, too, all they talk about is gang bangers. It gives us all a bad name. I mean there's mechanics and engineers and attorneys, too. Why don't they show more people like that teacher at Garfield High, Jaime Escalante? Why can't they include people who can show everybody, including the cops, that chicanos aren't all gang bangers?

Stereotypes like that make me want to contribute more to the community. I mean, I know what the bad things are, and I'm trying to make something good of my life. The L.A. marathon comes right through here, and I give some of my time to that. I joined the Catholic big brothers at one point. You have to give a lot of time, and you have to be careful what you say. The kid will tell you a problem and then ask you, "What should I do?" It's a big responsibility. I might try it again, maybe I could teach some kid that gangs are not it. They think that's it; they think gangs are everything. They think, This is *my* barrio. I tell them, "This is a street that the city owns. You gonna die for a street that the city owns?"

The whole gang thing just doesn't make any sense, and it makes racism worse. For example, one time, when I was at Berendo, we had all these different gangs, a lot of Hispanics, mostly chicanos. One day a black gang came to Berendo to fight. I wasn't going there at that time. Later, everybody called what happened next the

"three o'clock news." The black gang was very powerful, but all the different gangs at Berendo cooperated for once. They all got together to fight the invading gang out of their school. On the news they said that the different gangs were throwing cocktails. People are attracted to gangs for power; they never think about how dangerous it is, or about how it makes you stereotype people. Like the gangs in the "three o'clock news," they think belonging to a gang and fighting gives them power.

I'll tell you something that happened to me a few years ago. Every year our parish has a carnival. They never have it for the cinco de mayo, I don't know why, but that's okay. There were a couple of kids at the festival who were writing on the wall of the restroom. I said, "What are you doing. Stop writing on the wall. Degrading the church is not very nice." They answered, "Leave me alone or I'm gonna tell my home boy." They were wearing 18th Street clothes, and they were little kids, maybe twelve years old. I said, "Who're you going to tell?" One of them answers with a name, and I tell him, "Did you know that he's dead?" They said, "How do you know?" And I told them, "Because he was one of my home boys, and I went to his funeral two months ago." It scared them and they left, but that was the truth. I had gone to his funeral two months before that. They are so vulnerable at that age, they can be brainwashed easily. I wish I could go back and spend more time in school, to help me know more so I could help other people.

Knowing what I know now, if I went back to school and if I got crummy teachers or racist ones, or people approaching me to join a gang, I'd tell my mom that I want to go to a different school. There are six of us; four of us went to public schools, and the last two went to private schools. Now my little brother John is in college; he's the only one to go. He's pretty sharp, so he might have gone to college even if he'd gone to public school. I always told him to stay away from the gangs. At one time he started writing on walls, and I told him don't, to stop, and to keep going to school. I always try to give him advice. We talk a lot. John works part-time at the garage. My other brother Robert drives a semi truck. My sister Flora works at a hospital as an interpreter.

Right now you can't say that it's easy to be a mechanic. It's hard and it's getting more difficult to keep up with what's going on. Mostly all new cars have computers. About 90 percent of the cars now are fuel injection, and people are scared to work on them. But it's not that hard. I like trying things; you just have to go by trial and error. You look at the book and it tells you to do this; you do this, and it doesn't work, so you have to experiment and do what looks like it makes sense. I like being a manager, too. Most of my customers are regulars, they're mostly white, but I have some black and Hispanic customers too. They come to us because they trust us. My dad always told me never to lie, always be honest, tell them if you don't know something.

He said always be honest. Once, I was arrested for having my guns in my trunk. I collect guns—that's my hobby now—and I belong to the NRA. The guns were in their gun pouches inside a back pack. The only thing that was wrong was that they were loaded, all three of them. I was pulled over, and I had forgot my wallet. I was with a couple of girls and this cop pulled me over and took me to jail. The

attorney representing me was terrible, just awful. I got him through a friend. Some friend! I can laugh about all this now and about how embarrassed I was in front of those girls when he pulled me over and I didn't have my wallet. Anyway, the lawyer told me to plead guilty with an appeal. I wanted to know if I could get my guns back—that was really important to me—but I didn't have a permit for them. The cops said no. They asked me a whole bunch of questions, and I'm honest, so I told them the truth about everything, that I had been in a gang, that I smoked grass, things like that.

A month later I went to court. There were two courtrooms. I saw my name on one and went there and waited and waited. Then I went back over to the other one and they shouted, "Otto López." I said, "Yes, sir." Then they said that they'd been waiting for two hours and where was my attorney. Finally, he arrived and we went up to the front to the judge, who was excellent. He asked me why I had belonged to the gang, and if I'd ever been arrested for anything before. I told him, "I try to be a law-abiding citizen to the utmost. Once in a while, I fail here and there, I'm not gonna lie to you." So then he says, "Okay. Case dismissed, case dismissed, case dismissed." He dismissed my case and started dismissing everybody else's too. He was great.

Then I said to my good-for-nothing attorney, "Ask him if I can have my guns back." He asks and the judge said, "This courthouse does not return any weapons to anybody." Then I said to the judge, "Sir, as you can see, the report says that the guns were in gun pouches in the backpack in the trunk. I wasn't going to cause anybody any harm." He responded, "They were?" Then he asked, "Why did you have the guns?" I told him, "I'm a gun collector. As you can see, guns appreciate in value. They don't depreciate if you keep them in good shape, and I keep mine in good shape." So he told me, "Okay, we'll get your guns back." I got a court order to get the guns back. I was sort of on probation or surveillance for a year, but I didn't have to report, and that passed quickly. All my police officer friends had told me that I would never see my guns again. So, it does pay to be honest.

I have about five police officer friends. Some of them are scared; they don't even like to stop cars because they have to be so careful about what they say and do. Nowadays, if they even handcuff somebody, they feel like they'll get in trouble. They always ask me to join the force, but I'm fine where I am.

I have friends who always think that that white guy or that Jewish guy is going to use you. But I don't think that. I think that some people use you if you let them, but that most people are pretty good. Some things are unfair, but you can't get all upset about it. My dad told me that when he was working for Standard Oil, he was the lead salesman for eight months and then he got promoted. This other guy came and he was there for three months and they kept on promoting him. But then, my dad said to himself, "You are a good guy, and good guys are always needed." Later, he got the station. So it isn't that everybody's bad. You have to take some chances and trust people. You can't go around being afraid or suspicious or mad all the time. My dad says, "Why put yourself through all that. It just makes you sour." He's a hard man, but he's taught me a lot.

I really enjoy the work at the station. I love cars, and I love to work on them. I plan to stay here and at the garage. I also like to deal with people, to give them advice about their cars. It feels good to tell people what is wrong with their car and to give them an estimate of what's needed. Most people don't know anything about their cars, and they ask me, "Otto, do I really need this?" I know that they trust me. Some customers go out of their way to let me know they appreciate me. I've got some customers who, after I work on their car, they say, "Okay, I'm gonna take you to lunch now." It feels good. Of course you've also got your bad days like when this lady came in and wanted a smog check, but some of her equipment was disconnected. When I gave her an estimate, she said, "You're just a thief, you just want more money. You're a liar." I told my dad, and he said to get her car out of here now, that he didn't want to have anything to do with her. So I told her it would be better to take her car somewhere else. And she did.

But I've seen people who've been ripped off. One lady came in with a Honda. She had gotten her thermostat changed, and they had charged her ninety dollars to do it. That's ridiculous! At the most, I would've charged her thirty dollars with the part. But people make mistakes, too; I know I've made mistakes. I worked on one car, and the customer requested work which was not correct. His car had air suspension, and he wanted me to put the coil springs on it and to take the air bags off, and I did it. Then he asked, "Well, isn't the car unsafe?" I said, "Yeah, but I told you not to do it." Then he told me, "I want my money back." I gave him his money back, and I lost. I had told him not to do it, but he wanted it done anyway. I shouldn't have done the work at all, even though the customer wanted it, because I knew it wasn't right. I should've just said no. You live and learn. Sometimes things are difficult, cars are complicated and sometimes it takes a lot of work to figure out exactly what's wrong and to fix it. Most customers understand. You meet people and you get to know them in this business. Everyone is different. Just some are bad, not all or even most.

María Guadalupe Martínez Torres

By bus and by taxi, this busy Mexican woman shuttles back and forth across the Río Grande to participate in binational meetings on justice in the *maquiladoras*, or foreign-owned industries that line the U.S.-Mexican border, to testify before councils and commissions dealing with *maquiladora* issues, and to cover her designated Mexican territory from Matamoros to Coahuila where she organizes women workers to defend their rights, to insist on improved working conditions, and to agitate for stricter environmental controls.

Because of her commitment to community, to women, their families, their neighborhoods, and their environmental health, María Guadalupe Martínez Torres has taken on giant multinational corporations and placed herself at the center of controversy.

Interview

I was born in San Luis Potosí, and I came to Matamoros about thirty years ago. I'm forty-six years old. I came because we were very poor, and there were no opportunities at home. My *mamá* and I arrived here with empty hands. My *papá* had died much earlier. My mother is very strong and independent; I get my energy from her. I started working very young, *en la casa pues hacía mandados,* doing chores at home. Then I started going with my *mamá* to the other side to work as domestics in the homes of the *gente rica*, the rich people in Brownsville. We earned eight dollars a week, which was a good salary; the dollar was at 12.5 pesos them. We lived hidden in the houses where we were working. It was fine except that my mother was working in a different house, and I missed her. I was very young and I had no experience with children, but they asked me to care for six children, and the *más chiquito*, the youngest one, was only a month old. I became very attached to those children during the three years that I was there, and I was sad to leave them. Then I changed to another house, and then another, until finally I came back to this side looking for work in Matamoros.

I have always liked it better here on the Mexican side. I only went to school through the third grade here, but there were many patriotic *fiestas* and I always identified with Mexican history and culture. My mother would starch my petticoats and send me to the parties. I had a great childhood filled with love. I insisted that my mom and I return here from Brownsville because I wanted to work in the new electronics *maquiladora*. That was about twenty-five years ago. She thought that I would have a better life if I got married and lived in the U.S., but I insisted that we come here. In the meantime, we arranged to get temporary cards that allowed us to go across the border to work whenever we wanted. With our local cards we came and went as domestics for quite a while. We found a tiny house to rent here; it just had one room and the bed barely fit. We went out to eat because we couldn't buy a stove. Our first purchases were a *vaso*, a plastic glass which we still have, and a *vasija*, a pitcher for taking water from the spigot. The house is torn down now, and they've put something else up. We lived in it for a long time while *mamá* kept working on the other side and I looked for work on this side.

Unfortunately, I didn't find anything for quite a while. They were only hiring girls whose parents or families were part of a syndicate, sons and especially daughters, say, of the waiters' union. I went around getting letters of recommendation, letters from teachers, friends, but it was of no use. So I started working in a purse factory owned by an Argentine. It was a hidden factory, which means that it was illegal, not organized according to Mexican laws. It was in a *casa cualquiera*, an ordinary house. In the back was where about twenty of us worked in one big

room, seated on the ground on newspapers. I remember there were no chairs at all. We made *bolsas de tejido para tiendas elegantes*, woven fabric purses for elegant stores. Finally, someone reported us to the syndicate. The union reps arrived, violently barging in and pushing around the Argentine *señor* and his pregnant wife, and destroying the factory. *Lo corrieron*. They ran him off and said to us, "Those of you who want to work, come with us and join the union." They brought a little car around, and we all piled in it. I ran like a flash to be the first one in. That's how I joined the union, but it wasn't as easy as they said.

First they sent us to ECC, Electronic Control Corporation. I was so happy. The first day we got there, they took us on a tour of the factory. We all started working there, but they said that they would only be able to keep ten of us, and that the others would be permanently employed later. I was one of the "later" ones. But in the meantime, I worked my fingers to the bone for three months, because I wanted to be one of the ones chosen. The man had told me that if I worked hard, I would have the opportunity to stay. I was number one in production, and my hands were so swollen, because there was a little wheel and we had to thread it with a wire. It's a fine, repetitive movement like sewing; the product is electric coils. I stuck myself with the wire a lot. Most workers could make one boxful, but I would do three. We were all doing this work in hopes that we would be one of those chosen to be permanent. Of course, they had told us all that we would be permanent at the beginning. I was one of the *eventuales* even though I did the best work. It made me furious, because they had lied to me. Finally, they sent us to Union Carbide, and then I started off *con pie derecho*—on the right foot—and eager, because I went with a good recommendation from the other factory.

I always asked for the first shift, from 7 a.m. till 4 p.m. There we made energy condensers for NASA's moon exploration. I liked doing it, and I worked in the injection area. That's where they inject the liquid into the capacitor, and you have only fifteen minutes to work the epoxy. They gave me the smallest materials because they thought I was the most dexterous. They also put me on the epoxy line. It makes some people very ill, but it didn't bother me—of course, who knows in the long run. Some of the materials there were very harmful. For example, we used methylene chloride to wash the capacitors and to clean the table with, too. We didn't know that it was a carcinogen. Many of us washed parts in it regularly without any protective equipment, not even gloves. We just used our bare hands. The odor was horrible, and many people would get dizzy and faint. Some people would inhale the fumes and their heart would stop beating; they would have to have artificial respiration. But we still had to ask permission to go to the bathroom. They treated us very badly.

The supervisors were mostly Americans—some Mexicans, but not many at that time. There were two *gringos* who watched over us in the line and treated us like we were nothing. I began talking with some of the other *muchachas*, telling them that this was not right. I started asking them to go with me to the church where they were holding some orientation classes for us. They wouldn't go because they were afraid. I was incredulous! "What have you got to lose?" I kept asking them.

Zenith maquiladora, Matamoros

Finally, I got fifteen to go, and it was as if someone had opened the curtain and let the light shine in. That meeting marked the beginning of a flight that no one has been able to bring down. We keep learning and learning and learning, and what we learn we teach to others.

Our friend Eduardo was the one I met at the first of these meetings. We owe him so much. He and his wife were both there. The group had a religious base, but it was not a church project. That was the beginning. We learned that solvents are dangerous, to wash our hands, basic things like that. But over the years, we have learned that we have rights and that we have to defend them. We have learned to *valorarnos*, to value ourselves. We took a giant step forward the day that we brought Eduardo a label that listed the contents of one of the solvents. That was in 1984.

Soon after that, Union Carbide headquarters in New York sent inspectors to the *maquiladora*. They searched everything in all the work areas. The changes came immediately afterwards. They called us all together, because by then the Commission on Safety in the Workplace had come too, but this was really eye-wash on the part of the company, just to make them look good for finally doing what they should have done all along. I was in a delicate position because I was an outspoken leader of the workers and a member of the worker safety commission. I knew that if I used my name in any of the reports, that the union leaders would

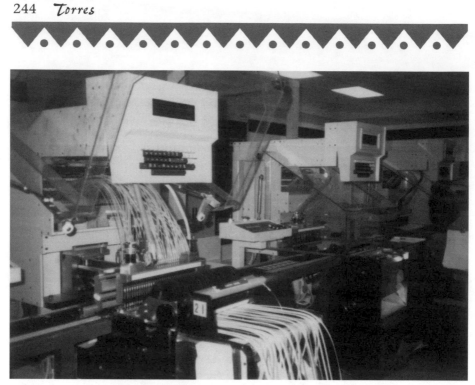

Delnosa maquiladora, Matamoros

see it and there would be reprisals. Sometimes the union is as much of a problem for workers as the *maquilas*.

Very soon after the inspections, our supervisors called us all together and said that things were going to change and that we would have a safe workplace. They made big changes, too. They began having safety inspections at regular intervals, every month. They replaced many of the floor bosses, managers, and assistant managers. They were still mostly Americans, but they were much better. The company put in big extractors to filter out gases and liquids. They kept the methylene chloride in tightly sealed containers. They provided safety goggles and gloves for protection from the heat and fumes. Those were things that we had been working for for a long time. Today, Kemet de México, as the firm is known here, *se autonombra líder mundial en seguridad*—calls itself a world leader in safety. That's a big exaggeration, but they did make important improvements. And they now respond to our complaints. What we have to do is continue to *concientiza*r, to raise workers' awareness of themselves as part of a group, because a hazard or poor condition does not only affect that one worker, it affects the whole group. There is strength in numbers, too. We have to train people always to use the protective materials, to be alert to hazards. If there is an exposed wire for example, to report it, take it to the safety coordinator. That *señor* takes our descriptions and works with us to train us and to tell us why we should use this or that safety measure. He is Mexican and speaks Spanish. Now most of the Americans speak enough Spanish so that you can understand them.

Zenith maquiladora, Matamoros

There are many more Mexican executives now, too. Most of the managers are still Americans, but most of the assistant managers are Mexicans, and many of these are women. But, I tell you, I would much rather *discutir*—argue—with a male supervisor than a female one. I feel that I can express myself better and defend myself better with a man. I can manipulate a man better, too. The problem is that the women supervisors go to your bathroom. They are always right there with you, they hear everything you say, and they spy on you. I have always been a hard working person, and I have left a lot of myself in that job, a lot of dedication, and to have these women spying on me is not right. So when they come in the bathroom, I say, *"Tú ¿qué quieres? ¿Quieres cagar o quieres cartular?"* "Hey you! What do you want? To take a shit or to take notes?" There was a woman who was *jefa de producción*, head of the production department, and she was terrible about hanging out in the bathroom and then distorting what we said. I started following her around and confronting her publicly with the lies that she had been telling about me especially. That was the only way to deal with her, openly, because she would rather go behind your back. She would always try to run away from talking to us face to face. We nicknamed her *la caballona*, "horsy," *porque era buena pa' correr*—because she was good at running! She would tell you something and before you could answer her back, *ppphhhhhhht*, she was gone.

We women organized ourselves and wanted to continue working on our own to make improvements, because when you join the union, *se agotan todos los recursos*—there go all your resources. Also, you are allowed only one delegate and one

alternate from each shift to represent your ideas. It's a big honor, but not very many people. However, we realized early on that we needed to join the union if we wanted to accomplish anything. At that time our immediate goal was to get air conditioning in the work area. We could hardly stand that hot work and those fumes without good air conditioning. We had an active planning group, and we met often in nearby cafés to plan. There were management *orejas*, spies [ears] in the group, but we learned more from them than they did from us. Without knowing, they would feed us valuable information about management. Soon a union representative began coming to our meetings to talk to us, and we realized that the union would be a great benefit to us. Their safety talks, for example, were, and are, very good, and so we joined. The problem is that union leaders earn a fortune. From just one maquiladora they get *cien millones de pesos por semana—por semana!* [one hundred million pesos per week, *per week!*] The labor leaders are the best maintained men in the world. What they give us, *la gente obrera*, the working people, is *muy poco*, very little. We have achieved a great deal through the union, but we need much more.

I'm now working full time with Eduardo and others in the CDTO, the Comité para la Defensa de las Trabajadoras Obreras, the Workers' Defense Committee. I am the director for this side of the border, from Matamoros to Coahuila. I go from place to place by taxi or bus, usually with some other *promotores*, or organizers, working with churches and ecumenical groups that help us with our program. The problem is that I always have to be dividing my time between these endeavors and my *mamá*. She says that I'm never there at home with her. She is eighty-five years old now, and she complains a lot, that's my problem. She doesn't have any company because no one can stand to be around her because she complains all the time. My work is very demanding and so is my mother. I can never talk with her about my problems, she just complains and criticizes everything, and she's in excellent health. I have had headaches for a long time; I don't know if it's from the chemicals over the years or what, but they've been getting worse. I have sinusitis because of the chemicals. The headaches are so bad that they make me dizzy and make me vomit. The doctor just gives me drugs that make me sleep. They've recommended an operation for the sinusitis, but I don't have time to be in the hospital. I suffer from low blood pressure and I get weak very easily. The heat overcomes me; every summer I get sick. I also have mood swings, *cambios de humor*, because of the low blood pressure. With the problems that my *mamá* gives me, the constant responsibility of my community organizing, and my physical problems, sometimes I get very, very depressed. When I go to the doctor, I don't know what to tell him, because it's so hard to tell all this to a man, also about menopause. I wish I had a woman doctor, but I don't know of any around here.

I'll tell you something that has affected me to this day and is a big limitation in my life. When I was very young, I had typhoid fever. I was sick for forty days with a raging fever. As a result, there are certain things that my mind cannot grasp. I'm very slow at getting numbers and dates. I spent many years in third grade. I feel very close to the *la gente de las colonias que no se le escucha*, the people in the poor

areas who no one listens to. When I am able to something for them, I feel good. All my work is here with the *maquila* women.

Something that has been wonderful for me personally and that has been a very successful organizing technique are the *sociodramas* that we do in people's homes. These are role-playing situations where someone plays the part of the worker, someone else the manager, and so on. The idea is to practice a likely situation before it occurs so that the worker is prepared and knows her rights. That way she can't be intimidated or caught off guard, and can cite the specific regulations that protect her in a given situation. For example, suppose the supervisor threatens to fire you if you don't work overtime tonight; or to dock your pay because there was a wait at the clinic where you took your baby; or to let you go because you accidentally used the emergency exit before you knew what it was. We practice such situations with dialogue and everything. We have a good time, and we learn how to defend ourselves, which gives us more confidence.

I'm also involved in a binational *comité de apoyo*, support group, and we get together often. They're from Edinburgh, McAllen, Brownsville, all from the Valley. You know, *el charquito que nos divide*, the little stream that divides us, is no longer so important. *Somos una sola cultura*, we are a single culture fighting against pollution. It's the same here as there, the same water and the same air. So we should not separate ourselves; we should feel united because our problems are the same. We, as Mexicans, are asked for our papers every time we cross the border, but not the pollution. It passes freely, without permission. We are supporting a group of *colonos*, residents of a very poor neighborhood, who are fighting against Química Fluor. Toxic wastes from the plant have contaminated the soil and the water of the surrounding community. The people have complained and asked that the company be moved. But instead of moving the plant, Química Fluor wants to move the people, who now face giving up their homes. The company won, but we are going to keep on challenging them.

Another problem that we need to address is a social one, I guess you could say. It has to do with the effects of the *maquiladora* system on the people as a whole, and on the family. For one thing, there is much sexual extortion on the job. It is a shame, but our own Mexican supervisors take advantage of these young girls who come here to work. There is so much ignorance. We are working on this everywhere, but progress is slow. The girls are so inexperienced. They come from the countryside from all over the republic with the dream of working in a clean, pretty job, well paid, with benefits. They come alone to live with a girlfriend; they leave their families behind. Soon they bring up a sister or a cousin, and then their parents. But it is a chaos because you know, in all Mexican families, the man es *él que manda*, the one in charge. He supports the family and gives his permission for everything. When the father comes here, he does not find work. He finds women, either in the factories or somewhere else, and he begins to drink and to throw away what his daughters bring home. He takes up with another woman and becomes a parasite. He feels bad about himself because the one who was in charge *ya no manda*, is no longer in charge, and he has no other role. He was probably a farmer

before and knows nothing else. The younger kids in the family ask for money from their sisters and not their father, and that wounds his pride, too. The youngest learn some trade, but the *papá* doesn't even know how to paint the outside of his house because he's never even picked up *una brocha*, a brush. He only knows how to plant and live in the country, not in the city. If the *papá* makes some friends, maybe they will invite him to work with them, but that doesn't happen too often. The mother also finds work easier than the father, in houses, either here or on the other side as a domestic.

If you get fixed up with a local card, you can go back and forth daily. You have to have a job, usually in a *maquila*, before they will give you one of those cards. They want to know that you have pay; they want you to have money to spend on both sides. On the other side, for example, many people buy used clothing in good condition, cheap, and bring it back here either for themselves or to sell to people who can't go to the other side. People also buy other things to sell here, such as tape recorders and radios. The first thing they get is a radio, the bigger the better. In San Luis, for example, in the ranchos, you can lack a table to eat on, a chair to sit on, but you have a *radio-grabadora*, a radio-tape recorder blasting out *música ranchera*. It's like the new altar.

We already have our own kind of free trade along the border. There is a lot of ignorance about what the proposed *libre comercio*, free trade agreement, means. I myself don't understand much of what's happening. Every day the newspapers talk about it because the Mexican government is so much in favor of it. But we know that it will never work as nicely as they say. The chemical wastes, the contamination, is overwhelming now. We are living in perilous times here along the border. There are canals with chemical waste running through them, and these canals go right through the *colonias* of the *gente humilde*. My people want to work and that's all some of them can think about, that free trade will mean jobs. Well, I want them to have work too, but *en buenas condiciones*, under good conditions. A job that allows them to live, but with dignity, without prejudicing the health of the children and pregnant women. However, the way we have seen things work here before is that the health of the workers is not an important consideration. The businesses are still throwing their chemicals wherever they will; they have no limits put on them. It's not right to put so many in jeopardy just so a few will benefit. I fear that this problem would continue with the free trade agreement. There would be so many more *maquilas* down here that it would be unbelievable. To have won all that we fought so hard for, only to *volver a agachar la cabeza*—to go back to hanging our head—*no señor*. And the small farmers in the Valley, what would happen to them? The labor unions in the U.S.? Would they collapse? What about the long-term effects on Mexico, if this part of the country is covered with *maquilas* and people keep moving here from all over the country? They paint everything so pretty, but we are afraid, and I especially am afraid because of the environmental and health aspects. When I first came here years ago, Matamoros was a pretty, tranquil town with very few cars. It has tripled in size since then, and more people are streaming in all the time. They are settling in desperately poor

colonias where there is no light, no water, no garbage pickup, no pavement, nothing. They come thinking that if they can't get a job in a *maquila*, then at least they can work as a domestic. If they don't find work at all, they think that they can always cross over to the other side. They have the idea that here in Matamoros everything will be great, with the backup that on the other side things will be better still, if you don't get caught.

The girl or very young woman is the one who works in the *maquila* because she, especially if she is a recent arrival from the countryside, is still brought up to do what her parents tell her and to obey all men. She keeps on obeying in the *maquila*. The young Mexican woman is typically *muy sufrida y muy fácil de manejar, muy callada*, very self-denying and very easy to control, very quiet. After two or three years, she is no longer the same as when she came. Now she looks around and sees how other people are living. Maybe she is ignorant and even foolish, but she wants to have what she sees others have. Another thing is that from very young, we are taught to *tejer*, to weave, and to do manual tasks at home, so we are very good at hand work. It's not that we work for less money, because here women earn the same as men; there are even women who are mechanics and electricians, and these women earn the same.

Usually the women work from about age fifteen to age thirty. Then they quit, but not because they have enough money, I'll tell you that. If they have two or three kids, the kids stay home alone while the mother works. They may stay a few hours with a neighbor, but really the children are alone, and they are very *despegados*, alienated, from their parents. This is a problem and a mistake. There is one huge child care center, but it's on the other side of town. To go there, and to pick up your children afterwards, takes a couple of hours. That is, if you can get there, plus you have to pay for transportation. Most times, the children stay by themselves, maybe in the care of an older sibling. If a woman has to quit her job in the *fábrica*, then she usually sells something. She sets up a little stall or she goes back to the plant where she used to work and sells food, clothes, or jewelry from a little stand. Such vendors abound; everyone who arrives here comes with something to sell. People come here from as far away as the capital and Oaxaca. They almost always can speak Spanish, but here there are many Marías, as they are called in the capital. They are Indian women who come to sell *dulces*, sweets, and they speak Spanish, but *un poco mocho*, a little mixed. Among themselves they speak their indigenous tongue. There is now an amnesty program in the U.S. and many people from San Luis, for example, are taking advantage of it to go to the other side to join their families. Many, many people are getting their passports in order to go. They feel betrayed by our government; they feel that our government is selling them out. So they leave, because they have become *braceros* in their own land. Everyone thinks that the PRI sells them out, that their vote doesn't matter. They don't have any trust in Salinas or in national politics. But PAN has won here locally three times in the past. PRD is the party that is the most popular now, Cárdenas's party. However, most people don't pay much attention to national politics because it is never for them. They don't go to political meetings, although we were obliged to

Maquiladora workers' colonia, Matamoros

go by the union, because the union is very close with the PRI. They don't make the workers attend meetings anymore, because they just stopped going, or else they would go, but then they would vote for the non-PRI candidate.

I was saying earlier that conditions have changed dramatically at Union Carbide, Kemet. That makes me optimistic about the environmental commissions I am involved in that are working on the pollution problem. We have had press conferences in Ciudad Juárez; Washington, D. C.; and in New York. We have had videos made, and I went with the Coalition for Justice in the Maquiladoras to Chicago where we talked to workers and to ecumenical groups. We have done many tests in the canals and have taken subsoil samples too. The coalition, churches in the U.S. and here, labor unions, and ecologists' groups are all working together on this. Pollution is not our problem, or their problem, it's everyone's problem. We just have one earth. What other world can we go to after we ruin this one? I want to stay here in this world. Maybe Salinas and Bush can go to another one, but I like the countryside and the flowers and the animals. We have to do the best we can with what we've got. The coalition is working for a life with dignity and justice for the workers, which they really do not have now.

Part 4
We Come Bearing Gifts:
Las Artes

Los Pleneros

La Sebastiana, sculpture by Horacio Valdéz

Barbara Carrasco's mural, "The Missing Peace"

El Señor Trujillo, master weaver, Chimayó, New Mexico

We Come Bearing Gifts: Las Artes

The arts can always be appreciated in their own right, but they are also an integral component of Latino communities. Bright splashes of color decorate the walls of *barrio* buildings. Community centers sponsor young artists who proclaim the story of their particular ethnic group in poetry, song, dance, and exuberant murals. Latino theater is the oldest and one of the most vital art forms in the U.S. It spans both the borderland and the *barrio* experiences and extends from the sixteenth century morality plays in northern New Mexico, to the farm workers' theater of the 1960s, to the political street theater of today. There has been a virtual explosion of writing by Latino authors in the U.S., many of whom are included in this anthology. Film festivals and filmmaking by Latinos round out the artistic enterprise, which, though increasingly universal in its appeal, still expresses the ethnic roots and sensibilities of its creators.

The following readings illustrate the particular and the universal aspects of the arts as we talk with a Mexican American museum director, a Mexican American mural artist, and a Cuban American painter; and as we read essays on Latino theater; the exigencies of being a Latino author, including the dilemma of whether to write in English or Spanish; and the folk origins of the plena, a distinctive Puerto Rican musical form.

The important point about the arts is that they are by *no* means marginal; rather, they are a *vital* part of Latino cultures. With the possible exception of some Cuban American artists, there is no clear line between "high" and "popular" culture in Latino arts. While it is true that the Latino arts reflect the personal views and emotions of the creators and express eternal truths, they also address a broad popular audience and help shape and interpret a dynamic and fluid social reality.

Dolores Prida

In this reading, Dolores Prida writes about her childhood in Cuba; the theater; the writing process; the portrayal of the Latino experience in her plays; her wish to be regarded as a playwright, not as a "Woman Hispanic Playwright"; and about what Prida considers the duty of the university community to bring Latino arts into the mainstream.

The Show Does Go On

Over ten years ago, when my first play was produced in New York City, I dragged my whole family down to a dank basement in the Lower East Side to see it. My mother, who never really understood what I did in the theater, said to me after the show was over: *"Todo estuvo muy bonito, m'ija, pero, en todo eso que yo vi, ¿qué fue exactamente lo que tú hiciste?"* I explained to her that I had written the play, that I was the *dramaturga*. She just said, "Ahhh," and shook her head.[1]

I fantasized about her, next morning, telling her coworkers at that factory in Brooklyn where she used to sew sleeves onto raincoats all day long, *"¿Oye, Rosalía, tú sabes que mi hija, la mayor, es dramaturga?"* And Rosalía answering, *"¿Dramaturga? ¡Ay pobrecita! Y eso, ¿tiene cura?"*[2]

My mother passed away three years ago, and I regret I never took the time to explain to her what being a *dramaturga* meant to me, and why it can't be "cured," that once bitten by the love of the theater, you are infected with it for the rest of your life.

Now it is too late to share with her why I put up with the long hours, the lack of money, the unheated basements: the thrill of opening night, the goose pimples when an audience laughs at the right lines, or when you can hear a pin drop at the right moment.

It is not too late to share some of it with you.

I didn't start off as a playwright. As a teenager, I wrote poems and short stories that nobody read. In fact, nobody knew I wrote them because I didn't tell anyone. Writing poetry wasn't the "in" thing among my peers. I am from a small town where there was one single bookstore and one single library, which was closed most of the time—I don't know why, maybe because it was right next door to the police station.

We had two movie houses, one that showed Mexican and Argentinean films, mostly three-hanky tearjerkers. In the other one—*el cine América*—you could watch the latest Hollywood films, with subtitles or dubbed into Spanish. I actually grew up believing that John Wayne was really from Madrid by watching movies in which he would speak perfect Castilian: *"Alzad laz manoz, matonez."*[3]

One thing we didn't have in Caibarén, Cuba, was a theater. I didn't get to see a live play until I came to New York. That was in 1961. It was a musical, and I became fascinated forever with the idea of people bursting into song and dance at the least provocation.

The first play I wrote—*Beautiful Señoritas*—was a play with music. And I wrote it in English.

⟨⟨⟨⟨⟨⟨⟨⟨⟨⟨⟨⟨⟨⟨⟨⟨⟨⟨⟨⟨⟨⟨⟨

In 1976, I went to Caracas, Venezuela, to cover an international theater festival for *Visión,* the Latin American news magazine. It was my first festival and I enjoyed every minute of it. I saw plays from over thirty different countries, many in languages I did not understand. But one peculiar thing caught my attention: not one of those plays dealt with "the women's issue." At the time, I was quite involved in the women's movement in New York and knew that *la liberación femenina* was also being hotly debated in Latin America and Europe. Yet, the stages of an international theater festival didn't reflect it. I decided, then and there, that when I got back to New York I would write a play about women. And I did.

Beautiful Señoritas was produced by DUO Theatre in 1977. It was a modest one-act musical play that poked fun at long-standing Latin women stereotypes—from Carmen Miranda to Cuchi Cuchi Charo to suffering, black-shrouded women crying and praying over the tortillas to modern-day young Latinas trying to redefine their images. The play was extremely well received—it went on to have many productions throughout the country, including a special performance at the National Organization for Women's national convention in San Antonio, Texas, in 1980.

From then on, most of my plays have been about the experience of being a Hispanic in the United States, about people trying to reconcile two cultures and two languages and two visions of the world into a particular whole: plays that aim to be a reflection of a particular time and space, of a here and now.

Of course, not all of my plays are women-oriented or totally Hispanic. Being a woman and being a Hispanic is neither an asset nor a handicap, but a fact. And, as an artist, I do not wish to be categorized just as a "Hispanic playwright" or a "Woman Hispanic Playwright," but rather as a person, a playwright who happens to be a woman and a Hispanic and who feels committed to writing on those subjects because they are part of the universe.

I find it particularly rewarding being able to write non-Hispanic characters, male or female, who are believable and authentic. And writing believable and authentic characters is what theater is all about. Of course, good theater also springs from writing about subjects and situations one knows best. And what I know best are the ups and down of being a Hispanic woman playwright living in New York City. And I am not contradicting myself.

Theaterworks

I consider myself a "theater worker" rather than a "theater literata." Theater is not literature; theater is to be "done," not read, seen, not imagined. Theater is people. Theater is teamwork. We need each other: playwright, director, designers, actors, choreographers, technicians, carpenters, composers, ticket takers, audience. We don't exist without each other. And I have tremendous respect and admiration for the skills and talent of everyone involved in bringing a production to the stage. I love actors. I adore choreography. I am awed by composers and musicians. Directors? Putting your play in the hands of a good director who has vision and understands your work—well, that's icing on the cake. Good directors, however, are few and far between.

ꙅꙅꙅꙅꙅꙅꙅꙅꙅꙅꙅꙅꙅꙅꙅꙅꙅꙅꙅꙅꙅꙅ

The first thing I did at Teatro the Orilla, a collective theater group in New York's Lower East Side, was to sweep the floor and collect tickets at the door. Then I ran the sound equipment, made lights from empty tomato juice cans and supermarket light bulbs, went shopping for costumes and props, filled out endless forms for grant money, and then, only then, I began to think I could write a play that would appeal to that particular audience: people who had never been to a theater before.

My theater life came into being soon after various Hispanic theater groups began to get established, thanks to newly available public funds in the late sixties and early seventies. It was all part of a process, a side effect of the ethnic and racial reaffirmation that followed the black civil rights movement, the women's liberation movement, the antiwar demonstrations.

I did not get into the theater for the "let's-put-on-a-show" fun of it, but because I felt I had things to say about immediate and relevant issues and I wanted to say them with comedy, with music, with songs. Live.

Besides those already mentioned, I have also written about gentrification (*Savings*), about antipoverty agencies (*The Beggar's Soap Opera*), about Hispanic theater itself (*La Era Latina*), about Latin soap operas and nuclear war (*Pantallas*), about cultural assimilation (*Botánica*). Waiting their turn are plays about AIDS (so many of my friends are gone) and teenage pregnancy (What happened to women's liberation? Have we failed the younger generation of women?)

Also, I've had plays canceled for the alleged "insidiousness" of my politics. "Maligned in Miami" is the Hispanic community's equivalent of "banned in Boston."

The need to use the theater as a medium to discuss relevant and immediate issues and experiences is not new, except in one sense; today, many Hispanic playwrights are writing about these experiences in English, whereas the earliest examples were in Spanish (of all my plays, only two, *Pantallas* and *Botánica,* are in Spanish).

There are two stories I always like to mention when speaking of the origins of Hispanic theater in the New World. One is fact, and one is fiction.

The fictitious event I like best, because it concerns the earliest example of Hispanic American musical theater. It comes from a passage of *El arpa y la sombra,* by the Cuban novelist Alejo Carpentier. One of the sections of the book, "La mano," is written as the travel diary of Christopher Columbus. Let me share it with you in its original splendor:

> Más adelante—fue durante mi tercer viaje—al ver que los indios de una isla se mostraban recelosos en acercarse a nosotros, improvisé un escenario en el catillo de popa, haciendo que unos españoles danzaran bulliciosamente al son de tamboril y tejoletas, para que se viese que éramos gente alegre y de un natural apacible. (Pero mal nos fue en esa ocasión, para decir la verdad, puesto que los caníbales, nada divertidos por moriscas y zapateados, nos dispararon tantas flechas como tenían en sus canoas . . .)[4]

6666666666666666666666

So here we see that one of the first, although fictional, Hispanic theater per-formers in the Americas (Christopher Columbus, producer) was a musical come-dy, and that it was panned by the audience.

The second—and much-quoted—story is fact, according to researchers. It docu-ments the actual first performance of what could be called a play, in what is today U.S. territory. In 1598, a group of *conquistadores,* led by Juan de Oñate, crossed the Río Grande from Mexico to take formal possession of all the kingdoms and provinces of New Mexico in name of King Philip of Spain. They struck camp on a spot near the present-day city of El Paso, Texas.

Among the group was a captain of the guard named Marcos Farfán de los Godos (how's that for a stage name!), who, besides being a soldier, dabbled in the art of "dramaturgy." That evening, he prepared *un espectáculo* to entertain his fel-low *conquistadores*. The theme of this presentation is reported to have dealt with the question of how the church would be received in the newly "discovered" lands of New Mexico.

This presentation is considered to be the first theatrical piece ever performed in what is today the United States of America. It predates, by sixty-seven years, the first recorded English play produced in the New World. It predates, by eight years, the French masque performed in Acadia, Canada, in 1606.

Both these theatrical events, whether fact or fiction, also sprung from the immediate reality of those first "Hispanics," and their experiences as *conquista-dores* in a new land. Had they not come here, they would not have written those particular plays. Therefore, they are "American" plays.

Today's Hispanic American playwrights, arriving at, or being born on, these shores more like *conquistados* than *conquistadores,* continue that tradition.

From a Miguel Piñero, who writes *Short Eyes* from inside the nightmare of a prison, to Eddie Gallardo's family in the South Bronx's *Simpson Street,* to Eduardo Machado's upper-class Cuban families arriving in Miami with suitcases chock-full of jewels, to Manuel Martín's working-class Cubans celebrating Thanksgiving in Union City, to Gloria González's *Café con leche,* to my own *Coser y cantar,* which deals with how to be a bilingual, bicultural woman in Manhattan and keep your sanity, to a host of as-yet-unproduced new plays by young Hispanics developing in the wings, Hispanic-American theater is slowly becoming a hall of mirrors in which our society and ourselves are reflected, sometimes documenting the intan-gibles of being a minority in the United States with more subtlety and depth than many an expensive sociological research paper.

However, much of this work is unknown or ignored, both by the Hispanic and the general community. For Hispanics, going to the theater is a tradition that gen-erally we do not bring along from our countries of origin. There the theater is, in most cases, for the social and intellectual elites. In coming here, we find that the arts are not necessarily considered a luxury, but perceived as being somewhat irrelevant, something for which one usually does not have time.

The need for many immigrants to struggle, survive, and adapt does not allow them the luxury of attending the theater. Going out means going dancing or to the movies—what they think is accessible and "fun." Regular escapist entertainment is found nightly in the never-ending *telenovelas* and in the weekly convulsions of Iris Chacón's hips. Only a minority within out community goes regularly to the theater. Many of our ninety-nine-seat houses are half-empty many a night.

Although non-Hispanics come to see our plays, it is more like a novelty, or a duty—as in the case of the classics. I mean, you have to see a García Lorca or a Lope de Vega play at least once in your lifetime, and, of course, the latest effort by novelist Mario Vargas Llosa.

In the Hispanic theater community, we are aware of the need to further develop our audiences. I believe the type of plays we are now writing, in which Hispanic-American audiences can identify with the characters and situations they see onstage, is contributing to that development (in 1986, *Bodega*, Federico Fraguada's first play, broke all box office records at the twenty-year-old Puerto Rican Traveling Theatre in New York City. Nearly every New York City *bodeguero* and his family went to see the play. It was presented again in the 1987 season). Musicals and comedies are attracting younger audiences who used to think that going to the theater meant they were in for a boring evening and opted to stay home and watch music videos.

Adding to the problem of lack of visibility and audience growth, we face the sad fact that in the Hispanic community we don't have a responsible media with responsible, knowledgeable writers who can discuss art and culture intelligently. American critics are, in most instances, either patronizing or insensitive to the work produced by Hispanics, even if it is in English.

The University's Universe

I feel the academic community has a large role to play in bringing Hispanic-American theater and literature into the mainstream of this country's cultural life. Fortunately, today there are many college professors who have a deep interest in our work, are studying it, writing papers, and struggling to include it in their curricula. This is a must. Because they are not only trying to enrich the lives of their students by exposing them to the art and culture of the soon-to-be-largest ethnic minority in this nation, but are also building theater audiences for the future.

Unfortunately, these few pioneers face many obstacles from within and without the walls of academia. From the outside, there is the problem of not enough published literary and theatrical works by U.S. Hispanics. From inside the walls, opposition, confusion, misunderstanding, and—why not say it?—plain, ugly racism from faculty and administrators.

Because they ask: What is Hispanic literature"? What is "Hispanic drama"? Is there such a thing? And, if so, where is it? Where does it belong in the curriculum? They don't know, or don't want to know, what to do with the whole darned big enchilada.

This metaphorical enchilada, like the small real ones, is meant to be eaten, and enjoyed! You can't worry about heartburn a priori! I say, what's wrong with bringing U.S. Hispanic literature and drama into the American drama department,

666666666666666666666666

along with black and Asian-American works? It also belongs as an interdisciplinary subject in Latin America departments. *¿Por qué no?*

My increasing theater contacts with Latin America and Spain reveal that there is a tremendous interest in what is happening in Hispanic theater in the United States. One of my plays, *La Era Latina,* a bilingual comedy I cowrote with Víctor Fragoso, won an award in Venezuela. Right now I am busy preparing an enormous amount of information on Hispanic theater in the U.S. for a book on Latin American theater, to be published next year by Spain's Ministry of Culture.

Yes, but What Is It?

I define Hispanic American theater, or literature, as that written by Hispanics living and working in the United States whose subject matter, whether written in Spanish or English or both, reflects their expressions in this country in the same manner that, before us, the Jews, the Irish, the Italians documented their experiences and their histories that came to be part of *the* history of this nation.

Hispanics are here for many different reasons. Many have been born here. Many were here before parts of this land came to be called the United States of America. Some came a lifetime ago. Some came yesterday. Some are arriving this very minute. Some dream of returning to where they came from. Some will. Some have made this place their home for good and are here to stay.

Millions of Americans live next door to a Rodríguez or a Fernández. They go down to the corner *bodega* and buy Café Bustelo and Goya Beans. They eat tacos and enchiladas (big and small) as if there were no tomorrow. They work shoulder to shoulder with millions of Hispanics at every level, every day.

However, in the schools, in the universities, these same Americans learn nothing about those strangers they ride the elevator with. They are not taught who they are, what they think, why they came here.

This is the place, and this is the time. And theater, and painting, and dance, and poetry can help bridge that gap.

In the theater, we have that saying—you know the one: "The show must go on." As I said before, soon Hispanics will be the largest ethnic minority in the U.S. Our presence here promises to be a long-running engagement—despite the bad reviews we get most of the time, despite the problems we may have with the lights, and the curtain, and the costumes, and the enter and exit cues. Despite all that, this show will on, and you might as well get your tickets now.

Nicholasa Mohr

Nicholasa Mohr is a highly regarded Nuyorican author whose numerous books for children and adults have garnered various awards. Works such as *Nilda* (©1973, Houston: Arte Público Press, 1991), *El Bronx Remembered* (©1975, Houston: Arte Público Press, 1989), *In Nueva York* (New York: Dial Press, 1977) and *Rituals of Survival: A Woman's Portfolio* (Houston: Arte Público Press, 1985) depict with realism the lives of Puerto Ricans in New York City. In this provocative essay, Mohr decribes the dichotomous existence of the Puerto Rican, discusses the crucial importance of the English language to her writing, and explains the differences between Puerto Rican writers on the island and those on the mainland.

Puerto Rican Writers in the United States, Puerto Rican Writers in Puerto Rico: A Separation Beyond Language

As a writer of Puerto Rican parentage who was born, raised, educated, and is presently living in New York City, one of the first questions asked of me is, "Why don't you write in Spanish?" And this question is asked not only by those persons of non-Hispanic background, but also by the island Puerto Ricans.

This past fall (1986) I was invited to be on a panel titled "Puerto Rican Women Fiction Writers" held at the Center for American Culture Studies, Columbia University, New York City. As I began to work on my presentation, I realized that I was the only Puerto Rican on the panel who writes in English. I decided to examine the differences that include and go beyond language, which exist between myself and those other Puerto Rican writers writing in Spanish that live in Puerto Rico or in other Spanish-speaking environments.

My birth makes me a native New Yorker. I write here in the United States about my personal experiences and those of a particular group of migrants that number in the millions. Yet all of these actualities seem to have little or no bearing on those who insist on seeing me as an "intruder," an "outsider" who has taken on a foreign language. Perhaps even taken it on much too forcefully, using it to document and validate our existence and survival inside the very nation that chose to colonize us.

Although a commonwealth of the United States, Puerto Rico continues to use Spanish as its official language. Puerto Ricans born in Puerto Rico, unlike other immigrants or migrant groups, hold the unique position of being United States citizens while still remaining part of the greater Latin American family. And, although their position in the hierarchy of Latin America is often assessed as one of low status because of their connected dependence to the United States (a sort of impoverished step-child of the Yankees), resulting in their government's dubious allegiance to Latin America, Puerto Rico is nonetheless considered a member of the Spanish-speaking world.

Thus, this status, singular in its kind, creates a dichotomous existence further exacerbated by the proximity of the island, which permits Puerto Ricans as United States citizens to travel frequently and cheaply from the Island of Puerto Rico to the mainland United States. Contact between the islanders and the Puerto Ricans here is a common occurrence. It follows that Spanish continues to be spoken in areas of the U.S. which are heavily populated by Puerto Ricans and today by the new political refugees coming in from Central and South America. One of the cities with the oldest Puerto Rican population and that is today inhabited by third and fourth generations of these early migrants, as well as other recently arrived Hispanic immigrants, is New York City. Consequently, New York is fast becoming a bilingual city. Public service messages and advertisements are now written in Spanish and English. Hispanic food is available in luncheonettes as well as in fine restaurants. Most merchants speak Spanish or have help which is bilingual to meet the needs of their customers.

In the U.S., and in New York in particular, there are many other immigrants and political refugees, and their children, who are not Hispanic. However, it is unlikely that a Greek American, an Irish American, or an Asian American, etc., could conceivably have monthly or even weekend visits overseas with their relatives. This frequent traveling is not unusual within the Puerto Rican stateside and island communities. Nor is it expected that these other ethnic Americans speak or write in the native language of their countries of origin. No matter how foreign these other groups may appear, their writers when documenting injustices or illuminating accomplishments, all do so by writing in English. Some examples are Joseph Conrad, Vladimir Nabokov, Jerzy Kozinski. . . . Others born and raised here are Maxine Hong Kingston, Philip Roth, and Mario Puzo.

These writers are not chastised or rejected because they use English. Nor are they expected to use another language of expression. Indeed, they are applauded for the way in which they master the English language. As a daughter of the Puerto Rican diaspora, English is the language that gives life to my work, the characters I create, and that stimulates me as a writer. It has also been a vital component in the struggle for my very survival. However, it is much more than language that separates the Puerto Rican writers that were born and/or raised here from the writers in Puerto Rico. And I will endeavor from my perspective to describe what I perceive as some of the major reasons for this separation.

In the books I've had published thus far, I have dealt with a period in time covering more than forty-five years of Puerto Rican history here in New York. When I started to write back in 1972, I realized that, except for a book or two that concentrated on the Puerto Rican male's problems and misfortunes, there were no books in the United States literature that dealt with our existence, our contributions, or what we as Puerto Rican migrants were about. I, as a Puerto Rican child, never existed in North American letters. Our struggles as displaced migrants, working-class descendants of the *tabaqueros* (tobacco workers) who began coming here in 1916, were invisible in North American literature. As I proceeded to record who we were, I addressed myself both to adults and children . . . and, of course, to women.

In my first book, a novel *Nilda,* I wrote about Puerto Ricans in New York City during the years of the Second World War. Through the various adolescent stages of the youngest child, a girl, I trace one family's position as they deal with their alienation as despised migrants, as well as their psychological, emotional, and physical attempts to sustain the family in a traditional Puerto Rican manner. We also see the beginning of the assimilation of Puerto Ricans in the U.S.

The works that followed included books recounting the problems, failures, and successes of the greatest influx of Puerto Rican migrants that arrived on the shores of the main land immediately after the Second World War. My work continued to trace the postwar migrants, many of whom arrived as small children or were subsequently born here. As the process of assimilation began, they inevitably began to understand that there was no going back; that *home* was here where they were working to materialize their own domain alongside their peers and immediate families. That Puerto Rico we were taught to believe in was largely based on the reminiscences of our parents and grandparents, many of whom had come from small towns and rural villages. They had nostalgically presented to their displaced offspring a "paradise" where sunshine, flowers, and ownership of one's own business or plot of land brought everyone abundant food and eternal happiness. This mythical island also boasted a population who knew no prejudice and where neither the dark color of one's skin nor one's humble birth were ever seen as a cause for rejection. All of this mythology had little or nothing to do with Puerto Rico, its inhabitants, and the reality of that culture.

Later, when some of us returned to the island, it was clear to see that, according to the position one's family held and the whiter the color of one's skin, the better your job and the higher your place in society. It was also evident that those children of the poor and dark migrants who had been forced out over two generations before and who returned either with intentions to relocate or merely to visit, were not always welcomed. They were quickly labeled and categorized as outsiders, as "gringos," and "Newyoricans." Indeed, proof of the false legacy that so many of us had inherited from our elders was painfully clear.

For me, the heart of my work has always dealt with my culture. Consequently, the players in my books have been the Puerto Ricans in this city, my people and my beloved Nueva York. Their failure and their triumphs are the core of what and who we are here today. I continue with my work examining the values I have inherited, always aware of the fact that I have come from an island people who have been colonized from the very onset of their being, and who to this day continue their dependency. As a Puerto Rican woman I must also reckon with the history of my patriarchal antecedents and work to heal the scars of *machismo* that have been etched into our fiber for centuries.

Within this framework, my obsession with people's ability to succeed and fail, to despise and cherish, to compromise and not yield, as well as all the other contradictions and incongruities inherent in the human species, fires me on to write. I often think I write very much as an investigative reporter to find out at the end what happened . . . to get at an answer that might give me a hint of the "truth." Yet I persist in using fiction as my medium. Fiction, as it is defined in the dictionary, is: "That which is feigned or imagined. An assumption of a possible thing as a fact irrespective of the question of its truth."

I am not an avid reader of the literature being published in Puerto Rico. However, throughout the years I have become mildly familiar with some of the work of these writers. Most of the time, I have found their work to be too obsessed with class and race, thus narrowing their subject matter into regional and provincial material. Their commonly used baroque style of writing in Spanish seems to act as filler rather than substance. Recently I read a story that attempted to deal with a working-class Puerto Rican woman from New York who goes to San Juan for a holiday. The use of what the author considered to be a cross between Spanish and English, which is referred to as Spanglish, was incorrect and ludicrous. No one here speaks that way. The story line was quite silly and the story rather farfetched and stupid, much like a cartoon. This writer had very little knowledge of who we are here, and I suspect holds quite a bit of disdain and contempt for our community. This author is not the only one with this attitude. Unfortunately, it is quite common among the island's intellectuals.

Yet, I have also recently read the work of Magalí García Ramis, *Felices días tío Sergio* (Editorial Antillana), whose language is very Puerto Rican and disarmingly complex despite her simple and unpretentious prose. Her subject matter deals with her privileged middle-class background with a depth that reveals much of the sickness that is prevalent in that class system. It is a system that continues to stifle attempts to eliminate the Spanish European–style legacy of race and class that was deposited on that island centuries ago. I also admire the work of Manuel Ramos Otero, who, without apology, self-consciousness, or inhibition, writes candidly and with compassion about his homosexual community. In his last book of poems, *El libro de la muerte* (Waterfront Press), he uses symbols and metaphors to bring the reader into the labyrinthine depths of his private world. I still treasure my copies of the early works of fiction by José Luis González, including *En Nueva York y otras desgracias* and *Cinco cuentos de sangre,* and the matchless poetry of Julia de Burgos. There are few writers from Puerto Rico with whom I feel I can share a sense of camaraderie. Most of what I read lacks the universality that bonds the common human family, regardless of language, class, or geography.

Here in the U.S., I find writers who continue to produce work that, although very specific, is also enlightening and inspiring. Their works introduce us to other Americans who ultimately share similar goals. Let me cite a few examples. Alice Walker in *The Color Purple* speaks to the reader in an exquisite black English about the power of female survival against the harsh domination of black machismo. In his short stories, Raymond Carver, with his minimal but powerful prose, shares with his readers a wide spectrum of lives of the working class white Americans. Tillie Olsen's books recount the personal struggles of European immigrants and their children, as well as the psychological and social obstacles females must overcome. Ishmael Reed's works explode with the rich vernacular of black English, creating a personal mythology which reflects the reality of the black male's struggles against emasculation in a white-dominated power structure. Finally, Denise Chávez, in *The Last of the Menu Girls* (Arte Publico Press) admirably incorporates the richness of Chicano Spanish, thereby further enriching our literature with the language of the peoples in the United States.

These are but a few examples of the writers (and there are many others I can include) who are not necessarily in the mainstream of the Anglo-American Writers Empire, but who nonetheless get published and speak about the realities and complexities of the varied ethnic groups who share our nation. All of these authors write in an American English that comes straight from their people. Their language represents and validates their experiences and those of the people who inhabit their books. None of them writes English like a "British subject," nor are they in any way trying to emulate the culture or the values of England. The rhythms of our American language are ever changing, representing the many cultures that exist in the nation. Those whose works speak to and about the peoples of color, and the other marginal communities that continue to struggle for equality in the U.S., are the writers I identify with.

Except for the attempts of a few writers, I do not see any significant literary movement on the island of Puerto Rico that speaks for the common folk, the working-class population on the island. I wonder if the obsession with race, class, Spain, and the use of baroque Spanish might not be a way for some intellectuals to attempt to safeguard their privilege and power against the strong North American influence which presently permeates Puerto Rico. If this should be the case, then it follows that, in safeguarding such status, a majority who are less fortunate must ultimately be excluded.

As I have stated, the separation between myself and the majority of Puerto Rican writers in Puerto Rico goes far beyond a question of language. The jet age and the accessibility of Puerto Rico brought an end to a time of innocence for the children of the former migrants. There is no pretense that going back will solve problems, bring equality and happiness. This is home. This is where we were born, raised, and where most of us will stay. Notwithstanding, it is my affection and concern for the people and the land of my parents and grandparents which is my right and my legacy.

Who we are and how our culture will continue to blossom and develop is being recorded right here, by our writers, painters, and composers; here, where our voices respond and resound loud and clear.

Sherezada "Chiqui" Vicioso

The Dominican poet Chiqui Vicioso
has published two books in Spanish. This
English translation of an interview given by
Vicioso at the University of Mayagüez in Puerto
Rico reveals the tremendous impact that her
years in New York City and her trip to Africa
have had on her development as a woman
and a poet, and on Vicioso's discovery of herself as a *caribeña*.

An Oral History

I started writing when I was very young and found out that the best way to pass Math was to write a poem to the teacher. . . . I began to become aware of the marginalized people in my country when I was an adolescent and worked in the *barrios* as part of a Christian youth volunteer group. Basically I am a poet, but I also write criticism about women's literature. I began to write in 1978 and published my first book of poetry, *Viajes desde el agua,* in 1981.

Up until about 1977, I regarded literature as a hobby of the petite bourgeoisie, but when I went to Cuba and spoke there with writers whom I very much admired, they showed me that a writer is also a cultural worker. Whereas I took note of this fact on an intellectual level, I realized it on an emotional one only when I went to Africa in 1978. I started writing criticism from 1982 on and published my second book in 1985 (*Un extraño ulular traía el viento*).

Both my books were written for Dominicans and were published in Santo Domingo. I never thought of publishing in the United States cause, as a Latina, I felt unable to deal with the publishing establishment in that country. My first book was presented at the Las Américas bookshop and other places for Latinos in New York. After all, New York is the second most important city for Dominicans. The island has six million inhabitants and half a million live in New York. Economically, it's the most important. I never felt far from Santo Domingo when I lived in New York.

I first came to the United States in April 1967. Initially, I had wanted to be a lay nun and work in the *barrios*. Marriage repelled me, especially when I looked at my aunts, practically all of whom were divorced. I couldn't stand the idiocy of the whole scene: the danger of getting mixed up with someone when you were thirteen or fourteen, worrying about not having a boyfriend when you were sixteen. To me, becoming a nun was my path to freedom. I also wanted to study medicine. The one year I planned to stay eventually became seventeen.

My mother, who had left a year earlier, said I should go to the States in order to improve my English and to get to know the world before embarking on becoming a nun. I was very angry with her at the time, but she was right.

I come from a very special family with an intellectual background. On my father's side, my grandfather was a journalist and a writer, and my father is a poet and a well-known composer. My mother is a better poet than I am, but has never dared to write. She is the daughter of a peasant woman who worked in a tobacco factory and a Dominican oligarch who owned the factory and literally bought her when she was sixteen. My mother is a hybrid of two very distinct classes. I felt this when I went to school in Santiago.

6666666666666666666666

In spite of having studied English in school, I found out, on my arrival in New York, that I didn't know very much. Like most Dominicans who come to the United States, I went to work in a factory: first a hat, and then a button factory (the acetone in which we had to wash the buttons damaged my eyes so that I have had to wear glasses ever since). I went to night school for a while, and then was accepted into a city-sponsored intensive English program, where I was paid to study.

My next job was as a telephone operator, and I quickly acquired a reputation as being extremely courteous to the customers, as my English still wasn't all that good and I said "Thank you" to everyone, even if they insulted me. Then Brooklyn College opened its doors to minority students. They responded to a policy, initiated under the Johnson administration, whereby colleges were paid federal funds to admit minorities. I was one of eight Dominican students admitted to Brooklyn College.

Since there were only eight of us, and it was very tough to survive in such a racist atmosphere, we joined up with other minority students, principally Puerto Ricans, blacks, other people from the Caribbean—we formed a Third World Alliance.

This was a real threshold for me; I had never known the people from Barbados or Trinidad, etc. My concept of the Caribbean, up to that time, had been limited to the Spanish-speaking part, and I discovered my identity as a *caribeña* in New York.

I was also racially classified at Brooklyn College, which was an interesting experience for me. In Santo Domingo, the popular classes have a pretty clear grasp of racial divisions, but the middle and upper-middle classes are very deluded on this point. People straighten their hair and marry "in order to improve the race," etc., etc., and don't realize the racist connotations of their language or their attitude. In the United States, there is no space for fine distinctions of race, and one goes from being "*trigueño*" or "*indio*" to being "mulatto" or "black" or "Hispanic." This was an excellent experience for me. From that point on, I discovered myself as a Caribbean *mulata* and adopted the black identity as a gesture of solidarity. At that time, I deeply admired and identified with Angela Davis, and ever since then, I have kept on identifying myself as a black woman.

This opened another door; I learned about Frantz Fanon and other Caribbean theoreticians, and that finished Europe for me. I learned about the triangular trade and how we had financed Europe's development. I realized that capitalism was an impossible model to follow in our development. For me, this was discovering a universe. I only became a feminist much later.

When I first became more radical I was very much put off by feminism and people like Gloria Steinem and Betty Friedan—to me they were representatives of the white U.S. middle class who were busy telling us how *we* were being screwed up by *machismo*. In a first stage I rejected this and, up to a point, I also had a false sense of solidarity with our men, who were racially oppressed as well. I felt that if we women criticized our men, we were only providing the racists with ammunition. This created a conflict of loyalties for me.

Discovering myself as a woman came much later. First I had to discover that I was part of a certain geographical area, and then, that I was Latin American. The great majority of the Latin American exiles converged on New York at that time—

the Argentineans, the Uruguayans, the Chileans (Allende fell during those years)—so that, for me, New York became a kind of great doorway to this Latin American world.

Being in New York was very essential to my development. I would not be the woman I am today had I not gone to New York. I would have been the classic *fracasada* (failure) in my country because I know that I would not have found happiness in marriage and having children. I would have been frustrated, unhappy in a marriage, or divorced several times over because I would not have understood that within me was a woman who needed to express her own truths, articulate her own words. That, in Santo Domingo, would have been impossible.

Nevertheless, for the first ten years that I lived in New York, I was engulfed by a great silence; I could write nothing at all. The only poem I salvaged from this era was one about two young Puerto Ricans, aged sixteen and seventeen, who were shot by a bartender they had robbed of one hundred dollars. I saw an article about it in the paper, and it made me terribly sad. The poem ends with the line, "sadness has never come so cheaply." New York was, for me, a crushing kind of silence.

Still, all these experiences were being stored up inside of me. It's that kind of a process; things go in stages.

It was going to Africa that restored my essence as a *caribeña* for me. I went for three and a half months to work on coordinating the first meeting of ministers of education of the Portuguese-speaking African nations, and discovered Amílcar Cabral, the outstanding African cultural and revolutionary theoretician. Up to that point, I had never understood the important role that culture plays in effecting change. This was a central experience for me.

When I returned to the States, I was a different person; I suffered from severe depressions, which I now realize marked the death of one Chiqui and the birth of another. I figured the only thing that could save me was to return to the university, so I decided, at that point, to get an M.A. in Education from Columbia. I tried to work one more year in New York, but it was no good, and I returned to Santo Domingo.

I was there for four years, until last year, when I returned to the States. Some very difficult things happened during that time. The man with whom I had planned to restructure my life died of cancer. I was working terribly hard in my job as an educational coordinator. Basically, I had a kind of breakdown. I returned to the States to recuperate, and then went back to Santo Domingo. I've been there three months now.

I have really wanted to be a literary critic, yet once again I am denying my condition as a writer. The African experience had awakened me to the terrible problems of illiteracy in my country; 40 percent of the population is totally illiterate, another 40 percent, functionally so. I've always moved in this atmosphere of crisis and tension [between the two drives in my life]. Even now, I am teaching not literature, but a course on Dominican education at the university.

I had to go back to Santo Domingo because, after a few years, living in the United States gave me a kind of physical malaise. . . . When you first get here from your country, full of strength and energy, you get involved in a first stage of learning, absorbing, discovering. Then comes a time when you have to go back in order to revitalize yourself. If you stay in New York too long, you begin to get worn down by it. Anyone who is in the least sensitive can't help but feel bruised by the destruction of our people. Really. I saw it all the time in the Dominican community. Even though I had already acquired all sorts of New York rituals—I took perfumed baths in a flowered bathtub, swallowed my B12 vitamins, was into meditation—none of it was doing me any good. I realized I had to leave.

The New York experience, which was so crucial to my discovery of my Caribbean and racial identity, has made me a very, very critical person with respect to my own society. Things I never noticed before, I now see. Like racism, for example. Class differences. Santo Domingo is a very societally structured city. The situation of women is atrocious. I get almost rude about this because I can't stand the kind of sexist behavior that exists in my country. And for that, you pay the price of ostracism. It's really hard. By dint of having lived in the United States, I am considered a "liberated woman," which means that the men feel they have a green light to harass me sexually while the women distrust me. That's the most painful part. You come back to your country with a sense of intimate relationship and find that, for the most part, the principal *machistas* are the women themselves. And that's terrible. You find yourself confronted by an immense hostility that is a product of their own frustration. At first you ask yourself, "What have you done to this woman to have her treat you like this?" And then you realize that you symbolize all the things that she has never been able to do, and perhaps never will: leave the country, study what she wants to. She may find herself tied down by three or four children, a husband that bores her, physical confinement, etc.; and you come along as a woman who can come and go as she wishes, write, be creative and productive, freely elect the man she wants to be with, and you become, for her, an object of hatred. It's really dreadful. And with the men, you represent a challenge to try and get you because you're different, but the real challenge is to dominate you. For the women, you are all they cannot be and that must be destroyed for survival. And you have to understand that so you don't self-destruct. You can laugh off the first two or three aggressions, but by the fourth time, it really hurts.

As a writer I haven't yet been able to talk about my experiences in the States. At some moment in the future I will. Remember that New York was an experience of great silence for me. I feel that a time will come when I will be able to surmount what happened to me in New York and will be able to write about it. Remember, too, that the things I'm telling you in such a light vein today were wrenching experiences for me, especially discrimination. I still can't talk about it, but because I now have a better understanding of the creative process, I have learned not to push the creative instincts so that they won't become artificial. I know I have to let things come to the surface. The time will come when I'll be able to do it. I've written some sociological essays and some journalistic pieces on New York for a Santo Domingo paper in order to let my people know what's happening there, but in terms of literature I haven't yet been able to draw out what I have inside.

Because so many of my potential readers live in New York, I am definitely moving more and more toward publishing in the United States. I think people on the island would be interested as well. . . . We cannot avoid the "invasion" of the Dominicans from the U.S. The whole country is changing: English is spoken all over—you feel the influence of the Dominicans who come back everywhere. I also think there will be interest in my writing in the States, first of all, because there are so many of us there, and second, because I will approach things with the particular viewpoint of a woman. I have a lot to tell about what New York did to my family. I had to assume a kind of paterfamilias role with respect to my siblings. A lot of it was very traumatic.

However, for the moment, I'm more interested in women's issues, and especially in testimonials by Dominican women. I'm working on a book that is a collection of women's testimonials from the four years when I was here earlier. I've collected testimonials from all classes of women: peasants, factory workers, etc. I would like to be the voice of those who have no voice. Later, I'll be able to speak about New York.

In Santo Domingo there is a need to create a market for women's literature. As women, we have not yet discovered out power as consumers of books, but someday, when we discover this, perhaps we'll manifest this power by supporting women who write.

Juan Flores

Juan Flores is a member of the Centro de Estudios Puertorriqueños at Hunter College, (City University of New York). His book *Divided Borders: Essays on Puerto Rican Identity* (Houston: Arte Público Press, 1993) is a collection of insightful essays on Puerto Rican identity and culture.

Our essay from this collection, "'Bumbún' and the Beginnings of Plena Music," explores the rural and working-class origins of plena music, an Afro– Puerto Rican musical form characterized by the *pandereta*, a hand-held drum or tambourine, and improvised social themes. Flores traces the evolution of the plena both on the island and in New York City.

"Bumbún" and the Beginnings of Plena Music

Mon, Rafa, and Maelo are gone. The death of those three master *pleneros*—Mon Rivera, Rafael Cortijo, and Ismael Rivera—in recent years marks the end of an era in the history of the Puerto Rican plena, that form of popular music which arose at the beginning of the century in the sugar-growing areas along the southern coast of the island, and which within a generation, by the 1930s, came to be recognized by many as an authentic and representative music of the Puerto Rican people. Despite the unfavorable odds dictated by its evidently African-based features and its origins among the most downtrodden sectors of the population, plena rapidly supplanted the traditions of both bomba and *música jíbara* as the favored sound among many poor and working people. Plena even superseded the *danza* as the acknowledged "national music" of Puerto Rico. Tomás Blanco's 1935 essay "Elogio de la plena" was a landmark in this process of intellectual and cultural vindication, which is itself part of a larger project aimed at acknowledging the fundamental role of African and working-class expression in the history of Puerto Rican national culture.

The story of the plena comprises three chapters, each spanning a period of about twenty-five years.[1] The first quarter-century, which extends to the earliest recordings of plena around 1926, saw the emergence and consolidation of the distinctive form and its spread to all regions of the island. Between 1925 and 1950, when Canario and then César Concepción were at their peak, plena continued to extend its popularity, reaching the salons and ballrooms, gaining intellectual recognition by sectors of the cultural elite, and establishing itself among Puerto Ricans in New York. In this period the onset of recording and radio were of key importance, and involved the commercialization of the music with an attendant departure from plena roots. The third stage, spanning the 1950s and 1960s, constitutes a return to those roots, both in the working-class point of reference and in the renewed moorings in bomba and Afro-Caribbean rhythms. Mon Rivera, Rafael Cortijo, and Ismael Rivera, while making full use of recording technology and contributing ingenious innovations to the style, brought plena back to the streets and among the poor workers and unemployed masses from whom it had sprung. The social world of plena, and the monumental significance of Cortijo, has been captured memorably in the testimonial account of Cortijo's funeral by Edgardo Rodríguez Juliá.

Though the story of the plena since the days of Canario is familiar to many, very little is known of that first, prerecording stage, when plena was first emerging from its folk roots and establishing itself as the most popular and typical genre of Puerto Rican popular music. Here the towering practitioner was the semi-

⌒⌒⌒⌒⌒⌒⌒⌒⌒⌒⌒⌒⌒⌒⌒⌒⌒⌒⌒⌒⌒

legendary Joselino "Bumbún" Oppenheimer (1884–1929), whose very name suggests his place in plena history: Oppenheimer, an unlikely surname for a black Puerto Rican worker, was adopted from that of German immigrant *hacendados* and attests to his direct slave ancestry, while the nickname "Bumbún" echoes the thudding beat of his *pandereta,* the tamborinelike hand drum which was idiosyncratic of the plena, especially in its beginnings. "Bumbún" Oppenheimer, a distant memory to the few remaining survivors of his times, was the pioneer of the whole tradition, the first "king" of plena, the forger of the style and creator of some of the all-time favorites of Puerto Rican song.

Bumbún was a plowman. For years in the early decades of the century he drove oxen and tilled the fields of the huge sugar plantations outside of his home city of Ponce. In the mornings he would leave La Joya del Castillo, the Ponce neighborhood where he lived, and be off along the paths and byways leading to Hacienda Estrella. He hitched up the plow and prepared the oxen for the day's work. Then he was joined by the *cuarteros,* the young laborers hired daily to help the plowmen by walking ahead to keep the oxen moving and by clearing the furrows of stones and cane stubble. Bumbún's cuarteros were always in earshot, though, for they also served as his chorus in the *coplas* (couplets) and plenas he sang to the beat of ox and mule hooves and the rhythmic thrust of the plow:

No canto porque me oigan	[I don't sing so that they will hear me
Ni porque mi dicha es buena.	Nor because my luck is good
Yo canto por divertirme	I sing to enjoy myself
y darle alivio a mis penas.	And to relieve my suffering.]

Bumbún composed many plenas while tilling the fields of Hacienda Estrella. Patiently he would teach the song choruses to his plowboys, who would repeat them in energetic response to the "musician-plowman" as he went on to sing the solo verses of his new song. After work, Bumbún would make his way back to La Joya del Castillo where, at night, he would introduce his latest compositions to the many *pleneros* and fans who gathered in the homes and storefronts of his neighborhood in those years. Thus the plenas of Bumbún Oppenheimer, rather than falling into quick oblivion, have endured as treasures of the plena repertoire.

The plowman Joselino Oppenheimer was king, *"Rey de la Plena."* In a history boasting such better-known royalty as Cortijo, Canario, and César Concepción, Bumbún stands at the threshold. In addition to his countless original compositions and performances of plena standards like "Cuando las mujeres quieren a los hombres," "Tanta vanidad," and "Los muchachos de Cataño," Bumbun led the first plena band and became the first professional *plenero* when he decided to set down his plow and dedicate full time and energy to music. He was also one of the earliest masters, some would say unsurpassed, of the *pandereta.* Though he could also play accordion or *güiro* as the occasion demanded, Bumbún was a virtuoso *panderetero.* In the midst of a vibrant improvisation he would rest it suddenly on his shoulder, bounce it off his head, or roll it along the floor, all the while twisting and jerking his body in a wild frenzy.

And La Joya del Castillo, Bumbún's neighborhood in Ponce, is the recognized birthplace of the Puerto Rican plena. There in the small wooden houses, bars, and supply stores is where the *pleneros* would gather for their nightly *tertulias,* sharing their latest compositions and renditions to the pleasure of an appreciative, bustling public. In the first decades of the century, musicians and enthusiasts from the surrounding areas, and eventually from all parts of the island, had to go to Ponce to find out about the plena, and La Joya del Castillo was the renowned hub of the action. The regal name, by the way, should fool no one; hardly a "jewel of the castle," La Joya del Castillo is actually a euphemism, in true plena spirit, for la "hoya" del Castillo: it was the "hole" occupying the ravine beneath the mansion fortress of the famous rum-baron Serrallés. Expectedly, La Joya del Castillo suffered the fate of so many working class *barrios* in twentieth-century Puerto Rico: it was eventually razed without a trace by the forces of progress and replaced by "modern" buildings and thoroughfares.

Most important to the birth of the plena, it was to that neighborhood, around the turn of the century, that families of former slaves from the British Caribbean islands of St. Kitts, Nevis, Barbados, and Jamaica began to arrive and settle, bringing with them musical styles and practices which were different and exciting to the native *Ponceños.* Among these new arrivals was a couple named John Clark and Catherine George. Mr. Clark and Doña Catín sang and played music in the streets of La Joya del Castillo and came to be known as *los ingleses,* the English people. Their daughter Carolina Clark, usually called Carola, was a foremost *panderetera* in those dawning years, and she and her husband, the popular *plenero* Julio Mora ("La Perla"), helped to fuse the novel strains introduced by *los ingleses* with traditions and styles native to Puerto Rico. Though it is not known how or why, it is clear that the "English" sound caught on in Ponce and sparked the emergence of a new genre of Puerto Rican popular music. Some theories of plena origins even contend that the very word "plena" derives from the English exclamations "Play Ana" or "Play now," which accompanied those early street performances.

However that may be, the historical significance of this "English" influence is paramount. After abolition the former slaves were set adrift throughout the Caribbean. They moved toward coastal cities and plantations and, increasingly as the century neared its end, abroad to other islands or neighboring regions on the continent. Venezuela, Cuba, and of course, Panama were common destinations, but Puerto Rico also drew contingents of immigrants, especially from the English-speaking Caribbean islands whose economies had been languishing since British imperial interests turned emphatically to India and Africa. The southern coastal city of Ponce was the main port of entry for these "free" laborers, particularly as of 1898 when that whole part of the island became blanketed by huge capitalist plantations in the hands of U.S. and creole-owned sugar corporations.

The Clarks and Georges and the other *ingleses* who settled in La Joya del Castillo were part of this migratory movement. The infusion of their musical expression into the popular music of Puerto Rico, though a mystery in its specifics, illustrates the multiple intersections and blending of cultures as working people scatter and relocate. New, "foreign" styles, instruments, and practices arrive, attract attention for their newness and find imitations.

The role of external sources in the beginnings of plena history, which has been ignored in most accounts of the tradition, deserves attention because it points up the regional, Caribbean context for the emergence of twentieth-century song forms in all nations of the area: *son,* calypso, merengue, and many other examples of the "national popular" music of their respective countries were all inspired by the presence of musical elements introduced from other islands.

As the case of the plena shows, the foreign influence served as catalyst. The real roots of plena, as is universally acknowledged, are in the bomba: all of the early *pleneros,* including Bumbún, were originally *bomberos,* and the most basic features of plena derive directly or indirectly from bomba. Moreover, the historical development of plena proceeded primarily in its interaction with other genres of the "national," Puerto Rican tradition, notably the *seis* and the *danza.* The varied musical expression of the slave population, the peasantry from the mountainous inland, and the national elite make up the direct context for the birth and growth of plena, while the "imported" elements brought by *los ingleses* constituted a spark igniting the appearance of a new genre at a time when the regional, racial, and class divisions underlying the relative separation of those traditions were in the throes of abrupt change.

The emergence of the plena coincided with the consolidation of the Puerto Rican working class; it accompanied and lent idiosyncratic musical expression to that historical process. The first two decades of the century, when plena was evolving from its earliest traces and disparate components into a distinct, coherent form, saw the gravitation of all sectors of the Puerto Rican working population—former slaves, peasants, and artisans—toward conditions of wage-labor, primarily in large-scale agricultural production set up along capitalist lines. More and more workers, formerly inhabiting worlds separated by place and occupation, came into direct association, both at the workplace and in their neighborhoods; their life experience and social interests were converging, and assumed organized articulation with the founding of unions, labor federations, and political parties.

Many of the best-known plenas, from the earliest times on, tell of strikes, working conditions, and events of working-class life; they give voice, usually in sharp ironic tones and imagery, to the experience of working people in all its aspects. Topical events, seized upon in all their specificity, take on general, emblematic meaning to Puerto Rican working people of varied stations, places, and times because of their shared social world and perspectives. Even the musical features of the plena, with its boisterous, syncopated rhythms, improvised instrumentation, and vigorous call-and-response vocal cadences, testify to this working-class base, as becomes clear in the derogatory outrage voiced so often by the cultured elites when reacting to the "primitive" and "vulgar noise" of plena.

Integral to the qualitative change in employment conditions, of course, was unemployment and the presence of a reserve of poor people without work. Working-class neighborhoods like La Joya del Castillo housed not only the regularly employed, but also, perhaps in still greater numbers, those living hand-to-mouth on earnings from a range of other sources—from odd jobs, street vending, and occasional or seasonal work to ragpicking, hustling, and prostitution. It was this sector, largely descended from slave backgrounds, that figured preponderantly in defining the flavor and texture of cultural life in the community. And it was among them, those most hardpressed and forced to the margins of the new socioeconomic order, that plena found its earliest and most characteristic social base. As one commentator has it, writing in 1929 when the plena was taking all classes of Puerto Rican society by storm, "The plena arose in the brothels; it was born in the most pestilent centers of the underworld, where harlots hobnob with the playboys of the bureaucracy. But the plena, after all, stands for the conception of art held by the common people, by the illiterate masses. The plena reviews the public events of the day with irony, and interprets them according to the effect they have on the lower classes."

The same conditions that engendered this structural excess of unemployed workers also propelled the emigration of growing numbers of Puerto Ricans from the island in search of work and opportunity. Migration, primarily to the United States, has been an inescapable fact of life for Puerto Rican workers since the first years of the century. It has also been a recurrent theme of plenas since early on. The notorious expedition of hundreds of workers to Arizona in 1926, arranged under contract and ending in dismal failure, occasioned several songs and versions, including one attributed to Bumbún: "Dime si tú no has pasado / por el Canal de la Mona / Ahora tu pasarás / cuando vayas pa' Arizona" ("Tell me if you haven't passed / through the Mona Canal / Now you will pass through / when you go to Arizona"). And when he learned of the support shown the destitute survivors of that voyage as they returned to the island, Bumbún composed "Los emigrantes": "Llegaron los emigrantes / pidiendo la caridad / Unos venían en el Cherokee / y otros en el Savannah" ("The emigrants arrived / asking for charity / Some came in the Cherokee / and others in the Savannah"). The well-known standard "La Metrópoli," also from those early years, is one of many plenas about the arrival in New York, treating the migration experience in more sanguine terms, though an undertone of irony is still present: "En esta metrópoli / se critica la vida / pero si nos vamos / volvemos en seguida" ("We criticize life here / in this metropolis / but if we leave / we come back right away").

Thus the plena tells of emigration, and it also emigrates, taking root in New York and enthusing audiences from all sectors of the Puerto Rican community by the late 1920s. The migration of some of the foremost *pleneros* and plena groups to New York, and the lure of recording possibilities, were decisive in this shift, as the metropolis itself became the center for the further popularization of the plena for the ensuing decades. The figure of Canario looms large in this new stage of the tradition, as recording and commercial incentives resulted in major changes in the sound and social function of the form. The hugely influential presence of Canario and his group in New York during the 1930s, and a decade or so later that of César Concepción, conditioned the development of the plena through mid-century, But already by 1929, when that early commentary appeared in the New York weekly *El Nuevo Mundo,* the plena had struck firm roots in the emigrant community: "accompanying the continual stream of Puerto Ricans to this city of the dollar," it says there, "like a ghost, or like some left-over that it's impossible to get rid of, there sound the chords of the plena. And at night in our Latin 'Barrio,' oozing out of the cracks in the windows and blasting from the music stores, there is the sound of the Puerto Rican plena, which has taken over everywhere, from the poorest and filthiest tenements of East Harlem to the most comfortable middle-class apartments on the West Side."

Despite the many changes marking the history of the plena—diffusion to all regions and social strata of Puerto Pican society, expanded and altered instrumentation and thematics, the influence of recording and commercialization, migration of its principal center of evolution to New York, continual intermingling with other musical styles—the humble beginnings of that story need to be called continually to mind. When Bumbún Oppenheimer composed his enduring songs while driving an ox-drawn plow across the cane fields of Hacienda Estrella, rehearsing his newly invented verses with his chorus of plowboys, he established the source of the plena in the process of human labor and interaction with nature. It was work and the life-experience of Puerto Rican working people that made for the substance and social context of the plena in the streets and bars of La Joya del Castillo where it was born, and it is that same reality which has remained the most basic reference point for plena music down to the present.

Helen Valdéz

A forceful advocate for Mexican and Mexican-American arts and cultures, Helen Valdéz has realized a tremendous achievement in the creation of the widely respected Mexican Fine Arts Center Museum in Chicago's predominantly Mexican Pilsen neighborhood. Among other things, the museum is well-known for its inclusion of both "fine" and "popular" arts.

In Valdéz's reflections, one learns the remarkable story of the museum, and one also sees the convergence of influences that led up to its founding: Valdéz's experience at the Jane Addams Hull House; the women's educational institutions that she attended; her exposure as a college student to the radical educational philosophy of Brazilian intellectual Paulo Freire; and her years as a math teacher in Chicago.

6666666666666666666666

Interview

I was born in Chicago in 1950. I was a Hull House child. I was the last generation of young people to go through the original Jane Addams settlement house. I started there as a baby, and stayed through 1963. My mom used the day care, nursery school, after school programs, sewing classes, cooking classes. She became a citizen through the Americanization program there. My dad wasn't as active in the Hull House as my mom, but she used it as an agency that provided social services, from health information and clinics, to camps. I grew up believing that everybody had a Hull House experience. It was wonderful! In the arts we had puppetry, skits, plays, piano lessons, ceramics. When someone asks me, "Where did you get the idea that the arts are important?" I respond "There, at Hull House."

The arts at Hull House were presented as an opportunity for everyone to be creative. There was no thought that we might not be the "right" people for these kinds of programs. It was a very positive appreciation experience. There was no judgment made about one's talent, just exposure and appreciation. I remember the plays, "The Tortoise and the Hare," for example. I was in quite a few plays because I could memorize my lines and I loved to dress up in costumes. We also had singing, folk songs from all over. It was in many ways a model program for youth.

So, Hull House represented a fun place that invited everyone to join in. My brother participated somewhat, and my sister a little bit less. I am the oldest of five, and I was the one who got the most out of it. I met kids from all kinds of ethnic backgrounds: African Americans, Italians, Germans, it was a real mix. As the years went on , the diversity trimmed down a bit. I have only good memories of nursery school, for example. We would have creative activities, nap time, cookies and milk, parties, just good times. It was a well-funded social agency. It had the benefit of being the founding settlement house in the city, so they received a number of contributions. At Christmas we would get stockings full of nuts and fruit. Through donations we went to plays, the Goodman Children's Theater; we had field trips to factories, museums—the kind of things that we know are good enrichment activites for youngsters. Certainly the arts were one of the vehicles for enrichment, so I enjoyed an extremely rich childhood. I lived in a safe block; we had a little group of kids who would play together. I lived on Arthington just east of Halstead for my first twelve years, and even then the arts were always there for me.

We had no intention of moving, but we were forced to because of eminent domain and the construction of the University of Illinois. Two of my dad's daughters and one of his sons lived in the building too. It was a six-unit, three-story brick home purchased for $14,000. Can you imagine? It was another world, but in those days that was a lot of money. Before they were married, my mom was shocked that my dad didn't have a place of his own. I'm sure that this is a rural value; you may not even have shoes, but you have a little plot, a little something, to call your own. So she put this pressure on him to buy a place. I think the primary reason is that the youngest of his six children were thirteen and twelve, and she felt that there needed to be a woman in the home to take care of them until they became young adults. Their mother had passed away. My dad was over sixty-five when he married my mom. Then I came along, and then there were four others, so there were five in the second family. My mom was old by Mexican standards, but young really; she married at twenty-two years of age.

My father was a strong, healthy man and never looked his age. He was retired from the New York Central Railroad. I remember we used to get free passes to go to Mexico. My brother and I would fight over the upper berth in the Pullman car. I loved to hear the bell ring and to eat in the dining car. I would enjoy doing that again. At one point Chicago was one of the stops for the railroad. I never really understood why he ended up in Chicago other than that.

Just to go back for a moment, we lived in a neighborhood block and there was an Italian family next door, and I remember the grandmother crying and crying because she didn't want to move. It was just horrible, that whole experience was one of anger toward that bigger entity coming in and moving a whole set of established people against their will. It destabilized the community so that it became dangerous and derelict, where before it had been a very stable family community. Years later, when I went back to Hull House to see the building that remains on the University of Illinois campus, it made me very sad. My memories of Hull House are so different from what it is now. When it came time to go to college, I most certainly did not want to go to the University of Illinois. To me, that would be a betrayal.

When we had to move, we moved to the Pilsen community. My mom by that time was already taking a stronger hand in the finances of the family, and found the building on Eighteenth and May where we moved. My parents are working-class folks. Neither my mom nor my dad ever finished grammar school. My father often used the X as his mark. My mom completed three or four grades in Mexico, and continued at the Hull House, writing and learning about the Constitution. Though they were not educated, both my parents were very wise and extremely resourceful in managing in an urban setting.

Besides Hull House, another central fact in my life has been school. I always liked school. It was a way of getting the kind of recognition that I seemed to need. I attended St. Mary's high school, the oldest Catholic girls' school in the city. From there, I went to Mundelein College. There was this one novitiate who I really admired at St. Mary's, her name was Sister Agnes Leonard. She had gone to Mundelein, so I decided, let's try Mundelein. When I heard that I could go to Mundelein, I was very happy. It was, in many ways, the perfect school for me. My mom didn't want me to go; you know, you finish high school and that's enough, was her thinking. Your brothers go to college, maybe, but you're a woman. But I convinced her. The college was close enough so that I could take the el, but far enough away so that I convinced my mom that I should stay on campus. I was able to swing it financially through the assistance of a lot of support systems, including Mundelein and my mom, because she ended up helping me. I said, "I'll be home every weekend mom." Soon it was every other weekend, and gradually less and less often. The fact that my parents at that time didn't need my financial assistance helped a great deal. They owned property, my father had a retirement fund, mom worked. Though we lived very modestly, still we had pretty much anything that we needed.

I had a strong background in math when I left high school. I wanted to concentrate in math in college. I wasn't sure what I wanted to do. I liked the idea of counseling, also social studies. The last two years of high school at St. Mary's were very experimental, which meant that they were extremely exciting and challenging. We had a course, one of my favorites, on Christian values, structures, and the arts. I was always being asked, "What do *you* think?" After high school, college was disappointing. When it came to more creative thinking, I found myself far ahead of most of the other students there.

One of the things that impressed me about Mundelein was the Continuing Education Program; it was one of of the very first ones anywhere. When I finally had some of the returning women in my classes, they were exciting. They were full of experiences, and for the first time it really shook me to realize that, okay, if I don't finish college—because I was always really afraid that somehow I wouldn't finish—I can come back later. No one had gone to college in my family, much less a woman; this was all uncharted territory. But I would meet these women who had been married, or had followed a different career first, and I saw that life didn't have to be sequential. I am very systematic and want to have a beginning, middle, and ending to everything. I especially like to have closure, so this was very good for me, being around these women. I saw that life could change; it was a big psychological relief. Of course, I did finish college, and I taught, so I did follow a sequence, but it was liberating to see that life didn't have to be this orderly. And the returning women were much more interesting students than some of my younger colleagues.

In terms of my identity as a woman, that developed in college, too. The Mexican woman is very strong. I think her strength is diminished by the overemphasis placed on *machismo*, which does exist, but the woman's role is very strong. When I think back, also going to an all girls' high school was very important. I could have easily become someone who took second place in the roles I had to do, especially in the field that I ended up in, math. If I had gone to a large university, the competition would've been greater, plus the tendency to consider math more a man's world than a woman's.

If you think about it, going to an all girls' school, and then to a women's college, was very important. At both places I had excellent women math teachers and role models. The only consideration was whether I could do the task or not; this was very positive. Also, the idea that women can do other things and come back to school was an eye-opener. Seeing women in leadership roles, doing interesting things, was the norm for me at St. Mary's and Mundelein.

It was an exciting time to be in college. Mundelein was changing from a conservative, almost finishing school, to a more liberal place. But we also had great fun.

We had the Unmilitary Ball, that was great. Then we had a Spiro Agnew birthday party. The older, more senior students spearheaded these things, and my friends María Elena, Beth, and Ann and I always gravitated to the more radical elements.

We went to Cuernavaca to study one summer on a program they had at Mundelein. Beth and I went; Ann had gone the year before. It was wonderful! When I first heard Paulo Freire speak there, I thought, "I love this man! He is articulate—he makes so much sense." His first language is Portuguese and when he spoke to the convocation in Spanish he had to speak slowly. I thought, perfect! It was the summer after my first academic year, and I was hanging on every single word that he said about oppression and conscientization. It was so exciting! I had Mexican history in Spanish, and the transference from many English cognates was immense, so I learned much. Ivan Illich spoke to us, too. He always spoke in the presentations at midday, he also taught a course. When I think of Mundelein, I think of all those exciting things, although, structurally, the college was still very conservative. But there were many wonderful people that the College could not control! Very exciting and fun!

There was a special lady at Mundelein, Sister Therese Avila. She approached me and said, "I'm so glad you're here." I knew what she was saying, that I was this kid from Chicago, of Mexican descent, that it was going to be tough for me, but that I could do it. She was the first person who actually talked about those things. I'm sorry, but I get emotional remembering her. She was always there for me to talk to. "Oh, I hope you take Spanish, you're going to need it," she would say, always very positive. She was a great lady. She shared with me some writing that she had done on Unamuno. That represented another jump for me. Had it been any other person, I would never have have attempted to read it. This is a lesson for the teacher in me who wants to structure things too much. You know, the strict teacher who wants to stick to exactly the right reading level for this student, and so on. But Sister Therese just gave the material to me, in Spanish, and believe me, my Spanish was minimal. She did this to show her genuine support for me.

So, college is a place where I met wonderful people and had great experiences. I sometimes felt that I was on the fringe, on the outside, and sometimes I sought that intentionally. I remember while I was in college I went to the demonstration in Washington, in '69, as part of the moratorium. Beth and I went, and I remember some people were shocked that we were going, but I didn't think it was that dramatic just to go to Washington. (It was there that I met the man who would later become my husband.) I also remember, it was after they killed the kids at Kent State, that somebody dropped a large amount of bright red paint on the angel statue of the college. A group of us were going to put up signs in the morning in an effort to close the school to protest the killings. There were many schools being closed then. It was kind of spooky because, you know, I said that we were the radical element of the student body. Now, however, all the folks in our dorms who hadn't been involved at all were suddenly supporting the idea of closing the school. We went out to put up a sign, and then we were going to go back inside for breakfast, because we would never forget our stomachs despite our great cause.

Suddenly, I looked down and there was this big pool of red paint at my feet. Then I looked up. By then we were all standing there looking up, open-mouthed. I saw that someone had dropped a huge amount of red paint from the second floor, so that it looked as if the statue had been bleeding. We were dumbstruck! We stood there looking at each other, like, "It's not me! Not me! I didn't do it!" And then we saw that someone had put a banner on the Christ statue by the bend in Sheridan Road. We saw all this and thought, "Oh, my God! They're going to blame us!" Actually, it was a very effective symbolic gesture. In hindsight, I see that we forgot the most important thing in our campaign to close the school and protest to the world the situation in Viet Nam, Kent State, everything. We had arranged for no publicity whatsoever, and when we saw the paint and the banner, we realized that we had missed a great opportunity. I heard later that motorists who passed by on Sheridan Road were outraged. They even called in to offer money to sandblast the statue. So I guess the event generated its own publicity.

You know, it's difficult to assess Hull House, St. Mary's, and Mundelein, because what I thought about them then is different from what I think now, and I'm trying to sort that out. However, I did know the *minute* that I moved to Pilsen that my experience at Hull House the first twelve years of my life was special, unique, because I didn't see *any* of those opportunities here. It wasn't like I could go somewhere else and find them either. They were lost forever.

After graduation, I taught at Bowen High School in South Chicago. It's isolated and is in the oldest Mexican community in Chicago. I got my first taste of politics there. I went for an interview, which was pretty much unheard of at that time. Usually, you just got your school assignment from the central office. The principal at Bowen was an old Irish woman, Dr. Marie O'Brien, who always had everything go through her. The first thing that she asked me was if I knew any of the Chico family from this neighborhood. I said, "No, I'm not from this neighborhood." And she asked me about my background, saying that she knew I was very qualified, she just wanted to know if I would "fit in." She asked me what I thought of the Chicano movement, which was interesting because in all my political involvement, I had never referred to myself as a Chicana. That wasn't the terminology. It was a plus that that was the case, though I tried to save my self-respect and explained that I was more interested in the Latin American question. All she was concerned about was the Chicano angle: Was I part of the militant Mexican community, or was I going to fit in? But it was such an insult. Afterwards, I thought, this is what I worked and studied for? What she was really saying is that my qualifications didn't matter; what matters is who I'm friends with or what I'm involved in. Well, I passed somehow and spent eight very good years there. We got along okay, and she retired before too long. The way I looked at it, the next best thing to having a good administrator was to have one who left you alone, and that's what happened.

There at Bowen got involved in bilingual education, which I had had no exposure to at Mundelein, except for when I went to Cuernavaca. *That* was *my* bilingual education, hearing material in Spanish for the first time and realizing that just because I hadn't heard the terms in Spanish before didn't mean that I had to start from scratch, because there was a transference. I thought if this can happen to me, it can also happen to these young people.

At Bowen I confronted the question—which is related to this museum; we're getting there—of what happens to the Mexican kids who are born here that makes them so alienated from mainstream American culture. I saw that deep alienation. Most Mexican kids don't see themselves as going to college. They don't see themselves as Americans. They hesitate to say they're Americans, but they don't feel Mexican either. In some cases, they begin to hate themselves, they hate each other, they hate the kids who speak Spanish, they hate the kids who speak English well. That is certainly not what you find with many of the young people who come from a Spanish-speaking country and who are in a bilingual program, which brings up another point. People often think that *all* the Mexican or Latino kids are in bilingual programs, but fewer than 25 percent were in the bilingual program in our school. There is no school even today where the entire Mexican or Spanish-speaking population is in the bilingual program. It has always been a small percentage. In fact, the program really has not been about bilingual education, but about learning English, and the sooner the better. In the process, we give the kids the idea that the Spanish language is second-rate. By extension, we are also telling them that their parents, their religion, their entire culture is second-rate.

One of the most striking examples, as I think back on it, concerned a kid named Bernardo from Mexico who enrolled late in the school year. I could see that Bernardo was a sharp kid and that he was going to go places. He had already had two years of *preparatoria* in Mexico, and he just needed to learn a little more English. Bernardo also played trumpet. I knew that our orchestra needed him, so I sent him to the band room. A few days later I heard that he had gotten into the orchestra. This kid George Muñoz in my homeroom—*mexicano*, born here, when he heard he exclaimed: "Mrs. Syman," that was my married name at the time, "Mrs. Syman, it's incredible, Bernardo can play the trumpet!" I said, "George, why are you so amazed that he can play trumpet?" George responded, "Well, he doesn't speak English!" At that moment I wanted to take George and put him on a plane and send him anywhere where they don't speak English and show him that the world turns in other languages. Some of our young people have this prejudice that, if you have an accent, that means you're not intelligent, you're not capable of thinking.

I did some things at Bowen that foreshadowed what I do here at the museum. We had a film festival; I brought *The Green Wall*. If you remember that film, there is one erotic scene, and I went through torment trying to get that film, but the kids loved it and accepted it. I actually had kids coming up to me and saying it was a wonderfilm film, really moving, how come we don't see more things like this. There was a dearth of opportunity to see things in Spanish about life, and even in English, when I think back.

At that point I was trying to do a bit of bridging between kids who were in the bilingual program and kids who came in just to study. It was not really a program, but a Bilingual Cultural Center, as the title says. I wrote a minicourse in Latin American History, other bilingual education teachers prepared other interesting minicourses, although, in the school as a whole, it was very obvious that we were just being tolerated.

From that experience, I learned a lot about how to bring about change. In terms of strategy, what you really have to do is convince the people who are involved in the structure to become part of that change. But what happened at Bowen, and across the whole city, was that change was something that happened *to* them. New personnel were brought in, with the result that there was no developmental change from within the structure. Even the teacher training program, which I got involved in later after Bowen: when you think of the history there, too, the strategy was very poor. All of a sudden the Congress of the United States decided there were to be bilingual programs, and so, somehow, tomorrow we're supposed to have them all in place. But, where's the research? Where's the body of resources, books, curriculum, teacher training? Nothing. It was as if instantaneously they had to appear. It wouldn't have been so bad, except that people sought to evaluate these programs as if they had existed for twenty or thirty years. So much of the research that was carried out was misguided and misleading.

I had my first experience of being under siege, so to speak, at Bowen. They were always watching us to see what we were doing. Actually, we in the Bilingual Center were envied because we had a team of people, and generally, no one works as a team in the public schools. We were accused of thinking we were superior to everybody else at Bowen, and of acting like the kids were our own. I would say, "You know what, they might as well be my own, because they look just like my cousins, my brothers, and my sisters."

The thing that gets me is that kids in Mexico would give anything to have the opportunity to go to a class with a teacher, chalk, people encouraging them, but those resources are not available. While here, we've got the resources, and people are encouraging the kids, telling them that they can do it, they can go to college, but the *ánimo*, the spirit, just isn't there. What happened? It's not that the kids lack talent, that is certainly not my experience. For example, I was so proud my first year, I had an algebra class, and I was going to teach the *best* algebra course ever. I was finally where I wanted to be, and I don't know if I expected a special ceremony or what, but all of a sudden there I was in front of this classroom and the responsibility hit me. I thought of all the time, effort, studying, sacrifice, and said to myself, well, this is it, here I am. I am responsible for these kids, so here goes. And they were wonderful! I had a mixture of kids, some who spoke mostly Spanish, and others who spoke mostly English. I was so interested in them; I wanted to motivate them. I guess I went a little overboard because I surveyed them, wanting to know what they were going to do with their lives. Three of them said they wanted to become math teachers, and I was so happy. Actually, one *did* become a math teacher. However, over the years I came to realize that even if I did a good job, the whole school did not function with that same motivation. Kids would go into other classrooms and they would begin to go down, to decline. So, this whole idea of the importance of the structures and the people supporting them was very marked for me. You know, it's a tough world, it's not easy to bring about change, and I have benefited from these practical experiences.

It was the low expectations for the Mexican-American children that just hit me in the face, that materialized themselves very concretely. For example, there are work-study programs designed for kids who are borderline dropouts, to get them involved on the job so they could see the relationship between school and work. Guess who they would recruit for those programs? The well-mannered Mexican kids—there were also some Puerto Rican kids too, so I should say nice Latino kids—who would go to work and not give any bad reports. The school wanted kids who would make *the school* data look positive and successful. But meanwhile, what they had done was take those kids out of a college track, so that they did not take that third or fourth year math, for example. They ended up going to business school and feeling good about it, when they could have gone to college. I knew what they could have done had they stayed in the track. And this is documented. I know kids who years later regretted that they did it that way. At the time I tried talking to them, but even so, the economics were too powerful a force. However, the fundamental problem was the low expectations for these kids within the system.

Just about the time I was looking around for a graduate program in math, I had a student teacher from the University of Chicago assigned to me. She was from Texas, she knew Spanish, and she wanted to see a bilingual program. She was very good, good-hearted, and she sold me on the program at Chicago. That's when I decided to go to the University of Chicago to get a master's in math education.

The math program was very useful. At that point I began to think that I wanted to go into teacher training in math. Unfortunately, there was an overflow of teachers and teacher-training programs were at an ebb, so I left those plans on the back burner. But I still am fascinated with how to teach math. I also got involved with what is now a raved-about program, a new curriculum that is being created out at the University of Chicago. My advisor is part of it. Had things been different, I might be doing that now instead of my work here at the museum. At any rate, the math program at UC was a very enriching experience. I learned what I was doing wrong, and I also learned another perspective in math. It opened my eyes and provided a very balanced math education program. This was part-time, summers; I was teaching full-time. I was the only one from the public schools there in the program. The problem is that it was a big financial burden. I pretty much put myself through the program. Even though there was tuition reduction for returning scholars, it was still hefty. But it was worth it.

I was married then. I met my husband in Washington in '69, got married in '71, and we divorced in '80. Many of those years were good. He was very supportive of my going to school. I left Bowen about two years before the drastic decline of the neighborhood. There were no efforts made by the school to assist students. There was a lot of racism. We had a mixed student body, one-third African Americans, one-third Latinos, mostly Mexican, and one-third whites of all ethnic backgrounds, such as Irish and Polish. But we never interacted, and the curriculum never reflected anything that would suggest that we live in a multiracial country. We ate lunch in segregated groups. There were riots; the adults completely lost control of the school.

Basically, there was no affinity at all between the administration and the student body. If anything, they pitted Latinos and African-American staff against each other. I remember the first time I heard an African-American teacher saying "those kids," and I wondered what kids she was talking about. So, I asked her and she said, "Oh, those kids from—," and named a neighborhood that was very poor. The better kids were those from better neighborhoods. So, you had class conflict. The teachers wanted the kids to be middle class, and their solution to the problem was to keep the poor kids out of the school. Many teachers were just as prejudiced as anyone else.

I met many teachers who were disappointed with the profession. That was quite a revelation because teaching had been an important goal for me. I finally reached it, and then I saw these unhappy teachers, especially the men. It was as if they had wanted to be doctors and what they were doing was second-best. There were so many frustrated teachers that I wondered how they could possibly motivate their students.

To get back to the question of why the Latino young people seemed to be the most lost, I think that part of the answer is that they needed to know that they could be proud of something, that they were part of a great culture, a great heritage, a great struggle of community and working people making a life for themselves in this country. They needed to strengthen their self-esteem. They needed to be helped to dream a little more, to reach for something beyond themselves. I think of the story of George all the time, and the film festivals and dances. We used to do a lot of things with music, and the kids were great. It is still very clear to me that we need a more holistic approach. Now, people are working to make the kids feel good about being Mexican, or Puerto Rican, and so on. However, I also see that teachers need to improve their teaching. It's not enough just to feel good about who you are. You've got to have both those things, self-esteem and knowledge. You also have to ask, "Are my teachers the best I could have?" There is little incentive in the system for the best to be teachers and for the best to stay the best. The respect for the teaching profession that is essential to support a system that makes teaching crucial to the development of young people is simply not there.

I'm basically a dropout of the school system. The stress and the overload were so much that there were times that I couldn't sleep. I even started sleepwalking; I just couldn't handle it. I had so much work, day and night, and then they offered me an accelerated class. I taught it at a junior high. It was partly sanity for me, compared to all the other things I had to do. Then there was counseling; they told me I had only three hundred students—can you imagine, three hundred—and that was a light load! But, any time a parent came in, especially if they were Spanish-speaking, I was called. I was also called in to deal with discipline, and this was supposed to be an honor. I was overwhelmed and exhausted.

By the time Marilyn Turkovich called me from the Urban Education Program, I said yes before she finished making her offer. That was also about the time my marriage was breaking up. I became a little more stable when I began to work for the Urban Education Program. I looked at education from a different perspective: How do we get teachers to become better human beings for the kids? I learned so much from Marilyn and from Peggy Mueller; they are wonderful people. They work on multicultural curriculum, exercises that sensitize people to different points of view, teaching through simulation, all kinds of techniques that are part of the multicultural education area. This was all very positive, but most of the people involved were nonminority, from very expensive liberal arts campuses, very few minority students. I felt somewhat alienated there. Not that I didn't feel like I was doing something positive, because I was working with these young people who were studying in order to be able help students. Still, I knew that every moment that I was working with them was time I could have spent teaching. I had been trained as a teacher and I was a darn good one, so why was I administering? I had a big job, covering thirteen campuses for the Urban Education Program of the Associated Colleges of the Midwest. I visited the different campuses, saw different qualities, perspectives, energy levels, survival techniques. I wrote proposals, worked on state accreditation for some of the programs in Illinois and Wisconsin. That was good for the time being, but I felt that I had something more urgent to do, and that was to teach instead of train teachers—in very small numbers, by the way.

So, I made a jump again, and at the same time, we got involved in this project, the museum. I like to do too many things at once. But anyway, the lady who years earlier had sent me to Bowen was now at Truman College. She called and said, "We need you. We're looking for math teachers." I responded, "How did you know I was looking for a job?" That was ten years ago now.

Truman, now, there's another world for you. It's like a United Nations. You have students from everywhere, the Middle East, Africa, Russia, Latin America, and about 30 percent are African Americans. The math department is pretty strong. Unfortunately, it's not because of our own high school graduates, but because of the Middle Eastern and Asian students who have very strong math backgrounds. Because of them, we have two years of the baccalaureate program in math, through linear algebra, and we actually offer these courses, we don't just list them like some places do. They asked me to teach calculus. Teachers there were very interested in teaching; I admired the staff. The ESL program is great. There are many good things about Truman. I have taught there for seven years; this year I am on leave.

Teaching while I was also working here at the museum has in some ways saved my sanity, because this job has its ups and downs. I certainly needed to make a living, plus, as you know, I find great satisfaction in teaching. Even a topic like fractions, which might be considered quite trivial, I think is a real challenge. It is quite another challenge to teach it well to adults. These are exciting challenges. Perhaps my only regret is that I could have been part of the cutting edge of math education now if I had stayed with it longer.

Now, to the Mexican Fine Arts Center Museum. In 1980, when we began the project, we didn't think that we would be starting from scratch. We had heard of previous efforts, one in particular called the Mexican Cultural Center. I was in charge of finding out what had happened to it. Carlos Tortolero, who had been my colleague at Bowen, Carlos and I had kept in touch and we began talking about how important it was to have a cultural center. We wanted to have something that wasn't a once-in-a-while operation where someone would do a film festival, or an exhibit, but an ongoing, year-round place. We knew that there were examples of this idea, that the Ukranians and Lithuanians had their museums, for example. From 1980 to 1982, we explored the concept and sought advice. We began September 15, 1982, with our first meeting of the board.

During the exploration phase, we found out that the last effort at a Mexican Cultural Center had all the who's who involved, and for a number of reasons it soured. We learned that if we were going to get anywhere, we had better not call ourselves the Mexican Cultural Center, because people would surely ask us questions, like, where did the money go for the first one! The other recommendation was that we not include people from the who's who of our community on the board because they are simply too busy, but that we involve them in an advisory capacity and to identify other people who could work with us to build a board.

We began the board with twelve and became incorporated. Our first board meeting was at the Benito Juárez High School conference room. The strategist in all of this was Carlos. He is a gamester, in the most positive sense. He loves football and baseball, and, to him, this enterprise is about winning. It's about moving forward, and, even with failure, to learn what went wrong and what we did right. Carlos has been a very intellectually stimulating colleague.

Our guiding objective was the same then as it is today: to sponsor exhibits and performing arts events that highlight Mexican culture. We wanted to have art education classes. We wanted to help artists. We saw them as important transmitters of culture, and we knew that they were building the traditions of the future, continuing the heritage. Primary during the first five years was to build our credibility within our own community and within the funding community, to convince them that we could do what we said we could do, especially in light of past failed attempts.

We decided to name ourselves the Mexican Fine Arts Center and then about five months later we added the word museum to our name. We construe the term "fine arts" very broadly. We didn't know the difficulty we would have where some purists would want to exclude from fine arts all folk art and film. We definitely used the broadest definition. The reason it wasn't *Mexican American*, but *Mexican*, is that the focus is Mexico. The term Chicano never became a popular term in this part of the country. I also think it is a divisive term, tending to separate the recent arrivals from those of Mexican descent. Within three years we had to address that issue very carefully, and we have had to define ourselves as that cultural expression that manifests itself both in Mexico and outside of Mexico. That's it. Basically, we don't recognize the border. We state it that way.

But as generous as that is, it is also offensive to some people on both sides of the U.S.-Mexican border. I've had people from Mexico say to me that I am not a real Mexican because I do not speak Spanish well and I was not born in Mexico.

They will stand right here in this building and say that to me. It's hard to respond. I take a deep breath and tell myself not to shout. All of a sudden, my Spanish improves three hundred percent. I tell them that we're here in Chicago, and that we are respectfully trying to serve the Mexican-American community, but that the institution and the community are linked in many ways to Mexico. At the other extreme, we have Mexican Americans come in and tell us that we bring in way too much art from Mexico, that this museum should be about us (Mexicans in the U.S.), our expression. What we are doing just with our name alone is challenging the status quo. It has also been significant that we have remained steadfast that this is not a Latino museum.

Now we find ourselves in a leadership position to move the culture, to teach. It's great, but it's also frightening, and I have the feeling that I often had at Bowen of being under siege, because what we are doing here, and what we did there, is about creating change, affecting the community's reality. Let me give you an idea of the important educational role we can play. I remember there was a gentleman, Carlos Cortéz, who came as a speaker when I was with the Urban Education Program. He talked about the societal curriculum, which is everything that happens outside of school. And to make his point, he said that in California there was a study done among young people about what they knew about gypsies. Now, these kids had never seen or studied about gypsies, but they knew every single stereotype about that group. "Now, where do you think they got those views?" he asked. Of course, it was from conversations, from their parents, TV—the outside. That example reminds me that there's an important role for this museum as a place that can teach others.

I remember it was such a big moment when we finally could afford a telephone for the museum. We still didn't have a place, we had a P.O. box, we were just a small group of committed people. But we didn't emphasize the need for a place. We emphasized progams, and we put on programs about every two months. Our first one happened accidentally at the Cultural Center of Chicago. We brought in an exhibit, "Mexico through the Eyes of Her Children." It's a lovely educational set, in English and in Spanish. SITES (Smithsonian Institute Traveling Exhibits) had brought together the original written materials and developed a traveling exhibit. So we brought it to the Cultural Center, and we also did a folkloric dance program there, and then something else at the Field Museum. We were at many places—also at the Benito Juárez High School—and we organized a film festival at the Art Institute Film Center. We were very busy. We worked with the staff at the Chicago Academy of Sciences on the first bilingual exhibit they ever did, on the people of the rainforest. It was another SITES exhibit, but we brought the famous scientist Gertrude Blum, who lives in Chiapas. Many, many school groups came. It was a very nice program, with a beautiful brochure.

It was critical that we always took an active role in fundraising, in audience development, and in program development, because organizations like the Field Museum wanted to reach out to the communities, but they didn't know how. There we were to provide the missing link. Actually, we wanted to do what they were already doing, so it was a great opportunity for us to develop our skills at the same time that we became the vehicle for bringing wonderful programs to the community. We learned that we could do it; it was not brain surgery. It was about people, about bringing a message to as many people as possible. I was the one always complaining that we didn't have a place of our own, because every time we approached a place about a show, we had to work it into their schedule, at the Field Museum or wherever. It was always a handicap in terms of our own scheduling, but it was wonderful working with the major museums of Chicago.

In 1988, I went to the Museum Management Institute at the University of California at Berkeley, an intensive four-week program sponsored by the Getty Foundation. About thirty museum professionals were there. I got good recommendations from the directors of the Field Museum and the Chicago Academy of Sciences. I thought that I would be very different from the other people at the institute, but I learned that I was not that odd, that there are a lot of people who come into the field at various points and from various careers. It was a great seminar. I learned a lot, and I also realized how much we were already doing right. Most other participants were career people, and I'm not, in the sense that I didn't train and study formally for this job. Some were striving to land a position at the Metropolitan Museum of Art, but I just wanted to be here. I wanted for the museum to survive and to grow. I still think it is very fragile.

One thing I learned there was that when I said that this museum is about people and about freedom, the others were shocked. To them, museum management is a career. They have their seven objectives, like ABC, but I said no, for me, this is about freedom. This is about breaking the stereotypes that limit not only our community but the whole country. It's about possibilities. It was spontaneous, what I said, and I think it was a good discussion for all of us there. It was spontaneous, but it came from my previous experience and my belief, like Paulo Freire, in the importance of empowerment, the conscientization of individuals, and the community becoming conscious of its culture, because it is there. We are not creating something that isn't already there. We are formalizing it, enhancing it, highlighting it, celebrating it.

You know, all those little *quinceañeras,* the celebrations of a girl's fifteenth birthday, that go on in church, the music, the beliefs, all those are parts of the culture in its most popular form and in its most sophisticated form as well. And I think that this is the other thing that the museum is about: connecting popular and high culture. A frequent criticism we get is that this is a nice place, but it shouldn't be here in Pilsen, it should be on Michigan Avenue. That's another problem. We didn't know how radical it was to locate the museum here and to make the statement that art is for everyone. You can be poor, but you can walk in here and stand alongside someone who is very wealthy and has a different lifestyle, and you can enjoy the same art.

I've always believed that education and art are for everyone, but I'm afraid that many others do not think so. We even had one contemporary Latina artist, a Cuban-American woman who is very accomplished, tell us that she was shocked that we allowed children in here. How does she think that we are going to get the community to appreciate and to validate their own cultural expression if they don't have access to it? Here's where my upbringing comes into play; I believe that art is for everyone, and this value has been strengthened over the years. Yet, we meet many artists who simply don't want to show here because they don't want to be associated with "this ethnicity thing"—it's one-dimensional; certainly it's not depth, it's not art; it speaks only to one group.

In the end, our position is pretty much that there should be validation from all sectors. It's important for our own community to make judgments on art, but certainly others should, too. I think the problem has been that in the Mexican-American community we have had people speaking for us, we haven't been analyzing for ourselves, making judgments for ourselves. When you lose control of that, you've lost control of an important dimension of your life.

I see that we have been an example in ways that I hadn't even imagined. I have a colleague at Truman, she's from Thailand, and she has been meeting with a group of people for lunch to try to create something similar for the Thai community. Another example is a woman from Turkey who lives in southern France. She came in and started talking to me about the universality of having minority cultures exist within the dominant culture, and the question of how they can coexist. The critical thing is that the dominant culture not survive at the expense of the minority cultures.

Part of the problem for minority cultures is equity, access, funds. There's all this brouhaha now about homophobia and eroticism, but what about people who don't even get to the table? There are not enough women who are allowed to be exhibited. There are so many screening processes, and art that shows the slightest cultural orientation is often thought to be inferior; this is a widespread prejudice. Have you ever gone to the South Side of Chicago? There are many African Americans who don't get a chance to be in galleries, but they're artists, they're producing, maybe some of them are not doing so on a regular basis, but that's because there are few support systems. The predominant belief is that there are the talented and the untalented, and somehow, the predominance of talented people are white males. This is something that we should examine.

Ours is meant to be an institution that provides access. Now, we have thirteen people hired, including myself. Most have never been in the museum field before, but they learn. Most of our exhibits have been curated by Mexicans, but for the Latino exhibit we didn't have a specialist, so we invited a non-Latina and coupled her with a Latino, because part of what we are about is access. If you want to present something, but you do not have a specialist in that field, you get the specialist because you've got to have quality, and you place a Latino alongside that person to learn. We employ more Latinos than any other arts organization, not only in the whole city, but in the whole state and country.

Our community still needs empowerment, our own first-person voice saying that we exist and this is how we see ourselves, but we also need integration. That's why when people ask me, Is this the solution, to create institutions like yours in every community? I say, "yes and no." Yes, if that's what the community wants. But no, because we also have to look for access to the mainstream. I am concerned, for example, that the Art Institute hire Latinos, Mexicans, African Americans, because that's important. It's not important just for us to do it. It's not this *or* the other, but both; everything is what we need. We also need to work actively to eliminate barriers. We don't have enough museum internship programs, for example. We need to use all avenues to improve the situation. And cultural arts is another area that's as political as everything else. Spike Lee made the statement, "Race has everything to do with how you live and die in the United States." It also has everything to do with the arts. Artists are usually considered very liberal and progressive, but they can be just as problematic as any other sector in our society, maybe worse if they don't admit to their prejudices.

The challenge which has been traveling with me all my life, especially my adult life in my career as a teacher, carries on here, in the pursuit of equal opportunity, dignity, and of high expectations for young people and families. We have a generation of kids who, now, because of our work to establish a museum, are growing up thinking that there has always been a Mexican Fine Arts Center Museum. These young people will grow up hearing the important things that we say about their culture through the arts.

Over 20 percent of the elementary public school population in Chicago now is Mexican. On my worst days, I think that having larger numbers in the public schools will mean only that we will suffer more because those kids won't be challenged, given a fair shake, educated, and, to boot, somewhere along the way they'll become convinced that they're just not good enough. On my best days, I think that maybe I'm giving the schools too much credit for the amount of harm that they can do! I also remember that there will always be good people going against that flow, really challenging the kids, doing different things with them, asking them questions, bringing them to a museum like this, letting them see people from their own background doing things like this, or coming here and seeing that there are well-to-do white kids from suburban schools coming here to learn, too, seeing that there is great value in the Mexican culture. We hope that we can break some of the stereotypes.

You can see the difference between the way I'm talking about this museum and the way some of the people at the Museum Management institute talked about their museums. They had no allegiance except to the career of being a museum director; in fact, about half of the them were in transition to another position or place, hoping to improve their résumés. They would also talk about the Mexican Fine Arts Center Museum as being second-rate, only they used a much more elegant term, "culturally specific." Then I would say, "You know, that's part of the problem I have because I believe your museum is culturally specific, too. I don't see myself represented there." They had not looked at it that way; yet many of these people would be the first to say that they are international and cosmopolitan.

The museum is a great project, and now we have expansion plans. I see the annex allowing us to do a better job in the areas of collection and education. We have so many talented artists, teachers, and community resources for curriculum development. One of my pet projects is a creative writing camp. Writing is one of the areas—another full circle for me—that has never been given full attention in my life. I've been lucky to have people help me with the technical aspects, and then later with the creative aspects. But it would be great to have kids involved in writing, to do multicultural, multiart kinds of experiences, to get them creating on computers. We have journalists, poets, and script writers in the community. I met a gentleman who works for Commonwealth Edison, a young *mexicano,* a wonderful spokesperson for writing. He says that he has been able to move up the ladder because he can write. He has his own kids write, and he would like to get the message across to other kids. He would be someone I would like to bring to such a group. That is, if I ever get that project started and can do something besides administrative work and networking.

The truth is that I also love the administrative aspects of my work because I have a vision for what I am doing. I thank you for this opportunity because it has made me take the time to reflect, which I almost never do. In earlier years, we had more opportunities like this; we would sit down and say what we did wrong here, or what went right there, and it was wonderful. We grew a lot that way.

This museum project has taught me a lot of things that I guess I knew but didn't want to deal with. Prejudice, for example. Now I'm talking about prejudice in our own Mexican community, in my own family even. I have had people become upset because there were too many Indians here. At first, I thought, What? But then I recalled that one of the biggest insults my mom could give me was to tell me that *me portaba como una india,* that I was acting like an Indian. I see that there is a problem within our own culture toward the indigenous cultures. Therefore, 1992 is an important year to try to articulate the counterview that maybe there are other things that we should be celebrating, like the victories of people to sustain their cultures, to survive some of the atrocities committed against them. We can't lose this opportunity, so we are having a pre-columbian exhibit, which came to us fortuitously. The Field Museum materials will be available to us, and some of them have never been shown before. It's going to be a powerful exhibit early in 1992. Later in 1992, the Art Institute is also presenting a fantastic, magnificent exhibit with beautiful, outstanding pieces. Then we're also going to have an exhibit that deals with what's Mexican. We're doing an exhibit—for the first time one that's being produced by a Mexican institution and curated by Mexicans. It will focus on contemporary U.S.-Mexican artists. Most art shows that have been coming out with a Latino theme have been sponsored by beer companies or universities, so there's no community control, and there have been many heated controversies. Well, this will be a national show that we hope will travel. We are raising funds for it ourselves. The biggest cost will be the transport of materials. First to Chicago; then, hopefully, it will travel to California; Texas, to San Antonio or Austin; and to New York, where the Museo del Barrio is interested.

I guess the only other thing that comes to mind is that, in the arts community, we feel that the term Hispanic is more a word that has been laid upon us, actually it means belonging, or of Spain, and that offers too much recognition to Spain and too little to the indigenous cultures. Not that Latino does the trick either, so here in Chicago we prefer to use the term Mexican. Unfortunately, that presents even more controversy. Politically, there's a tendency to use Latino or Hispanic more to disguise some other people's agendas than to illuminate a coalition. Not that there's that great a unity among the different groups in the first place. If we were to bring to the public's attention that there are differences between Cubans, Puerto Ricans, and Mexicans, that we don't automatically get along, they would be surprised. They think we are all the same. In the Latino community, we don't talk enough about the truth. In other words, there is a lack of communication, of honest recognition of differences, the very thing we want from the mainstream. The amazing thing is that there are many non-Latinos who are on the Mexican-American and the Latino's side, and who support our right to name ourselves.

We have the responsibility here to protect and nurture Mexican cultural identity in an institutional way so that it can develop. We feel that we have a leadership role to play in providing a strong forum for discussion, and in supporting the artistic expressions and voices of our community. In the end, that's all we have.

Barbara Carrasco

Barbara Carrasco has been drawing ever since she can remember, from her earliest days in El Paso, to the housing projects in Los Angeles, to her participation in the Upward Bound program as a high school student, through her years as an art student, and certainly during her continuing involvement with farm worker and Chicano/a issues.

Carrasco is known both for her mastery of technique and form, and for the bold themes that she expresses in her work, the most striking example being her controversial mural *L.A. History—A Mexican Perspective,* the subject of national attention in the press and in the artistic community. In the following interview, Carrasco discusses the censored mural as she recounts the formative influences on her development as an artist.

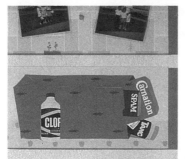

*Codex Carrasco, 1992
by Barbara Carrasco*

Interview

I was born in El Paso; my folks were born there, too. On my mother's side, her father was born in Durango, but I'm not sure where my dad's family was from. They've been in Texas for a long time. My mother's great-great-grandfather was German; that's why I have light hair, skin, and eyes. Yet my sisters are very dark; you would not believe we are related. One of them even has freckles. One sister and I worked together at the University of California at Los Angeles and no one thought we were related because she's really dark with long black hair. We had problems growing up because people thought she was black, and a lot of times they thought I was white. I had my first fight when I was about thirteen, with a girl who said that I thought I was better than anybody else since I was light-skinned. We lived in Mar Vista Gardens Housing Project in Culver City. I don't know exactly why we left El Paso, but we lived in the projects for a very long time, all the way through high school. It's now considered one of the most dangerous ones, with drug trafficking and gangs. When I was growing up it wasn't that bad; it was dangerous, but it's much worse now. My mother was very strict, very traditional. I was literally in the house for eighteen years with my mother. She wouldn't let me go to parties, she was very, very strict. She was afraid because a lot of kids were into fighting and drugs.

I was born August 5, 1955. My father died when I was twelve, and my mom was thirty-five with five children to raise by herself. I can't imagine taking care of five kids between thirteen and three years old. He died of a heart attack. He smoked about seven packs a day, and he had had a couple of heart attacks before the last one. He played a very important part in my life. He used to have these long talks with me about the fact that he was a bus driver and he hated being poor. He was always apologizing for us living there in the projects. He felt like we should have a better environment to grow up in. He told me that anybody can be a bus driver, but not everybody can be an artist. I was very young when he told me that. I have been drawing since before kindergarten. My mom has kept all those earliest drawings. Some of them are funny; I had one of my parents kissing with their lips interlocked. They had a beautiful marriage; I think that's why my mom wore black for two whole years after he died. They were an unusual couple. They met at a downtown department store in El Paso called the Popular. She saw him going up in the elevator, and she said she knew immediately that they would get married. Six months later they were married. I remember them kissing all the time, and laughing. My brother is a year older than I am; he's *güero*, fair, like I am. He looks a lot like me, but the other three, my other brother and two sisters, are dark. I used to have trouble with my color. I don't have any problems with it now, but when I was younger I kept asking why I wasn't dark. I wanted to be dark; I had the reverse complex of most people. That's because I grew up in the projects where everybody was dark; they were blacks and Asians, all dark poor people.

Actually, they got along very well. I think that many of the problems that existed were in in fact instigated by the local police. They used to drive up on the lawns, for no reason at all, just to intimidate us. My mom played an important role for the kids in the projects because she would divert our attention from things like that. She was excellent at getting all the kids to do things together, like play volleyball. She went out and got two inner tubes, filled them with cement, put a pole in each one, got a net, and made it possible for us to play volleyball. She did a lot of things like that for all the kids in the projects. She made snow cones for the kids; she was a great mother, in those days! She became a little too strict as I got older!

In fact, in the ninth grade, I was going to Marina Junior High School and I got a scholarship to go to Oldef Art institute. I was very excited about it, but my mother made me turn it down because she didn't think it was right for a young girl to ride on the bus! I was about fourteen at the time. I held a grudge against her for a long time because of that, especially since she had told me that her grandmother had made *her* turn down an art scholarship when she was young. She had wanted to go to art school, too, but she later went to nursing school. At the time, she was living with her grandmother because her mother had passed away, and she had a very hard time being raised so strictly by her grandmother. She even went with my mom to her prom! Really bad! It's like a cycle that repeats itself. I remember her telling me how she felt when her grandmother made her turn down that scholarship, and then she did the same thing to me. How could she do it! I never said anything to my mother for eighteen years, but when I got older you can be sure that I brought it up. We had it out and she hadn't realized that it bothered me so much, that's how well she had trained me never to talk back. I held it in, but I wondered why she repeated something that was so hurtful to her. I could have benefited a great deal from going to Oldef at an early age.

Instead of going to art school, I later attended UCLA. You see, there was a program in high school called Upward Bound. It was great. They bused us to UCLA every weekend during my eleventh and twelfth grades. Summers we would live in the dorms taking art classes and college preparatory classes. We took Latin, Greek studies, essay-writing courses, classes that helped later on when I attended college. We just had a reunion; I hadn't seen some of those people for eighteen years. My sister was in the Upward Bound program, too, and we both graduated from UCLA. We're the only two out of our family who graduated from college. Others started but didn't finish. Two of them got married, and the youngest one, she's twenty-seven, is not interested in college at all. She became a legal secretary without going to college, and she's making more money than all of us put together.

In college, my sister and I were also involved in MECHA, the Chicano student organization. I was the first woman editor of the Chicano newspaper on campus, *La gente*. It was founded in 1970 and had all male editors every year. Then I came along in 1978; it was a challenge to me, and I felt that I had to do a better job than the previous editors. I was on the *Daily Bruin* news staff as well, that's the regular student newspaper. *The Daily Bruin* had students working on it who I would never interact with normally. They were not my type of friends. They were upper middle class, and they were the sort of students who would never pick up the Chicano newspaper and read it, so I felt like there were a lot of communication problems. I did articles on artworks for the *Daily Bruin*. I also wrote a big article on the Cinco de Mayo for them. They put great graphics with it. I did a lot of research on that piece. My Spanish is not as good as it should be, but a friend of mine who teaches Spanish translated things from this detailed book for my article. My parents spoke Spanish together at home, but they thought it better not to teach us because in El Paso they were not allowed to speak Spanish in school. I wish they had taught me, because now I can understand it, but I can't speak it. I also did caricatures for the *Bruin*, but it wasn't like I was being asked to write for them often. I was treated well by the staff, and I think one reason is that I am light-skinned. Even today, I'm very conscious of being so white. A friend of mine and I have both applied several times for the same job openings, and she looks very Mexican. I have always gotten the job over her. I'm convinced it's because of color, because she's the sweetest person in the world, never says a negative thing about anybody.

I guess you heard about the mural I did, *L.A. History—A Mexican Perspective,* for the CRA, Community Redevelopment Agency, in 1981. I was on staff already. I was one of six artists working at CRA in the graphics department where we used to do topographical maps for the city. One day John López from the McDonald's on Fourth Street came to the CRA and proposed that a mural be painted on the side of his building. One of the architects asked if I was interested in doing it, and then the mural got approved. The CRA commissioned the mural for display during the 1984 Olympics in Los Angeles. I was just twenty-six years old, and I threw myself into the project, but the whole experience turned into a very painful one that left me deeply depressed long afterwards. I did a huge mural on movable wooden panels that depicted scenes from the minority history of the city, both the persecution and the victories, all woven into the strands of a woman's flowing hair. But the city of L.A. censored it. They objected to fourteen scenes, such as the ones depicting Japanese-American internment camps and the lynchings of Chinese in the late 1800s. The city said that these scenes would offend Asian visitors to the Olympics.

The city also disliked my depiction of the whitewashing in 1932 of the mural on Olvera Street by the famed Mexican muralist David Alfaro Siqueiros. The Siqueiros mural was painted over by the city after it was finished because it portrayed an American eagle preying on a crucified Mexican peasant. My mural was whitewashed, too, and I was very angry about it. In my mural you can see a paint roller coming down on the painter Siqueiros, number one, because his mural was whitewashed fifty years before mine; his was the first. I am number two, and the roller came down on me exactly fifty years later. His mural, *América Tropical,* is precisely the same size as mine, sixteen feet high and eighty feet long. Isn't that a weird coincidence! I had already designed my mural and then I got permission to go see the Siqueiros mural. You had to have permission because it's all boarded up. When I got the dimensions I couldn't believe it—the exact same size. I had already graphed mine out and everything, and then I went to see Mrs. Siqueiros, who passed away a couple of years ago—this was about ten years ago that I went to see

Barbara Carrasco in front of her mural "LA History—A Mexican Perspective"

her—and she just loved my mural of the history of L.A. in a woman's hair. Too bad that the city didn't feel the same way. They censored it because they said that certain parts were negative and inflammatory. I refused to take them out, and the unfinished mural is still in storage at the farm workers' headquarters in Bakersfield.

The mural took eight months to do, and I had seventeen kids and four artists working on it. Then the CRA started saying we want this and this removed completely. Their reason for eliminating Siqueiros is that he was a communist. I said, "Excuse me, but Picasso was a communist, too." The sketch of the mural is five feet long and they had it on the wall with images outlined in red and purple. The purple were to be considered for removal, while the red were images they definitely wanted removed.

Another image they wanted cut was the last black slave in L.A., Betty Mason. They didn't want to be reminded of her, but Betty Mason was great. She came to California from Ohio in the late 1800s, because the guy who owned her stopped over in California temporarily and was going to take her to Texas where she would be a slave. By that time, California had a law against slavery. Betty Mason sued her owner, and won her case. Then she became the largest landowner in L.A. She owned most of the downtown. She also started the first black African church here in L.A. But the CRA censor wanted her out of the mural. I couldn't believe it!

The CRA issued a two-page press release saying that they vehemently denied every single accusation about censorship or copyright. You see, there were three issues at stake, copyright ownership, censorship, and ownership of the mural itself. Copyright ownership I won immediately because there are laws to protect artists' rights with copyright. I also won ownership of the mural. But I lost the exhibit site. How's this for a reason—because the CRA owns the parking lot in front of the McDonald's building, they said that they also owned the air space, and the two and one half inch thick mural jutted out, violating their air space. So I lost the exhibit site. This was in 1983. The story was on the front cover of *USA Today*, and every single TV station covered it. McDonald's corporation—here's the strangest thing—McDonald's headquarters in Chicago approved the entire mural. I had no problems with Chicago at all.

I was deeply depressed over this whole mural thing, and Dolores Huerta was a wonderful friend to me during that stressful time. There were certain artists here in the city, respected Latino artists, who didn't support me at all. A couple of them said that if they signed their name to my mural or spoke up for me that it might jeopardize their chances for getting a mural project from the city. These were guys I had worked with before on different projects. I told them that this could happen to them some day, and it did. A few years later, Shell Oil bulldozed one of their murals. This is a serious problem with mural art; it gets bulldozed and redeveloped, razed, and defaced. I was thirteen when I was in Catholic School and I selected St. Joan of Arc for my confirmation saint. I must have had some idea of the future!

In 1983 I went into two years of depression. I didn't do any work at all. I was terribly hurt by the lack of support of other artists. I got support from educational groups, labor, auto workers, steel workers, longshoremen, so much support from labor, probably through César [Chávez] and Dolores, and from some artists, but there were a lot who didn't support me. I was supported more by national artists than by those here in L.A. The thing that hurt was hearing people say that they would like to help but that they just couldn't. After the controversy died down a little, someone wanted to make a movie about the mural. I turned that down because a producer from Hollywood wanted to have my character fall in love with the city official in the movie. I said, "No, thank you, I don't want to sell out at this stage of the game." And the weird thing was that my sisters were very upset that I turned down the offer.

I just withdrew for those two years; I lost faith. Father Olivares was a good friend during that period. I used to talk to him a lot. I was severely depressed then. If you put so much effort into something, then you feel like a failure and like you let everyone else down when you lose. Last summer, the mural had a special exhibition for one month, and PBS did a program on the mural. I was amazed at the opening of the exhibition because Peter Sellars showed up; he was the one who had selected it as part of the L.A. Festival and he was very supportive. When I saw the mural all up at once, the whole thing, I started crying. Anyway, the mural is now history; it's in storage again. The new Latino museum is interested in purchasing it and putting it up. Originally, Union Station was interested, but they have a lot of asbestos there, not to mention the fact that councilman Richard Alatorre has always been against the mural.

I added Martin Sheen to the mural because he saw one third of it at a museum, fell in love with it, and wanted to be in it, so I put him in it. All the seventeen kids who painted are in the mural. They were tough kids but I dealt with them just fine. You set up certain rules, like, if there's a fight I don't care who started it, but you're off the project. And I said that if the section they worked on was messy that at the dedication I would announce their names to everyone. They were very careful after that.

I had good influences, role models, and special opportunities when I was growing up, and I want to help offer some of those same things to the kids who are growing up now. All this made a difference to me in setting goals, and because of the positive supports, I always had high expectations for myself. There was a summer sports program in the housing projects when I was twelve years old. My father had just passed away, and the program couldn't have come at a better time. They bused kids from all the housing projects in L.A., Watts, East L.A., and West L.A., where I was from. They took us to UCLA where we ran track and field, had relay races, and ate lunch in the cafeteria. Some of our counselors were famous athletes , like the basketball player Henry Spivey; the gold medalist discus thrower Olga Connelly, and Wilma Rudolph. I had a feeling that I was going to wind up going to that university, I liked it so much. I continued going to UCLA through the Upward Bound program. Those programs were great for socialization. We met kids from other parts of the city, we had a positive sense of competition, and we had great counselors. It's an experience that other kids don't have. And now, of course, the buses are getting shot at. I told the director that I had never realized how important this project was; I am very grateful for it.

The major result or effect of growing up in the projects is that we saw a cycle where families want to leave but can't—the sons and daughters of parents who were basically blue collar workers would try to get out, but couldn't; and then their kids lived there, too. It's a cycle. I told myself early on, "There's no way I'm going to wind up staying here." On the other hand, there were times that living in the projects was like being in a great extended family. But there were too many negative things. Do you know that *thirteen* of my friends were killed in the projects as a result of gang violence or problems with the police? Thirteen! I remember that my friends' parents wouldn't allow their kids to visit the projects because bad people lived there. I wished I had had a house, a backyard, all that kind of thing, but I was having fun in the projects, too, if you can imagine. I was always doing art. My mother was a Girl Scout leader, and she was always coming up with great ideas for us to work on.

When I went to UCLA, I thought their art department was terrible. Very traditional still life and figure drawing. There were a few very good professors there. I had transferred from a junior college after two years, and I entered as a junior. I was denied acceptance into the Art Department but accepted into the school. I petitioned to get into the Art Department, but I had an unusual way of petitioning. I went to the dean—I was very upset, I was only nineteen or so, my older brother was with me—and I told the dean that the Art Department was racist. I had gotten an ethnic breakdown from the planning office, and there were just a few minority students in the department. I was accepted two weeks later. I guess I had a strong political consciousness fairly early, but it wasn't in my art at all. I was a typical art student. I used to do drawings of women with very beautiful clothes as a teenager, and even when I petitioned the Art Department I was doing very traditional work.

⑥⑥⑥⑥⑥⑥⑥⑥⑥⑥⑥⑥⑥⑥⑥⑥⑥⑥⑥⑥⑥⑥⑥⑥

It was UCLA that made things exciting for me, not the department, and I became involved with the farm workers my first year on campus. They were there setting up a table for signatures for a petition, so I stepped right up. Working with the farm workers has changed my outlook a lot. While I was still at West L.A. Junior College, before going to UCLA, I had a boyfriend who was editor of the Chicano newspaper at UCLA. I was doing front covers, illustrations for *La Gente* a year before going to UCLA. They were eleven-by-fourteen-inch drawings. *La Gente* was a bilingual monthly. I enjoyed working on the paper; the first couple of years I just did illustrations. Then I started doing some articles; and then I became the editor. I remember a number of the guys dropped out when I became the first woman editor; they just couldn't face it. The UCLA communications board selected me based on the fact that I was pushing strongly for some change in the newspaper. It had been produced in a nonartistic manner; the layout was pretty bad; the content was basically on campus issues; and it was a very political newspaper. I wanted to introduce different types of art and change the layout, and they were impressed with that. But it was harder than I thought it would be to take on that additional responsibility and still maintain my school work.

UCLA was a training ground for me for a lot of things. Within the art department, I encountered some pretty overt racism, I'd say, not just professors, but fellow students. Once, I was learning lithography and I did a print. I was always trying to experiment with different kinds of paper, and I printed on rice paper, but everybody else printed on traditional paper. The lab technician there said, "Next thing you know, Barbara is going to be painting on green, white, and red paper," the colors of the Mexican flag. I looked at him like I couldn't believe him. He's still there, and you don't forget things that people say. Some of the same professors I had are still working there. They would say, "Your work is in the tradition of the Mexican muralists," but it was nothing like that at all, the technique was different. I knew the difference, because I was always going into the Chicano Studies library, and they had good books on Diego Rivera and all the Mexican masters. I knew my work was not influenced by them, because I hadn't seen their work at all growing up. I was not exposed to that material, but to Michelangelo and traditional artists. It was not until I got to UCLA that I became exposed to the muralists and Mexican artists. The first time I saw Frida Kahlo's image was in the Chicano Studies library. Anyway, it was strange seeing the response of other students to my work. There were just a very few non-Anglo students in the department, practically no women professors, and no professors of color at all.

I think we learned a lot from the visiting professors, like Ian Culberson from England, who taught a printmaking and a painting course. I took his class both years. He was very hard on me, and I didn't understand why because I was a lot more disciplined than most of the other art students. But he encouraged me to go to the L.A. County Museum and to look at what other people are doing outside of this campus. He really encouraged me to broaden myself, to look at art, and he was very encouraging about my art, telling me that I was good and to keep it up. No one had said that before. Another professor, Gary Lloyd—and this is a curious coincidence because I was just hired by the Children's Hospital here in L.A. and my boss, she's going out with him, one of my former professors—and he was like Ian Culberson, very supportive. He also mentioned that I could be a role model, he was very positive. Jim Valerio, who is a really good painter, and John Stucey, who just passed away of cancer, were very helpful. John was very critical of my work, but he taught anatomy the way it should be taught, from the skeletal system to the muscle system. That's what's lacking in many artists, that training and knowledge. I can see it in their work. My training was very traditional, but it was good because these four professors were all fine artists outside the campus; they were practicing artists. It was very good of all of them to show students their own work; I respected them a lot more for it, especially when they critiqued my work.

As soon as I graduated I started working, but I wanted to work with Chicano artists. I was twenty-three, and I saw two artists working on a mural on the Aquarius Theater on Sunset and Vine in Hollywood; it was 1978 when *Zoot Suit* came out. The play was much better than the movie. I met Eddie Olmos when I was doing the *Zoot Suit* mural and got to know him and Luis Valdéz very well. I practically invited myself to work on that mural. I saw these two artists and I said, "How come you guys don't have a Chicano working with you?" They said, "Well, let's see your work." They liked my work, and they hired me. They sandblasted that mural after about a year and a half. It's been documented in slides, so it still exists in that sense. That mural was an exciting breakthrough for me. We were on an electric scaffolding system, and it was scary but exciting.

I went nine years to Catholic school, and I have to admit that I really hated those years. There were certain nuns I liked a lot. There was one in fourth grade, Sister Mary Ann, who used to give three of us free milk every day. She let me attend summer school free; she was great. I got in trouble with another nun in seventh grade because I raised my hand to her when she grabbed me. I didn't slap her, but she said I did. My mother came in and I had to go see the mother superior—all because I was wearing a half slip instead of a full slip and was tempting the guys. That's ridiculous! I was a tomboy, total, complete. I played basketball. Another thing I remember was in second grade when the nun asked me to stand in front of the whole class and tell her what I ate for breakfast that morning because I wasn't very alert. I said that I had a glass of Kool Aid and one scrambled egg. Everyone cracked up; they all started laughing. I started crying because I didn't know what they were laughing about. I guess it was an unusual breakfast. My mother really tore into that nun later. But those things stay in your memory.

I'm doing this show about growing up in Catholic school; it's going to be called *Thirteen Stations of the Double-Cross*. It begins with zoom lens images of first communion. I interviewed lots of people from twelve to forty-five years of age trying to get Catholic growing-up experiences for this piece. This one woman in New York told me that when she was making her first holy communion she thought she was going up to the altar to be married and she started crying. One guy told me as an altar boy he was molested by a priest. There are a lot of stories; some are humorous, some are not. And baptisms, with the pagan baby thing—do you know about that? We had this thing in Catholic school called pagan babies, where you would get a poor kid from Africa or Central America, and there's this photograph of them and the class who raises the most amount of money can name that child. A lot of people haven't had this experience of pagan babies, the unbaptized babies, but a lot have. There was a guy who went to school in Chicago, to Kresge School, and he told me that they had the pagan babies experience at their school too, and he had some great stories. He was also hit with a ruler on several occasions. I'm working on this project right now. It's taking a lot of time and energy, but I should finish it in about a year.

I graduated several months ago with an M.F.A. from California Institute of the Arts. Unfortunately, I gained a lot of weight while I was a student. I need to lose about twenty pounds and get in good shape for this strenuous project. I have wanted to do the Catholic school images theme for a long, long time. It will be cross-cultural; a lot of people will be able to relate to it, not just Latinos. I'm going to send out a one-page questionnaire to people I know who went to Catholic schools. I'll deal with things that are familiar to me—not just unpleasant things, but nice ones, too. I found an old-fashioned desk where you put your books underneath, and I'll use that in the show. I've been collecting things, like Virgin Mary rings and necklaces, Virgin Mary wall lights. The Santa Monica Museum is interested in having the show; it's a big space and a good location. I need a big space because I'm going to be making pews also, and it's going to cost a lot of money. I have practically no financial resources, but every once in a while I sell work and I put that money into my art. Right now I'm an artist in residence at the Children's Hospital in L.A. I work twenty hours a week there, but they pay well. It's a special program to allow artists to have time to do their work.

Recently, there was a show called "Image and Identity" at Loyola Marymount featuring five Chicana artists. That was the first time I had put anything really personal in a painting, and I called it *Torture Tradition*. It showed my mother combing my hair, and my eye was pulled all the way over to the side. It went over very well at the show; people actually laughed out loud because they remembered that experience themselves. There was another image of the Virgin Mary and Joan of Arc burning at the stake. I also did a triptych—I'm continuing that series—featuring a Barbie doll image, Wilma from the Flintstones, and Mary McCall. She was a paper doll from McCall's magazine, and I did a painting of her. On the Barbie doll, there's a little tag on her ankle that says "Property of Toy Loan." Inside the projects we had this thing called Toy Loan, where you could borrow a toy for up to a week. If you took good care of the toy, you got a star next to your name. After ten stars you would get a free toy, your very own. They don't have that anymore, but the housing authority used to sponsor it. It was a good program, because we were so poor we didn't have any toys. My mom was very resourceful, though. She was always finding paper and art materials for me, a lot of nontraditional art materials, too. She would get photographs, a few pieces of Scrabble, and she would pour resin in it. Like magic, it became a desk pen holder for my dad's birthday.

All of my background shows up in one way or another in the materials and subjects I choose to express myself as an artist and a Chicana.

Humberto Calzada

This prominent Cuban-American artist is known for his architectural paintings that highlight the themes of time and the imagination and invite the viewer to reflect nostalgically upon the past, while simultaneously envisioning the future. Calzada uses the blue Caribbean sea and sky, as well as certain characteristic elements of Cuban architecture, such as the *vitral,* or colored glass, and the black-and-white tiled floor, to visualize a place and to suggest a sense of loss for a place that can only be recreated in the mind's eye.

In this interview, Calzada speaks with energy and humor about his life and his art, and the relationship between the two.

Interview

I arrived here in 1960, when Castro had been in power a little more than a year. My father had been an executive of the American Power and Light Company, and for that reason we were persecuted from the beginning.

I'd like to tell you the reason I paint what I paint. In Cuba, I was a very protected, sheltered child. I had more time to observe my surroundings than the typical child. My father was fascinated by Cuban history. He was born in 1912 and his father had been a veteran of the Cuban war for independence. My father was very, very Cuban and he transmitted that to me. On my mother's side, there was my uncle, who loved to collect artifacts of Cuban history, especially typical styles of architecture, and he transmitted that to me.

When I came here, even though I had been to the U.S. every year as a child, still it was a big adjustment. In Cuba, I had gone to St. George's American school in Havana, which was in English from kindergarten on. I finished my sophomore year of high school in Cuba and then came here for the last two years. Even so, the fact of losing my country was very difficult. As a teenager you dream about your future and you dream about it in your own country. Here we have reconstructed friendships, food, much of our culture, but we have not rebuilt the visual part. As a teenager, I always thought I'd become an architect. But economic necessity made me forget all that and study industrial engineering and finance, neither of which I have any passion for. After a while, I realized I was a fish out of water working in these areas and as a building contractor.

So, as a hobby, I started painting. I had never been interested in painting in Cuba, just in observing. In 1972, twelve years after arriving here, I began to paint. I've kept my first work, which I painted with a watercolor set that I bought for a dollar at Eckerd's drugstore, and I haven't stopped since. I wasn't just a Sunday painter, I became hooked right away. Three years later, in 1975, I had an exhibit sponsored by the Bacardí Company. I sold ten or fifteen pictures, and I couldn't believe it. Two years later, I was a full-time painter and could stop building houses, which is what I had been doing until then.

I never studied art. I am ignorant of artistic culture. When I started, I didn't know anything about Cuban art either. I knew what I liked and that was it, and what I liked was certain types of Cuban furniture and houses. I know nothing at all about art history, and I think actually it's better that way because perhaps I am a little freer than I would be otherwise. I do try to borrow the ambience, the feeling of the surrealists, the eeriness of their settings. I guess in some sense it's because, well, I've been here thirty-three years, and to this day it doesn't seem real to me. If someone had told me then that I would never ever return again, I wouldn't have believed it, and to this day it seems impossible that I am here. I think you can see that combination of unreality and nostalgia in my art.

There's no such thing as a Cuban school of painting in Miami. We are a very diverse group of artists, from different generations, with different experiences and different artistic sensibilities. I guess that the common thread is the experience of exile, but there are as many different modes of expression as there are artists. My influences have been very personal. I think that the influences of the young Cuban artists arriving lately have come largely from foreign art magazines from Europe and the United States, because Cuba is so isolated. Also, I think you see a lot of anger in the work of the younger artists, while you see more nostalgia in that of the older ones. My dream would be to return, but I think it is totally unrealistic; further, the Cuba that we love and remember exists here now.

What there is in Miami is a feeling of camaraderie among the artists from all over Latin America; Cuban artists by no means dominate the scene. Many Latin American artists live here, while others merely come here to exhibit. Similarly, many Cuban-American artists exhibit in Latin America. For example, I have exhibited in Panama, El Salvador, Venezuela, Peru, Chile, and when I do, I look up artists that I have met here. It's a bit like a fraternity. I've also exhibited in Chicago, Atlanta, San Francisco, Sarasota, and in a group show in New York. I've had the best reception in Miami, where both Cubans and Americans buy my work.

One interesting thing about the art world in Miami, though it is not the center of Latin American art that some people claim, is that it is a great art market. For example, within the U.S. there is a large market for Latin American art, and people come from all over the country to buy here. By the same token, you will find Latin Americans coming here not only to exhibit, but also to buy Latin American art. In other words, it's not unusual for an Argentine, for example, to come to Miami to buy Argentine art. The truth is that Latin Americans do not travel much in Latin America; they travel to the United States and Europe.

The inspirations for my works come from many different sources. I have files and files and files of ideas. Sometimes, an idea will hit me and I'll make a sketch of it. Other times, I'll see a photo of something that appeals to me, and later I'll transform that photo into something totally unrecognizable. I have had several different stages; the first one was from about 1972 to '81, my "anecdotal period," in which I was trying faithfully to reproduce the Cuban past. Starting about 1981, I began my "stairs" period, trying to develop a more imaginative, inventive art. Then, in about 1984, I began to create new spaces and to include in them old paintings of mine hanging on the walls, for example, to suggest another perspective. Later came a kind of "deconstruction" period, in which I painted ruins, as an allegory of the situation in Cuba, as in my series "The Gardens." My "water" period came afterwards, with ponds, reflections in the water, and floods, all highly symbolic. Water is a very powerful symbol of destruction and purification.

We Cubans are a funny people, nostalgic, arrogant, and talkative. For example, it doesn't seem possible, but my children feel nostalgia for Cuba, my daughter especially. It's as if you could inherit nostalgia. Cubans are different from other

*The Invitation II, 1982,
by Humberto Calzada*

Latin Americans. Once a professor from Georgetown University said at a conference on Cuban history that Cubans are the way we are because we are islanders. We are very self-centered, like the Japanese or the English. For example, in the last century there was a big storm in England that lasted a week and cut communications with Europe the whole time. Afterwards, the London headlines read, "Continent without Communications for a Week." That's the way the Cuban are, too. Nor do we mix much. If you put in one room clusters of, say, Americans, Irish, Cubans, and other Latin Americans, everyone except the Cubans will mix sooner or later. Yet, at the same time, we fight among ourselves like cats and dogs; it's like we have a fatal attaction. And do we like to talk! It's the national pastime. You know that the one thing you can't find in the Caribbean is a Cuban mime!

I have never understood why art sometimes seems like a fashion. I don't think it should be; I think it should be very personal. Why should I paint in the style currently in vogue if I don't feel it, if it's not my style? Basically, I view artists as a kind of filter, with a sensitive radar that captures what is happening in our society. We ingest it, and then we transform it. We are part of the culture of our time, and we act as visual historians and critics, too, because art has a social function. Any society that doesn't value art remains at the primitive, animal level. Art touches the soul of a culture.

Part 5
In the Belly of the Beast:
(Im)migration and Exile

Border crossing

Sara and Jesus Sánchez

Bay View Detention Center, Bay View, Texas

Taos Mountain

Last hand-pulled ferry—Rio Grande crossing, Los Ebanos, Texas

In the Belly of the Beast: (Im)migration and Exile

Give me your tired, your poor,
Your huddled masses yearning to
    be free,
The wretched refuse of your teem-
    ing shore.
Send these the homeless, tempest-
    tost to me,
I lift my lamp beside the golden
    door![1]

These moving words engraved on the Statue of Liberty proclaim the United States as a nation of immigrants and a beacon of freedom. However, the continuing viability of this historic mission in our time is being seriously questioned by many North Americans, who express great concern about the increasing numbers of immigrants—legal and illegal—to the United States. The 1980s saw the largest wave in *legal* U.S. immigration since the beginning of the century. From 1981 to 1990, six million people immigrated into the United States legally; of these, 44 percent were Asian, 40 percent were Latin American (13 percent from Mexico and 27 percent from other Latin American countries), 14 percent were European and Canadian, and 2 percent were from other areas.[2] These were the officially accepted new arrivals, but millions more entered, or tried to enter, *illegally*. Approximately 77 percent of illegal immigrants during

the 1980s were from Latin America. Roughly 55 percent of these were Mexican, while the rest were from other Latin American countries, mostly Central America.[3] However, most of these Mexican illegals, nine out of ten, do not stay permanently in the U.S. They are sojourners who come for a few months to work, or to visit far-flung family members, and then return to Mexico.[4]

As we have seen, movement north from Mexico is as old as the borderlands themselves. It continues today, not only because of economic stress in Mexico and relative opportunities in the United States, but also because, as Carey McWilliams points out, it is deeply rooted in American history. The migration follows ancient trails and predates by centuries the creation of the river border between the two countries. Psychologically and culturally, Mexicans are not *emigrating* to the Southwest; they are *returning* there, or, perhaps more accurately, migrating within one homeland. To McWilliams, the border that separates Mexico from the United States is one of the "most unrealistic" in the Western Hemisphere.[5] Jesuit theologian Allan Figueroa Deck takes the argument a step further by declaring that the current United States policy of regarding Mexican immigrants as aliens is a "self-serving exercise in historical amnesia."[6]

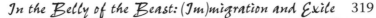

Illegal immigration peaked in 1986, rising to between three and five million, and dropped following the passage of the Immigration Reform and Control Act (IRCA) in 1986. This act made it harder for illegal aliens to find employment in the States and allowed more than three million illegals already in the United States to obtain legal status through an amnesty program. However, since 1989, the influx of undocumented persons has again increased dramatically, rising to somewhere between two and one half million and four million people in 1992.[7] Though their children born in the United States are eligible for assistance, illegal immigrants themselves may not receive food stamps, unemployment compensation, or federal welfare payments. They are legally entitled to income-tax refunds owed them, but very few file, fearing that they will be deported. Undocumented workers come to the United States in search of jobs, not welfare payments.[8]

The resurgence in illegal immigration began in 1964 when the bracero guest worker program ended. After that, the Mexican population began to build up along Mexico's northern border. Some of this number were attracted to irrigated agriculture in the northern part of Mexico, however, there were more people than jobs, and the population of border towns such as Matamoros, Juárez, Nogales, and Mexicali swelled to bursting. The demographic shift to border towns created pressures in those cities and gave rise to a big business in transporting people across the border. There are *coyotes,* those who make plans with the emigrant at the Mexican border; *pateros,* those who help one cross the river; and

polleros, those who help the emigrant across land borders. Organizing illegal crossings, for many years an informal business, has become an organized, lucrative, and dangerous one that often involves payoffs to the Mexican police. As the demand in the United States for farm workers declined (it is estimated that only 9 percent of illegal immigrants are pickers, for example), more Mexicans sought employment as domestic workers, or in low-wage border industries, including furniture, clothing, and food service.[9]

Attempting to reduce the number of illegal emigrants, the Mexican government created manufacturing districts along the border, beginning in 1966. The plan was to bring jobs to the Mexican workers and thus keep them in Mexico. This Border Industrialization Program (BIP) led to the proliferation of *maquiladoras,* foreign-owned assembly plants that require labor-intensive work. In 1970, there were two hundred *maquilas* with 19,000 workers; by 1986, there were nine hundred *maquilas* employing 255,000 people.[10] These factories have not reduced internal migration, nor have they slowed emigration; instead, they have probably aggravated both.

During the 1970s and 1980s the American public became alarmed at the increasing number of illegal immigrants. The Immigration Reform and Control Act is one result of those fears. This law allowed undocumented aliens who could show proof of continuous residence since before January 1, 1982, and who satisfied other criteria, to become legalized. It also provided sanctions against employers who knowingly hired undocumented workers, in an attempt to eliminate

the incentive for illegal immigration. The law has had both mixed and unintended results. First, since 1986, illegal immigrants have been receiving lower salaries than ever before. There are an estimated five times more "hiring corners" than before—these are street corners where immigrants congregate in hopes of being hired as day laborers—and new underground sweatshops have sprung up in cities with large populations of Latino immigrants.[11] Daily, even the most casual observer in, say, Houston or Los Angeles, can see Latin Americans on certain street corners, hiring themselves out as manual laborers, factory workers, or *mariachis*. Second, almost overnight, there occurred a proliferation in the production of fraudulent documents. Always an annoying problem to the United States government, it has become a big business since 1986. Third, the IRCA has increased job discrimination against United States citizens and green-card holders because of their presumed ethnicity. This is because some employers would rather hire no one who looks remotely Latino than to take a chance on hiring someone who may be illegal.[12]

During the 1980s, Salvadoran and Guatemalan immigrants were added to the illegal list, on grounds that they were not legitimate seekers of political asylum, since their governments were ostensibly democratic and were supported by the United States. As these people fled persecution and chaos in their homelands, many found protection in the sanctuary movement, an ecumenical religious alliance that used churches as places of asylum and sought to call attention to what sanctuary supporters regarded as the mistaken

United States immigration and foreign policies with regard to Central America.[13] The sustained public pressure and court cases of the sanctuary alliance succeeded in 1989 in convincing the United States to reconsider the cases of tens of thousands of Central Americans who had previously been rejected for asylum. The peace treaty ending El Salvador's civil war, signed on January 16, 1992, slowed to a trickle the Salvadoran immigrant population; however, Guatemalans are still emigrating.

Although the issue of illegal immigration is still unresolved, its overall effect in economic and cultural terms can be seen as positive. By many recent calculations, illegal immigrants generate more dollars than they cost the United States taxpayer.[14] Further, they come bearing gifts in art, music, literature, cuisine, and cultural values that enrich our entire human enterprise. The problem is one of pressure on social institutions such as schools and hospitals, and on job opportunities for the nonimmigrant population, that is, competition for scarce work.

The interviews, poems, and short story in this chapter give poignant and stirring expression to the courage of migrants and exiles from Mexico, Puerto Rico, Cuba, El Salvador, Nicaragua, Chile, and Argentina who have started over in a sometimes hostile milieu, determined to make a go of it. Selected readings also acknowledge the gifts of the agricultural laborers, teachers, writers, and university professors who have brought their considerable talents with them. The United States continues to be a nation of immigrants; the Latino experience, while fascinating in itself, is but another chapter in that historic saga.

Jesús Sánchez

For almost forty years, Jesús Sánchez traveled back and forth countless times from his native Texas to Mexico to Chicago and back to Texas again, taking whatever work he could find, but seeking out factory work for its benefits of union membership. Sánchez's experience as a unionized worker in Chicago proved to be crucial in his later decision to work as a UFW organizer when he eventually settled in California, where he was shocked by the conditions in which farm workers lived and worked.

Sánchez's story is that of a thoughtful, caring person who migrated for many years and who, inspired by *la causa* and the personal example of UFW leader César Chávez, put the experiences and wisdom gained "on the road" to the service of the larger community.

Interview

I was born in Corpus Christi, Texas, in 1924. I went to school in Mexico, in Nuevo Laredo, because my papá moved us across the border in 1930 during the Depression when there were no jobs here on this side. My father sold vegetables and my older brothers learned their trades there. One is a barber, one is a baker, another shines shoes. They had steady work and it helped support the family. Later, I worked for several years on the U.S. side of the border again, in Laredo, in a customs house.

In 1944 an aunt from Chicago came down to visit and she encouraged us to go to Chicago because there were jobs to be had there. My uncle was working in a defense plant there. So my brother and I came to Chicago and we got jobs, thanks to my uncle, at Bethlehem Steel. We forged iron, did piecework, gathered scrap; we made a certain type of screw that they use in bridges; and we made rudders for great ships. We also helped the welders with their acetylene torches. It was all defense work, and we earned good wages.

After the war, we had several different jobs. We worked on the Chicago North-western Railroad on the track, replacing the ties and rails. We worked for Wisconsin Steel in South Chicago at the open hearth and in the yard. Then we worked in a quarry with jackhammers. This was on 26th Street; it's now a Mexican neighborhood, but then there were Italians, Poles, and Yugoslavs. We worked there until we were laid off, and I went back to Laredo for a year. Then I returned to work in the Doray Lamp Company on Michigan Avenue, making lights for trucks and also making traffic lights.

Soon after that, I went back to Old Laredo and married my wife Sara, who had a beauty shop there. We came back to Chicago, and the next year our first son, Jesús Junior, was born. I kept working, this time for Material Service, in the quarry on 26th Street, until 1960, when I was laid off and we went back to Laredo again, where our second son was born.

Back in Laredo I worked at a gas station until my brother-in-law came to visit from California and said, Why don't you try your luck there? So in 1962 we came to California looking for work, and I, for the first time, went into the fields to work. I saw immediately that people were paid only ninety cents per hour, that they had no break, vacations, protection, insurance, nothing. I had always worked with the union in Chicago, and I knew that things could be better than this. We had no clean water to drink; we had to carry dirty water from where they irrigate. There was no break at all; it was just work, work, work. And on payday, we didn't have enough to make ends meet. It was robbery, and they never gave us receipts, either. Everything was in cash, no checks, so that there was no record of

anything. It was highway robbery! Another thing that they, the growers, did was to have people bring beer and sodas to the field and sell them to us for $1.50! Since we were thirsty, we would buy the drinks. If anyone complained, they were let go. At that time I was working in the fields picking oranges, running up and down the ladders, because the trucks would not wait and the "pusher's" job was to hurry us up, to prod us, so that we would pick faster.

Because of all of this, César Chávez planned the march from Delano to Sacramento in 1966, and he passed through here, through Parlier, on foot. When we found out that the march was coming this way, we all took radios out to the fields where we listened to the progress of the march. It was thrilling! At noon they were to arrive at Orosi, and we finished work early that day. My wife worked with me in the fields, too, and that day I said to her, "Let's go meet César." And we went. The marchers arrived very tired, hungry, thirsty, with blisters on their feet, and with a huge group of followers. There were also ranchers there with big dogs, just looking for a pretext to let those dogs loose. But César just said not to pay any attention to them, that all they want to do is provoke us so that we will be put in jail.

Then I went home and got my pickup and went around to all the streets in my neighborhood announcing that César was coming. When he arrived here in Parlier, we put up a big sign on Manning Street saying, "Welcome to Parlier!" And the ranchers were furious. People kept joining the march at every town, and we joined at Parlier. When we finally arrived in Sacramento there were many, many families to greet us with food, sodas, and ice water. It was very festive. And there in the church when César spoke, people were moved to tears. We slept in the big church there—there were more than 10,000 of us—at the capitol. Governor Pat Brown refused to wait for the marchers to arrive; instead he went to Palm Springs to play golf. Dolores Huerta gave a speech in which she said that if Governor Brown doesn't have time for us, then we won't have time for him on election day. His son, Governor Jerry Brown, later was a good friend to the farm workers.

The whole experience changed my life because, from then on, I have dedicated myself to organizing for the farm workers' union. It's totally voluntary, we pay for our own gas, it's on our own time. Sometimes to put an announcement on the local radio station about an upcoming meeting we have to go asking our neighbors to help collect the fifteen dollars, but that's how we've been managing. And the same thing is true for all the other organizers as well. They are *campesinos* like myself. But little by little, with hard work, we got our first contract, in March 1967 with Christian Brothers wines. But it is a constant struggle, and it has at times been very unpleasant. You know that five members of the union have been killed just from this area. They are martyrs. But this has only caused us to unite and for our numbers to grow. But there were many strikes first. We called field strikes, general strikes, work stoppages, and we would picket.

I remember one strike against Roberts Farms when we picketed. We didn't let anyone enter the fields, day or night. The peaches were very ripe, and it was 115 degrees. It was so hot that the peaches on their own just fell to the ground and rot-

ted. Then the growers became angry. They decided to bring workers from Delano to pick the crops. So I got in my pickup and drove to Delano and told the brothers not to come because the growers only wanted to break the strike and divide us. I had never spoken in public in my life, and I only have a few years of schooling, but there was no other way. I was very nervous, but I talked to the meeting of workers and urged them not to get in the buses that would be coming for them tomorrow. That same night, I drove back here to be on the picket line.

The next morning we were all picketing and the police were everywhere, ready to take us to jail for the slightest cause, because the sheriff was in the employ of the grower. Then we saw that the buses were coming that the growers had sent to Delano, and that they were full of workers. We thought, This is the end of all our efforts if they get off the bus. Then we all began to shout at them that this is a strike, don't enter the fields. But the workers got out of the buses. Then the police and the ranchers shouted at them to go in the fields, but they didn't move. They just stood there. Then they said that they were not going to enter the fields because they had been lied to, that the contractor had not told them that they were coming to break a strike. So then I cried out, "Let's march," and we all marched around the buses and in the street, and not one person entered the fields. At that point, Roberts Farms talked to César and told him they wanted to sign a contract.

This was a big improvement because now we couldn't be let go except for just cause; we got two breaks of fifteen minutes each; clean ice water in the fields; toilets in the field; soap; and clean, not irrigation, water, for washing our hands. We also were given overtime. We were paid $1.75 per hour instead of the previous ninety cents. We also had a medical plan and the right to a week's vacation after a year. It was a huge success.

Then Robert Kennedy came here, and I volunteered for him. I got seventeen people in my pickup to go to Delano to meet him there. He greeted me and shook my hand. I'll never forget it. But then they killed him. We were so sad because he was a good man and really wanted to help the farm workers.

Things began to heat up about that time. The more contracts we got with growers, the greater the resistance to the union and the more the sheriffs and police would harass us, looking for an excuse to beat us or arrest us. It got to where we couldn't say the word *huelga,* strike, or they would put us in jail. That's when our friend Sister Carol Frances Jegen and other nuns and priests and religious from all over came to join the front lines of the strikes, and they were jailed with us in 1973. We were dragged from the fields where we had been kneeling in prayer and taken to the court where the judge wanted us each to put up a $400 bond ! Can you imagine? When we didn't have enough to buy food for our families. We were in jail for two weeks, thousands of us.

Then we were freed on the condition that we not join any picket lines. We agreed because, by that time, several of our people had been murdered and César decided that the way to go was the boycott, not pickets because the people were being exposed to too much danger. That was the time that young López in my

town was murdered as he was walking the picket line. A brother of the grower hired a Mexican to kill him. The assassin drove up in his van, lowered the window, called to López, who came over and the guy shot him . He fell dead on the spot.

We also had trouble during the strikes with the Teamsters who would pay motorcycle gang members to come and beat up our people just for being on the picket line. They would run their motorcycles over them after they had beaten them.

Because of the growing violence, the boycott was the way to go. So, since then, we have been involved in a long struggle. We have targeted large chains in many cities nationwide and the results have been good. We have also gained widespread public support.

The problem is that with the recession things are very difficult now, and the growers are canceling contracts, hiring cheaper labor, and we are hurting. There's just not enough work for everyone. There are fewer and fewer jobs for more and more people, and it is difficult.

Another problem that we continue to have is pesticides. The owners spray the fields. They used to spray them while we were working; now they spray at night, but the next day, the poison is still there. We come to pick apples or whatever and our skin starts to burn and we get eruptions and itching on our arms and faces. Plus the insecticides are washed into the ground and contaminate the wells that we drink from. There have been children born with defects, without arms, or without legs, because their mothers had worked in fields that had been sprayed. My wife has not escaped, either. She was just in the hospital because she got a sudden unbearable itching and a rash and welts on her arms that was driving her crazy. They gave her some medicine and told her not to worry about it, that it was probably just an insect bite! But we know that our environment is contaminated. For example, our doctor told us several years ago to drink only purified water, not water from the tap because it is polluted.

Recently, the growers that my wife was working for let all the workers go, just like that, all of them, from one day to the next. So my wife is now working for a packing company. It's not unionized, and if they knew she was a sympathizer they would fire her. All the other workers in the packing company are migrants; the majority are illegals from Mexico. They are employed while the farm workers are let go. It's serious and very bad for the union. Some growers are good to work for; they sign contracts with the union, and they try to avoid using harmful pesticides, but others are impossible. I'm just thankful that we were able to educate our sons so that life will be easier for them. For example, Juan José is a supervisor for Head Start programs in the nearby towns of Visalia and Tulare. And our grandchildren are excellent students, so I know they will make something of themselves, too.

The big question now is are we going to have a contract or not. Because if we don't have a contract, then we work day by day, as day laborers. That's the way I started out when I came here thirty years ago from Laredo and Chicago. I'd hate to lose now all that we have fought so hard to gain.

Judith Ortiz Cofer

Judith Ortiz Cofer was born in Puerto Rico and grew up in New Jersey.

Her poetry, which has appeared in numerous journals and anthologies, treats these two basic facts of her life as does her acclaimed personal narrative, *Silent Dancing: A Partial Remembrance of a Puerto Rican Childhood* (Houston: Arte Público Press, 1990). The following poems, "Arrival" and "Birthplace," from the collection "Reaching for the Mainland" (in *Triple Crown: Chicano, Puerto Rican, and Cuban-American Poetry,* Tempe, Ariz.: Bilingual Press/Editorial Bilingüe, 1987) express the experience of migration and return, using powerful symbols that evoke the emotion-laden journeys here and there.

Arrival

When we arrived, we were expelled
like fetuses
from the warm belly of an airplane.
Shocked by the cold,
we held hands as we skidded
like new colts on the unfamiliar ice.
We waited winter in a room sealed
by our strangeness.
Watching the shifting tale of the streets,
our urge to fly toward the sun
etched in nailprints like tiny wings
in the grey plaster of the windowsill,
we hoped all the while
that lost in the city's monochrome
there were colors we couldn't yet see.

Birthplace

There is no danger now
that these featureless hills will hold me.
That church sitting on the highest one like
a great hen spreading her marble wings
over the penitent houses does not beckon to me.
This dusty road under my feet is like
any other I have traveled,
it leads only to other roads.
Towns everywhere are the same when shadows thicken.
Yet, each window casting a square of light,
that grassy plain under a weighted sky turning to plum,
tell me that as surely as my dreams are mine,
I must be home.

Jesús Martínez and Ricardo Murillo

Ricardo Murillo

The stories of these two immigrants, who initially entered the United States illegally from El Salvador, represent odysseys in some ways as remarkable as that of Cabeza de Vaca himself centuries ago. Martínez traveled on foot from El Salvador to Texas, was deported, returned, and eventually made his way to Florida. Murillo, after close encounters with unscrupulous coyotes and Mexican police, also ended up in Florida (and in jail), but via the indirect route of California and Idaho.

Interview

Jesús Martínez

Everybody calls me Don Chuy, but my name is Jesús Martínez, and the Murillo family are my *amigos*. I came here from El Salvador in 1982. I came by myself, and as I had no money, I had to walk all the way from the Department of Aguachapán, El Salvador, to the United States. The main reason was because of the disruptions caused by the war in my country. There was violence everywhere, factories and businesses were closing down, everything was just collapsing. The only hope was to go north.

I worked awhile in Mexico, in the Federal District, in a small village very near the capital. Then I went to Monterrey. There I worked doing odd jobs for a *señor* who was a farmer. I felt right at home working for him because I had been a farmer back in El Salvador. From Monterrey, I went to Laredo. I worked with another *señor*, a truck farmer, and he got me a space with seven other men to cross over. We got in the *panga*—it's like a big plastic boat—and someone had a pole and we made it across. No police or anything because these guys knew everything about the best day, hour, and minute to cross. And I didn't have to pay a *centavo*. The man I was working for paid for me. He was a good man.

Of course, I didn't have a *centavo* either. I was now on the other side with no funds, so I started working on a nearby ranch, the Rancho Loma Larga, to make enough money to go on a little further. The *tejano* I worked for was another very good man. I took care of his horses and cows and I rode a beautiful white horse. I thought, what freedom! Riding all day long in the countryside, *puro campo*. The ranch was huge; it had three parts, like three separate ranches really. The *caporal*, or overseer, asked me please to stay, that I was a good worker, and besides, what was I going to do if I went somewhere else. But I always had the idea of moving on to see what was ahead and if I could get a better job. The *tejano* was very good to me. I didn't pay for anything, not rent, not food, nothing, but I didn't make much either. The other guys I was working with kept on saying, "Come on, come on, let's go to Houston."

So I got all enthused and went to Houston, and I loved it. *Ooooo, qué va!* Wow! I liked it so much that I stayed five years. I worked in many jobs—roofing, putting on shingles, tarring roofs, painting, putting in Sheetrock, doing gardening, planting and mulching. I also worked in a plastics factory.

I have to confess that the real reason that I didn't remain at any of these jobs for very long was that at that time I had a terrible vice, alcohol. I guess it was because I was lonely and far from home. Alcohol was my ruin. In Houston, I had good jobs

and I earned good money, but my vice wouldn't let me be. Every weekend, Friday, Saturday, and Sunday, I would be drinking. Monday I would wake up still drunk, and be unable to go to work. In the company, you could miss once and they would give you another chance. If you were a very good worker, you could miss twice, but the third time, no way. You were out. And that's what kept happening to me. Then I would sign up for another job, get drunk, and lose that one, too. Once, I got a great job *indoors*, in an office building downtown, with good pay, but my habit—I didn't know how to control it, and it ended up controlling me.

After Houston, I came to Florida. The reason I came here was that I needed a *mica*, a green card. They were charging $500 in Houston, but I heard that they charged less in Florida. A *señor* came to where I was working in Houston and won me and some Mexican friends over; he sold us the cards for three hundred each. I came to Florida with the contractor himself. We paid for the ride, $150 each, in a van; we were seven people. Once we began to work here in the fields, they paid us little by little. We made between $50 and $75 per week. I worked in Wahneta for one season. The following season, I came here to the Winter Haven area, and this is where I've been ever since, like a member of the Murillo family. I plan to stay, if God wills. I am not working now, but when I'm working I pick oranges—that's what the work is here, *pura naranja*.

The truth is that I have been very lucky. It was not easy to leave EL Salvador in '82, because of the war, but I escaped on foot. *En el camino no tuve piedra*—there was no stone in the road. And I had no problems with the *migra* until Houston. The first time they caught me I was with some Mexican friends and they took us to the border in a big van. We were all locked up in there, and I was afraid. I didn't know where they were taking me, and I had vivid memories of what happened to people in El Salvador. I saw the Mexicans as brothers because we were in the same situation. At first I was panicked by the *migra*, but by the third time I wasn't afraid any more. I finally learned to tell them that I was a *salvadoreño*. Then they didn't pick me up any more. Instead, they gave me a little paper and told me to present it to the *migra*. It was so small that I lost it, but it doesn't matter now, anyway, because we have our cards.

Ricardo Murillo

My story is a little different from Don Chuy's, though I, too, left El Salvador in '82. My brother, José Dimas, and I left in the predawn darkness on January 15, leaving everyone and everything behind. I worked in the army headquarters called El Paraíso —Paradise—in the northern zone of the country. I was not a soldier, but an employee, a bricklayer, one who builds houses. I worked making repairs on the officers' casino and other things at the *cuartel*, or headquarters. I loved this work.

The reason I left it was because each day we had to travel quite a distance to get to and from work, and it kept getting more and more dangerous every day. We never knew if we would make it home alive from one day to the next. Every day we

encountered danger in the streets, either with the *guerrilleros*—the rebels—or the government soldiers. It was too tense and dangerous to keep on working. If the *guerrilleros* had found out that I was working in the headquarters, they would've taken me out and killed me then and there. They didn't want anyone to collaborate in any way with the military. The *guerrilleros* just see you and they kill you on the spot, that's that. No questions asked. The worst thing was if they found out that you worked in some way for the government; that was the biggest crime.

Sometimes, my brother and I got in trouble. There were many tense moments when we had to decide what to say and what not to say, and hope that we would not contradict each other. On one occasion some friends of ours tried to defend themselves by saying that they worked for the government, and they showed their government ID cards. What they hadn't realized was that the *guerrilleros* were disguised as soldiers. Right before our eyes they murdered our friends. You never knew who were the soldiers and who were the *guerrilleros*. They went around dressed alike. You didn't know whether to show your ID or not in order to defend yourself. You couldn't trust anyone. That's when José Dimas and I decided to leave the country. I told my wife and my mother, "I think that God wills it. The road will be difficult, but with the help of God we will continue. We will be long in returning home, but we will be alive." And then we set out. We hardened our hearts, because it is almost unbearable to leave your parents, your wife, your children. But there are moments of truth in our life when we have to make painful decisions.

We went as tourists. We got our passports and tourist visas in El Salvador to enter Guatemala and Mexico. It was all legal to Mexico. We worked in Guadalajara for several months and made good friends there. We worked very hard there in jobs that I had never done before in El Salvador. Some days we loaded trucks with stones, big stones, and the higher the load in the truck, the higher we had to lift, and then throw, the heavy stones. Those first months, we weren't tired from that heavy work, but we were exhausted from worrying about our families who we had left behind. We wrote them letters every day, but had no idea if they were getting through or not.

We also helped gather cane tips, because these make good fodder for the animals. We earned two hundred pesos a day, not enough to eat on. Impossible! On other occasions, I was able to work in construction, but one had to accept what was available in order to survive. Sometimes we became so despondent that we would ask ourselves what we thought we were doing, and what was the point of going on. But we had to keep on to achieve our goal and to keep it foremost in our mind, and that was to get to the United States. To Idaho, really, because my cousin was working there, and it was he who had been sending us money ever since we left El Salvador. On our own, we didn't even earn enough money for food, much less to be able to leave Mexico. Everything costs money, and we had to pay the *coyote* $700 each to cross us from Tijuana to Los Angeles.

Finally, my cousin called us in Guadalajara and said that it was now time for us to travel. The reason we had waited was because it was cold up there in the north.

We had arrived in Guadalajara on January 20, and *estaba el mero frío*, it was freezing cold in Idaho then. So we waited until March 3 to leave Guadalajara, and then we were in Los Angeles by March 5.

Crossing was dangerous business. A friend—well, he said he was our friend, but he was not—who we had met in Guadalajara, said that he would cross us for $1000 total. We trusted him, and since we had known him in Guadalajara, we gave him $500 and said that we would give him the other $500 when we reached Los Angeles. Then this "friend" locked us in a room, there in Tijuana, and he himself turned us in to the Mexican federal police. However, since we had spent some time in Guadalajara and had the experience of talking like Mexicans, this helped us out. The police thought that we were Central Americans and they were going to kick us out. However, they couldn't do it because we knew the colors of the flag, who was governor so-and-so, and we showed them how much we knew about Mexican history, and we did so with a Mexican accent and vocabulary. We had bought a birth certificate that said that we were children of so-and-so, and that we were from such and such part of Mexico. *En México todo lo compraba con dinero*—in Mexico you could buy anything. They finally got tired of the whole thing, charged us five thousand pesos each, which was robbery, but we had no choice. And the *señora* in charge of the rooms where we were staying became worried for us and said, "I'll get someone to take you across right now, I mean right now, *pero rápido pa'l otro lado*, quickly to the other side, *antes que nos vayamos a volver a morder*, before they return for another bite [bribe]."

I think that the *coyotes* and the Mexican government work together because the police agent knew the entire area and he knew that we were carrying money that my cousin had sent us. I was, by then, in debt to my cousin for a total of three thousand dollars; I didn't think I would ever make enough money to pay him back. But that *señora*, I remember her name was Josefina, said that she would get a *coyote* for us right away and she did. But he came up and he said, "*No más tengo cupo para uno*,"—I only have room for one of you. But we were two. And then my brother said to me, "'*Mano, te vas tú. De otro lado me mandas a traer*,"—Brother, you go, and after you cross, send for me. He convinced me and I left. But then, when it was time to go, I couldn't go through with it. I told the *coyote*, "*Yo no me voy. Si hay para los dos, me voy, si no, no*."—I'm not going. If there's room for two, fine; if not, I'm not going. He said, "Okay, okay, okay," and returned to pick up my brother, who he had left in a *locked* room. We picked him up and that night, about eight o'clock, we crossed through a hole in the fence and a cable which runs right along the border.

The coyote said, "When I say run, run; when I say stop, stop and hide." When we crossed to the other side, there were *migra* all over the place shining their blinding lights, shouting at us, helicopters overhead. We ran and hid in the woods, and then we walked all night, *puro caminar,* through the woods, not along the highway. There were about twenty-eight of us and two *coyotes*, one in front and one in back. Our only objective was to arrive, just to arrive. Dead on our feet we arrived about 6 a.m. in San Diego. At 9 a.m. a car came and put six of us in the trunk. Six people! I couldn't believe my eyes! And it was a small trunk. Well, that's

how we got from San Diego to Los Angeles. It took about three hours; we couldn't move and we could hardly breathe. We arrived stiff and sore, exhausted, and nearly starving, but we arrived. *Uno sufre mucho en la vida*—one suffers a great deal in this life—but, even so, we were luckier than most.

We carried two hundred dollars, *well* hidden, because if they see you taking money out of someplace, then it's *adiós* and to the hospital with you. But I had to hide our money or else we would have nothing, so I unstuck the heel of my shoe and hid it there. We stayed in Los Angeles for three days waiting for my cousin to send us our plane tickets. They just gave us one meal a day, at 6 p.m. We had to stay locked up; we couldn't go outside. We were in one of those little sheds where people store their tools; they had put a sofa in it. There were ten people waiting for someone to pick them up and pay for them. Everybody had their goal to arrive at a certain destination, and *nos iban regando a distintas partes*—we were sprinkled around to different places.

Finally, my cousin sent our tickets, and we went to the airport in Salt Lake City, in Utah. He came by car from Idaho to pick us up; it was not far from the border with Utah. We stayed there until October, working in the fields, irrigating, planting, harvesting sugar beets, wheat, beans, everything. My cousin worked on a mink farm in Idaho. He left El Salvador in '79, and moved to Idaho because when he arrived at the border there was a man there who was offering passage for Mexicans to harvest in Idaho. So he ended up in Idaho, and he liked it because he was able to get year-round work, very stable, and the boss gave him many benefits. His salary covered an apartment in good condition for only $100 a month. He had his social security that he had bought in Los Angeles; it was not legal, but his boss didn't mind.

Meanwhile, I was still worrying about how I was going to pay back that three thousand dollars in one lifetime! And the *patrón*, the boss, gave us the money! After the growing season was over, we were trying to decide what to do and there was this Pentecostal family that was going to Florida. They took us there for $600. You see, it was difficult to find a ride because nobody wanted to get in trouble with the law. The family took us, but they never let us go into a restaurant to eat. They would just bring us sodas or little snacks, which we paid for. Three days like that, without being able to get out except to go to the bathroom.

We arrived in Wahneta because that's where the Pentecostal family lived. We didn't know a soul, but this nice *señor* showed up and said, "If you have money, I will find you a place." We had money because the season had finished and we had worked in Idaho. This man got us a trailer, bought us the gas, everything. Then the next problem, how to get work? And, how to get a ride to work? But, God is everywhere, and a *señor* came up and offered to pick me up and bring me home and said that he would ask his boss if I could have a job. This man is a friend; his name is Jaime.

That was our odyssey, but it only lasted a year, 1982. We arrived here in Wahneta at Halloween. But there have been many years of struggle since then. I worked first in oranges; *era naranjero*—I was an orange picker. I wanted to do other jobs that I was qualified for, such as being a mason, but the problem was our immigration papers. We still didn't have them. The next year we got them: June

27, 1983. But first, we were picked up by the *migra* when we went to North Carolina to work. They took us to Miami where we were detained for two months. There were 1,500 prisoners there, from twenty-eight countries, all detained for being illegals. There were two guys there, lawyers, who took a kind of census of how many were from each country and so on. One was from Colombia and the other was from Panama. And whenever we got word that someone was going to be released, these two collected funds from all of us and gave it to the people who were being released so they would leave with some money. When I left they collected $60 for me. The Colombian was there for contraband; not for being a criminal, but for carrying marijuana. He had loaded a boat with fifty tons of marijuana, can you imagine? He did five years in prison and was free on bond, paying $75,000 *por la pura fianza*—just for bail! When his time was up in jail, they sent him to Miami, where we were because he was also an illegal immigrant. So, he had served his time for his offense, but he had not yet finished his time as an illegal. He's been there a long time.

Life in prison, well, it's not difficult. Of course, *no deja de ser prisión*; it's still prison, because one has no freedom, but conditions were very good. Health was very important there; each individual had to take care of his personal hygiene. If you didn't, then they would make you, because every morning, early, you had to bathe, brush your teeth, comb your hair, and then have breakfast at seven o'clock. Then you had recreation, games, weights, whatever you liked, to entertain yourself. At eleven they locked us up again, and then at twelve we formed a line to go eat. Then we were free until four, and at five we had to line up again to eat. They let us have free time until eight, when they locked us up again. They changed your bedding every day. It was very clean. José Dimas and I were there together, but we were locked in a very large room with others, about two hundred people in this one room. They had big fans for ventilation and two policemen on duty all the time so that no one would rob you.

The guards were good; there they respect the prisoner. Sincerely, I'm not going to complain about them, because the truth is that they really respected you there. Those of us who were religious could go and listen to talks by evangelicals or by a Catholic priest who came on Sundays. Saturdays, from two to four in the afternoon, they had dances, if you liked dancing. They would bring a band; the women prisoners were there nearby and they danced with us. We all had the same bright uniform; we were all bright orange.

Here, in this country, one can live in peace. If I have to choose which country I love more, of course, I have to say my country. But there I could not be free, it was like being tied up and afraid all the time. Here at least I am free, I can go to the movies or anywhere I want. But there you can't do that even at three in the afternoon much less at seven in the evening, because of the violence. Sometimes there is a curfew, but there is always violence, and your life is worth nothing in the dark. It was too much. But with God's help, I made it here.

After we got out of Miami, we came to Wahneta, without a penny, nothing. The reason we came back here was that at least we had met some people who had

been good to us. My brother by then had a girlfriend, and she came to pick us up when they let us out, and she brought us back. She didn't have money for gas, but we had the sixty dollars they had given us. Once we were back here, since some people knew us, they gave us credit while we worked to get ourselves established again. If you don't have money, you can't do anything.

Meanwhile, my wife Rosa was still in El Salvador. This was 1983. She arrived here November 8, 1984, two years after José Dimas and myself. We were all along sending our families a little money to maintain themselves on. When we left Miami, finally we got our permissions. It was a receipt to show in order to be able to work legally, like a voucher. You could also leave the country with it, but you could not get back in. There are newer ones now where you can return as well. I would love, if God wills, to return to visit when this orange season is over. I have applied for permission for my parents to come here, but I haven't heard anything yet. I paid a lawyer for this; if I am lucky it will turn out. My *papá* works in the fields; my *mamá* no longer works, but before, she worked in the home. That's the hard part for me, to know that they are getting older, and maybe God will take them away before I can see them again. And to know that I would not be able to go to them if they were in trouble or dying because I could not come back to my family here. But one has to trust in God.

My children need a future for their tomorrow and my wife also, and the schools there were often not even open because of the violence. Maybe you studied for nearly a whole year, but you couldn't complete it; then your whole year is lost. We decided that we needed to do everything possible for our children. I told my wife that we must make the effort for them. My *papá* knew the day that my wife and kids left to join me that I would never return, and he was right. But I told him that we are looking to our kids' future, and I do not regret it. Our son here, Hugo Alexander Murillo, is an excellent student. He has won himself a scholarship to high school, and look at this plaque they awarded him for outstanding scholarship. He speaks very good Spanish and English. He's working hard in order to learn, and in Michigan, where we spend part of the year, they are giving him classes in French and Japanese, too, in the seventh grade. When the season is over here, we go north, around Traverse City, where we pick strawberries, cherries, pears, and apples. The change of schools is not hard for the children. They use the same books both places, and they have friends they look forward to seeing in Michigan and in Florida.

We have much to be grateful for. This house is new; it was built for us by Habitat for Humanity. One day a *señora* came and told me that they would like to help me, that they had $700 from a Methodist church in Michigan, and that they would start in two days if that was okay with me. They're through now. The carpenters were very good, but I did the finishing touches myself in the evenings after work.

Roberto Durán

The California poet Roberto Durán has been involved in political action work; served time in jail when his protests on behalf of farm workers got out of hand; and written mordant, witty poetry critical of hypocrisy, social injustice, and indifference to the suffering of others.

The poems "Border Towns" and "Super Freak," from the collection "Feeling the Red on My Way to the Rose Instead" (*Triple Crown: Chicano, Puerto Rican, and Cuban-American Poetry,* Tempe, Ariz.: Bilingual Press/Editorial Bilingüe, 1987), illustrate Durán's sharp, epigrammatic style as they describe his view of the "welcome" given the immigrant and exile in the United States.

Border Towns

Border towns and brown frowns
and the signs say
get back wet back
souls are searched at night by silver flashlights
gringos and greasers play cat and mouse
and I still wonder why
do apple pies lie?
the signs say live the american way
visit but don't stay
be a friendly neighbor hire good cheap labor
as rows and rows of illegal star war aliens
are aligned and maligned
as the morning shouts fill the morning chill and still
they will not
no way José go away

Super Freak

And the song says do the freak do the super freak
as show-town sneaks into our pockets
meanwhile more South American refugees flee
as once again military men blow off another brother's knees
with government rockets
as they make their way into our cities
escaping the torture and rape
we in America put on our headsets and tape
and the song says do the freak and dig that funky beat

Francisco Javier Savallos

Francisco Javier Savallos

Disillusioned by the gross corruption of senior officers in the Nicaraguan air force, Savallos, after two previous abortive attempts, finally arrived in the United States, where he was immediately picked up by the *migra* and taken to the Bay View Detention Center on the Texas border. There, he met Delio Toro, who fled his native Honduras when the government began cracking down on the human rights group with which he was working. The experiences of Savallos and Toro both speak volumes about the tremendous hardships borne by the people of Nicaragua and Honduras.

Delio Toro

Interview

I was born in Managua in 1962 of a poor family. My *papá* is a taxi driver and my *mamá* sells clothes in a kiosk in the Roberto Huembey Market in Managua. She has supported myself and my five brothers and sisters ever since my father abandoned us when I was five years old. It was through her efforts that we learned how to work and get ahead.

I studied for a while in the Instituto Loyola secondary school, but when they found out that I was an FSLN sympathizer, they threw me out. I also studied in the Colegio Simón Bolívar, which is where I became involved with the MES, the Secondary Student Movement, and I did things like handing out Sandinista flyers and giving political talks to other students. This was in 1978 and '79.

When the Insurrection broke out in 1979, they sent me to Masaya, where I was assigned to help set up the CDS, the Sandinista Defense Committees. Unfortunately, on July 15, just four days short of the victory, Somoza's *guardia* picked us up. They had a command post there in the Centro Comercial Managua where they beat and tortured prisoners, and that's where they took me. They repeatedly struck me on the head with their rifle butts. Then they heated the gun barrels and burned me with them. Here, you can still see the burns. They kicked me in the testicles and beat me all over my body, especially my face, so that I was completely swollen and unrecognizable from head to toe. I begged them to take me to the hospital, but they paid no attention, even though I was hemorrhaging. It turns out that a distant cousin of mine worked in Somoza's security. He showed up, cursed me, and said I was a disgrace to the family. Then he gave the guards some marijuana, and they finally took me to Manolo Morales Hospital. I have never fully recovered; I still have blinding headaches and only one functioning kidney.

I went back to school and finally graduated from high school the following year, but I remained in the reserves of the Sandinista Army. I began university studies in agronomy, but was soon sent to Cuba to study aviation for the military. I was there from 1982 to 1987, and I graduated as an electrical engineer in aviation. When I came back they sent me to military operations in Matagalpa, where I was stationed from '87 to '89. Then they transferred me to Managua, which is when my problems began.

First, they awarded me militant status; it's a tremendous honor, and I earned it by the sweat of my brow and deep devotion to the Revolution. But it became clear that some others got their militancy by wrapping themselves in the flag; by glorifying themselves; and, in the air force, by cheating, stealing, and misusing funds. It was staggering to me to realize the extent of the corruption. There were officers who were pocketing money, selling oil and tires, trucks, even the prefabricated

houses that were supposed to be for us. A few officers were stripped of their status as militants, and Colonel Javier Pichardo was sent to a remote administrative post on the Atlantic Coast, but that's all. There was no punishment. When I saw the degree of the abuse of power and the corruption, I wanted to speak out, but if I had, they would have called me a reactionary and there was *nothing* you could do against that accusation. Plus, I was having recurring problems from my earlier beatings at the hands of the *guardia,* and that's when one of my kidneys collapsed. I was very ill, but they refused to give me a discharge. My only recourse was to desert, so the next year, in '90, I left the country.

I was headed for the U.S., but the first time I had bad luck and didn't make it. I went to Guatemala and was there when the elections took place in Nicaragua, the ones that brought in Chamorro and turned out the Sandinistas. Up until that time, my mother told me that security kept coming to the house looking for me. But after the elections, I went back, thinking things would be better. Unfortunately, it was a different government, but the same security apparatus. They arrested me for desertion and for illegal possession of a weapon. I showed them my gun permit, but they took my weapon anyway. Then they asked me if I wanted to stay in the military in the new government, but I said no, that I wanted nothing more to do with the military because of all the deception, cruelty , greed, and corruption I had seen. I wanted to be a civilian and work and live a normal life, not feel like a failure, a *fracasado.* They transferred me to the heavy transport squadron and sanctioned me for forty-five days.

Toward the end of July of 1990, Colonel Javier Pichardo tried to bring about a revolt against Humberto Ortega. I was asked if I wanted to be part of the movement, and I said *de ninguna manera,* no way, because I haven't robbed with you! The movement failed, and the entire air force was detained one entire day. Humberto came to where we were and explained everything to us. *¡Qué lástima la situación de mi país!* What a shame, the situation of my country!

I then left the country again, going through Guatemala to Mexico. There was a wonderful Mexican family in Tampico that gave me shelter for one entire month. But Mexican immigration caught me and returned me to Guatemala. I tried again and finally made it to Brownsville. I was going to take a plane to New York where I have a friend, but *la migra* picked me up in Harlingen.

I've been detained here for over four months now. My family doesn't have the money to get me out. The workers here at Proyecto Libertad have a lawyer who is trying to help me. I'm asking for political asylum because I'm afraid to go back. I'm not the exception in my group that was sent to Cuba to study. There were one hundred of us, and only twenty-five are still in Nicaragua. They all left for similar reasons. You know, the officers would even steal our pay. We ate rice if we were lucky, while they were eating and drinking in the *cantinas.* We were poorly fed and fighting for a cause that we believed in and helped create. But they turned their backs on us and on the Revolution. I'm not disillusioned with the Revolution, but rather with the intermediate level officers and political officials who destroyed it by becoming thoroughly corrupt.

Bay View Detention Center, Bay View, Texas

I hope that in these years of reconstruction we will see the rebuilding of the Sandinista Front. It is possible that they can become something positive again in the next six years. If my country's situation were to change for the better, I would return at once—that is, if desertion charges against me were dropped. If not, I will stay here, working at whatever I can and building the future that I did not have the opportunity to build in my own country. I am bitterly disappointed because I have put a large part of my life into the Revolution. I am twenty-eight years old now. I am still ill, but the doctor here at the detention center says that my problems can't be cured; they can only be treated.

I am waiting every day for word that I will be released. In the meantime, I watch TV, or do the various jobs we are assigned, such as cutting the grass, working in the recreation room or in the laundry area. This jail is in no way like those in Nicaragua; the problem here is the psychological anguish of being deprived of freedom. But there is absolutely no physical mistreatment at all. And the prisoners all get along, too. We are mostly Central Americans, so we are like brothers.

I have become good friends with a guy from Honduras named Delio. He had to leave his country because he had been working for a human rights organization and the military kept picking him up and beating him. The last time they tortured him, and he nearly died. He's still a very nervous person. They told him that the next time they were going to get his family. That's when he left to come here. Immigration picked him up in McAllen, where he was trying to get a plane to

Houston, where someone had told him there was a safe house. Delio writes to his family all the time, and when the priest comes, he gives him letters to pass on to people who are going down to Honduras. He's been here for four months, too, and still hasn't heard from his family, so he doesn't know if they are all right, or disappeared, or if they have gotten his letters. Nor has the human rights group he worked for sent the *constancias,* official papers, that he has asked them for. We talk a lot about our feelings and about our countries, which are absolutely lost, *perdidos.*

We all get along here, but there are very few Nicaraguans. Most are from Honduras and El Salvador. I'm putting all my hopes on getting out of here and finding work. If I'm granted asylum, and if I get a job, then maybe I can bring my family here to begin a new life. Families should never be separated.

Ariel Dorfman

Acclaimed novelist, essayist, short story writer, journalist, and poet, Ariel Dorfman has had many of his numerous creative works and critical essays translated into a variety of foreign languages. Of those writings that have been translated into English, *The Empire's Old Clothes: What the Lone Ranger, Babar, and Other Innocent Heroes Do to Our Minds,* trans. Clark Hansen (New York: Pantheon Books, 1983), *Widows* trans. Stephen Kessler (New York: Pantheon Books, 1983), and *The Last Song of Manuel Sendero* trans. George R. Shivers and Ariel Dorfman (New York: Viking, 1987) are among the best known.

Dorfman left his native Chile for the United States during the long period of harsh repression under the regime of dictator Augusto Pinochet, during which time thousands of Chileans were routinely deprived of their civil rights, tortured, murdered, and "disappeared." The painful experience of exile is vividly called forth in Dorfman's emotionally piercing collection of poems, *Pastel de choclo, Last Waltz in Santiago and Other Poems of Exile and Disappearance* trans. Edith Grossman and Ariel Dorfman (New York: Viking, 1988), from which the following selections are taken.

Something Must Be Happening to My Antennas

I find myself crying at the end of General Hospital
I swear it's true
the worst soap opera on TV
the cheapest song
a good-bye on a platform
or a broken balloon in a child's hand
are all it takes
and I get a lump in my throat
my eyes burn like acid
my nose itches
my heart pounds
my breathing becomes irregular
maybe tears will come
and my eyes grow red

> I know the tricks and techniques of the movies
> I've studied how the violins manipulate us
> I spent my life denouncing Doris Day

but during General Hospital
something clouds over inside
and something wet and salty runs down my cheeks

I'm like a stone when I receive the news of your death
lists of crippled people come off the plane
        your best friend limping
I learn that they killed your sister on a street corner
the children in the slums eat cats and dogs
if they can find them
you haven't worked for fifteen months
another worker clubbed
the noise of a stick on a shoulder

and I am not moved
I am not moved
      I must be very sick
I'm afraid
I'm afraid
      I'm afraid of what's happening to me
I'm afraid
      so afraid
      of what's happening to me

Prologue: That Deafening Noise Is the Garbage Truck

Today the cup broke;
how could I be so clumsy.

It made me very sad when it broke,
it was the one we had bought right after
                we left the country,
one that we were fond of,
you could say it was almost
                our friend,
bright red with white spots
for drinking café con leche
                in the mornings,
those first mornings at the beginning.

So that there wouldn't be any slivers left,
any sharp bits to surprise us afterwards
in our soup, our feet, our eyelids,
I picked up all the tiny fragments
                squatting
at first and then on all fours,
with the infinite care of a punished child
doing a chore over again
                quietly, quietly,
and slowly.

                We had it for
                more than four years.

Today I broke a cup
and my exile began.

Beatriz Badikian

Beatriz Badikian was born in Bueno Aires, Argentina, and lives in Chicago. She has won numerous literary fellowships and has been published in *Third Woman, Imagine, The Americas Review, Iowa International Women's Issue,* and *Spoon River Quarterly,* among others. She is the author of the chapbook, *Akewa is a Woman,* and the forthcoming collection *Mapmaker.*

Badikian's poem "Ragdale Evenings," from the mini-anthology *Emergency Tacos* (Chicago: MARCH/Abrazo Press, 1989), describes the poet's discomfort at feeling out of place in a wealthy suburban mansion and her desire to return to her own home.

Ragdale Evenings

Buenos Aires: violins, guitars, the bass,
Piazzolla and his "bandoneon."
and me, surrounded by trees,
Lake Forest ladies and mansions
large enough to hold a small town in.

The sun barely out today:
a small boy who hides behind
drapes, shy of visitors.
I want to hide, too,
in this room,
forever, behind lamps
and pillows, inside the yellow
wallpaper or under the rug
of leftover threads woven
into a multicolored bird.
Between day and night, when
the sky is indecisive between
dark and light, a quilt of clouds,
books and hours slip from my lap.
I sit by the window: fuchsias droop
beyond the lace curtains, wind
shakes oak leaves after rain.
Darkness arrives unnoticed:
my bed narrow, the mattress high.

And from here I fly very fast,
not passing Chicago, like
sneaking behind a husband's back
to Buenos Aires and laugh,
dreaming of trapeze artists and acrobats.

Juan Armando Epple

Juan Armando Epple is a Chilean exile who came to the United States in 1974. His stories have appeared in anthologies such as *Chilean Writers in Exile* (Trumansburg, N.Y.: Crossing Press, 1982).

The following story, "Garage Sale People" (in *Paradise Lost or Gained?* [Houston: Arte Público Press, 1990]), describes with humor the nostalgic reinventing of the exile's beloved homeland, and offers a unique method for dealing with reality when it threatens to intrude upon one's fantasies.

Garage Sale People

I'm going for a spin, he said, and before I could ask him where he was heading, he had the car in reverse and was backing out over the daffodils he himself transplanted when we moved from Springfield. The daffodils suffer whenever he's angry or confused about one of the assignments they give him to write; he starts enthusiastically, but then drops them saying he can't find the right tone.

My daddy's typewriter is like my mom's sewing machine that she bought at a garage sale; it works okay for a while and then breaks down. My mom says when he writes nonstop for an hour it's because he's answering a letter from one of his friends, those ten-page epistles they like to send to each other. And when he writes for a few minutes and then there's a long silence in his room it's because he's thinking over some problem . . . like homework Miss Greenfield gives us? . . . and we know at any minute he'll come downstairs and cruise through the kitchen uncovering the pots on the stove or head straight out to the yard to water his tomatoes, saying it helps him concentrate.

"I bet your papa wanted to watch the news and you changed the channel on him," I said to Marisol who had settled in front of the TV with a package of cookies and Def Leppard records scattered around her, glued to one of those music programs where singers change scenes every verse.

"No, he told me he had to write some letters. Besides, the only program he likes is the news at seven. I went in to ask him why he didn't write Granny, too, and let's get her here finally, even if it's just for a visit. That's when he jumped up from his chair and pumm . . . was gone. You think he went to the post office?"

Since I don't understand anything about American football, much less baseball, and it's even harder for me to understand English in the movies (it's like speaking while you chew potatoes, Marta says, trying to imitate a phrase), the only way I can deal with Marisol's questions is to get out on the streets to warm up my muscles. Even this metaphor doesn't fit, because every time I catch myself in a mirror, it confirms that I'm gaining several pounds a year, and my first gray hairs have already arrived. It's the most interesting age for a man, Marta says; at the same time she runs her finger along my incipient double chin. Besides, every time I decide to go running I find myself competing with hundreds of athletes all wearing their Nikes, and convinced that Eugene is the running capital of the world and every one of them—even the modest—truly believing they can win the New York marathon. So I finally opted for the classical wheelchair of this country, even if only to imagine that we are discovering new routes, gliding through these

rigorously laid-out streets with traffic lights and patrolmen regulating my exercise, swearing loyalty to this car which was so shiny at the beginning and now moves by jerks, like a Pinto with the flu.

When I was learning to drive and Chinaman (Chinaman was from Antofagasta and even he didn't know why he had the nickname) taught me a few basic maintenance tips like checking the pressure in tires, changing the oil and putting antifreeze in the radiator, I thought it would be a good idea to get myself some of those tools he carries in the trunk of his convertible (this is a real convertible, my friend, he exudes, flashing a sleeve over the canvas top . . . from the good old days, you can even turn it into a bed should the occasion arise), so I stopped once at one of those little signs that say "Garage Sale," looking for extra equipment for the car. Bit by bit my curiosity became an obsession as I discovered that garage sales are small family markets *gringos* set up in their garages or on their lawns, where they put out second hand and even some new things, acquired on their tourist safaris no doubt or at those irresistible sales in the big department stores, stuff they accumulate until their boundless desire for new things forces them to offer it all up for a few bucks to make room for new purchases. My first few times out I got carried away by enthusiasm, enthusiasm for the variety of objects set out on little tables or casually placed on the picture post card lawns. I started bringing home unexpected trophies; Marta's reactions went from compassion to concern: a plow from the era of the gas engine (the farm in the South we had to sell in a hurry to get out of the country in time), prints, fishing lures, picture frames, a new Mexican *guayabera* shirt which I wore even in midwinter, not so much to imagine how life would have been in that country had our visas arrived in time but mainly to relive the good-byes in the Bomba Bar, jot down addresses, go over the coded language we would use to communicate with one another, and *gringo* Hoefler looking warily at the chairs—every day one more was empty—his mind made up to remain till the last for some secret ancestral reason, and now a toast to the "Scourge of Puebla," a pair of imitation Colt 45s made out of tin, like those idealized in the westerns written by Marcial Lafuente Estefania who turned out to be a Spaniard who never left his own country, earning his living writing stories of the Far West which he diagrammed with the help of a map taken from *National Geographic,* Frankie Avalon or Cinco Latinos records, and those best-sellers so passé people have to throw them in a box in hopes that someone will cart them off free, help yourself. I put a halt to my casual purchases one day when, coming home with a terrific mannequin worthy of a place in my office, there was Marta in the midst of putting our own junk away in the garage, trying to make some room: "If you keep up this sport of yours, I'd appreciate it if you would bring home something a little more useful. I asked you a long time ago to get me some canning jars, or a vacuum cleaner that works since you don't want to buy a new one."

In our years away from Chile we had to change countries twice (in some countries to get a resident's visa you need to have a work contract first; in others you have to have the residency in order to get a job, and then there are other countries where they don't want us even as tourists), and once in the United States we had

lived in more than five states before we finally got something more or less permanent in Eugene. Oregon drew us immediately, like a secret force, because it looks so amazingly like the South of Chile. Our moves had us packing and unpacking, selling or giving away what little furniture we acquired, crating and uncrating Dario's books, because there's one thing for sure—a woman can say good-bye to her vacuum, the pots, and even the china, but Mr. Big's books have to be put in the coziest part of the truck. We'll buy it all new there, dearie, don't worry. Then we had to send our new address to family and to the friends for whom we still existed, take Marisol's vaccination certificate and school records to yet another school; she didn't even know what to put anymore in the "country of origin" section. She ended up writing MARISOL (which guaranteed her a spot in the geography class), and even planning a little garden spot in the backyard to put in some cilantro and basil. For sure, these proud exiles are always ready to travel, "looking for New Horizons," but wherever they go they keep longing for the *empanadas* and *humitas* Granny used to fix for them. When he got into these garage sales it didn't bother me too much because it seemed harmless entertainment, but when he began to sing praises of these "Persian markets" as he called them in front of other Chileans, I had to rein him in. Hilda told me confidentially that people were now calling us "the Persians."

In school nobody knows where Chile is, so they call me Hispanic, or Latin sometimes. One time I told the English teacher that it was a beautiful country with a lot of mountains and fruit trees, and she smiled and said how true, she had wonderful memories of a trip to Acapulco. Maybe they don't know where it is because it's so small on the map, kind of like a string bean, and that's why so many Chileans have had to go abroad to live. What I don't get is, if it's so small, how come everything there is so big. Any time Chileans get together at my house —everywhere we've lived there's a group of Chileans who call each other every day and get together to eat—they create a country I don't think exists on any map. The watermelons there are bigger and sweeter than the ones at Safeway; grapes are the size of plums there; Mt. Hood doesn't come up to the ankle of Aconcagua; there's nothing like a stew of *congrio*, which must be an enormous fish like a shark but tasty; the wine they sell here tastes like sweet ink or the beer tastes like piss; and there is no comparison between bread baked in the South and that plastic stuff they sell here. One day they got together to discuss something about passports and to look at a list Uncle Romilio brought, inventing surnames that began with the letter "L" (like Lunatic, Limpid, Lolosaurus, Lucifer, Laborious, Lanco, Liberator, and so on). We kids began to draw. I drew a mountain range and went to show it to my papa. He looked at it a long time, then he became serious, and corrected my mountain range, saying it was much taller and more difficult to cross. He didn't see that I had also drawn an airplane. That afternoon he criticized everything my aunts and uncles were saying—we have to call all grownups from Chile aunt and uncle—saying that *empanadas* are originally from Chile and the *cueca* is a dance brought to Chile from Africa. Finally our visitors had had enough and left, and one of the uncles shouted at my papa that the only thing clear was that we considered ourselves Persians now.

Marisol had put us on the spot again with her innocent logic, just that sunny day with raspberry pie, when I said something about the flour they sell at the supermarkets, and she spoke up to say that if Granny knows how to make better pies, why don't we go to Chile to see her? Dario stood up and walked to the kitchen, Does anyone want more coffee?, giving me that "You brought it up, you answer her" look. But at this point in exile it's hard to explain to a girl who grew up in this country what it means to have an L on your passport—I mean, we don't even know what the "L" stands for—so I tried to explain that airfares were out of sight these days, that Papa had been trying to save money, but we barely have enough for one ticket and it's not fair for just one of us to go back to Chile, right? I don't know if I convinced her, but she ate an extra piece of pie, played with her napkin a bit, then announced that she was reserving the television until twelve.

I closed myself up in my office, but in a while she came up, lifting my papers as if interested in what I write and then looking out the window. She proposed: "Why don't we invite Granny to spend the summer with us? It's just one ticket, right? And this girl for whom we have spent years painting a country filled with specific tastes and odors, fixed and obsessive memories, faces which still seem just around the corner, and above all family presences which grow even as they fade in time, how can we jump up and tell her her grandmother died a few months after we left Chile? I gently mussed her hair and said, "Good idea, Miss, let's see what we can do," and I left.

That day I hit a couple of garage sales not seeking anything in particular, and I stopped at one house to take a look at some gardening tools they had, with prices precisely marked on those little white papers, in hopes of finding a hoe. I was about to go back to the car when I found the old woman, installed on a reclining chair, staring off into a world prior to all Sundays filled with questions and garage sales. At first I thought she was another mannequin, artfully arranged on the chair to show off a blue velvet dress with lace or the box of Hindu prints on her lap. But when I drew closer to inspect some shirts and look at her, I was surprised to see her reach out her hand for the twenty-five-cent souvenir-of-Seville fan, and begin to fan herself energetically with perhaps a bit of coyness.

Seeing me stretch the collar of a shirt, the owner of the house came up with an ear-to-ear smile and the typical supermarket question: "May I help you?" The shirts were practically new; their daughter had gotten married, and they had decided to sell off some of their belongings because they were moving to an apartment, he offered. You know, he added, as you get older to need less space.

Impulsively responding to my dilemmas, I pointed with my finger and asked him:

"How much are you charging for that granny over there?"

The man stared at me, then quickly disappeared into his house.

I started retreating fast, fearing well-deserved insults which might improve my grasp of the English vernacular, but before I got around the corner I heard him call me, almost sweetly. A blond lady was standing beside him, wiping her hands on an apron.

.

Putting a friendly hand on my shoulder and dropping his voice at the numbers, he said, "What about five hundred bucks?" like he was making the deal of the year.

Taking my confusion as a bargaining ploy, the woman added, "She's really worth much more. To tell you the truth, we weren't even thinking of selling her."

"And besides, she's completely healthy," her husband interjected. "She's just started to use glasses. A month ago we got her a complete checkup and the doctor said she'd live for many more years. In her condition, the doctor predicted . . ."— my possible relative was about to let out an approving guffaw, but his wife cut him off with her elbow—"she might outlive us all."

"You really want to sell her?" I asked in perplexity.

"The thing is, the apartment is so small and the only way was to send her to a retirement center, and really, she's so used to family life she just doesn't deserve to end up there. We hadn't imagined that there might be another solution: a young family, full of plans, because you, judging by your accent, must be a Hispanic immigrant, right? You can give her a new opportunity, and in a Latin environment where you value the old ways . . ."

"How much can you offer for her?"—the woman went on—"Besides, we'll give you all her personal effects and you can't imagine how much of value she's accumulated over her lifetime. And we'll throw in some kitchen items because you wouldn't believe what great apple pie she makes, from a secret recipe she inherited from her mother, and she likes to cook with her own pans."

We spent a couple of hours on the deal, and after working out a way to pay, we agreed that I would come back for her in a couple of weeks. A wise decision, because you can't just up and make these changes from one day to the next.

That night during dinner, I noticed that Dario was quieter than usual, and he even drank *mate,* which he practically never does because he says it gives him insomnia. Looking at Marisol who was drawing something on her napkins, he suddenly started proposing a series of changes in the house routine, asking if we still had that cot we bought when Heriberto El Chilote came from California to visit us.

Anticipating the surprise, I casually allowed, "Because we've got to get another bedroom ready. I booked a reservation for Granny today, and she'll be making us a visit in two weeks."

Then I went outside into the backyard because it was still light, and the hills surrounding the Willamette Valley intensified the degrees of green, stretching towards the last golden sparks of the sun. It was like being on Lake Llanquihue once more, smelling the secret rhythms of the seasons, but without being there.

But I also went outside because I wanted to make sure that the beans were climbing up the stakes, that the danger of frost had passed, and that the hoe was really of good quality—that hoe my new Northamerican relatives threw in as an extra.

—Translated by R. M. Jackson

Achy Obejas

The Cuban American Achy Obejas is a free-lance writer, journalist, and poet who lives in Chicago. Her work has appeared in a number of journals, anthologies, and newspapers. In our reading, "Sugarcane" (in *Woman of Her Word: Hispanic Women Write,* ed. Evangelina Vigil [Houston: Arte Público Press, 1983]), Obejas uses swaying, rhythmic repetitions and popular speech to contrast the canefields of Cuba with the slums of Chicago, while also observing the striking similarities between the people in both locales—brown, black, and, for Obejas, "bros."

Sugarcane

can't cut
cut the cane
azuca' in chicago
dig it down to the
roots sprouting spray paint on the
walls on the hard cold
stone of the great gritty city
slums in chicago
with the mansions in the hole
in the head of
the old old rich left behind
from other times lopsided
gangster walls overgrown taken
over by the dark
and poor overgrown with no
sugarcane but you
can't can't cut
cut the water
bro'
from the flow and
you can't can't cut
cut the blood
lines from this island
train one by one throwing off
the chains *siguaraya*
no no
no se pue'e cortar
pan con ajo quisqueya
cuba y borinquen no
se pue'en parar

I saw it
saw black a-frica
down in the city
walking in chicago *y*
la cuba cuba
gritando en el solar

I saw it
saw *quisqueya*
brown
uptown in the city
cryin' in chicago
y borinquen
bro'
sin un
chavo igual but
you can't can't cut
cut the water
bro'
from the flow and
you can't can't cut
cut the blood
lines from this island
train one by one throwing off
the chains *siguaraya*
no no
no se pue'e cortar
pan con ajo quisqueya
cuba y borinquen no
se pue'en parar
¡azuca'!

Carolina Hospital

This Cuban American poet and writer lives and works in Miami. She edited the volume *Cuban American Writers: Los Atrevidos* (Princeton: Ediciones Ellas/Linden Lane Press, 1988), which includes our selection "Dear Tía," a poem about the pain of forgetting those that one has left behind.

Dear Tía

I do not write.
The years have frightened me away.
My life in a land so familiarly foreign,
a denial of your presence.
Your name is mine.
One black and white photograph of your youth,
all I hold on to.
One story of your past.

The pain comes not from nostalgia.
I do not miss your voice urging me in play,
your smile,
or your pride when others called you my mother.
I cannot close my eyes and feel your soft skin;
listen to your laughter;
smell the sweetness of your bath.
I write because I cannot remember at all.

Pat Mora

Texan Pat Mora has had her poems widely published in various reviews and is the author of two prize-winning collections, *Chants* (Houston: Arte Público Press, 1984) and *Borders* (Houston: Arte Público Press, 1986), as well as her more recent *Communion* (Houston: Arte Público Press, 1991). Our reading, "Elena," from the anthology *Woman of Her Word* (Houston: Arte Público Press, 1983), expresses a crucial aspect of the immigration experience: the need to learn English, not just to get along, but also to be able to communicate with one's children.

Elena

My Spanish isn't enough.
I remember how I'd smile
listening to my little ones,
understanding every word they'd say,
their jokes, their songs, their plots.
       Vamos a pedirle dulces a mamá. Vamos.
But that was in Mexico.
Now my children go to American high schools.
They speak English. At night they sit around
the kitchen table, laugh with one another.
I stand by the stove and feel dumb, alone.
I bought a book to learn English.
My husband frowned, drank more beer.
My oldest said, "*Mamá,* he doesn't want you
to be smarter than he is." I'm forty,
embarrassed at mispronouncing words,
embarrassed at the laughter of my children,
the grocer, the mailman. Sometimes I take
my English book and lock myself in the bathroom,
say the thick words softly,
for if I stop trying, I will be deaf
when my children need my help.

Part 6
My Roots Are Not Mine Alone:
La Identidad Cultural

Mariachi musicians in San Antonio, Texas

Abuelo

Celia Cruz

Orange grove, Wahneta, Florida

Folk dancer

My Roots Are Not Mine Alone: La Identidad Cultural

The experience of (im)migration and exile, as we have seen, profoundly affects every aspect of Latino life in this country, but most of all, it affects the question of cultural identity. Joseph Fitzpatrick has characterized identity as the points of reference that we use to define ourselves in relation to other people and the world; it is an awareness of who we are and where we belong. Some Latinos, of course, identify themselves completely with United States culture. A few do not identify with the United States at all. The majority occupy places along a spectrum between these two positions. For those who are immigrants or exiles, the points of cultural reference include the shared condition of being uprooted. For all Latinos, points of reference come from family, religion, community, and various artistic expressions. These are the sources that the Latino refers to for answers when asking the basic question, "Who am I?"[1]

The working out of one's identity is made more difficult when one is transplanted from one culture to another as many Latinos have been. Like plants, human beings suffer trauma—the loss of those roots, points of reference, values, and persons through which one defines oneself and one's world. The emigrant or exile Latino must try to transplant some of his or her native culture to new soil. If that is successful, the transplanted culture retains some of its original essence while also reflecting adaptations to a new way of life and to new reference points.[2] Such is the process and the problem of identity for people who have been torn from their native culture, whether they are intellectuals from Uruguay or *campesinos* from Honduras.

The questions that all Latinos must ask as they seek signposts for identity often involve pitting traditional against modern values. The process of adaptation often involves juxtaposing a personalistic, religious, spiritual, integrated, hierarchical, communitarian, static view of the world and one's place in it to a worldview that is impersonal, secular, materialistic, fragmented, egalitarian, individualistic, and in constant flux. For that clash is exactly what is involved when the *machista* male has to accept his wife's paycheck; when the sheltered wife has to take the subway to work; when the obedient daughter wonders why her brother can stay out all night but she cannot go out at all; and when both brother and sister prefer English to the language of their parents. The fact that such adjustments are taking place in a climate of racism and economic uncertainty only aggravates the situation.

Yet what is striking about the theme of Latino identity is not the onslaught of the forces of Americanization, but the determined retention by Latinos of particular aspects of their own ethnic identity and heritage. They identify with those facets of United States life that they either choose or need to accept, while they reject others and close ranks around those values of their native cultures that they insist on retaining—family, religion, community, and the importance of the arts. This process is an eclectic, or selective, assimilation; it involves donning the outer garments that bring acceptance and advancement, while protecting an intact inner core. Sometimes that inner core is more an imagined than a real entity. Especially in second and third generations, one sees a nostalgia for something never experienced but only longed for, an Aztlán or Varadero Beach of the mind. Much as wishing can make something so in creating community, so, too, can one will oneself an identity. If being Irish is a state of mind, then so, too, is being Latino.

The arts address the issue of identity by giving concrete expression in murals, painting, sculpture, music, theater, film, and literature to the experience of being, or becoming, bicultural, of having a dual identity. The community demonstrates and helps create cultural identity by the colorful and dramatic public events that commemorate religious occasions that celebrate the accomplishments of Latin American heroes such as Benito Juárez, Ramón Betances, and José Martí, and that mark the independence observations of Mexico, Puerto Rico, and Cuba. The family, of course, is at all times and in every way dealing with and shaping one's identity, personal and cultural, for the family provides the basis for one's sense of self and for how one fits into the larger world.

In this chapter, readings by Mexican Americans, Cubans, a Salvadoran, a Puerto Rican, a Chilean, and an Ecuadorian treat the difficult problems of affirming one's cultural identity in the face of racism, sexism, cultural loss, uprooting, and language and economic barriers, while, at the same time, highlighting the strong sense of self, pride, faith, place, history, and destiny that make the Latino cultural identity a positive force for the future.

Gustavo Pérez Firmat

This widely published Cuban American, Gustavo Pérez Firmat, lives and works in North Carolina. He is the recipient of various awards and is well-known both for his poetry and for his works of literary criticism, such as *Literature and Liminality: Festive Readings in the Hispanic Tradition* (Durham, N.C.: Duke University Press, 1986), *The Cuban Condition: Translation and Identity in Modern Cuban Literature* (Cambridge and New York: Cambridge University Press, 1989), and *Do the Americas Have a Common Literature?* (Durham, N.C.: Duke University Press, 1990).

His poetic themes revolve around the question of identity and often treat the subject of language, as in the poem that follows, "Dedication," in *Triple Crown: Chicano, Puerto Rican, and Cuban American Poetry* (1987).

Dedication

The fact that I
am writing to you
in English
already falsifies what I
wanted to tell you.
My subject:
how to explain to you
that I
don't belong to English
though I belong nowhere else,
if not here
in English.

Sister Elizabeth Avalos

The themes of language and identity are brought up again in the story of El Salvador–born Sister Elizabeth Avalos, who emigrated with her family when she was very young, and who longs to recover the Spanish language and cultural identity that she feels were denied her, growing up as she did during the peak influence of the melting pot ideal.

Through her social service work with Latino groups in Los Angeles and San Francisco, Sister Elizabeth endeavors to recover and recreate lost ties.

Interview

I was born in 1941 in El Salvador and came here in 1944 when I was three. I don't know why my parents left El Salvador exactly. I believe it had to do with an insurrection against the president at the time, Martínez, who was a good friend of my grandfather. Also, my dad had worked in the shipyards in California for a year of so after I was born. When he went back to Salvador, he tried to make a go of it working in a bank and also as a tailor. I don't know if he made it or not, but for some reason, he decided to come back here and work in the "shipiyards" as he called them. Neither of my parents have ever returned to El Salvador. They broke totally with their past, their culture, their language. They left it all behind.

What they always stressed at home was education and English. It was decided from the beginning that my brother and I would go to college. I went to St. Paul's High School in the Irish neighborhood. There were only a handful of Hispanics there. It was because of my parents' desire to improve themselves, to fit in, and to give us a future that I lost my past. I am still dealing with that sense of loss. As I look back on it, I see that the issue of my own cultural identity has influenced or determined many important decisions that I have made in my life all along. For example, at Mundelein College in Chicago I took Spanish from a wonderful teacher named Kateri O'Shea. Because of her, I fell in love with *Don Quijote.* That experience helped me recapture my culture. When I went to San José State, I got my master's in education with an emphasis in history, which had been my undergraduate major. I did one of my papers there on César Chávez, and that was a big step in reclaiming my identity.

Later, I went to Our Lady of Loretto High School in Los Angeles as a teacher and as the principal. It's about 90 percent Hispanic, and that was a definite turning point. I had worked with Hispanics at Holy Family High School for girls in Glendale, and I had met some Hispanics when I was in Chicago at Holy Name. But Loretto was my first total immersion and opportunity to understand some of the traditions and values up close. It's the little things I observed that made the most impact. For example, at Christmas the students gave the teachers *tamales* as gifts. Food is a very important part of one's culture, and this custom was brand new to me. Another thing I observed was when mothers would come to pay their tuition, they would stick their hand in their sock and plunk down three hundred dollars in cash because they didn't have a checking account. They would stand there counting out the ones and fives. That was very powerful because it suggested a whole set of experiences and a way of living very different from mine. All of us at Loretto tried to promote Hispanic culture. We wanted the students to be proud of their culture so that they would have enough self-esteem and pride to make it in

the broader, more alien culture. That atmosphere says a lot to me about the positive role of schools like Loretto. There's so much criticism now that you're isolating the kids, that it's not like this in the real world. But the fact is that in these formative years, it gives people from minority cultures a chance to develop a strong sense of identity, to appreciate who they are.

These past two years at PUENTE (People United to Enrich the Neighborhood Through Education), a school for adults, have also been wonderful in terms of learning about Hispanic culture. It's the simple things that I treasure, such as learning to appreciate the importance of touching and to be able to hear the beauty of the Spanish language. I also admire the spontaneous warmth of the adult students. For example, teacher appreciation day at the center is May 16, but, of course, most of the students don't even remember it until they get to class. Now, the Anglo way is to have it organized three weeks ahead of time, with an agenda and a program. But these people came to class and then they remembered. So I got from several people, *"Perdón tícher*, but I have to leave right now." A little later, they came back with flowers and guitars and *mariachis*. They played and sang for all the teachers.

Experiences like that one make me more determined to learn the language better. Next year I'm going to go back to school and take Spanish. I haven't told my mother, and I don't know what she will think about it. We have had practically no contact for the past two years. My mother would not be upset if I tried to improve my Spanish. She does believe that if you come to the United States you should learn English. She could only get a job as a seamstress in a factory when they came here because she didn't speak English. I know that was hard considering how well educated she was and that she had been an elementary school teacher in El Salvador. Well, as an ESL [English as a Second Language] teacher, I'm dedicated to English too. But I must get in touch with that part of me that has been denied. It's strange, because we never kept any of the customs at home, but on my sixteenth birthday my mother asked me if I wanted to have a *quinceañera*, the special celebration for a Hispanic girl's fifteenth birthday. She was Americanized enough to ask me if I wanted a party for what we call the sweet sixteen birthday here, but she was Hispanic enough to call it a *quinceañera*. I think she asked me because a friend of mine was keeping all the traditions, but I didn't have any idea what she was talking about. I didn't know what a *quinceañera* was! That's how alienated I was from my culture. As you can see, mine was not the typical immigrant experience of coming to the United States and continuing the family traditions.

Being at PUENTE has put me in touch with the more typical immigrant experiences. In the first place, many people at the Center are undocumented. The first thing I tell them is that the *migra* won't come here; they cannot walk into this classroom because the school is a sanctuary. We never ask anyone if they're here legally or not. That's not our place. We're here to provide services to anyone who walks in off the street. The second thing that I tell them is to decide what name they would like to use and to use it all the time in their documents. Some of their experiences are painful. One young woman, she's about eighteen and she finished the *prepa*, roughly equivalent to high school, in Mexico. She's very bright

and is already up to level two in English after being here only a few months. Unfortunately, her dad, who is an alcoholic and who has been drinking more than usual lately, has arbitrarily decided to send her back to Mexico. For no reason—just because he wants to. She has several married sisters here, but she won't stay with them. She's going to obey her father and go back to Mexico. I thought to myself, if she were American she would stay here. I was taken aback by the strength of that cultural rule which says that the father is the one who controls the family, whether he is a responsible person or not.

That brings me to the reason that we have many of our programs during the day, especially the English classes. On a rotating schedule we offer parenting skills, reading and math readiness for preschoolers, computer literacy, teacher certification, literacy classes, ESL, and job placement. Many of the women, if they don't know English, they are not going to leave the house, right? Well, some of the husbands want just that because they do not want their wives to learn English and get a job. I had to call the police the other day because a husband was beating his wife because she wanted to come to English class. He's in jail now, but *she* feels bad about it. The classes offer a great support system for mothers; they bring their children and we have child care. It is also a social event, an opportunity to get out of the house and to meet people.

I'm coming into contact with things that I've never experienced before in my life. The people I am working with will retain their language and their culture, both the positive and what you could call the negative aspects. For me, however, that was never an option. I'm a product of an age when other cultures weren't accepted. It was a time in American history where you assimilated. If you didn't, you were suspect; there was something wrong with you. My parents did not want me to associate with Mexicans because they were lower class. Friends of mine about my age, Salvadorans, friends of my parents, have experiences like mine. Catholic school or public school, you tried to be part of the dominant culture and not to keep, or even acknowledge, traditional values.

I had some very good friends when I was growing up. There were four of us and we would have a good time together even though my parents were unbelievably strict. It wasn't until I was a *senior* in high school that I got to use the car on the weekends, and then it was only once a month. But since there were four of us, we could go out every weekend. For me, the only reason that I could go to my senior prom and stay out until 1 a.m. was that I was with friends that my parents trusted. Of course, it wasn't that way for my brother George. His upbringing was very different, with a great deal more freedom. He's eleven years younger than I am and from the time he was in the third grade I was away at school. He understands Spanish but does not speak it. He is interested in his heritage but it is not a priority in his life.

Part of the reason my parents moved from our first neighborhood was to get away from the Mexican "element." That's when they bought a house in the Irish ghetto. My mom will still go back and shop in the Hispanic neighborhood, but she didn't want to live there. My parents had worked very hard toward their goal, my mom in the factory and my dad in his tailor's shop. It was a nice area of San

Francisco, mixed, but with few, if any, Hispanics. Had my parents chosen not to assimilate, but to retain their culture and do the best they could, I probably would not have gone to college. The reason I say that is because had we lived in an area of the city where the schools were not good; I would not have gotten an education. I would not have been pushed, and there would not have been such high expectations for me. It was always an accepted fact that I would go to college.

English has been an important fact of life in my family for a long time. My grandfather was an English professor at the National University in El Salvador, where he emigrated to from Cuba. My mother read English—she would read the books in his library—but she could not speak it until she came here. Both my parents were determined to learn English. They insisted that I speak to them in English. So they learned English from me and from their work. I learned English first, and then I taught it to them. They would speak Spanish when they were talking about personal or family things, but all other times they spoke English. After my brother was born they became United States citizens, and I did too. This was during the McCarthy era, and they didn't want to be deported. I was thirteen years old, and to me, the fact of citizenship for the three of us was like closing a door on our culture and heritage. One thing I see at PUENTE, and this is one reason why I say that I have learned so much from my students, is that they have not learned English from their children. They want to keep their culture, and so they maintain their Spanish. Of course, some people can take it to an extreme. One woman was telling me that her English would be much better except that her husband forbids any of them to speak English at home. But that gives you an idea of how much things have changed, from being forbidden, or at least discouraged, from speaking Spanish, to being forbidden to speak English!

The Loretto experience was all important to me. I mentioned that it was nearly all Hispanic. The BVM—that's my order, the Sisters of Charity of the Blessed Virgin Mary—the BVM faculty there were very close; we were all in our twenties and thirties and we were very idealistic. But I am one of the few minorities in our community. Personally, I have had some real problems with that. Think of all the years that we BVMs have spent in Hispanic and black communities, but we have not attracted many minorities. I feel that there has not been a genuine acceptance of other cultures. It's unconscious, but in the past we were greatly influenced by Irish culture. At St. Paul's, which went from grade school through high school, over a seventy-five year period, *ninety-five* women became BVMs! Not all stayed, but that's a huge number. St. Paul's, you remember, was in the Irish ghetto. You can imagine how entering an Irish community has added yet another dimension to my quest for identity! For a while, I felt like I was living two different lives. Now, however, I am very comfortable. I also speak up and say that we need more diverse perspectives in our community, and people are very receptive to that. We have begun a Hispanic Ministry Network. Those of us who are involved or interested in Hispanic Ministry meet once a year to discuss issues in our ministry. This shows me how far our Congregation has come since I entered.

I keep coming back to the importance of language to my identity. What has happened in my case is that learning Spanish has jarred my memory. Words like "fender" and "pencil sharpener," for example, take me back and then I remember more words. What I remember are words associated with early childhood, because of course I didn't speak Spanish as an adult at all. Studying the language has brought back my childhood vocabulary and many emotional associations. I remember when I was three years old in El Salvador hiding under the table when the soldiers and tanks went by. I have a Bible in Spanish, and sacred language to me is much more personal in Spanish.

If I were coming to the U.S. today, my experience would be very different. I would probably discover an acceptance of my heritage because the times are so different now. There's more of an acceptance of diversity. Even in social studies classes, we're no longer into assimilation; we're not the melting pot. Now we are multicultural; that's the new emphasis. The culture of the recent Salvadoran immigrant is probably not the culture that I would have had because they are *campesinos* and I was from a professional family. I haven't run into too many Salvadoran professionals. Those Salvadorans that I have dealt with, especially in San Francisco, working in the sanctuary movement and on the Latin American Task Force, were the very poor. I was on the task force for two years, and we tried to make people in parishes aware of the need—this was in the early eighties. We worked with sanctuary to help raise consciousness, because people didn't realize how desperate the Salvadorans were.

But I didn't come to the United States today; I came nearly fifty years ago. As a result, my strong identification with Hispanic culture is not grounded so much in lived experience as a Hispanic as it is in nostalgia, determination, and the career choices I have made. For example, there is a program in San José that I will be working with beginning next year. It's geared to jobless and homeless Hispanics. Many people here at PUENTE are making it just fine; they have developed good survival, study, and social skills, or they will in time. This other program is for those who have fallen through the system and have no resources of any kind, social or cultural. I am committed to the Hispanic people. I didn't grow up on beans and tortillas, but it's the food of the people I identify with. In the midst of the early memories and associations that the Spanish language recalls to me, there is a profound sense of loss, a feeling that something that should have been mine was taken away. But little by little, I am salvaging shreds of what was and what could have been, and using them to fashion my own, unique Hispanic identity. If all goes well, I plan to visit El Salvador before too long as a critical part in this whole process of recovery.

Rudolfo Anaya

The eminent Rudolfo Anaya is the author of numerous prize-winning short stories and novels including *Heart of Aztlán* (Berkeley, Cal.: Editorial Justa Publications, 1976), *Bless Me, Ultima* (Berkeley, Cal.: Tonatiuh-Quinto Sol Publications, 1972), *Tortuga*,(1982); *Cuentos/ Tales of the Hispanic Southwest*; (Santa Fe, N.M.: Museum of New Mexico Press, ©1980), and *Albuquerque* (Albuquerque, N.M.: University of New Mexico Press, 1992). He has also edited essays on Chicano identity, such as *Aztlán: Essays on the Chicano Homeland* (Albuquerque, N.M.: University of New Mexico Press, 1989, with Francisco Lomelí), and anthologies of New Mexican literature.

Anaya's most famous work, *Bless Me, Ultima*, is the classic novel of growing up in New Mexico. In our excerpt, Tony, the young narrator, experiences his very first day of school; through Tony, the author treats the themes of language, identity, and assimilation.

from *Bless Me, Ultima*

On the first day of school I awoke with a sick feeling in my stomach. It did not hurt, it just made me feel weak. The sun did not sing as it came over the hill. Today I would take the goat path and trek into town for years and years of schooling. For the first time I would be away from the protection of my mother. I was excited and sad about it.

I heard my mother enter her kitchen, her realm in the castle the giants had built. I heard her make the fire grow and sing with the kindling she fed to it.

Then I heard my father groan. "*¡Ay Dios, otro día!* Another day and more miles of that cursed highway to patch! And for whom? For me that I might travel west! Ay no, that highway is not for the poor man, it is for the tourist—ay María, we should have gone to California when we were young, when my sons were boys—"

He was sad. The breakfast dishes rattled.

"Today is Antonio's first day at school," she said.

"Huh! Another expense. In California, they say, the land flows with milk and honey—"

"Any land will flow with milk and honey if it is worked with honest hands!" my mother retorted. "Look at what my brothers have done with the bottomland of El Puerto—"

"Ay, *mujer,* always your brothers! On this hill only rocks grow!"

"Ay! And whose fault is it that we bought a worthless hill! No, you couldn't buy fertile land along the river, you had to buy this piece of, of—"

"Of the *llano,*" my father finished.

"Yes!"

"It is beautiful," he said with satisfaction.

"It is worthless! Look how hard we worked on the garden all summer, and for what? Two baskets of chile and one of corn! Bah!"

"There is freedom here."

"Try putting that in the lunch pails of your children!"

"Tony goes to school today, huh?" he said.

"Yes. And you must talk to him."

"He will be all right."

"He must know the value of his education," she insisted. "He must know what he can become."

"A priest."

"Yes."

"For your brothers." His voice was cold.

"You leave my brothers out of this! They are honorable men. They have always treated you with respect. They were the first colonizers of the Llano Estacado. It was the Lunas who carried the charter from the Mexican government to settle the valley. That took courage—"

"Led by the priest," my father interrupted. I listened intently. I did not yet know the full story of the first Luna priest.

"What? What did you say? Do not dare to mention blasphemy where the children can hear, Gabriel Márez!" She scolded him and chased him out of the kitchen. "Go feed the animals! Give Tony a few minutes extra sleep!" I heard him laugh as he went out.

"My poor baby," she whispered, and then I heard her praying. I heard Deborah and Theresa getting up. They were excited about school because they had already been there. They dressed and ran downstairs to wash.

I heard Ultima enter the kitchen. She said good morning to my mother and turned to help prepare breakfast. Her sound in the kitchen gave me the courage I needed to leap out of bed and into the freshly pressed clothes my mother had readied for me. The new shoes felt strange to feet that had run bare for almost seven years.

"Ay! My man of learning!" my mother smiled when I entered the kitchen. She swept me in her arms and before I knew it she was crying on my shoulder. "My baby will be gone today," she sobbed.

"He will be all right," Ultima said. "The sons must leave the sides of their mothers," she said almost sternly and pulled my mother gently.

"Yes, Grande," my mother nodded, "it's just that he is so small—the last one to leave me—" I thought she would cry all over again. "Go and wash, and comb," she said simply.

I scrubbed my face until it was red. I wet my black hair and combed it. I looked at my dark face in the mirror.

Jasón had said there were secrets in the letters. What did he mean?

"Antoniooooo! Come and eat."

"Tony goes to school, Tony goes to school!" Theresa cried.

"Hush! He shall be a scholar," my mother smiled and served me first. I tried to eat but the food stuck to the roof of my mouth.

"Remember you are a Luna—"

"And a Márez," my father interrupted her. He came in from feeding the animals.

Deborah and Theresa sat aside and divided the school supplies they had bought in town the day before. Each got a Red Chief tablet, crayons, and pencils. I got nothing. "We are ready, Mamá!" they cried.

Jasón had said, look at the letter carefully, draw it on the tablet, or on the sand of the playground. You will see, it has magic.

"You are to bring honor to your family," my mother cautioned. "Do nothing that will bring disrespect on our good name."

I looked at Ultima. Her magic. The magic of Jasón's Indian. They could not save me now.

"Go immediately to Miss Maestas. Tell her you are my boy. She knows my family. Hasn't she taught them all? Deborah, take him to Miss Maestas."

"Gosh, okay, let's go."

"Ay! What good does an education do them," my father filled his coffee cup. "They only learn to speak like Indians. Gosh, okay, what kind of words are those?"

"An education will make him a scholar, like—like the old Luna priest."

"A scholar already, on his first day of school!"

"Yes!" my mother retorted. "You know the signs at his birth were good. You remember, Grande, you offered him all the objects of life when he was just a baby, and what did he choose, the pen and the paper—"

"True," Ultima agreed.

"*¡Bueno! ¡Bueno!*" my father gave in to them. "If that is what he is to be then it is so. A man cannot struggle against his own fate. In my own day we were given no schooling. Only the *ricos* could afford school. Me, my father gave me a saddle blanket and a wild pony when I was ten. There is your life, he said, and he pointed to the *llano*. So the *llano* was my school, it was my teacher, it was my first love—"

"It is time to go, Mamá," Deborah interrupted.

"Ay, but those were beautiful years," my father continued. "The *llano* was still virgin, there was grass as high as the stirrups of a grown horse, there was rain— and then the *tejano* came and built his fences, the railroad came, the roads—it was like a bad wave of the ocean covering all that was good—"

"Yes, it is time, Gabriel," my mother said, and I noticed she touched him gently.

"Yes," my father answered, "so it is. Be respectful to your teachers," he said to us. "And you, Antonio," he smiled, *"suerte."* It made me feel good. Like a man.

"Wait!" My mother held Deborah and Theresa back, "we must have a blessing. Grande, please bless my children." She made us kneel with her in front of Ultima. "And especially bless my Antonio, that all may go well for him and that he may be a man of great learning—"

Even my father knelt for the blessing. Huddled in the kitchen we bowed our heads. There was no sound.

"En el nombre del Padre, del Hijo, y el Espíritu Santo—"

I felt Ultima's hand on my head and at the same time I felt a great force, like a whirlwind, swirl about me. I looked up in fright thinking the wind would knock me off my knees. Ultima's bright eyes held me still.

In the summer the dust devils of the *llano* are numerous. They come from nowhere, made by the heat of hell. They carry with them the evil spirit of a devil, they lift sand and papers in their path. It is bad luck to let one of these small whirlwinds strike you. But it is easy to ward off the dust devil, it is easy to make it change its path and skirt around you. The power of God is so great. All you have to do is to lift up your right hand and cross your right thumb over your first finger in the form of the cross. No evil can challenge that cross, and the swirling dust with the devil inside must turn away from you.

Once I did not make the sign of the cross on purpose. I challenged the wind to strike me. The twister struck with such force that it knocked me off my feet and

left me trembling on the ground. I had never felt such fear before, because as the whirlwind blew its debris around me the gushing wind seemed to call my name:

Antonioooooooooooooooo . . .

Then it was gone, and its evil was left imprinted on my soul.

"¡Antonio!"

"What?"

"Do you feel well? Are you all right?" It was my mother speaking.

But how could the blessing of Ultima be like the whirlwind? Was the power of good and evil the same?

"You may stand up now." My mother helped me to my feet. Deborah and Theresa were already out the door. The blessing was done. I stumbled to my feet, picked up my sack lunch, and started towards the door.

"Tell me, Grande, please," my mother begged.

"María!" my father said sternly.

"Oh, please tell me what my son will be," my mother glanced anxiously from me to Ultima.

"He will be a man of learning," Ultima said sadly.

"¡Madre de Dios!" my mother cried and crossed herself. She turned to me and shouted, "Go! Go!"

I looked at the three of them standing there, and I felt that I was seeing them for the last time: Ultima in her wisdom, my mother in her dream, and my father in his rebellion.

"¡Adios!" I cried and ran out. I followed the two she-goats hopping up the path ahead of me. They sang and I brayed into the morning air, and the pebbles of the path rang as we raced with time towards the bridge. Behind me I heard my mother cry my name.

At the big juniper tree where the hill sloped to the bridge I heard Ultima's owl sing. I knew it was her owl because it was singing in daylight. High at the top by a clump of the ripe blue berries of the juniper I saw it. Its bright eyes looked down on me and it cried, whoooo, whoooo. I took confidence from its song and, wiping the tears from my eyes, I raced towards the bridge, the link to town.

I was almost halfway across the bridge when someone called "Race!" I turned and saw a small, thin figure start racing towards me from the far end of the bridge. I recognized the Vitamin Kid.

Race? He was crazy! I was almost halfway across. "Race!" I called, and ran. I found out that morning that no one had ever beaten the Vitamin Kid across the bridge, his bridge. I was a good runner and I ran as hard as I could, but just before I reached the other side the clatter of hoofbeats passed me by, the Kid smiled a "Hi Tony," and snorting and leaving a trail of saliva threads in the air, he was gone.

No one knew the Vitamin Kid's real name, no one knew where he lived. He seemed older than the rest of the kids he went to school with. He never stopped long enough to talk, he was always on the run, a blur of speed.

I walked slowly after I crossed the bridge, partly because I was tired and partly because of the dread of school. I walked past Rosie's house, turned, and passed in

front of the Longhorn Saloon. When I got to Main Street I was astounded. It seemed as if a million kids were shoutinggruntingpushingcrying their way to school. For a long time I was held hypnotized by the thundering herd, then with a cry of resolution exploding from my throat I rushed into the melee.

Somehow I got to the schoolgrounds, but I was lost. The school was larger than I had expected. Its huge, yawning doors were menacing. I looked for Deborah and Theresa, but every face I saw was strange. I looked again at the doors of the sacred halls but I was too afraid to enter. My mother had said to go to Miss Maestas, but I did not know where to begin to find her. I had come to the town, and I had come to school, and I was very lost and afraid in the nervous, excited swarm of kids.

It was then that I felt a hand on my shoulder. I turned and looked into the eyes of a strange red-haired boy. He spoke English, a foreign tongue.

"First grade," was all I could answer. He smiled and took my hand, and with him I entered school. The building was cavernous and dark. It had strange, unfamiliar smells and sounds that seemed to gurgle from its belly. There was a big hall and many room, and many mothers with children passed in and out of the rooms.

I wished for my mother, but I put away the thought because I knew I was expected to become a man. A radiator snapped with steam and I jumped. The red-haired boy laughed and led me into one of the rooms. This room was brighter than the hall. So it was like this that I entered school.

Miss Maestas was a kind woman. She thanked the boy whose name was Red for bringing me in, then asked my name. I told her I did not speak English.

"*¿Cómo te llamas?*" she asked.

"Antonio Márez," I replied. I told her my mother said I should see her, and that my mother sent her regards.

She smiled. "Anthony Márez," she wrote in a book. I drew closer to look at the letters formed by her pen. "Do you want to learn to write?" she asked.

"Yes," I answered.

"Good," she smiled.

I wanted to ask her immediately about the magic in the letters, but that would be rude and so I was quiet. I was fascinated by the black letters that formed on the paper and made my name. Miss Maestas gave me a crayon and some paper and I sat in the corner and worked at copying my name over and over. She was very busy the rest of the day with the other children that came to the room. Many cried when their mothers left, and one wet his pants. I sat in my corner alone and wrote. By noon I could write my name, and when Miss Maestas discovered that she was very pleased.

She took me to the front of the room and spoke to the other boys and girls. She pointed at me but I did not understand her. Then the other boys and girls laughed and pointed at me. I did not feel so good. Thereafter I kept away from the groups as much as I could and worked alone. I worked hard. I listened to the strange sounds. I learned new names, new words.

At noon we opened our lunches to eat. Miss Maestas left the room and a high school girl came and sat at the desk while we ate. My mother had packed a small

jar of hot beans and some good, green chile wrapped in tortillas. When the other children saw my lunch they laughed and pointed again. Even the high school girl laughed. They showed me their sandwiches which were made of bread. Again I did not feel well.

I gathered my lunch and slipped out of the room. The strangeness of the school and the other children made me very sad. I did not understand them. I sneaked around the back of the school building, and standing against the wall I tried to eat. But I couldn't. A huge lump seemed to form in my throat and tears came to my eyes. I yearned for my mother, and at the same time I understood that she had sent me to this place where I was an outcast. I had tried hard to learn and they had laughed at me. I had opened my lunch to eat and again they had laughed and pointed at me.

The pain and sadness seemed to spread to my soul, and I felt for the first time what the grownups call, *la tristeza de la vida*. I wanted to run away, to hide, to run and never come back, never see anyone again. But I knew that if I did I would shame my family name, that my mother's dream would crumble. I knew I had to grow up and be a man, but oh it was so very hard.

But no, I was not alone. Down the wall near the corner I saw two others boys who had sneaked out of the room. They were George and Willy. There were big boys, I knew they were from the farms of Delia. We banded together and in our union found strength. We found a few others who were like us, different in language and custom, and a part of our loneliness was gone. When the winter set in we moved into the auditorium and there, although many a meal was eaten in complete silence, we felt we belonged. We struggled against the feeling of loneliness that gnawed at our souls and we overcame it; that feeling I never shared again with anyone, not even with Horse and Bones, or the Kid and Samuel, or Cico or Jasón.

Pat Mora

These two sensitive poems by Pat Mora express, respectively, the determined struggle of an older woman to learn English ("Señora X No More"), and the reflections of a grown daughter on her mother's childhood, courage in coping with a new language, and success in adapting to a new culture ("A Voice"), both from *Communion* (Houston: Arte Público Press, 1991).

Señora X No More

Straight as a nun I sit.
My fingers foolish before paper and pen
hide in my palms. I hear the slow, accented echo
            How are yu? I ahm fine. How are yu?
of the other women who clutch notebooks
and blush at their stiff lips resisting
sounds that float gracefully as
bubbles from their children's mouths.
My teacher bends over me, gently squeezes
my shoulders, the squeeze I give my sons,
hands louder than words.
She slides her arms around me:
a warm shawl, lifts my left arm
onto the cold, lined paper.
"*Señora*, don't let it slip away," she says
and opens the ugly, soap-wrinkled fingers
of my right hand with a pen like I pry open
the lips of a stubborn grandchild.
My hand cramps around the thin hardness.
"Let it breathe," says this woman who knows
my hand and tongue knot, but she guides
and I dig the tip of my pen into that white.
I carve my crooked name, and again at night
until my hand and arm are sore,
I carve my crooked name,
my name.

A Voice

Even the lights on the stage unrelenting
as the desert sun couldn't hide the other
students, their eyes also unrelenting,
students who spoke English every night

as they ate their meat, potatoes, gravy.
Not you. In your house that smelled like
rose powder, you spoke Spanish formal
as your father, the judge without a courtroom

in the country he floated to in the dark
on a flatbed truck. He walked slow
as a hot river down the narrow hall
of your house. You never dared to race past him,

to say, "Please move," in the language
you learned effortlessly, as you learned to run,
the language forbidden at home, though your mother
said you learned it to fight with the neighbors.

You liked winning with words. You liked
writing speeches about patriotism and democracy.
You liked all the faces looking at you, all those eyes.
"How did I do it?" you ask me now. "How did I do it

when my parents didn't understand?"
The family story says your voice is the voice
of an aunt in Mexico, spunky as a peacock.
Family stories sing of what lives in the blood.

You told me only once about the time you went
to the state capitol, your family proud as if
you'd been named governor. But when you looked
around, the only Mexican in the auditorium,

you wanted to hide from those strange faces.
Their eyes were pinpricks, and you faked
hoarseness. You, who are never at a loss
for words, felt your breath stick in your throat

like an ice cube. "I can't," you whispered.
"I can't." Yet you did. Not that day but years later.
You taught the four of us to speak up.
This is America, Mom. The undoable is done

in the next generation. Your breath moves
through the family like wind
moves through the trees.

Viviana Carballo

Viviana Carballo has created a special niche for herself through her skill as a chef and her talent for associating cuisine with identity, both personal and cultural. Carballo, who earned the prestigious Grand Diplome at the Cordon Bleu in Paris, worked as a chef and ran a catering business in New York before moving to California, where she also worked as a chef and developed recipes for companies such as General Mills, Kraft, and NutraSweet. Currently, Carballo lives in Miami, where she is resident chef for "Club Telemundo", a Spanish-language television show, and author of a cooking column that appears in the *Miami Herald* and *El Nuevo Herald*.

In the brief interview that follows, Carballo describes the cultural and culinary ingredients of Cuban and Caribbean cooking and includes two essential recipes for us to enjoy.

Interview and Recipes

I've always been interested in food and in cooking, ever since I was a child in Havana. I loved to be in the kitchen. Of course, they never let me actually do anything, but at least they let me play there amid all the activities and aromas. Some of my fondest memories and cultural identifications I associate with the kitchen and with typical dishes. I guess that's not too surprising because food is an emotional and personal topic, associated with family, community, ritual, offering, and celebration, prominent qualities in Caribbean culture.

Actually, there's really no such thing as Cuban cuisine; I mean, we have a few dishes, but that does not make a cuisine. We have no natives, because they were decimated by the Spaniards, so our influences are mostly Spanish and African. What we have is Caribbean cooking, which I like to describe as very opportunistic because it assimilates, integrates, and adapts all that it encounters, taking advantage of the availability of ingredients, resources, and time. The first inhabitants of the Caribbean were the Arawak and Carib Indians who hunted birds, fished, and cultivated corn and some root vegetables. They smoked and stewed their foods and are believed to have invented the barbecue.

After Columbus came waves of Spanish settlers, English pirates, Dutch merchants, French adventurers, African slaves to work in the sugarcane fields, and indentured servants from China and India. Each group contributed its own foodstuffs and methods of cooking. Caribbean cuisine is the result of evolution, invention, recreation, and cross-cultural integration. It extends far beyond lime juice and cilantro, offering surprising combinations in the rich, uninhibited bounty of the unexpected, such as the tamarind, mamey, mango, guava, plantain, yucca, and malanga.

Though Caribbean cooking is diverse, I see more similarities than differences in island cuisines. The commonalities are strong, distinctive tastes; rich textures; depth and complexity of flavors. Often, a certain island specialty is known by a different name elsewhere, and while there may be differences in spicing or seasoning, or in the addition or deletion of a certain ingredient, the basic preparation remains the same.

An example of a basic food whose preparation varies slightly is *ropa vieja,* old clothes, which is basically shredded beef cooked with onions, tomatoes, and garlic. Also, chicken with rice and any number of stews fall into this category. Perhaps the best example is *sofrito,* meaning lightly fried, which came from Spain and starts out with oil or lard, onions, garlic, and sometimes tomatoes and peppers in the Caribbean, but in Mexico it is dominated by a variety of chiles. Here's

a *sofrito* recipe to use with the *fricasé de pollo,* skillet chicken. Give it a try; it's a delicious, basic Caribbean dish.

It is the distinctive flavors and aromas of Caribbean cooking that express cultural and emotional identifications and associations while cutting across national borders. Cooking is in a class by itself as an indicator and reminder of where we come from and who we are.

Sofrito is the linchpin of Caribbean cooking, an indispensable preparation made simply of chopped and lightly sauteed vegetables. *Sofrito* forms a flavor base for many soups, stews, potages (thick bean soups), and almost everything else.

The word comes from the Spanish verb *freir,* to fry. *Sofreir* implies to lightly fry in a small quantity of fat. The method, too, is Spanish in origin. Though onion and garlic are always present, other ingredients—including the type of fat—vary widely from kitchen to kitchen. The Catalans have their *sofregit,* cooked very slowly to almost melting and used as a base for sauces. In Portuguese cooking, this basic preparation is known as *refogado.* In the Italian kitchen, it is called *soffritto* or *battuto* and includes celery and carrots.

In the Caribbean, the basic *sofrito* is sometimes referred to as *condimento molido* and *recao* or *recaito.* As with any *cocina del pueblo*—common, everyday cooking—recipes vary greatly. Almost all recipes in the Spanish Caribbean begin: *"Haga un sofrito con . . ."* or "Make a sofrito using . . ." Many cooks make their basic *sofrito* in large quantities and refrigerate to use as needed, adding different ingredients demanded by the particular dish being prepared. This allows greater flexibility in building layers of flavors and results in a wonderfully subtle and complex preparation.

For my taste, the best of these basic preparations is the Puerto Rican *sofrito.* This basic recipe is from my friend Aurelia Alvarez, who makes it in industrial quantities and ships it cross-country to her children and ex-husband. When she is cooking, she adjusts the recipe by adding the *alcaparrado,* or capers and pimiento-stuffed olives, along with tomato for any meat dish.

The essential ingredients are cilantro and culantro, distinguishing this *sofrito* from the Cuban version, which uses neither. Cilantro, also known as Chinese parsley, has a lacy leaf and looks like parsley. Culantro has a large leaf 2 to 5 inches long, dark green, broad, shiny and with ragged edges. Both plants have a similar aroma and taste, but culantro is stronger and more pungent. If you can't find culantro in the market, increase the amount of cilantro. But try to find and use the culantro; it's an interesting herb.

Aurelia's Sofrito

2 tablespoons olive oil
1 large onion, diced
1/2 green pepper, diced
1 *aji dulce,* diced (see note)
4 garlic cloves, minced
1/2 bunch cilantro, minced
3 culantro leaves, minced
1/2 teaspoon black pepper
1/2 teaspoon oregano

Heat oil in a frying pan and add the ingredients in the order listed. Cook for 15 to 20 minutes over low heat, stirring occasionally. If making a large batch, cook very slowly for about 1 hour and don't forget to stir often. Makes about 1 1/2 cups.

Optional: According to personal taste, you may add all, some, or none of the following ingredients. Experiment and change to suit your palate.

1 bay leaf
2 tablespoons *alcaparrado* (capers and pimiento stuffed olives)
1/2 cup diced fresh tomato or 1 tablespoon tomato paste
1/4 cup diced slab bacon
1/2 cup ground baked ham

Note: The *aji dulce* is a small ornamental chile also known as fiesta or fips. It is related to the cenne and Tabasco chiles. They vary in flavor from mild to sweet and intense and add just a touch of zip. You may substitute half a ripe jalapeño or Scotch bonnet pepper, though these two are both much hotter.

Fricasé de Pollo (Skillet Chicken)

This dish refrigerates well but loses flavor if frozen.

2 pounds chicken thighs and/or legs, skin removed
1 tablespoon olive oil
Salt, pepper and paprika to taste
2 tablespoons Aurelia's Sofrito
1/4 cup *alcaparrado* (capers and pimiento-stuffed olives)
1/4 cup tomato sauce
1/4 cup raisins
1/2 cup chicken broth

Heat olive oil in a frying pan over medium heat, then cook the chicken pieces until lightly browned. Pour off excess fat. Season with salt, pepper and paprika.

Add Aurelia's Sofrito and stir to coat the chicken. Add the rest of the ingredients, stir and cover. Cook over low heat about 30 minutes. Adjust seasoning and serve with white rice. Serves 4.

Carolina Hospital

In the following poem by Cuban American Carolina Hospital, we see the reluctant admission that the north is now more familiar than the south, and we wonder with the poet what this realization signifies with regard to "Finding Home" (in *Paradise Lost or Gained? The Literature of Hispanic Exile* [Houston: Arte Público Press, 1990]).

Finding Home

I have traveled north again,
to these gray skies
and empty doorways.
Fall, and I recognize
the rusted leaves descending
near the silence of your home.
You, a part of this strange
American landscape with its
cold dry winds,
the honks of geese and
the hardwood floors. It's more
familiar now than
the fluorescent rainbow on the overpass,
or the clatter of *politicos* in the corners,
or the palm fronds falling by the highway.
I must travel again, soon.

Gloria Anzaldúa

Texan Gloria Anzaldúa is a prominent lesbian feminist poet and writer of fiction who has coedited the prizewinning *This Bridge Called My Back: Writings by Radical Women of Color* (1981) and edited the volume *Making Face, Making Soul: Haciendo caras: Creative and Critical Perspectives by Women of Color* (San Francisco: Aunt Lute Book Co., 1990).

In "To live in the Borderlands means you . . . ," our reading from Anzaldúa's *Borderlands/La Frontera* (San Francisco: Aunt Lute Book Company, 1987), the poet describes her sense of alienation from both Mexican and United States culture, and offers a suggestion for how to "survive" in the borderlands.

To live in the Borderlands means you . . .

are neither *hispana india negra española*
ni gabacha, eres mestiza, mulata, half-breed
caught in the crossfire between camps
while carrying all five races on your back
not knowing which side to turn to, run from;

To live in the Borderlands means knowing
that the *india* in you, betrayed for 500 years,
is no longer speaking to you,
that *mexicanas* call you *rajetas,*
that denying the Anglo inside you
is as bad as having denied the Indian or Black;

Cuando vives en la frontera
people walk through you, the wind steals your voice,
you're a *burra, buey,* scapegoat,
forerunner of a new race,
half and half—both woman and man, neither—
a new gender;

To live in the Borderlands means to
put *chile* in the borscht,
eat whole wheat *tortillas,*
speak Tex-Mex with a Brooklyn accent;
be stopped by *la migra* at the border checkpoints;

Living in the Borderlands means you fight hard to
resist the gold elixir beckoning from the bottle,
the pull of the gun barrel,
the rope crushing the hollow of your throat;

In the Borderlands
you are the battleground
where enemies are kin to each other;

you are at home, a stranger,
the border disputes have been settled
the volley of shots have shattered the truce
you are wounded, lost in action
dead, fighting back;

To live in the Borderlands means
the mill with the razor white teeth wants to shred off
your olive-red skin, crush out the kernel, your heart
pound you pinch you roll you out
smelling like white bread but dead;

To survive the Borderlands
you must live *sin fronteras*
be a crossroads.

América Paredes

Master storyteller and pioneering folklorist, Américo Paredes wrote extensively on the customs, music, myths, and history of the Río Grande Valley. His writings include *The Hammon and the Beans and Other Stories* (Houston: Arte Público Press, 1994 edition), *George Washington Gómez* (Houston: Arte Público Press, 1993 edition), and *"With His Pistol in His Hand": A Border Ballad and Its Hero* (Austin, Tex.: University of Texas Press, 1958), the classic account of border hero Gregorio Cortéz and the source of our reading.

Gregorio Cortéz was a ranch hand who, because of a translator's error, was wrongly accused of stealing a horse, and who ended up killing a sheriff in an altercation. The dramatic story of Cortéz's flight, capture, trial, imprisonment, and ultimate pardon captured the imagination of Valley balladeers who, in an infinite number of variants, sang, and still sing, of the exploits of the outlaw/hero. The following reading describes the unique and deeply rooted oral tradition that has helped shape the cultural identity of the Valley, points out similarities and differences between the balladry of the Río Grande and that of Mexico and Europe, and reproduces the music and the words of one of the best-known variants of the "Ballad of Gregorio Cortéz."

from "With His Pistol in His Hand": A Border Ballad and Its Hero

"El Corrido de Gregorio Cortez" has been presented as a prototype of the *corrido* of border conflict, a ballad form developed on the lower border of the Rio Grande. There a ballad community much like those of medieval Europe existed during the nineteenth and the early part of the twentieth centuries. Cultural homogeneity, isolation, and a patriarchal, traditional way of life made the existence of a native folk balladry possible. In discussing the Spanish border ballad, Entwistle says that the earlier *romances fronterizos* were composed under "classic conditions of balladry," being the songs "of small communities, intensely preoccupied with their own immediate dangers and successes."[1]

The Lower Rio Grande communities were just these sorts of closely knit small groups, interested in their own affairs. Morley notes that most British ballads are of "limited, localized import."[2] Entwistle classifies the Montenegrin Serbs as a postmedieval folk because their social unit was a small one, the tribe or the family state. They had no elaborate society and were isolated in the mountains.[3] The isolated, patriarchal character of the Rio Grande folks has been mentioned.

Folklorists have also noted the democratic spirit in the folk communities of medieval Europe. Vicuña Cifuentes notes that the Castilians, in the times before Spain became an empire, "saw in each peasant an hidalgo" and that plebeians and nobles were identified in the same aims.[4] In the term *pueblo* Milá y Fontanals includes not only the Spanish peasants but the "military aristocracy, which was also uneducated and extremely rude."[5] The border *ranchero* also lived in a rude and egalitarian society.

The nonliterate character of the folk does not need documentary support. Balladry, like most other folk arts, depends on a society that finds its entertainment in oral form. It went into decline in Europe when the habit of reading for religious purposes, and then for entertainment, became widespread. The lower border people were not Bible readers, and they preferred the oral to the written word.

The Lower Rio Grande people lived under conditions in which folk cultures develop. They lived in isolation from the main currents of world events. They preferred to live in small, tightly knit communities that were interested in their own problems. Their type of social organization was the family holding or the communal village, ruled by patriarchal authority under a kind of pre–eighteenth-century democracy. And their forms of entertainment were oral. But they were not unique in this respect. Other frontier areas of New Spain, such as New Mexico,

produced folk communities of the same type. The New Mexican folk communities are much older, and they preserved their isolated, individual character much longer than did the communities of the lower border. New Mexico, however, did not develop a balladry of a distinctively heroic type. Like most modern ballad areas, it maintained for the most part the traditions brought over from Europe.

It is my belief that before 1836 a balladry of the New Mexican type existed along the Lower Rio Grande, and all evidence available supports this theory. What subsequently made the balladry of the lower border different was the Texas Revolution and the annexation by Texas of the Nueces–Rio Grande part of the old province of Nuevo Santander, one-half of the home area of the Lower Rio Grande people. Thus a border was created, and the bitterness resulting from events that occurred between 1836 and 1848 provided the basis for a century of conflict.

In the histories of European balladries one finds the heroic ballad also arising in frontier areas where small, cohesive folk groups are in conflict with another people. The *romance,* direct ancestor of the lower border *corrido*, developed in Castile, where the efforts to reconquer Spain from the Moors came to a focus, and where border conflicts were daily fare for centuries. Scottish balladry also was of border origin. In Russia the *bylini* arose from the border struggles of the Russians against the nomads of the steppes. Entwistle speaks of the Akritic age in Greek balladry as "the oldest stratum of European balladry: an age when the Greek frontier was on the Euphrates and the Saracens were their enemies."[6] It would appear then that the "oldest stratum of European balladry" was also a balladry of border warfare.

The Rio Grande ballads had as their immediate models the ballad forms brought over from Spain. In its verse form, language, and objectivity of style and its restriction for the most part to men singers, the border *corrido* resembles its ancestor, the Castilian *romance.* Occasionally one finds reminiscences not of the Spanish marches but of the Scottish border country, in tone and emphasis and in the way the hero and his background are seen by the ballad-maker. The tradition and the ballad patterns are Castilian, but the social and physical conditions of the border *corrido* were more like those of Scotland. Unlike the Spaniards, but like the Scots, the Russians, and the Greeks, the border ballad people ended on the losing side of their conflict. Unlike the Russians and the Greeks, but again like the Scots, the border people were not engulfed by an alien invasion. They were plagued over a long period of years by a comparatively small number of invaders, who settled down among them, often learned their language, and picked up many of their habits, and who could have been defeated but for the protection of a powerful state and a strong army. Again like the Scots, the border people were faced by a more numerous people with a more advanced technology. The Texan's six-shooter had its counterpart in the Englishman's longbow. If the Scot was able to mount a strong attack and score some local victories, he always lost in the end to a superior army from the south. The same situation faced the Mexican border raiders. It was the Scot, usually on the losing side, who produced the most stirring of the British border ballads. On the Rio Grande it was only the losers in the conflict, the border Mexicans, who produced ballads.

In sum, the balladry of the Rio Grande border was not like the Castilian, a border balladry of military victory, but like the Scottish, one of the resistance against outside encroachment. The Russians and the Greeks also had balladries of the resistance rather than the victory type. But like the Spanish, they took a more national view of their struggles on the frontier. Castilian counts, Russian princes, and Greek generals led armies against the foe. The conflict on the Rio Grande, like that on the Scottish border, was most often on an individual rather than a national scale. The fighters operated in small bands, or they were individual fighting men. Morley thinks that an important difference between the *romance* and the British ballad is that the British ballad is "of limited, localized import."[7] The British ballad poetizes the exploits and the feuds of individuals rather than of nations. Its heroes were scarcely known in their own day outside a narrow region. The same may be said of the *corrido* of the lower border.

Here is a balladry, resembling in many respects that of medieval Europe, which developed partly in the twentieth century, within the memory of living men. Though it flourished independently of newspapers and other written material, it existed side by side with them, allowing many opportunities for a comparison of written records and oral tradition, something not always possible with medieval balladry. "Gregorio Cortez" and the ballad tradition it represents offer some living evidence concerning points that have been discussed by scholars in relation to the balladries of the past. One sees the effect of social conditions in the development of the balladry of the lower border. A type of society similar to that of the European folk groups of the Middle Ages produced a balladry similar to that of medieval Europe. The importance of border conflict in the development of heroic balladry is illustrated. One also sees evidence of the emergence of a dominant ballad form (given sufficient time) that replaces or assimilates other forms. Before the border-conflict period, it was the *décima* and to a lesser extent the *copla* that were the ballad forms native to the Rio Grande people, as they were to other peoples of Mexican descent. With the *corrido* also came the *danza,* another competitor. Toward the end of the ballad period on the border, the *corrido* is dominant and has begun to replace the other ballad forms. In response to conditions similar to those which produced the *romance* in Spain, the dormant, half-forgotten *romance* tradition in America revived in the *corrido* and was well on the way to becoming a uniform corpus when the ballad period ended.

In the variants of "El Corrido de Gregorio Cortez" one has concrete evidence of the ballad tendency to develop from comparatively long originals into shorter variants. Since "Gregorio Cortez" obviously could not have been composed before 1901, its rich development of variants has taken place within a surprisingly short time, fifty years at the most. The collective imagination of the *guitarreros* and other gifted ballad singers has carved short, rounded compositions out of the longer ballad much as the action of a stream turns a rough, jagged stone into a smooth pebble. In both cases the time consumed in the transformation is less important than the ductility of the material and the amount of friction brought to bear. One often thinks that the old European ballads took centuries to go

through their changes. But a ballad sung constantly by a large group of people, learned and relearned by singers of varying talents, a ballad which is part of the life of a folk group as a whole, may change more rapidly in forty years than one preserved by a few singers may change in two hundred. Some of the ancient ballads may well have undergone their important changes in forty or fifty years.

A question that should be of interest to Mexican ballad students is the place that "El Corrido de Gregorio Cortez" and the border tradition that it represents should occupy in the whole of Mexican balladry. Unaware, it seems, of the existence of a well-established *corrido* tradition on the Lower Rio Grande, Mexican ballad scholars have viewed the *corrido*'s appearance among the Spanish-speaking people of the United States as a late manifestation. Professor Mendoza says of the Greater Mexican *corrido* in the United States: "In the border states of the South and in the industrial cities of the North, such as Detroit . . . it has given rise to the creation and the derivation of new types, which already begin to show local characteristics."[8] Mendoza's statements, made in 1954, are true enough as they refer to other parts of the Southwest and to the large cities of the North, where the *corrido* is truly a late importation, brought in with the *braceros* that have come from Mexico. On the Lower Rio Grande, however, we have a *corrido* tradition that is at least as old as the Greater Mexican, if not older.

It may even be that the Greater Mexican heroic *corrido* has been influenced by the border heroic tradition which "El Corrido de Gregorio Cortez" epitomizes. Some data has been given in support of this assumption. It must remain nothing more than an assumption, however, because there is not yet sufficient material available to arrive at any sort of conclusions. The balladry of the lower border of the Rio Grande needs further investigation. A more complete collection not only of oral variants but of old manuscripts, documentary references to ballads, and like data is still needed. The balladry of Greater Mexico has received the attention of some very able literary historians and musicians, but they have concentrated their efforts to a great extent on the collection of broadside material and ballads from other nontraditional sources. In Greater Mexico much remains to be done in the collection of oral variants in the field. The fact remains though, that both on the border and in Greater Mexico the *corrido* springs from the roots of the *romance*, gaining hegemony over the *décima*, as a result of special conditions, border conflict in the one case and the Mexican Revolution in the other. The necessary conditions were present on the lower border many years before they appeared in Greater Mexico. The heroic tradition is already in full vigor in "El Corrido de Gregorio Cortez" ten years before the Revolution.

It was a peculiar set of conditions, prevailing for a century, that produced the lower border *corrido*, an international phenomenon straddling the boundary between Mexico and the United States and partaking of influences from both cultures. The most important single influence on the border *corrido* was the *romance*, though it owes a great deal to the Greater Mexican balladry as well. But the English-speaking culture also had its influence on border balladry. The Anglo-American served first of all as a reacting agent. The most important ballads produced on

the border have to do with cattle driving and interracial struggles. The Anglo-American influenced the border *corrido* in other ways. The concept of the *corrido* hero, pistol in hands, is "in the American style," as "El Corrido de Cananea" puts it. The English language affected the *corrido,* as can be seen in "Gregorio Cortez." And the border Mexican's attitudes about the Anglo-American and his customs became part of border folklore. The American folklorist, particularly the folklorist of Texas, finds the balladry of the lower border as much his province as that of the Mexican ballad student. Transcending national boundaries, the border heroic *corrido* belongs to Texas as much as to Mexico. A product of past conflicts, it may eventually serve as one of the factors in a better understanding.

El Corrido de Gregorio Cortez

1

En el condado de Carnes	In the county of Karnes,
miren lo que ha sucedido,	Look what has happened;
murió el Cherife Mayor	The Major Sheriff died,
quedando Román herido.	Leaving Román badly wounded.

2

Serían las dos de la tarde	It must have been two in the afternoon
cuando la gente llegó,	When people arrived;
unos a los otros dicen:	They said to one another,
—No saben quién lo mató.	"It is not known who killed him."

3

Se anduvieron informando	They went around asking questions,
como media hora después,	About half an hour afterward,
supieron que el malhechor	They found that the wrongdoer
era Gregorio Cortez.	Had been Gregorio Cortez.

4

Ya insortaron a Cortez	Now they have outlawed Cortez,
por todito el estado,	Throughout the whole state;
que vivo o muerto se aprehenda	Let him be taken, dead or alive;
porque a varios ha matadao.	He has killed several men.

5

Decía Gregorio Cortez
con su pisola en la mano:
—No siento haberlo matado,
lo que siento es a mi hermano.

Then said Gregorio Cortez,
With his pistol in his hand,
"I don't regret that I killed him;
I regret my brother's death."

6

Decía Gregorio Cortez
con su alma muy encendida:
—No siento haberlo matado,
la defensa es permitida.

Then said Gregorio Cortez,
And his soul was all aflame,
"I don't regret that I killed him;
A man must defend himself."

7

Venían los americanos
más blancos que una paloma,
de miedo que le tenían
a Cortez y a su pistola.

The Americans were coming,
They were whiter than a dove,
From the fear that they had
Of Cortez and of his pistol.

8

Decían los americanos,
decían con timidez:
—Vamos a seguir la huella
que el malhechor es Cortez.

Then the Americans said,
Then they said fearfully,
"Come, let us follow the trail;
The wrongdoer is Cortez."

9

Le echaron los perros jaunes
pa' que siguieran la huella,
pero alcanzar a Cortez
era seguir a una estrella.

They set the bloodhounds on him,
So they could follow his trail,
But trying to overtake Cortez
Was like following a star.

10

Tiró con rumbo a Gonzales
sin ninguna timidez:
—Síganme rinches cobardes,
yo soy Gregorio Cortez.

He struck out for Gonzales
Without showing any fear,
"Follow me, cowardly rangers,
I am Gregorio Cortez."

11

Se fué de Belmont al rancho,
lo alcanzaron a rodear,
poquitos más de trescientos,
y allí les brincó el corral.

From Belmont he went to the ranch,
They succeeded in surrounding him,
Quite a few more than three hundred,
But there he jumped their corral.

12

Cuando les brincó el corral,
según lo que aquí se dice,
se agarraron a balazos
y les mató otro cherife.

When he jumped their corral,
According to what we hear,
They got into a gunfight,
And he killed them another sheriff.

13

Decía Gregorio Cortez	Then said Gregorio Cortez,
con su pisola en la mano:	With his pistol in his hand,
—No corran, rinches cobardes,	"Don't run, you cowardly rangers,
con un solo mexicano.	From just one Mexican."

14

Salió Gregorio Cortez,	Gregorio Cortez went out,
salió con rumbo a Laredo,	He went toward Laredo
no lo quisieron seguir	They decided not to follow
porque le tuvieron miedo.	Because they were afraid of him.

15

Decía Gregorio Cortez,	Then said Gregorio Cortez,
—¿Pa' qué se valen de planes?	"What is the use of your scheming?
No me pueden agarrar	You cannot catch me,
ni con esos perros jaunes.	Even with those bloodhounds."

16

Decían los americanos:	Then the Americans said,
—Si lo alcanzamos ¿qué haremos?	"If we catch up with him, what shall we do?
Si le entramos por derecho	If we fight him man to man,
muy poquitos volveremos.	Very few of us will return."

17

Allá por El Encinal,	Over by El Encinal,
según lo que aquí se dice,	According to what we hear,
le formaron un corral	They made him a corral,
y les mató otro cherife.	And he killed them another sheriff.

18

Decía Gregorio Cortez	Then said Gregorio Cortez,
echando muchos balazos:	Shooting out a lot of bullets,
—Me he escapado de aguaceros,	"I have weathered thunderstorms;
contimás de nublinazos.	This little mist doesn't bother me."

19

Ya se encontró a un mexicano,	Now he has met a Mexican;
le dice con altivez:	He says to him haughtily,
—Platícame qué hay de nuevo,	"Tell me the news;
yo soy Gregorio Cortez.	I am Gregorio Cortez."

20

—Dicen que por culpa mía	"It is said that because of me
han matado mucha gente,	Many people have been killed;
ya me voy a presentar	I will surrender now
porque eso no es conveniente.	Because such things are not right."

21

Cortez le dice a Jesús	Cortez says to Jesús,
—Ora sí lo vas a ver,	"At last you are going to see it;
anda diles a los rinches	Go tell the rangers
que me vengan a aprehender.	To come and arrest me."

22

Venían todos los rinches,	All the rangers were coming,
venían que hasta volaban	Coming so fast they even flew,
porque se iban a ganar	For they wanted to get
los mil pesos que les daban.	The thousand dollars they were offered.

23

Cuando rodearon la casa	When they surrounded the house,
Cortez se les presentó:	Cortez suddenly appeared before them,
—Por la buena sí me llevan	"You will take me if I'm willing,
porque de otro modo no.	But not any other way."

24

Decía el Cherife Mayor	Then the Major Sheriff said,
como queriendo llorar:	As if he was going to cry,
—Cortez entrega tus armas,	"Cortez, hand over your weapons;
no te vamos a matar.	We are not going to kill you."

25

Decía Gregorio Cortez,	Then said Gregorio Cortez,
les gritaba en alta voz:	Shouting to them in a loud voice,
—Mis armas no las entrego	"I won't surrender my arms
hasta estar en calaboz'.	Until I am in a cell."

26

Decía Gregorio Cortez,	Then said Gregorio Cortez,
decía en su voz divina,	He said in his godly voice,
—Mis armas no las entrego	"I won't surrender my arms
hasta estar en bartolina.	Until I'm inside a jail."

27

Ya agarraron a Cortez,	Now they have taken Cortez,
ya terminó la cuestión,	Now matters are at an end;
la pobre de su familia	His poor family
lo lleva en el corazón.	Are suffering in their hearts.

28

Ya con ésta me despido	Now with this I say farewell,
a la sombra de un ciprés,	In the shade of a cypress tree;
aquí se acaba cantando	This is the end of the singing
el corrido de Cortez.	Of the ballad of Cortez.

Father Jerome Martínez

Father Jerome Martínez is a devoted student and exponent of New Mexican cultural history. In this interview, he describes the settlement and development of the state, the mentality of the New Mexican people, their sense of rootedness, and the particular values and historical experiences that have shaped their strong sense of identity.

Interview

I am a native New Mexican. My family, as far as I have been able to trace the genealogy, goes back at least ten generations. They were "Martín" after the conquest of this area by the United States. During the census many names were changed—that was very typical of what happened on Ellis Island too. My family changed to Martínez, which was more common—that's why there are so many Martínezes in New Mexico. Through church documents I've been able to do some research on this back to 1680, the time of the Pueblo Indian revolt. My father has a fond saying, "We never crossed the border; one day the border crossed us." In other words, we were first part of the Spanish empire as Hispanics, and then part of the República Mexicana, and then later on, by conquest, we became part of the United States. I think it's important to understand that makes us very different from any of the other people who inhabit the United States. They're an immigrant society; that is, they chose to leave their ancestral homeland and come here, as did our ancestors originally, but so far off in the remote past that it's hardly a collective memory. But many of my classmates in seminary are third, second, first generation; I mean, they can remember grandparents and great-grandparents who just came over on the boat. Theirs is an immigrant mentality where people actually leave the home country to make a whole new beginning here, and in a sense, forsake all that they have left behind to start anew. It's very different here, where we were a conquered people, and we became assimilated to a country that we had no desire to be part of. We also wanted to maintain our culture and our traditions and our language; that's a very important key to the New Mexican mentality.

The whole myth of Aztlán as a rediscovery of Aztec culture is a phenomenon of this century, and it has very little to do with the historical consciousness of Spanish-speaking peoples up to this century. In a sense, it is also part of the Mexicans' attempt to create a history. I'm not saying that's invalid, but one has to take it with a grain of salt. The Aztecs were a great people, but they were also butchers, and they were not the greatest of the indigenous peoples who lived in the valley of Mexico. Certainly, the Toltecs were far greater. The Mexican government's attempt to erase three hundred years of history under Spanish rule is understandable, but it is also pretty intellectually illegitimate. We are a combination of two, and we have to appreciate and understand how they mixed and created a third people. Here, in New Mexico, Aztlán, the recapturing of our Aztec ancestry and noble lineage—well, it's forced. I dare say it may be forced elsewhere where you have a culture that's been here so long, that antedated the American conquest, that antedated Mexican independence. It's a little forced.

There are some key differences between the Hispanic populations in California and New Mexico. I think those Hispanics who antedated the Mexican defeat in California were quickly overwhelmed by the flood of people who came there, especially for the gold rushes. They were criminally displaced in the new culture, and they became very rapidly a kind of marginalized minority. They would be using this consciousness about Aztlán or anything else to reclaim their heritage. They are angry, they haven't been heard from, they are voiceless. Here, because New Mexico is an unforgiving climate, it's very hard for us to make a living. Americans did not flood in. There was no gold, no agricultural community here; there was nothing. As a consequence, up until this century, the Hispanic population was still a majority, and this is not to say that there was not some suffering and some incredible injustices that were committed on the part of the American conquerors, especially at the time of the Treaty of Guadalupe Hidalgo. There were the displacements of whole peoples, the taking away of the land grants, the disenfranchizing from voting, the denial of the permission guaranteed under the treaty of Guadalupe Hidalgo to return to Mexico—but it was not permitted because so many people applied.

One thing you have to say for New Mexicans, they learned the politics fast; we are a very political—not politicized—people. Some of the first governors of New Mexico were Spanish-speaking: the first governors of the territory, and the first governors of the state. To this date 40 percent of the New Mexico legislature is Hispanic, and the clergy is Hispanic in great numbers. In other words, we learned to play the system well because we learned that we have to survive, and since there was not a flood of Anglos, we became an important part of the political system. We voted; we still vote—that was seen as the way to get on the school board, or whatever. We also became educated; we became teachers. My grandfather, for example, never went to formal school, but he taught himself to read. He bought the Encyclopedia Britannica and read it from cover to cover, all twenty-four volumes at the time, passed the examination to become a school teacher, taught school, then taught himself to be a lawyer. Education was seen as the key. So, no, we are not as angry I would say as *californios* or *tejanos* would be, because we haven't gone through the same experience, but we are skeptical and reserved. We have been burned, and, as a consequence, there is kind of a latent resentment about the white people coming in to take the church away, at least the institutional part of it, and sometimes they have taken governments away. So, there's resentment, especially in small communities.

You can't believe how unjust it was when the land grants were taken away. It happened to the Indians, too, but the Indians recovered their lands. A land grant in the Spanish colonial system was an *ejido,* and they were never given as a proprietary sort of thing to one person, but to a community. If they were given to an individual, it was so that person could organize a bunch of families and go settle a certain valley. What he did then was he portioned out the little valley next to the river, and irrigation rights would be provided and crops could be raised. But the vast majority of the land grants were *ejido* common land, which was used for

watershed, for wood, for pasture. When the American government took over, they declared the *ejido* eminent domain and took up jurisdiction by the Bureau of Land Management. In doing so, they destroyed the wherewithal by which that little village could sustain itself as an independent community. An entire way of life was taken away. Is there any wonder that poverty engulfed that little community, or that that one policy condemned entire villages in the north and throughout New Mexico to subsistence farming and extraordinary poverty? Now they had to pay for the privilege to pasture their animals, and now they have to battle the people of El Rico in the far north, the people of Santa Fe or Albuquerque who have no need of wood to heat their homes, or people from either of those towns for pasture, because they only give out so many permits. That's why these communities were settled in the first place, because of their proximity to those kinds of resources. No one has taken up that issue of Spanish land grants to restore them. They've taken up the issue for Native Americans; it's very popular and it was quite fashionable around the turn of the century. Eventually during the forties and fifties Congress gave back many of the Indian land grants on the basis of religious use. No one has taken up the issue of the Spanish land grants, which were given under the same authority and confiscated under the same authority. So, there is a smoldering resentment and a feeling of skepticism about outsiders. That's why New Mexicans on the whole are not effusive, not gregarious; they're a reserved people. That, of course, comes back to many generations before that, but it has been fueled by injustices and oppression since the conquest.

The other issue that gives rise to New Mexican reserve is that they were isolated, and still are. We were the furthest outpost of the Spanish empire. Spain, not so badly, and Mexico, worse, just abandoned us. We got one wagon train a year. That was the only news we had, and it had to cross some inhospitable deserts and hostile indigenous peoples to get here. As a result, the people here have developed their culture almost in a parallel fashion to that of the valley of Mexico. I don't think radically different, but different; our language is different. Our language, when we speak it, and unfortunately it is being lost, is very archaic—*yo traiba* instead of *yo traía, ojalá que haiga, murre de bien* instead of *muy bien, yo sebo* instead of *yo soy*; its roots are very Latin. Some of the words are Indian, too, like *colquets,* the Zuni word for coffee. Chimney we say *chiflon,* and wood-burning stove, *fogón.* We adapted because we were so isolated and we kept our Spanish very archaic.

The first colonization was 1598 here; that was nine years before Jamestown. We were very different from the English colonies, too, which had constant commerce because of the ease with which maritime commerce occurred. Not here. Commerce occurred between Veracruz and Sevilla, maybe, and then a tortuous overland journey of several years to get here. So, what remained of Spanish culture was inherited in the genes; it wasn't commerce. The archaic language we speak, also our religiosity, it is medieval, by which I don't mean middle ages, dark, primitive. For example, our spirituality is definitely not influenced by secular humanism. There is no division between religion and your daily life. My grandfather would go out in the morning before he went out to work, and he would sing

the *alba* to the rising of the sun. He would go out and work in the field, and before he came home at night, he would kneel down on the ground that took his energy that day and give thanks. It was a whole web, a way of seeing the divine interpenetrate into everyday life and interpreting it as such: seeing the saints as daily, constant companions, the voice of God as constantly present, asking what is the message of God in this event or in that event. Religion was not something you did on Sunday and you forgot about the rest of the week; it penetrated every aspect of your life. If the saint didn't give you what you wanted, here in New Mexico we'd turn him to the wall, put him in the corner, or put him in the underwear drawer. It was that personal. It wasn't idolatry; it was a personal relationship with the saints. The same thing with God, though God was seen as altogether very distant, the great creator, but at the same time, this is where we learn a little bit from the Indians. He was called *tata, tatita Dios,* Our Father, Daddy. But then Our Lady became very near, because sometimes *tatita Dios* was too far away.

Our Lady was important in New Mexico from the beginning. But Our Lady of Guadalupe is not anywhere near as important in New Mexico. In fact, her devotion is quite late. Even in Mexico she became very popular only after 1810 as a symbol of independence for the mestizos. The earliest church devoted to Our Lady of Guadalupe in New Mexico is 1776. You've got to consider her appearance was 1531—that's over two hundred years later. The most popular representation of Our Lady in New Mexico is *Nuestra Señora de los Dolores,* Our Lady of Sorrows, and this illustrates another feature of New Mexican spirituality. They can identify a great deal with the passion of Christ and with suffering because this was such a harsh society; death was a constant reality. We didn't become morbid about death like the Mexicans; I think they were much more influenced by the sense of fatalism of their indigenous peoples. That preoccupation with death—it was very true of the Aztecs, for example. I think that was rolled over to the Spanish, who had a kind of morbid fatalism as well, but here the native Americans weren't that preoccupied with death. It was a gentle reality. Here, though the Spanish were also concerned with death, it didn't become a morbid preoccupation. We had figures of death all over the place, but the *día de los muertos* is not a big thing for us. We may or may not go visit the cemetery; it's not a big day. There certainly are not picnics in cemeteries; that would be so foreign, so foreign. But death was a constant companion because any one of us could die of famine, disease, Indian attacks, and these attacks lasted very late, until 1913.

Here's another part of the revisionist history that I have a little trouble with. Of course the Spanish did commit atrocities against the Native American peoples, but it also went the other way. I mean, it's a very complex issue; Columbus has been blamed for everything, including the ozone layer being depleted, but there would've been the clash of cultures in any case, with or without Columbus.

In any case, the Hispanics here have a gentle relation with death, and they used to call her *La Comadre Sebastiana*—she was like a godmother, a member of the family. That is still true. They would represent her dressed in skeletal form during Holy Week and covered in a black gown. She represented different ways one could die. For example, there was the arrow, which symbolized a quick death;

and the lance, which was a death that was not so quick and painless, but painful and drawn out. You wished for the quick death, like a *flecha,* or arrow. *La Comadre Sebastiana* was oftentimes carried in a *carreta,* or cart; she would be bouncing in the back. She would be pulled through the streets during Holy Week to remind us of our mortality. Santiago and *El Niño de Atocha* are also very popular here.

Much more than an allegiance to Spain as some kind of political entity, or to the king of Spain, the people here brought it in their genes. It is not a coincidence that people settled in the areas that were similar to the ones they came from in Spain. You know, if they were from the high plains from around Madrid, they would settle in similar areas here. The plateaus of Spain are like New Mexico, so this was a collective remembrance of what they had been. It was that collective memory, I think; Paul Horgan writes about it very well in his book *The Great River.* He has a beautiful chapter on the collective memory the Spanish brought here from Spain. At the same time, this collective memory was opened to learning from the indigenous peoples as well. He says so well, "The Spanish came to conquer. They remained to submit to the same influences that have formed the indigenous peoples." Because there were so few of them and existence was so harsh, they "submitted," whereas in Mexico, I guess with their greater numbers, the Spanish continued to be oppressive. But here, they didn't; they had to dialogue.

In fact, New Mexico is one of the only places in the U.S. where the Indians actually won a war against the Europeans—that was the Pueblo revolt of 1680, in which they actually drove the Spanish out. The Spanish returned in 1692 and reconquered and resettled the area, but they came back much chastened. It is my contention that the beginning of *New* Mexican culture was 1692, because the Spanish were willing to learn, not to be so arrogant. They were the dominant political power, but they were learning from the Indians. It's evidenced in many ways. The Franciscan friars no longer came back looking to destroy all that was uniquely characteristic of Pueblo culture. Instead, they would take the religious practices of the Indians, like the dances and their symbolism and their ritual, and they would baptize them and they would make it uniquely Catholic. Whereas the Franciscans who came before the revolt were rigid, very Eurocentric, but afterward, they had learned their lesson. Also the Spanish government began to see that the greatest importance New Mexico had was its missionary endeavor. There was no wealth. It was also a safety valve to relieve population either from Mexico or Spain by sending them to the frontier, most of them society's dregs. If they were so good over there in Spain, why did they risk their fannies here on the very edge of the world, why did they risk coming? The people who came here were for the most part very poor, second sons who had no hope of maintaining the land; they were either criminals or Jews who were not trusted; they were religiously suspect and, in this regard, many of them were Jews and Arabs. Most New Mexicans have significant Arabic and Jewish blood because this was *la frontera,* this was where the *conversi* came, those who were forcibly converted and decided to remain Spanish rather than leave Spain after the expulsion in 1492. My contention is that by 1692, the Spanish had to submit to the same influences that they had fought before.

There were also some technological benefits of working with the Europeans. What happened is that prior to the Spaniards ever arriving, the Indians had many different languages, at least five different Pueblo languages, not to mention the native Navajo, Apaches, or anybody else. So they couldn't communicate, not even Pueblos living next to each other. When the Spanish came, they gave them a common language, which was a great benefit. It also helped them unite against the Spaniards. The other thing is the in-fighting that occurred. The Navajos and Apaches were the big nomadic tribes. They began to prey on the Pueblo Indians and very possibly could have wiped them out had it not been for Spanish intervention. There was an alliance of agricultural peoples against nomadic ones, so they began to throw their lot in together. As a consequence, there was such an intermixture of cultures that what we consider Spanish now and Indian now is exactly the opposite in origin. For example, we consider this kind of silver ring Indian jewelry, but the Indians didn't know how to work metal; they learned that from the Spanish. Food: we consider our food Spanish, but it's mostly Indian. Hot chiles and corn, mixed with *carnes,* meats, and with some eggs, vegetables, and fruits that were brought from Spain; it's a unique combination. For example, Indian bread that we bake in the *hornos* outside. The Indians didn't have wheat before the Spanish arrived, nor did they have the technology to build those beehive ovens that we received from the Arabs. It's marvelous, the history of technology is really the history of cultures, and you see wonderful combinations in that one little example.

However, our religion is not Indian at all. There was often intermixture and intermarriage, but if you moved from that side over here you became Spanish, and if you moved from that side over there you became Indian; it was like never the twain shall meet. And that was a result of the Council of the Indies laws that resulted from the great atrocities that were committed by the Spaniards in Mexico. By the time New Mexico was colonized, the Council of the Indies forbade intermarriage between Indians and Spaniards, and it forbade Spanish encroachment on Indian lands to the point here in New Mexico that the Indians who have lived together since the time the Spaniards arrived still have their same ancestral lands. The laws were enforced brutally; to encroach on Indian land meant to have your head chopped off, very Arabic.

After the 1692 revolt when all these laws came into effect, there was a peaceful coexistence between Pueblos and Spanish. There was a great exchange of culture, architecture, foods, religion—though the religion was mostly the Spaniards trying to influence the natives. But the Native Americans also gave the Spaniards a sense of peace, of respect for the land, and a sense of fatalism, of quietude. That's why I say that my contention is that by 1692 *New* Mexican culture began. Before that, it was two peoples living in antithetical hostility, and one trying to impose its will on the other. In the end, 1692 saw the two peoples admitting, reluctantly, that they could not survive without each other. In some areas Hispanic culture is dominant; in some, it is the Indian culture. One area where the Hispanic is dominant is in religion. The Indians saw many parallels between Catholicism and their

native religions. You know, with the whole view to the sacred, images, smoke, holy water, rituals, that kind of thing. Today, they will say, "We are better Catholics than you." And it's probably true. Today when they celebrate the twelve days of Christmas, they celebrate, they take off work, they dance, they consecrate the days. The same is true of other religious holy days. We've lost that.

New Mexicans don't leave New Mexico. We have a great homing instinct. We have this dirt running in our veins. If we do leave, we want to come back, sometimes to great economic deprivation. I have friends who studied law and who are well educated elsewhere, and could be making a hell of a lot of money, but they come back. I studied at the monastery in Indiana and also in D.C., but I came back.

The history of Catholicism in New Mexico is unique for many reasons, especially for the important role played by the *penitentes*. There is, of course, a rich tradition in Europe, especially in Spain and Italy, of the *penitentes*. They practiced mortification, self-penance in the imitation of Christ. Again, that's the medieval mentality: that as they went through a reenactment of the sufferings of our Lord Jesus, it was like an analesis, it became present. The mystery of salvation was palpable, present, and living, kind of a kairos time, you know what I'm saying? It's not merely a remembering, but a calling to mind, making it happen. That sort of mentality is very much part of Hispanic spirituality, and this came here to New Mexico in the form of the third order of St. Francis. In every community where the Franciscans were established, the third order was established. The first order was the clergy and brothers, the second order was the poor clerics, the third order being lay people who wanted to live and emulate the ideal of St. Francis in their own lay state of life.

What happened is that these third orders more or less flourished under the Franciscan influence. By 1776, there were forty-six priests serving here, the missions were well stocked and supplied by the Spanish crown. There was no separation between church and state, of course. What happened is that the great turmoil in Mexico resulted in the independence revolution, and all the Franciscans in New Mexico were Spanish born. Laws enacted in Mexico in 1827 and 1828 expelled all Spanish-born citizens who did not renounce their Spanish citizenship. Many of these were Franciscan friars, and the number of priests in New Mexico plummeted from forty-three to about eight in the early 1800s. Then the Spanish crown stopped supporting the missions, as the Mexican Republic either disagreed with the missionary system or could not afford it. As a consequence, all the churches in New Mexico began to fall into disrepair. The great missionary endeavor of educating the people, providing them with the basic rudiments of the faith, fell. There was no diocesan clergy to fill the void because the Vatican followed a singularly unwise course in trying to punish Mexico to go back to Spain by refusing to ordain Mexican bishops. There was actually a ten-year period in Mexican history where there were no bishops. We had a few of our own priests who had been trained at the diocesan seminary in Durango, Mexico. A few of our own native sons ended up being extraordinary priests, leaders of the people, like *Padre* Antonio José Martínez, or *Padre* Felipe Ortiz, or *Padre* Manuel Gallegos. They

brought in, for example, printing presses; they established the first public schools, the first newspaper, the first seminary. They were great and visionary leaders, but there were very few of them, and living in great penury.

So what happened is that the church survived not only because of the great vision of a few priests, but because of these lay organizations, these third orders, which took on the responsibility for the maintenance of the faith that was like fire. Each of the communities where the third order established themselves maintained a mutual assistance society whereby they helped each other with food or whatever need there was. If a house burned down, the people would get together and rebuild it; they would provide for the widows and orphans. We call them confraternities, but *La Fraternidad Piadosa de Nuestro Padre Jesús de Nazaret,* the Pious Brotherhood of Our Father Jesus of Nazareth, is the full title. They did not want to be called *penitentes* because everyone is a penitent. So they are called *hermanos.* They provided for mutual assistance; they provided for teaching the faith to the children, gathering the communities together for high holy days, especially during Lent, and to reenact the Passion—that was the main, but not the only, activity. I think it has been sensationalized to emphasize death, but no, they were year-long organizations. What they did was, through beautiful prayer forms, beautiful music called *alabados,* they were able to keep the people's faith alive, gather together for funerals, gather together for main events in Christian life, and most important, to have prepared the community for when a priest would arrive.

The reason I love to lecture on New Mexico is so our own people begin to realize how unique their heritage is. I grew up in a period when we were punished for speaking Spanish, and when we were made to feel less because we had dark skin. We were made fun of for being as dark as we are; the pressures to become American and to jettison all that is Hispanic were very strong. I still think that attitude is prevalent, perhaps accelerated even more so in the last twenty years. So, whenever I go somewhere and speak of the history of our culture, when I tell the story of our people's history and spirituality, it is a rebirth, a born-again experience.

Joaquín F. Blaya

A native of Santiago, Chile, Joaquín F. Blaya is currently president, chief executive officer, and a director of the Spanish-language television network Telemundo Group, Inc. Blaya has distinguished himself for his commitment to producing domestic programming, sponsoring public service campaigns, promoting the importance of education for Latino families, pioneering Spanish-language news programming, and fostering a sense of shared identity among United States Latinos. He serves on the board of directors of the Smithsonian Institution, among others, and was recently awarded the Rubén Salazar Award for Communications by the National Council of La Raza for his efforts to present a positive, accurate portrayal of Latino cultures in the media.

In the following interview, Blaya shares his vision for the future of Spanish-language television and relates his observations to the theme of cultural identity.

Interview

I feel that in my position I have a special reponsibility to the Hispanic community, which is a very different responsibility than that of my general market counterparts in English-language television. Spanish-language television can and must fulfill a social mission for the Hispanics of this country, and it is a mission which we can never take lightly.

The inventors of Spanish-language television in the U.S. were Don Emilio Azcárraga, founded of the Mexican television empire Televisa, and René Anselmo, who today is owner of PanAmSat, the only privately owned commercial satellite. The idea then was to bring in, at very low cost, programs produced in Mexico, for broadcast in U.S. markets with sizeable Hispanic populations, such as San Antonio and Los Angeles. From the very beginning, Spanish-language television was intended as a *service* to the Hispanic population. These were the roots of what later came to be Univisión, the enterprise that I directed up until about a year ago.

What I have developed is the concept of Spanish language television produced in the U.S. which responds to the realities of the Hispanics who live in this country. I've always felt that there has to be a balance between domestic programming and simply transmitting programs from Mexico. So, I stimulated the development of television in Spanish, produced by and for U.S. Hispanics.

I believe that Spanish-language television must be a reflection of the Hispanic community. I think that we have a fundamental responsibility in this regard that goes far beyond the normal responsibility of television as a medium that should entertain and inform. In general, English-language television has no social responsibility and it accepts none. That's not a criticism, simply a statement of fact.

Spanish language television, on the other hand, *has* to have a social responsibility. We do everything possible to help create a community of Hispanics who feel and act like first class citizens. By this I mean a community which is fully equipped to take full advantage of all that this country has to offer. It's interesting, to the degree that Spanish language television improves the quality of our programming—to the extent that we have done and are doing that—Hispanics begin to "come out of the closet." Finally, there exists a medium in which they see themselves and of which they can feel proud. Our responsibility is *enormous*, and the one who does not accept this responsibility is not complying with the requirements of the job.

This is a fundamental philosophical difference, for example, between the network that I directed before, Univisión, and the one that I am in charge of now, Telemundo. You see, we have to *destacar a nuestra gente*, highlight our people, make them stand out, make them feel like first-class citizens. We have to encourage them to participate in the process, we have to inform and educate them with regard to the responsibilities, obligations, and rights that they have in this country.

For example, we are now involved in a national outreach campaign called *De Padres a Hijos*—From Parents to Children—which basically teaches parents the responsibility that they have to participate in their children's education. At the same time, we are informing them about the rights they have within the system—participation in the PTA, for example, which is a foreign concept to many Hispanics, especially those immigrants who come from poor countries.

In large measure, the recent success of Spanish-language television is due to the fact that we have accepted a commitment to the Hispanic community and we have respected our viewers. We have done so with important educational campaigns, such as stressing participation in the national census; public forums; and talk programs, like that of María Laria. Now, some people get upset that "culturally taboo" themes are discussed. They don't want to see that we have mental illness, homosexuals, AIDS. But, for the first time, these crucial issues are discussed on television. Of course, there is sensationalism in all these things, and one has to be careful, but their social value is important.

I also believe that Spanish language television fulfills some of the same functions that national television in English does. Let me explain. When I came to the U.S. about twenty-six years ago, there were tremendous, fundamental regional differences in this country. Today, and I'm not saying that it's necessarily a positive thing, but today there exists a uniformity at the national level that is the result of having had in this country a national communications system over the past forty years. In one way or another, the communications media have made uniform the standards for just about everything. The obvious example is that if you go from place to place in this country you will see that all the news programs and announcers sound just alike; all of them talk like Walter Cronkite, regardless of whether they came from Massachusetts or Oklahoma. It's virtually impossible to say where they are from. Language has been made uniform.

Tastes with regard to programming, which originates in Hollywood, have also become uniform. *Roseanne* is the number one program, obviously a fierce criticism of the cultural standards of this country, but, well, this is a subject for another conversation. The fact is that the network media, in addition to entertaining and informing, have created the concept of mass distribution and marketing, such that if one arrives at the airport of a city and covers one's eyes, one sees the same Holiday Inn, Pizza Hut, Hyatt, McDonalds, and if one gets on the expressway, it's the same thing. American cities have lost their individual characteristics and their personality. This is the massification of culture that stems from the mass media, and it has positive and negative aspects.

One positive aspect of massification for the Hispanic community is the growth of the mass information media in Spanish. This has permitted, for the first time and unlike any place else in the world, Hispanics to understand each other, to see that our similarities are greater than our differences. For example, I'm a Chilean and I have lived half my life in Chile, but the lack of understanding between Chile and Argentina, which was just one hour away by plane, was enormous. Now, however, such distances become smaller every day.

As a national and international network, we are breaking barriers. I hope we are going to create more uniform standards, not in the negative aspect that I mentioned earlier, but in a positive way. We need to understand that we have a common ancestry, common cultural bases: religion, the extended family, the language, the way in which we celebrate, our fervor for music. There are many similarities that we Latinos share, so that if someone says *frijol* for *bean* and another says *gandul*, those are minimal differences; we still have the vertebral column of a culture, the language. With regard to how we program, we do it with our commercial mandate in mind. We are not PBS; if we were, no one would watch us. If we just programmed things like documentaries on Cervantes or Goya, no one would tune in. We can do things like that from time to time as *un saludo a la bandera*, a salute to the flag, but it brings no audience. If, on the other hand, we run a Mexican cowboy film, we get a big audience. We have to remember that although we have a national viewership, it is in its majority Mexican American. We base programming decisions on Nielsen ratings; that's how we sell. One has to remember that this is a business that has to make a profit for the investors. So, business success is measured that way; personal success is measured by making a contribution to the development of our people.

I think that the negative aspects of massification could result with Latinos, too, in the distant future. But one has to remember that the Hispanic in the U.S. has access to another culture and another language, which is not the case for the monolingual American. Hispanics have the opportunity for a more global understanding of other Hispanics. In fact, I can already see this beginning to happen. Recently, I went to a meeting of the Congressional Hispanic Caucus in Congress, and for the first time there were representatives of different Latino groups within that organization working together, having realized that they are one. What appeared impossible just ten years ago is now happening.

Part of the responsibility of those of us in the media is to encourage people to register and vote, to get their citizenship, and so on. This year we have had mass voter registration and education campaigns. Some people are cynical. They don't think their vote counts because that's the way it was in their country. These attitudes don't change overnight, but what we are doing is using the media as a responsible agent for generating change.

I've heard it said that Spanish-language television will prolong the ghettoization of the Latino population, but those who say that are ignorant of the facts. If you live in the heart of the Hispanic community, you realize immediately that it would create devastating problems if there were no Spanish language media to inform, to permit Hispanics to feel proud of their heritage. We do not promote total assimilation, the melting pot, because we believe that it reduces the individual to being just another number, and because we believe that contributions from other cultures enrich this country. Therefore, we think in terms of "culturization," not assimilation.

It is obvious that English is predominant in this country, and we constantly promote the need to be fluent in English. But we stress *both* languages because we

believe that a person's individual identity is fundamental. The social pressures in this country are so great that English is practically going to come naturally—that's the reality; that's the market research. Those who fear that Spanish-language television will keep people from learning English don't read the statistics.

My five kids speak only English with me. For the first three years they spoke only Spanish. They went to school, and within two weeks, *two weeks*, they were speaking English. I always speak Spanish to them. I ask them in Spanish and they answer me in English. They ask me in English and I answer them in Spanish. Recently, however, I have seen my twenty-one-year-old, who is a *gringa total*, watching *novelas*, soaps in Spanish, and she likes Luis Miguel, and Manuel, but also Michael Jackson, and she watches *Home Improvement*. That is participating in both cultures. It's wonderful. And it's not at all the same as it was in the past when if someone said, "Is your name Blaya?" you would say, "No, it's Smith," and thus amputate an extremely rich cultural limb and make people feel ashamed of their past.

Our people's self-esteem is fundamental to their positive sense of identity, and it is something that is not reinforced by any state institution or agency. History is full of cases in which kids were sent to classes for the mentally retarded because they did not speak the dominant language. This is like slapping the left-handed person on the hand with the ruler because he can't write with his right hand. That behavior produces a generation destined to become second-class citizens. Self-esteem is fundamental in the development of the person, and that is exactly what we promote. When we talk about the social role of television in Spanish, that is the role that we should be playing.

Spanish-language television is not merely a reflection of the Hispanic reality, but also a projection toward the future, toward something better. This is completely absent from English-language television because they do not accept this as their responsibility. What reigns is extreme individualism and the present. For example, no English-language network is conducting any educational campaign whatsoever, and this when education is the most serious problem this country faces. We are creating a society of illiterates, of people incapable of holding jobs that require technical skills, and the media are doing nothing. All our other problems stem from this lack of education.

For us at Telemundo, education is a fundamental mission. We are investing millions of dollars in it, plus our time, lots of time. Next week, for example, we are having a meeting here with Joe Fernández of New York, Leticia Quesada of Los Angeles, and other well-known Latino educators to evaluate student scholarship applications. We are going to give special recognition to these kids in eleven markets across the country, announcements in the newspaper, a dinner, keynote speaker, all these things to let people see the kind of graduates that we can produce in our community. None of this is a business; we are not earning any money from it. In the long run, maybe, but now, it's just costing money. But that's okay if we don't have an immediate response to our efforts. Our problems are long-term and so are the solutions.

Unfortunately, in this country we want results right now. We haven't invested in the long run, and we are spending now the chips of the future. Education is a

major, long-term investment. I once thought about using the experience I gained from working with Monseñor Salcedo of Venezuela in a very successful mass literacy campaign that he headed there and developing a series of literacy programs here. However, I ran into the enormous obstacle that I would be promoting a literacy campaign here in *Spanish*, and that had insurmountable political implications. That's a subject that one simply cannot touch. However, in the U.S., unlike Latin America, we can operate within the established bases of the system. At least here schools exist, and education is accessible to everyone. We're not talking about a situation in which you live in the mountains and the nearest school is three hundred kilometers away.

I know that this administration is now focusing on the problem of health care, which is a tremendous problem, but education in this country is in a desperate state. Just think of the cost of crime alone; no other society pays such a cost for violent crime. The bottom line is that it is a problem of education. Here—in any city—one lives in fear. People do not respect each other and they do not respect themselves. On the whole, religious leaders in the U.S. have not provided much leadership in this area. Here, as in literacy work, I think we can learn from Latin America. There is much to criticize in the role of the Catholic Church in Latin America in retarding various areas of development, but you have to give them credit for having established ethical standards. These include the concepts of respect for oneself and for others, especially within the family, something that scarcely exists in this society. We have a lot to learn from Latin American culture.

Over the past twenty-three years, I personally have lived the difficult experience of not being accepted. When I came to Miami from New York they didn't accept me here because I wasn't Cuban. They said I was a communist for having left Chile, and they put bombs in my car during that time—this was about 1972. But, eventually, I came to be a hero to the Cuban community. When I took charge of the network, I then encountered problems on the West Coast. To them, I was unacceptable because I was Cuban, at least, that's how they perceived me. I've felt all this prejudice and conflict personally, but I've also seen changes, and I've done everything I can to help create these changes through the media.

But the huge changes in the media, these have not occurred over the past twenty-three years, only over the past seven. That's when we began programming in the U.S. instead of just importing from Mexico. I made this change when I was at Univisión. I also created news programming at Univisión; sponsored various community service campaigns; invented the programs, *Sábado Gigante* and *Cristina*, among others. Now, I've been here at Telemundo about a year and I'm creating not only a national news organization, but another network for international news. I'm working on a news organization for the whole hemisphere that will be something like CNN in Spanish, with news twenty-four hours a day, world news, but with a focus on Latin America. It should be in place before too long.

You can see that I am very serious about the responsibility of Spanish-language television to promote self-esteem, education, and dialogue among the U.S. Hispanic populations. These are basic to a positive personal and cultural identity.

Robert W. Pazmiño

Robert Pazmiño is of Ecuadorian, Dutch, and German heritage. He is an ordained American Baptist minister and faculty member at Andover Newton Theological School. Pazmiño is the author of *Foundational Issues in Christian Education: An Introduction in Evangelical Perspective* (Grand Rapids, Mich.: Baker Book House, 1988) and *The Seminary in the City: A Study of New York Theological Seminary* (Lanham, Md.: University Press of America, 1988).

The essay we are reading comes from the collection *Voces: Voices from the Hispanic Church,* ed. Justo González (Nashville: Abingdon Press, 1992); it explores various types of education, opting for a model that affirms both one's cultural identity and one's participation in the broader world.

Double Dutch:
Reflections of a Hispanic North American on Multicultural Religious Education

I am a Hispanic–North American, a new-breed Hispanic. My ethnic roots are Ecuadorian in my father's lineage, and Dutch and German from Pennsylvania in my mother's lineage. Given the fact that persons from German lineage in Pennsylvania are called Pennsylvania Dutch, my three-and-a-half-year-old daughter names this strand of our family heritage from my mother's roots "Double Dutch." It is an appropriate naming because double dutch is also the term for a rope game played with two jump ropes which are turned in tandem. My active daughter, Rebekah, observes and practices this rope game, which requires a unique combination of jumping and coordination to balance one's position successfully between two ropes rotating in opposite directions and converging on the person whose turn it is to jump. This image of jumping double dutch is appropriate for considering the status of minority persons in public and religious education in the United States within a dominant Anglo middle-class ethos.

A person who is Hispanic–North American is conscious of being at a point represented by the position of the hyphen in that term, the position of navigating and balancing the convergence of two cultures, which rotate in distinct orbits and require careful coordination and balance. In our pluralistic society with various cultures converging, the image of jumping between two ropes provides insights for negotiating the interaction of elements in multicultural education. Yet this image is particularly helpful for the new-breed Hispanic population which Virgilio Elizondo describes as *mestizaje,* the origination of a new people from two ethnically disparate parent people.[1]

Like the rope game of double dutch, my life represents the tandem play of two cultures because I grew up in close association with my father's extended family and cultural roots due to a distancing and disassociation from my mother's family. Yet these extended family ties were immersed in the world of an Anglo-dominant local community and culture.

Elizondo vividly describes my status and that of others in relation to the experience of persons with mixed blood, not unlike the status of being a Galilean in first-century Palestine. Like Galileans, new-breed or new-generation Hispanics are looked down on both by Latin Americans for their cultural impurity, and by Anglos for their ethnic ties. New-breed Hispanics are Hispanic in their approach to life, but their first and dominant language is either English or "Spanglish," which

is a mixture of English and Spanish. In most cases they are not at home in Anglo society and struggle with the status of being modern day Galileans.[2]

Galilee at its best was a crossroads of cultures and peoples with an openness to each other, not unlike some small communities and associations in the city of my origin, New York. But Galilee at its worst resulted in the exclusion and division of those who were different, not unlike the experience of a vast majority of minority persons in the United States and a number of cultural groups in New York City. This experience of exclusion was heightened for me through my marriage to a woman of pure Puerto Rican descent. I feel Puerto Rican as an adopted member of my wife's extended family and as a result of six years of ministry in a predominantly Puerto Rican church in East Harlem, New York. Being Puerto Rican and being Hispanic in that context requires nurture through a constant effort to re-own one's cultural heritage within a dominant culture that has generally sought to squelch it and assign it to an inferior status.

For those of new breed status who are second, third, and fourth generation Hispanics in the United States, the distinct challenge is to recover those aspects of Hispanic language and culture which were decimated through decades of racist and discriminatory practices, components of which are ever present in individual and corporate life. This recovery must occur while actively participating in a wider society which devalues this very renewal of Hispanic culture as evidenced through, for one example, the increased opposition to bilingual education. Such recovery is subject to numerous factors which must be addressed. One factor is the potential danger of further ghettoization where the maintenance of an ethnic enclave results in alienation from the wider society and an inability to impact upon that society in constructive ways. A second factor is the unwarranted perception by those in the wider society that the affirmation of one's ethnic identity inherently represents an immature longing for one's home group with the attending feelings of security and connection. A third factor is the complex of shifts in a multicultural global existence which necessitate interaction and dialogue on a daily basis across ethnic and cultural divisions. Additional factors can be cited, but the challenge remains to broaden our understanding for addressing such realities. One source for understanding is embodied in the promise of Galilee as Elizondo has prophetically suggested.

The Promise of Galilee

The promise of Galilee at its best can be discerned through exploring some of its history. Galilee, literally denoting a ring or circle, referred to a region comprised of Gentiles and foreigners, of persons from various nations. It was a region that was constantly experiencing infiltration and migration. At various times in its history, Galilee was controlled by Babylon, Persia, Macedonia, Egypt, Syria, and Assyria. In the first century, Galilee with a population of approximately 350,000 persons had a large slave element and about 100,000 Jews who were largely Hellenized. The primary language at this time was Koine Greek, although Jews spoke Aramaic. Thus the Galilean Jews represented a bilingual community.

Galilean Jews were lax in the matter of personal attendance at the Temple in Jerusalem, in part for the obvious reason of distance, and this attitude was symbolic of the modified orthodoxy of Jews in Galilee of the Gentiles.

It is significant that much of the teaching of Jesus, directed primarily to those living in this context, was not acceptable to the orthodox interpreters of Judea, for he gained a reputation for unusual and controversial interpretation. Jesus manifested a freshness and independence of mind as to the meaning and application of the Law, consonant with the religious spirit of Galilee. This region was occupied by a mixed population and had a reputation for facial variety and mixture in and around its borders.[3]

It was in this very context of Galilee that God chose to be incarnate in the person of Jesus of Nazareth. Yet it is the very nature of this multicultural context which is so often ignored in considering Christian religious education today. Nevertheless promise is realized for educators who take heed to the nature of Galilee which is inclusive of ethnic and cultural diversity. The existence of this region assumes that some form of boundaries were set to define this space and/or the persons occupying this space. By focusing on the question of boundaries which is ever present in human interactions, the religious educator can explore dimensions of ethnicity and religious faith, particularized in this case from the perspective of the Christian faith.

Anya Peterson Royce points out that the maintenance of ethnic identity involves the use of symbolic boundaries from within a group to distinguish it from other groups. Those groups maintaining these boundaries celebrate their differences among peoples as distinctive and affirm the place of beauty in their culture and ethnic heritage. But at the same time other boundaries are imposed by external groups upon an ethnic group, thus reinforcing distinctions. These distinctions too readily become a source of trouble for ethnic groups, fostering ethnic stereotyping, discrimination, and racism. These secondary boundaries isolate differences among peoples as deficits as compared with the positive distinctives maintained by the groups themselves. Thus there often exist double boundaries or two ropes with which ethnic groups must contend.[4] Ethnic groups that have developed boundaries to define themselves, often in response to a hostile context, can find that additional boundaries have been set which divide them from others. The struggle then becomes how to maintain one's identity and integrity as a member of a minority group and yet fully participate in the larger society both across defining boundaries and dividing boundaries imposed by that larger society. Those dividing boundaries perpetuate oppression and injustice with a host of complicating factors for ethnic minorities. The struggle becomes how to play double dutch in being both Hispanic and North American and wanting to play in a way that affirms the significance and integrity of both realities. This conflict is not unique to Hispanic–North Americans because similar issues can be posed for those who seek to be Black and American, Asian and American, or even Christian and North American. Yet the current historical context of the United States and the corresponding emphases upon global and multicultural education provide a

unique setting in which to consider the emergence of a new people, new-breed Hispanic–North Americans who have experienced the joys and pains of emergence. This emergence offers the opportunity for dialogue and interaction across various cultures in addressing the need for religious education which seeks to be multicultural. Both the historical and sociological studies of general and religious education have revealed various models of education which have functionally emerged and have been perpetuated in education. Each of these models of education, formulated in relation to ethnic and cultural differences, have primarily patterned themselves after the larger communal contexts of which they are a part.

Models of Education

The various models of ethnic or cultural education are manifest more at the level of the hidden or null curriculum than that of the explicit curriculum.[5] An investigation of the explicit written curriculum of religious education, as helpfully undertaken by Charles Foster, reveals a progression of models which increasingly favors multiethnic and multicultural pluralism.[6] On the basis of this history of the actual written materials used in religious education, one could conclude that significant progress is being made in the area of addressing ethnocentrism in religious education. But if a researcher explores the actual experiences of minority persons and considers what areas of ethnic studies are being forgotten in terms of the null curriculum, a very different impression is gained. Whereas the explicit curriculum may affirm a multicultural education, the hidden and null curricula may operate effectively to undermine that emphasis. This is too common an experience for ethnic groups who experience the wide gap between what Lawrence Cremin has termed the stated intentions of the explicit curriculum and the revealed preferences of the hidden and null curricula.[7] Such is an inevitable consequence of life within a society which does not consistently address the existence of institutional racism in its educational efforts.

The works of both Ricardo García in general education and Charles Foster in the history of church education suggest the following four models which currently operate despite a national commitment in the United States to integration and the elimination of some of the effects of racism.[8]

1. Anglo Conformity Model

This model maintains that some persons are inferior and marginal because of their cultural, racial, and/or ethnic origin. Such a model perpetuates racial and social exclusion either intentionally or unintentionally and devalues the heritage, identity, and experience of persons who do not belong to favored ethnic groups. Whereas the vast majority of educational efforts in the United States do not intentionally emphasize conformity at the explicit or stated level, the hidden and null curricula reveal contradictory evidence.

A few examples from personal experience will suffice to illustrate the presence of this model which operates functionally for minority persons. My family and I lived in a New England small town community with such a small percentage of

minority persons and a parochial ethos that it essentially functioned from an Anglo conformity model. The educational experience of our son in the local middle school was typified by the comment of its principal as to why only French was being taught to the exclusion of Spanish in the school's curriculum, the explicit curriculum. The principal's response was that Spanish was only needed to use at a local chain restaurant to order Mexican food. One can imagine the extent to which Latin American heritage gains access in this school at the levels of the hidden and null curricula. A similar experience awaited the family in a local church where our daughter was often neglected in her nursery and Sunday School class in overt preference to children with Anglo heritage. The differential treatment extended to the point where our daughter was actually once physically struck to deal with her crying. Upon confronting the teacher with our daughter's account, she initially denied the incident. No Anglo children in this class received such treatment. These examples could proliferate to illustrate the subtle and not so subtle messages that persons of ethnic differences received. We were not welcome in the public and religious education programs in this community.

Richard de Lone's work, *Small Futures,* describes the functional caste system in the United States which isolates blacks, Native American peoples, Mexican Americans, and Puerto Rican Americans.[9] My family and I experienced the realities of casting in terms of the hidden and null curricula of the public and religious education offerings in this locale sufficiently to indicate the presence of an Anglo model.

2. Melting Pot Model

Historically this model characterized the educational rationale in the United States prior to the 1960s. As García indicates, the melting pot model began to show signs of collapse in the 1960s when Nathan Glazer and Daniel Moynihan published the book *Beyond the Melting Pot.* By 1975, the melting pot model had become intellectually outmoded, but not functional inoperative.[10] A melting pot or ethnic synthesis model maintains that all cultures melt down to a common denominator, which in the case of the United States has been Anglo-dominant and English speaking.

The melting pot functions very selectively and can be illustrated by the comments of a black seminary student who shared with me about the number of well-intentioned peers who said to him that they no longer saw him as black, but as a Christian brother. The place of *koinonia* or community is to be affirmed, but not at the loss of recognition of persons as they have been created by God. Ian Malcolm, an Australian religious educator, has appropriately identified the drive to cultural or ethnic uniformity in the melting pot model as rooted in human pride and arrogance. From his perspective, ethnic diversity reflects an appropriate relationship between a transcendent God and a finite humanity.[11]

The melting pot works to eliminate ethnic distinctives in the effort to develop a unified identity. It does so not to the extremes of the Anglo conformity model; nevertheless, distinctives are merged in a way that inevitably favors the dominant culture. From the perspective of the minority person this model might best be

compared with a meltdown of a nuclear reactor in terms of the destruction of that which is to be preserved in an ethnic heritage. Whereas the Anglo community model seeks to deny and/or obliterate ethnic distinctives that are not Anglo, the melting pot model serves to diminish seriously these distinctives in relation to the perceived higher good of unity. Whereas the Anglo conformity model stresses uniformity, the melting pot allows for a unity which at least at the ideational level seeks a muted and distorted diversity. These two models choose the higher value for unity over against diversity. But this unity is realized at a great cost to persons of ethnic backgrounds not viewed as the favored majority. The hidden curriculum of a major portion of the educational settings and programs in the United States affirms the values of this melting pot model.

One may not expect the revolutionary social changes initiated in the 1960s Civil Rights Movement and resulting legislation to make significant inroads in the value system and ethos of educational institutions in the United States within such a short time. Some progress has been realized at the level of the explicit curriculum, but addressing the hidden and null curricula is a task of long-term magnitude. Work and struggle must continue in this area, but realistic expectations must also be maintained. The recent rise of racial incidents on university (and I might add seminary) campuses is a reminder of the continued efforts which must be extended to realize a more equitable education for minority persons in the United States.

3. Cultural Pluralism Model

This third model stresses the inclusion of racial and ethnic minorities into the life of the nation, community, school, or church. It seeks to have a representative ethnicity as a means by which to pattern global or national realities. At various points in the actual practice of this model, Anglo superiority emerges, but the effort is made to mute paternalism.[12] Various ethnic heritages are recognized, but the implicit expectation is that with maturity one's ethnic heritage will no longer be emphasized. The message is that people have a right to maintain their ethnic identities, but no one must be carried away with this emphasis, in the interest of genuine dialogue and affirmation of a unity which transcends the existent diversity.

This third model is a welcome alternative to the first two described, yet it still expects of minority persons the denial or submergence of one's heritage rather than its enrichment as it is offered as a gift to other peoples. A unity is sought which essentially displaces one's ethnic identity rather than a unity which coexists in the midst of one's heritage. The choice is posed between either maintaining one's ethnic identity throughout one's life or diminishing its importance in the interest of engagement with the larger cultural plurality. Such terms are not in actuality applied equitably to all ethnic groups in the United States because the heritage of some groups is maintained in the existing plurality to a much greater extent. Such a situation parallels the one in George Orwell's description in *Animal Farm*, where the position of some is more equal than that of others. The lack of emphasis upon some ethnic heritages is tantamount to their obliteration in a societal context steeped in racial and cultural domination. For example, if Armen-

ian Americans do not emphasize their cultural heritage, then it will no longer be a gift to this nation or the world because of the genocide experience of this group.

Plurality is encouraged in this model of cultural pluralism, but within the bounds defined by the dominant culture and circumvented by the press for a maturity and a unity ill conceived. A vastly diminished particularity of ethnicity is promoted which for the Hispanic–North American represents a contradiction in terms and commitments. Educationally, this model operates to welcome the participation and contributions of representative ethnic groups without addressing the long-term implications of the inclusion and nurture of their ethnicity. Ethnic diversity in this perspective becomes a long-term detriment in favor of a universal agenda that is too narrowly defined. For one to project a point of maturity in which I no longer emphasize my heritage and identity is to deny my person as created by God, even within the purview of the new creation of Jesus Christ.

4. Multicultural Model

As García defines this model, it suggests a type of education committed to creating educational environments in which students from all cultural groups will experience educational equity. Multiethnic education is a specific form of multicultural education. It includes not only studying ethnic cultures and experiences, but also making institutional changes within the school setting so that students from diverse ethnic groups have equal educational opportunities.[13] This type of educational format assumes that ethnicity is a salient and continuing part of national and personal life. In this emphasis, a multiethnic or multicultural model moves beyond the model of cultural pluralism. This is the case because those who support multicultural education value the continuing significance of ethnicity throughout the maturing process. Ethnic diversity is maintained and not diminished in the interest of realizing a narrowly defined unity.

A multicultural model suggests two educational movements, the maintenance of both being essential for a proper rhythm and balance. The initial movement is that of emphasizing one's ethnic identity and definition. The complementary movement is that of seeking a common ground for community, for life in a global village grappling with the realities of ethnic and cultural plurality. This second movement involves a quest for universality, for unity, but not at the expense of diversity. The model of cultural pluralism diminishes the first movement in favor of emphasizing the second. This second movement in the multicultural model does not deny one's identity, but embodies that identity in dialogue with others from distinct ethnic backgrounds. By its very nature it includes exploring ethnic heritages other than one's own heritage and learning to appreciate them. This dialogue assumes that one has had the luxury and space for grounding one's ethnic identity. This luxury and space have not been afforded to everyone in the United States, and both the securing and the maintaining of that space are crucial in the context of a continuing racially divisive environment. Such racism is perpetuated on the institutional and personal levels of North American society, even with the explicit advocacy of a multicultural model.

This description of two complementary movements in multicultural education suggests the imagery of double dutch. A careful coordination of both movements is needed in order to maintain the proper balance of both diversity and unity. The other three models described have in one way or another sacrificed diversity in the interest of unity with a resulting loss of ethnic distinctives which provide an essential ground for identity. Such unity has been maintained at an unacceptable sacrifice to minority persons in the United States. This fourth model is a welcome alternative with its complementary emphases on diversity and unity.

With the description of a multicultural model, there remains the question of the basis for unity amid the vast diversity of ethnic and cultural groups encountered in our world. The Christian claim is that unity is found in Jesus Christ the Galilean. The resurrected and exalted Christ at Pentecost gifted his followers with the Holy Spirit. The experience of Pentecost points to a multiplicity of ethnic groups and tongues as the first sign of the Spirit's action in bringing healing to a divided world. Pentecost represents the reversal of the divisions of Babel, with persons from diverse ethnic and language communities finding unity amid their diversity as each person hears the gospel in his or her own tongue. The Spirit on that birthday of the Christian church points to a new source of human understanding and unity, a source embodying persons from every race, culture, and language. That source is the Lord Jesus Christ.[14] Personal and communal ethnic identities are not nullified or forgotten with Christian maturity, but are transcended in Jesus Christ. This transcendence does not entail the denial of the gift of ethnicity, but the sharing of that gift with others while receiving the gifts of their heritages as described in a multicultural model. This is Galilee at its best, present in Jerusalem.

In conclusion, one can see that a multicultural model of education is to be sought. Double dutch can be played through incorporating both movements of multicultural education: the one which affirms one's identity, and the one that affirms one's participation in the larger world. Double dutch is played at risk, but the risk is worth the taking if one is to be faithful in the task of educating in a pluralistic world. An image of double dutch distinct from the rope game and more in tune with the dominant North American culture is that of sharing equally the costs of one's outing on a date with friend. It is a multicultural model that assumes each contributing ethnic group can equally share its heritage and gain from those of others in a climate of mutual respect. To do otherwise is to deny the full implications of the gospel of Jesus Christ and to refuse to address the ethnocentrism resident in each of our lives.

Virgil P. Elizondo

Father Elizondo is a trailblazer in the development of a United States Latino theology. He is the founder of the Mexican American Cultural Center (MACC) in San Antonio and the author of several influential works, including *Christianity and Culture: an Introduction to Pastoral Theology and Ministry for the Bicultural Community* (San Antonio: Mexican American Cultural Center Bookstore, 1975), *Galilean Journey: the Mexican-American Promise* (Maryknoll, N.Y.: Orbis Books, 1983), and *The Future is Mestizo: Life Where Cultures Meet* (Bloomington, Ind.: Meyer-Stone Books, 1988), the source of this reading on the enriching possibilities of the new *mestizaje*, the synthetic cultural identity of the future.

from *The Future Is Mestizo: Life Where Cultures Meet*

The poor who migrate into a richer nation do not pose a threat to the local culture. In fact, the very opposite is true. The threat is to their own self-image and cultural identity. They come because they want to better their lives. Thus they try to take on the traits of the host culture. The adults may fantasize about the great life in the old country, but members of the new generation often abhor their racial and cultural identity because of the ridicule they suffer at school, in the neighborhoods, and even in the churches. Everything in the new society makes the children feel different and odd. The dominant society quite naturally projects images of its own people as normative. Those who are different often experience a deep sense of shame and inferiority.

As the children grow up, they often strive to get rid of everything that in any way is linked to the old ways and take unto themselves the traits of the new culture. They will even make efforts so that their own children will not be "contaminated" with the language and cultural traits of the culture of the old country. Yet in time, the children of this first generation, who grew up totally in the new culture, sometimes reclaim the culture of their parents in a deeper and even more radical way. In many ways, though, they already belong to the new culture. It is here that the cultural *mestizaje* begins to emerge.

Mexican immigrants to the United States often want their children to become more United States–American than any native-born citizen. They do not want their children to have to suffer the insults and hurts they had to endure. But the culture of our parents is so deep that it is transmitted in an almost biological way. We can adjust to a new culture and even assume many of the traits of the new culture we have moved into, but we can never totally cease being who we are.

New generations discover that certain aspects of their national and cultural identity are so much a part of their inner selves that they are not free to give them up. The new *mestizaje* occurs when they take unto themselves the new culture while combining it with their own inner selves. If they return to the ancestral home, they quickly discover that they are now foreigners in their own land, for they have taken on the cultural personality of the new country. At first, this bicultural personality is difficult to live with, but in time it provides the basis for a new synthesis.

This new synthesis is easy to talk about, but it never takes place easily. There is first a deep and profound loneliness, the loneliness of not even being able to con-

ceptualize and verbalize the reasons for the social alienation. Attempts will be made to "unbe" in order to be. Games will be played. The inner self will be suppressed into an almost total silence. Finally, through struggle and suffering the new identity will begin to emerge and the self will be able to shout out with joy: *"I am."* This new identity does not eliminate either the original culture of the parents or the culture of the new country. On the contrary, it enriches both by opening up each to the possibilities of the other.

Aurora Levins Morales

This Jewish Puerto Rican feminist poet possesses a very rich cultural heritage. Levins Morales's assertive pride in who she is and in the many strands that converge to form her identity is expressed with vivacity and an impressive mastery of language in our selections "Puertoricanness," and "Child of the Americas" from the collection *Getting Home Alive* (1986), which Levins Morales coauthored with her mother, Rosario Morales, whose spirited and humorous "I Am What I Am" concludes this volume.

Puertoricanness

It was Puerto Rico waking up inside her. Puerto Rico waking her up at 6 a.m., remembering the rooster that used to crow over on 59th Street, and the neighbors all cursed "that damn rooster," but she loved him, waited to hear his harsh voice carving up the Oakland sky and eating it like chopped corn, so obliviously sure of himself, crowing all alone with miles of houses around him. She was like that rooster.

Often she could hear them in her dreams. Not the lone rooster of 59th Street (or some street nearby . . . she had never found the exact yard though she had tried), but the wild, careening, hysterical roosters of 3 a.m. in Bartolo, screaming at the night and screaming again at the day.

It was Puerto Rico waking up inside her, uncurling and shoving open the door she had kept neatly shut for years and years. Maybe since the first time she was an immigrant, when she refused to speak Spanish in nursery school. Certainly since the last time, when at thirteen she found herself between languages, between countries, with no land feeling at all solid under her feet. The mulberry trees of Chicago, that first summer, had looked so utterly pitiful beside her memory of flamboyan and banana and. . . . No, not even the individual trees and bushes but the mass of them, the overwhelming profusion of green life that was the home of her comfort and nest of her dreams.

The door was opening. She could no longer keep her accent under lock and key. It seeped out, masquerading as dyslexia, stuttering, halting, unable to speak the word which will surely come out in the wrong language, wearing the wrong clothes. Doesn't that girl know how to dress? Doesn't she know how to date, what to say to a professor, how to behave at a dinner table laid with silver and crystal and too many forks?

Yesterday she answered her husband's request that she listen to the whole of his thoughts before commenting by screaming, "This is how we talk. I will not wait sedately for you to finish. Interrupt me back!" She drank pineapple juice three or four times a day. Not Lotus, just Co-op brand, but it was *piña*, and it was sweet and yellow. And she was letting the clock slip away from her into a world of morning and afternoon and night, instead of "five-forty-one-and-twenty seconds—beep."

There were things she noticed about herself, the Puertoricanness of which she had kept hidden all these years, but which had persisted as habits, as idiosyncrasies of her nature. The way she left a pot of food on the stove all day, eating out of it whenever hunger struck her, liking to have something ready. The way she had lacked food to offer Elena in the old days and had stamped on the desire to do so because it *was* Puerto Rican: *Come, mija . . . ¿quieres café?* The way she was em-

barrassed and irritated by Ana's unannounced visits, just dropping by, keeping the country habits after a generation of city life. So unlike the cluttered datebooks of all her friends, making appointments to speak to each other on the phone days in advance. Now she yearned for that clocklessness, for the perpetual food pots of her childhood. Even in the poorest houses a plate of white rice and brown beans with calabaza or green bananas and oil.

She had told Sally that Puerto Ricans lived as if they were all in a small town still, a small town of six million spread out over tens of thousands of square miles, and that the small town that was her country needed to include Manila Avenue in Oakland now, because she was moving back into it. She would not fight the waking early anymore, or the eating all day, or the desire to let time slip between her fingers and allow her work to shape it. Work, eating, sleeping, lovemaking, play— to let them shape the day instead of letting the day shape them. Since she could not right now, in the endless bartering of a woman with two countries, bring herself to trade in one-half of her heart for the other, exchange this loneliness for another perhaps harsher one, she would live as a Puerto Rican lives *en la isla,* right here in north Oakland, plant the *bananales* and *cafetales* of her heart around her bedroom door, sleep under the shadow of their bloom and the carving hoarseness of the roosters, wake to blue-rimmed white enamel cups of *jugo de piña* and plates of *guineo verde,* and heat pots of rice with bits of meat in them on the stove all day.

There was a woman in her who had never had the chance to move through this house they way she wanted to, a woman raised to be like those women of her childhood, hardworking and humorous and clear. That woman was yawning up out of sleep and into this cluttered daily routine of a Northern California writer living at the edges of Berkeley. She was taking over, putting doilies on the word processor, not bothering to make appointments, talking to the neighbors, riding miles on the bus to buy *bacalao,* making her presence felt . . . and she was all Puerto Rican, every bit of her.

Child of the Americas

I am a child of the Americas,
a light-skinned mestiza of the Caribbean,
a child of many diaspora, born into this continent at a crossroads.

I am a U.S. Puerto Rican Jew,
a product of the ghettos of New York I have never known.
An immigrant and the daughter and granddaughter of immigrants.
I speak English with passion: It's the tool of my consciousness,
a flashing knife blade of crystal, my tool, my craft.

I am Caribeña, island grown, Spanish is in my flesh,
ripples from my tongue, lodges in my hips:
the language of garlic and mangoes,
the singing in my poetry, the flying gestures of my hands.
I am of Latinoamerica, rooted in the history of my continent:
I speak from that body.

I an not african. Africa is in me, but I cannot return.
I am not taína. Taíno is in me, but there is no way back.
I am not european. Europe lives in me, but I have no home there.

I am new. History made me. My first language was spanglish.
I was born at the crossroads
and I am whole.

Rosario Morales
I Am What I Am

I am what I am and I am U.S. American   I haven't wanted to say it because if I did you'd take away the Puerto Rican but now I say go to hell   I am what I am and you can't take it away with all the words and sneers at your command   I am what I am   I am Puerto Rican   I am U.S. American   I am New York Manhattan and the Bronx   I am what I am   I'm not hiding under no stoop   behind no curtain   I am what I am   I am Boricua as Boricuas come from the isle of Manhattan and I croon sentimental tangos in my sleep and Afro-Cuban beats in my blood and Xavier Cugat's lukewarm latin is so familiar and dear   sneer dear but he's familiar and dear   but not Carmen Miranda who's a joke because I never was a joke   I was a bit of a sensation   See! here's a real true honest-to-god Puerto Rican girl and she's in college   Hey! Mary   come here and look she's from right here   a South Bronx girl and she's honest-to-god in college now   Ain't that something   who woulda believed it   Ain't science wonderful or some such thing   a wonder a wonder.

And someone who did languages for a living stopped me in the subway because how I spoke was a linguist's treat   I mean there it was yiddish and spanish and fine refined college educated english   and irish which I mainly keep in my prayers   It's dusty now   I haven't said my prayers in decades but try my Hail Marrry full of grrrace with the nun's burr with the nun's disdain   it's all true and it's all me   do you know I got an English accent from the BBC   For years in the mountains of Puerto Rico when I was twenty-two and twenty-four and twenty-six   all those young years   I listened to the BBC and Radio Moscow's English english announcers announce and denounce and then I read Dickens all the way through three or four times at least and then later I read Dickens aloud in voices and when I came back to the U.S. I spoke mock-Dickens and mock-British especially when I want to be crisp and efficient I know what I'm doing and you can't scare me   tough   that kind   I am what I am and I'm a bit of a snob too   Shit! why am I calling myself names   I really really dig the funny way the British speak   and it's real it's true   and I love too the singing of yiddish sentences that go with shrugs and hands and arms doing melancholy or lively dances   I love the sound and look of yiddish in the air   in the body   in the streets   in the English language   nooo   so what's new   so go by the grocer and buy some fruit   *oye vey*   *gevalt*   gefilte fish   *raiseleh*

oh and those words   hundreds of them dotting the english language like raisins in the bread   *shnook* and *shlemiel*   *zoftik*   *tush*   *shmata*   all those soft sweet sounds saying sharp sharp things   I am what I am and I'm naturalized Jewish-American   wasp is foreign and new but Jewish-American is old shoe familiar   *shmata* familiar and it's me dears it's me   bagels blintzes and all   I am what I am   Take it or leave me alone.

Appendix

Table 1

Expected percentage growth in selected ethnic populations, 1992–2050:

Asians and Pacific Islanders	412.5%
Latinos	237.5%
American Indians, Eskimos, and Aleutians	109.1%
African Americans	93.8%
Whites	29.4%

Robert Pear, "New Look at the U.S. in 2050 . . ." *New York Times*, 4 December 1992, sec. A, p. 10.

Table 2

Distribution of Latino population by state as of 1990:

State	Latino population	% of state population	% of U.S. Latino population
California	7,687,938	25.8%	34.4%
Texas	4,339,905	25.5%	19.4%
New York	2,214,026	12.3%	9.9%
Florida	1,574,143	12.2%	7.0%
Illinois	904,446	7.9%	4.0%
New Jersey	739,871	9.6%	3.3%
Arizona	688,338	18.8%	3.1%
New Mexico	579,224	38.2%	2.6%
Colorado	424,302	12.9%	1.9%

Jeffrey S. Passel, "Demographic Profile," *Report on the Americas,* vol. 26, no. 2, (September 1992), p. 21.

Table 3

Distribution of Latino ethnic groups in New York City, Los Angeles County, and the Miami metropolitan area:

New York City

	% of city population	% of city Latino population
Puerto Rican origin	12.2%	50.3%
Dominican	4.5%	18.7%
Colombian	1.2%	4.7%
Ecuadorian	1.1%	4.4%
Mexican	.8%	3.5%
Cuban	.8%	3.1%
Total:	24 %	

Los Angeles County

	% of county population	% of county Latino population
Mexican	28.4%	76.2%
Salvadoran	2.9%	7.7%
Guatemalan	1.4%	3.8%
Cuban	.5%	1.4%
Puerto Rican	.5%	1.2%
Total:	37.3%	

Miami Metropolitan area

	% of metropolitan area population	% of metropolitan area Latino population
Cuban	28.6%	59.4%
Nicaraguan	3.8%	7.8%
Puerto Rican	3.8%	7.6%
Colombian	2.8%	5.6%
Total:	49.2%	

Report on the Americas, vol. 26, no 2, (September 1992), pp. 28, 35, and 40, respectively.

Table 4

Generation, Nativity, and Language Use Among Selected Foreign-Language Origin Groups, 1976

Ethnicity	Age	% Born in United States	Mother tongue only	Mother tongue mainly	English mainly or only
Mexican	5–17	89%	3%	19%	78%
	18+	68%	21%	23%	56%
Cuban	5–17	42%	1%	26%	73%
	18+	3%	33%	41%	26%
Central and South American	5–17	60%	7%	19%	74%
	18+	7%	26%	29%	45%

David E. López, *Language Maintenance and Shift in the United States Today*, vol. 1, (July 1982), quoted in Portes and Rumbaut, *Immigrant America*, pp. 206–207.

Table 5

Monolingualism and Bilingualism Among Hispanic Adults in the United States, by Nativity, 1976
Language Usually Spoken (%)

Ethnicity	18 years +	Mother Tongue only	Mother Tongue mainly	English mainly or only
Mexican				
Foreign born	32%	50%	28%	22%
U.S. born	68%	7%	21%	72%
Puerto Rican				
Island born	80%	27%	41%	32%
Mainland born	20%	0%	16%	84%
Cuban				
Foreign born	97%	34%	41%	25%
United States born	3%	1%	19%	80%
Central American and South American				
Foreign born	93%	27%	31%	42%
United States born	7%	0%	4%	96%

David E. López, *Language Maintenance,*vol 3 (July 1982), quoted in Portes and Rumbaut, *Immigrant America*, p. 208.)

Table 6

Family Statistics: Latinos, Latino ethnic groups, and non-Latinos

	Median family income	below poverty level	single female head
All Latinos	23,446	23.4	23.1
Mexican	22,245	19.6	25.7
Puerto Rican	19,933	30.4	38.9
Cuban	31,262	12.5	18.9
Central and South American	25,460	16.8	25.0
Non-Latino families	35,183	9.2	16.0

NACLA, *Report on the Americas,* vol 26, no. 2 (September 1992), p. 24.

Bibliography

Part 1 The Ties That Bind: *La Familia*

Victor Villaseñor. *Rain of Gold*. Houston: Arte Público Press, 1992, pp. 362–364, 366, 381–385, 536–539.

Rolando Hinojosa. "Sweet Fifteen," *Texas Monthly*, vol. 16 (1988): pp. 96–99.

Sandra Cisneros. "Papa Who Wakes Up Tired in the Dark," "Alicia Who Sees Mice." *The House on Mango Street*. Houston: Arte Público Press, 1985, pp. 53, 32.

Edward Rivera. *Family Installments*: *Memories of Growing Up Hispanic*. New York: Penguin, 1982, pp. 202–219.

Danny Santiago. *Famous All Over Town*. New York: Simon & Schuster, 1983, pp. 103–111.

Carlos Cumpián. "After Calling." *Coyote Sun*. Chicago: MARCH/Abrazo Press, 1990, p. 12.

Roberto G. Fernández. "Raining Backwards." *Raining Backwards*. Houston: Arte Público Press, 1988, pp. 142–149.

Part 2 *Buenos Días, Mi Dios: La Religión*

Roberta Fernández. "Filomena." *Intaglio*: *A Novel in Six Stories*. Houston: Arte Público Press, 1990, pp. 63–87.

Carlos Cumpián. "Coyote Sun." *Coyote Sun*. Chicago: MARCH/Abrazo Press, 1990.

Tomás Rivera. *Y no se lo tragó la tierra . . . And the Earth Did Not Devour Him*. Tr. by Evangelina Vigil-Piñón. Houston: Arte Público Press, 1992, pp. 114–117, 135.

Moisés Sandoval. "The Future of the Hispanic Church." *On the Move, A History of the Hispanic Church in the United States*. Maryknoll, N.Y.: Orbis Books, 1990, pp. 131–136.

Virginia Sánchez Korrol. "In Search of Unconventional Women: Histories of Puerto Rican Women in Religious Vocations Before Midcentury." *Unequal Sisters: A Multicultural Reader in U.S. Women's History*. Edited by Ellen Carol DuBois and Vicki L. Ruiz. New York: Routledge, 1992, pp. 322–332.

Eldin Villafañe. *The Liberating Spirit: Toward an Hispanic American Pentecostal Social Ethic*. Lanham, Md.: University Press of America, 1992, pp. 112–119.

Part 3 All for One and One for All: *La Comunidad*

Dolores Prida. "Savings." *Beautiful Señoritas and Other Plays*. Edited and introduced by Judith Weiss, Houston: Arte Público Press, 1991, pp. 71–116.

Part 4 We Come Bearing Gifts: *Las Artes*

Dolores Prida. "The Show Does Go On." *Breaking Boundaries: Latina Writing and Critical Readings*. Edited by Asunción Horno-Delgado, Eliana Ortega, Nina M. Scott, and Nancy Saporta Sternbach. Amherst: University of Massachusetts Press, 1989, pp. 181–188.

Nicholasa Mohr. "Puerto Rican Writers in the United States, Puerto Rican Writers in Puerto Rico: A Separation Beyond Language." *The Americas Review*, vol. 15, No. 2 (Summer 1987): pp. 87–92.

Sherezada "Chiqui" Vicioso, "An Oral History." *Breaking Boundaries: Latina Writing and Critical Readings*. Edited by Asunción Horno-Delgado, Eliana Ortega, Nina M. Scott, and Nancy Saporta Sternbach. Amherst: University of Massachusetts Press, 1989, pp. 220–234.

Juan Flores. "'Bumbún' and the Beginnings of Plena Music." *Divided Borders: Essays on Puerto Rican Identity*, Houston: Arte Público Press, 1993, pp. 85–91.

Part 5 In the Belly of the Beast: (Im)migration and Exile

Judith Ortiz Cofer. "Arrival," "Birthplace," In Roberto Durán, Judith Ortiz Cofer, and Gustavo Pérez Firmat, *Triple Crown: Chicano, Puerto Rican, and Cuban-American Poetry*. Arizona State University, Tempe, Ariz.: Bilingual Press/Editorial Bilingüe, 1987, pp. 88, 84.

Roberto Durán. "Border Towns," "Super Freak." In Roberto Durán, Judith Ortiz Cofer, and Gustavo Pérez Firmat, *Triple Crown: Chicano, Puerto Rican, and Cuban-American Poetry*. Arizona State University, Tempe, Ariz.: Bilingual Press/Editorial Bilingüe, 1987, pp. 59, 33.

Ariel Dorfman. "Something Must Be Happening to My Antennas," "Prologue: That Deafening Noise Is the Garbage Truck." In *Last Waltz in Santiago*. Translated by Edith Grossman with author. New York: Viking Press, 1988, pp. 63–64, 57.

Beatriz Badikian. "Ragdale Evenings." In Badikian, Cisneros, Cortéz, Cumpián, Gallaher, López-Castro, and Niño, *Emergency Tacos*. Chicago: MARCH/Abrazo Press, 1989, p. 9.

Juan Armando Epple. "Garage Sale People." Translated by R. M. Jackson. In *Paradise Lost or Gained? The Literature of Hispanic Exile*. Edited by Fernando Alegría and Jorge Ruffinelli. Houston: Arte Público Press, 1990, pp. 69–75.

Achy Obejas. "Sugarcane." In *Woman of Her Word: Hispanic Women Write*. Edited by Evangelina Vigil. Houston: Arte Público Press, 1983, pp. 48–49.

Carolina Hospital. "Dear Tía." In *Cuban American Writers, Los Atrevidos*. Edited and introduced by Carolina Hospital. Princeton: Ediciones Ellas/Linden Lane Press, 1988, p. 169.

Pat Mora. "Elena." in *Woman of Her Word: Hispanic Women Write*. Edited by Evangelina Vigil. Houston: Arte Público Press, 1983, p. 61.

Part 6 "My Roots Are Not Mine Alone"*: *La Identidad Cultural*

*From Aurora Levins Morales and Rosario Morales, *Getting Home Alive,* p. 109.

Gustavo Pérez Firmat. "Dedication." In Roberto Durán, Judith Ortiz Cofer, Gustavo Pérez Firmat. *Triple Crown, Chicano, Puerto Rican and Cuban-American Poetry.* Arizona State University, Tempe, Ariz.: Bilingual Press/Editorial Bilingüe, 1987, p. 127.

Rudolfo Anaya. *Bless Me, Ultima.* Berkeley: Tonatiuh-Quinto Sol, 1972, pp. 48–55.

Pat Mora. "Señora X No More," "A Voice." *Communion.* Houston: Arte Público Press, 1991, pp. 15, 74–75.

Carolina Hospital. "Finding Home." *Paradise Lost or Gained? The Literature of Hispanic Exile.* Edited by Fernando Alegría and Jorge Ruffinelli, Houston: Arte Público Press, 1990, p. 109.

Gloria Anzaldúa. "To live in the Borderlands means you . . ." *Borderlands/La Frontera, the New Mestiza.* San Francisco: Aunt Lute Books, 1987, pp. 194–195.

Américo Paredes, *"With His Pistol in His Hand": A Border Ballad and Its Hero.* Austin: University of Texas, 1958, pp. 5, 241–247, 154–158.

Robert Pazmiño. "Double Dutch: Reflections of a Hispanic North American on Multicultural Religious Education." *Voces/Voices from the Hispanic Church.* Edited by Justo González, Nashville: Abingdon Press, 1992, pp. 137–145.

Virgil P. Elizondo. *The Future Is Mestizo: Life Where Cultures Meet.* Bloomington: Meyer Stone Books, 1988, pp. 99–100.

Aurora Levins Morales. "Puertoricanness," "Child of the Americas." Rosario Morales. "I Am What I Am." Aurora Levins Morales and Rosario Morales. *Getting Home Alive.* Ithaca, N.Y.: Firebrand Books, 1986, pp. 84–86, 50, 138–139.

Notes

Preface

1. David González, "What's the Problem with 'Hispanic'? Just Ask a 'Latino'," *New York Times*, 15 November 1992.

Introduction: Latinos, Past and Present

1. Robert Pear, "New Look at the U.S. in 2050: Bigger, Older and Less White," *New York Times*, 4 December 1992, sec. A, pp. 1, 10.

2. Ibid.

3. Roberto Suro, "Generational Chasm Leads to Cultural Turmoil for Young Mexicans in U.S.," *New York Times*, 20 January 1992, sec. A, p. 11.

4. Ibid., p. 10.

5. See Appendix, Table 2.

6. Allan Figueroa Deck, S. J., *The Second Wave* (New York: Paulist Press, 1989). See also *Report on the Americas*, vol. 26, no. 2, (September 1992), p. 18. See also Appendix, Table 3.

7. Karen De Witt, "Minority Enrollment in Colleges Rose in Late 1980's, Report Says," *New York Times*, 20 January 1992, Sec. A, p. 11.

8. Alejandro Portes and Rubén Rumbaut, *Immigrant America* (Berkeley: University of California, 1990).

9. Ibid., pp. 202, 204. See also Appendix, Tables 4 and 5.

10. Carey McWilliams, *North From Mexico,* 2nd ed., updated by Matt Meier (New York: Praeger, 1990).

11. Ibid., p. 18.

12. Ibid., pgs. 30–35. See also Alvar Nuñez Cabeza de Vaca, *Adventures in the Unknown Interior of America* , tr. Cyclone Covey (New York: Collier Books, 1961).

13. McWilliams, p. 33.

14. Ibid., p. 41.

15. Deck, p. 48, and Moisés Sandoval, *On the Move, A History of the Hispanic Church in the United States* (New York: Orbis, 1990), p. 27.

16. Sandoval, p. 29.

17. Ibid., p. 51.

18. Ibid., p. 53.

19. Sandoval, pp. 54–55, also McWilliams, pp. 221–231.

20. Kitty Calavita, *Inside the State, The Bracero Program, Immigration and the I.N.S.,* (New York: Routledge, 1992).

21. McWilliams, p. 315.

22. Ibid., p. 279.

23. Sandoval, p. 98.

24. See Jorge Huerta, "Labor Theatre, Street Theatre and Community Theatre in the Barrios, 1965–1983," in Nicolás Kanellos, ed., *Hispanic Theatre in the United States* (Houston: Arte Público Press, 1984), pp. 62–70.

25. Matt S. Meier, "Politics, Education, and Culture," in McWilliams, p. 292.

26. Rudolfo A. Anaya and Francisco Lomelí, eds., *Aztlán: Essays on the Chicano Home-land* (Albuquerque: University of New Mexico Press, 1989).

27. Sandoval, pp. 52–53, 108.

28. Ibid., p. 108.

29. "Puerto Rico Again Embraces English," *Chicago Tribune*, 23 January 1993.

30. "'Inglés, No!' Puerto Ricans Shout," *New York Times,* 25 January 1993.

31. Joseph P. Fitzpatrick, *Puerto Rican Americans: The Meaning of Migration to the Main-land*, 2nd ed., (New York: Prentice-Hall, 1987), p. 20.

32. Ibid., p. 21.

33. National Public Radio program "Casitas: Little Houses in the Barrio," 23 June 1992.

34. Fitzpatrick, p. 11.

35. Ibid., p. xii.

36. Ibid., p. 12.

37. Ibid., p. 45.

38. Ibid., p. 92.

39. Ibid., p. 100.

40. Ibid., p. 56.

41. Ibid., pgs. 55–57.

42. Sandoval, p. 106; also José Llanes, *Cuban Americans: Masters of Survival* (Cambridge, Mass: Abt Books), 1982, pp. 8,9, 135.

43. See Appendix, Table 6. For an account of the persecution of homosexuals in Cuba and of the extremely difficult experience of adjusting to exile in the United States, see Reinaldo Arenas, *Before Night Falls,* trans. Dolores M. Koch (New York: Viking, 1993).

44. Portes and Rumbaut, p. 115.

45. Earl Shorris, *Latinos: A Biography of the People* (New York: W. W. Norton & Company, 1992), p. 74.

46. Ibid., p. 65.

47. Llanes, p. 206.

48. Shorris, p. 66.

49. Ibid., p. 74.

50. Portes and Rumbaut, p. 118.

51. Ibid., p. 92.

52. Ibid., pgs. 20–21.

53. Ibid., p. 21. See also Alejandro Portes and Alex Stepick *City on the Edge: The Transfor-mation of Miami* (Berkeley: University of California Press, 1993).

54. Llanes, p. 131.

55. Ibid., p. 132.

56. Ibid.

57. Ibid., p. 201.

58. Ibid., p. 206.

59. Deck, p. 95.

60. Fitzpatrick, p. 9.

61. Virgil Elizondo, *The Future Is Mestizo: Life Where Cultures Meet* (Bloomington, Ind.: Meyer Stone Books, 1988).

Part 1   The Ties That Bind: *La Familia*

1. Deck, p. 11.

2. See Appendix, Table 6.

3. Fitzpatrick, pp. 68–91. See also Norma Williams, *The Mexican American Family, Tradition and Change* (Dix Hills, N.Y.: General Hall, Inc., 1990).

Part 2   *Buenos Días, Mi Dios: La Religión*

1. Fitzpatrick, p. 120.

2. Fitzpatrick, p. 119.

3. Fitzpatrick, p. 120.

4. See Joseph M. Murphy, *Santería: African Spirits in America* (Boston: Beacon Press, 1993).

Moisés Sandoval, "The Future of the Hispanic Church"

1. Maria de Jesus Ybarra, "Los Hispanos en el Noroeste: Primera Migración, 1774–1820," an unpublished paper citing research by Erasmo Gamboa and T. J. St. Hilaire.

2. Edward P. Dozier, *The Pueblo Indians of North America* (New York: Holt, Rinehart & Winston, 1970), p.45.

3. Frederick Webb Hodge, George P. Hammond, and Agapito Rey, *eds., Fray Alonso de Benavides' Revised Memorial of 1634* (Albuquerque: The University of New Mexico Press, 1945), p.68.

Virginia Sánchez Korrol, "In Search of Unconventional Women: Histories of Puerto Rican Women in Religious Vocations Before Midcentury"

Reprinted with permission from the author and the *Oral History Review*, vol 16, Fall 1988.

1. Oral histories with the Reverends Leoncia Rosado and Aimee García Cortese were taped during the winter of 1985 by the author and Dr. Benjamín Alicéa, New Brunswick Theological Seminary, with the purpose of elucidating a little-known period in the history of the Puerto Rican community in New York City. The interview with Reverend Rosado was conducted in Spanish and translated by the author for this essay. The interview with Sister Carmelita was conducted and taped, by Professor John Vazquez, New York City Technical College, when he directed one of the earliest oral history projects on the Brooklyn Puerto Rican Community in Conjunction with the Brooklyn Historical Society.

2. Joseph P. Fitzpatrick, *Puerto Rican Americans: The Meaning of Migration to the Mainland,* second edition. (Englewood Cliffs, N.J.: Prentice-Hall,Inc., 1987) p. 135.

3. Virginia Sánchez Korrol, *From Colonia to Community: The History of Puerto Ricans in New York City, 1917–1948* (Westport, Conn.: Greenwood Press, 1983), ch. 4. See also: "On the Other Side of the Ocean: Work Experiences of Early Puerto Rican Migrant Women in New York," in *Caribbean Review* (January 1979): pp. 23–30. Altagracia Ortiz explores the role of women in the garment industry from the 1940s to the fifties in "Puerto Rican Women in the ILGWU, 1940–1950," paper presented at the Women's Studies Conference, Brooklyn College, April 1984. For a broader and

comparative analysis see Palmira Ríos, "Puerto Rican Women in the United States Labor Market," *Line of March,* no. 18 (Fall 1985).

4. Numerous articles have appeared on notable women in Puerto Rican society. Among the most substantive are Isabel Picó de Hernández, "The History of Women's Struggle for Equality in Puerto Rico." and Norma Valle, "Feminism and Its Influence on Women's Organizations in Puerto Rico," in Edna Acosta-Belén, *The Puerto Rican Woman: Perspectives on Culture, History, and Society* (New York: Praeger Press, 1986). For an overview of exceptional women in New York, see: Virginia Sánchez Korrol, "The Forgotten Migrant: Educated Puerto Rican Women in New York City, 1920–1940," in *The Puerto Rican Woman.*

5. Interview with Sister Carmelita Bonilla, Puerto Rican Oral History Project, Brooklyn Historical Society, Brooklyn, N.Y., 1977. See also; Anthony Stevens-Arroyo, "Puerto Rican Struggles in the Catholic Church," in Clara E. Rodriguez et al., *The Puerto Rican Struggle: Essays on Survival in the U.S.* (Maplewood, N.J.: Waterfront Press, 1984).

6. Interview with Sister Carmelita Bonilla.

7. One of the best sources for the Puerto Rican experience in the U.S. during this early period is Cesar Andreu Iglesias, ed., *Memorias de Bernardo Vega* (Rio Piedras, Puerto Rico: Ediciones Huracán, 1977). English translation, *Memoirs of Bernardo Vega,* by Juan Flores, Monthly Review Press, 1984. See also History Task Force, Centro de Estudios Puertorriqueños, *Labor Migration under Capitalism: The Puerto Rican Experience* (New York: Monthly Review Press, 1979), and Sánchez Korrol, *From Colonia to Community,* ch.2.

8. Sánchez Korrol, *From Colonia to Community,* ch. 3. Another account of the community from the twenties to the forties is Jesús Colon's *A Puerto Rican in New York and other Sketches* (New York: International Publishers, 1982). The Federal Writers Project, *The WPA Guide to New York* (New York: Pantheon Books, 1982) offers interesting observations regarding the Manhattan Puerto Rican community.

9. Fitzpatrick, *Puerto Rican Americans,* ch. 8.

10. Ann María Diaz Ramírez, " The Roman Catholic Archdiocese of New York and the Puerto Rican Migration, 1950–1973: A Sociological and Historical Analysis." Ph.D. dissertation, Fordham University, 1983. See also Anthony Stevens-Arroyo, "Puerto Rican Struggles in the Catholic Church," in Rodríguez et al., *The Puerto Rican Struggle,* and Fitzpatrick, *Puerto Rican Americans,* ch. 8.

11. Interview with Sister Carmelita Bonilla. A number of individuals interviewed in my research, including Elizabeth Guanill, former Commissioner of Human Rights, Suffolk County, New York, credit Sister Carmelita for guiding and encouraging them.

12. The Puerto Rican Oral History Project yielded other life experiences which supported Sister Carmelita's perspective. Among these was the interview with Doña Honorina Weber Irizarry.

13. Lawrence R. Chenault, *The Puerto Rican Migrant in New York City* (New York: Russell and Russell, 1970), p. 129. Refer also to the dissertation in progress of Reverend Benjamin Alicéa, "The Puerto Rican Protestant Churches in East Harlem: 1912–1980," Union Theological Seminary, Columbia University, New York.

14. Fitzpatrick, *Puerto Rican Americans,* pp.135–36.

15. Interview with Reverend Leoncia Rosado Rosseau. First Reformed Church, Queens, N.Y., November 1985.

16. Sánchez Korrol, *From Colonia to Community,* ch. 2. See also: History Task Force, *Labor Migration Under Capitalism,* ch.2.

17. Numerous studies have appeared on the migration experience of Puerto Ricans dur-

ing the fifties and sixties. Among these are C. Wright Mills, Clarence Senior, and Rose Goldsen, *The Puerto Rican Journey: New York's Newest Migrants* (New York: Harper & Bros., 1950). Also Elena Padilla, *Up from Puerto Rico* (New York: Columbia University Press, 1958), and Dan Wakefield, *Island in the City: The World of Spanish Harlem* (Boston: Houghton Mifflin, 1959). Personal narratives include Piri Thomas's *Down These Mean Streets* (New York: Alfred Knopf, 1967), Nicholasa Mohr, *Nilda* (New York: Bantam, 1973), and Edward Rivera, *Family Installments* (New York: William Morrow & Co. 1982).

18. Interview with Reverend Leoncia Rosado Rosseau.

19. *Ibid.*

20. Anthony Stevens-Arroyo, "Religion and the Puerto Ricans in New York," in Edward Mapp, ed., *Puerto Rican Perspectives* (Metuchen, N.J.: The Scarecrow Press, Inc. 1974), pp. 119–31.

21. Interviews with missionaries Doña Virginia Martínez, New York, Doña Celina Díaz, Brooklyn, N.Y., and the Reverend Aimee García Cortese, Cross Roads Tabernacle Church, Bronx N.Y., December 1985.

22. Interview with Reverend Leoncia Rosado Rosseau. Reverend Rosado Rosseau's achievements, particularly with the Christian Youth Crusade, were highlighted in an article by Howard Broady, "The Power of Faith," Associated Press, 1959.

23. Interview with Reverend Aimee García Cortese, December 1985.

24. *Ibid.*

25. *Ibid.*

Eldin Villafañe, from "The Liberating Spirit: Toward a Hispanic American Pentecostal Social Ethic"

1. See Eldin Villafañe, *Liberating Spirit: Toward an Hispanic American Pentecostal Social Ethic* (Lanham, Md.: United Press of America, 1992).

2. Joseph P. Fitzpatrick, *Puerto Rican Americans: The Meaning of Migration to the Mainland* (Englewood Cliffs, N.J.: Prentice Hall, 1971), p. 117. Some explain the apparent contradiction of a religiosity that does not attend mass at the institutional church (one Boston study indicated only 31 percent of Hispanic Catholics attended mass regularly, while 69 percent considered itself "Catholic but non-practicing") with a "personal" folk religiosity expressed at home—*velorios* (wakes); *imágenes o altares en el hogar* (religious images and altars); *velas* (candles), *rezar el rosario* (pray the rosary).

3. Melvin Delgado and Denise Humn-Delgado, "Natural Support Systems: Source of Strength in Hispanic Communities," *Social Work* (January 1982), p. 84.

4. See June Macklin, "*Curanderismo* and *Espiritismo*: Complementary Approaches to Traditional Mental Health Services," in Stanley A. West and June Macklin, eds., *The Chicano Experience* (Colorado: Westview Press, 1979).

5. John A. Mackay, *The Other Spanish Christ: A Study on the Spiritual History of Spain and South America* (New York: Macmillan, 1933), p. 98.

6. Orlando E. Costas, *Theology of the Crossroads in Contemporary Latin America* (Amsterdam: Editions Rodopi N.V., 1976), p. 97.

7. Fitzpatrick, *Puerto Rican Americans*, p. 116.

8. Renato Poblete and Thomas F. O'Dea, "Anomie and the 'Quest for Community': The Formation of Sects among the Puerto Ricans of New York," *American Catholic Sociological Review* 21 (Spring 1960): pp. 18–36.

9. Moisés Sandoval, "The Latinization Process," in Moisés Sandoval, ed. *Fronteras: A*

History of the Latin American Church in the USA since 1513 (San Antonio, Tex.: Mexican American Cultural Center, 1983), p. 451.

10. Leo Gebler, Joan W. Moore, Ralph Guzmán, *The Mexican American People* p. 468.

11. Sandoval, "The Latinization Process," p. 451.

12. See Carlos Rosas, "La Música al Servicio del Reino," *Apuntes* 6 (Spring 1986), pp. 3–6.

13. Octavio Paz, "Reflections," *The New Yorker* 17 November 1979, quoted in Ruben P. Armendariz, "Hispanic Heritage and Christian Education," *ALERT* (November 1981): p. 26.

14. Virgilio Elizondo, *Galilean Journey: The Mexican-American Promise* (Maryknoll, N.Y.: Orbis Books, 1983), p. 43.

15. Joan W. Moore and Harry Pachon, *Hispanics in the United States* (Englewood Cliffs, N.J.: Prentice Hall, 1985), p. 96.

16. See Ada María Isasi-Díaz and Yolando Tarango, *Hispanic Women, Prophetic Voice in the Church: Toward an Hispanic Women's Liberation Theology* (New York: Harper & Row, 1988).

17. Mackay, *The Other Spanish Christ,* p. 102.

Part 3   All for One and One for All: *La Comunidad*

1. quoted in Llanes, p. 205.

2. Benedict Anderson, *Imagined Communities,* 2nd ed. (New York: Verso, 1991).

Part 4   We Come Bearing Gifts: *Las Artes*

Dolores Prida, "The Show Does Go On"

This article is partly based on a lecture given at Rutgers, The State University of New Jersey at Newark, February 1987.

1. That was all very nice, dear, but what exactly did you do in what I just saw? *dramaturga* = playwright.

2. "Hey, Rosalía, did you know that my oldest daughter is a *dramaturga*?" "*Dramaturga!* Poor thing! Can it be cured!"

3. Hands up, you bullies.

4. Later on—it was during my third trip—when I noticed that the Indians of a certain island were suspicious of us and reluctant to approach us, I improvised a stage on the stern of the boat, forcing some Spaniards to dance noisily to the sound of drums and castanet, so they could see that we were happy and peaceful people. (But to tell the truth, it was not a very fortunate occasion. The cannibals, unamused by all the heel-tapping and arm-waving, shot all the arrows they had in their canoes at us.)

Sherezada "Chiqui" Vicioso, "An Oral History"

This interview with Dominican poet Chiqui Vicioso was taped and subsequently translated by Nina M. Scott at the Segundo Congreso de Creación Femenina, University of Mayagüez, Puerto Rico, on 17 November 1987. Sincere thanks go to the staff of the University of Mayagüez who aided in the making of the tape.

Juan Flores, "'Bumbún' and the Beginnings of Plena Music"

First published in *Centro Boletín,* 2/2 (Spring 1988): pp. 16–25. It also appears in *Salsiology,* Vernon W. Boggs, ed. (New York: Excelsior, 1992), pp. 59–67.

1. The main source for information on early plena is the book by Félix Echevarría Al-

varado, *La plena: origen, sentido y desarrollo en el folklore puertorriqueño* (Santurce: Express, 1984). Based on interviews with many of the surviving pioneers of the *plena* and their families, and containing photographs and song texts, this unassuming work provides crucial new insights into the history of the form and sets the record straight on many counts. The most valuable historical and political analysis of the *bomba* and *plena* tradition to date is Jorge Pérez, "La bomba y la plena puertorriqueña: ¿Sincretismo racial or transformación histórico-musical?" *Anales* (Havana, Centro de Estudios del Caribe, 1988). Pérez's essay is a first effort to set forth a periodization of the *plena* tradition and also takes issue with many methodological and theoretical assumptions underlying the treatment of the *plena* in the standard writings on Puerto Rican popular music: María Luisa Muñoz, *La música en Puerto Rico* (Sharon, Conn.: Troutman, 1967); and Héctor Campos Parsi, *La gran enciclopedia de Puerto Rico: Música,* vol. 7 (Madrid: Ediciones R, 1976).

Plena has become the topic of broad cultural and sociological interest among Puerto Rican writers over the past decade or so. In his *Literatura y sociedad en Puerto Rico*(1976), José Luis González signaled the key importance of the *plena*, "the most representative genre of modern Puerto Rican folklore," for the study of Puerto Rican literature and culture in the twentieth century, and announced plans for a book on the subject. More recently, Edgardo Rodríguez Juliá's excellent testimonial, *El entierro de Cortijo* (Río Piedras: Huracán, 1983), has done much to kindle interest and understanding among a wide readership, while the ongoing research by such scholars as Angel Quintero Rivera and Rafael Aponte-Ledée promises to add significant new knowledge and approaches.

The present sketch on *plena* beginnings was intended as part of a longer essay to accompany the film on *plena* produced by Pedro Angel Rivera and Susan Zeig. Collaboration on the film project and conversations with my generous and knowledgeable friends René López and Jorge Pérez guided this effort.

Part 5   In the Belly of the Beast: (Im)migration and Exile

1. Emma Lazarus, "The New Colossus," in *Collier's Encyclopedia,* vol. 14 (New York: Collier/Macmillan), 1990, p. 557.
2. *Congressional Quarterly Researcher,* vol. 2, no. 16, (24 April 1992): p. 368.
3. *CQ,* p. 372.
4. *CQ,* p. 374.
5. McWilliams, pp. 62–63.
6. Deck, p. 18.
7. *CQ,* p. 364. See also *Report of the Americas,* vol. 26, no. 1 (July 1992).
8. *CQ,* p. 365.
9. *CQ,* p. 374, and McWilliams/Meier, pp. 317–318.
10. McWilliams/Meier, pp. 317–318. See also Robert Lee Maril, *Poorest of Americans,* (University of Notre Dame Press, 1989), pp. 65–72.
11. *CQ,* p.374.
12. Ibid.
13. See Ann Crittenden, *Sanctuary: A Story of American Conscience and the Law in Collision,* (New York: Weidenfeld & Nicholson, 1988).
14. *CQ,* p. 361. Also, Portes, pp. 235–239, and McWilliams/Meier, p. 317.

Part 6   "My Roots Are Not Mine Alone"*: La Identidad Cultural

*From Aurora Levins Morales and Rosario Morales, *Getting Home Alive.* (Ithaca: Firebrand Books, 1986), p. 109.

1. Fitzpatrick, pp. 8–9.

2. For information on how Cuban and Mexican immigrants view life in the United States, see Alejandro Portes and Robert L. Bach, *Latin Journey: Cuban and Mexican Immigrants in the United States* (Berkeley, Cal.: University of California Press, 1985).

Américo Paredes, "With His Pistol in His Hand": A Border Ballad and Its Hero

1. William James Entwistle, *European Balladry* (Oxford: Clarendon Press, 1939), p. 160.

2. Sylvanus Griswold Morley, "Spanish Ballad Problems: The Native Historical Themes," *Modern Philology* 13 (December 1925): p. 208.

3. *European Balladry,* p. 5.

4. Julio Vicuña Cifuentes, *Romances populares y vulgares recogidos de la tradición oral chilena* (Santiago de Chile: Imprenta Barcelona, 1912), p. xi.

5. Manuel Milá y Fontanals, *De la poesía heroico-popular castellana* (Barcelona: Líbrería de Alvaro Verdaguer, 1896), p. 395.

6. Entwistle, *European Balladry,* p. 310.

7. "Spanish Ballad Problems," p. 208.

8. Mendoza, *El corrido mexicano,* (México: Gráfica Pan-americana, 1954).

Robert W. Pazmiño, "Double Dutch: Reflections of a Hispanic North American on Multicultural Religious Education"

1. Virgilio Elizondo, *Galilean Journey: The Mexican-American Promise* (Maryknoll, N.Y.: Orbis Books, 1983).

2. Orlando Costas, "Evangelizing An Awakening Giant: Hispanics in the U.S.," in *Signs of the Kingdom in the Secular City,* comps. David J. Frenchak and Clinton E. Stockwell, ed. Helen Ujvarosy (Chicago: Covenant Press), p. 57.

3. K. W. Clark, "Galilee," in *The Interpreter's Dictionary of the Bible,* ed. George A. Buttrick (Nashville: Abingdon Press, 1962), pp. 344–347.

4. Anya Peterson Royce, *Ethnic Identity: Strategies of Diversity* (Bloomington: Indiana University Press, 1982), pp, 18–19.

5. Elliott Eisner makes these distinctions in *The Educational Imagination: On the Design and Evaluation of School Programs,* 2nd ed. (New York: Macmillan Publishing Co., 1979), pp. 87–108.

6. Charles Foster, "Double Messages: Ethnocentrism in the Education of the Church," *Religious Education* 82 (Summer 1987): pp. 447–467.

7. Lawrence Cremin, *Public Education* (New York: Basic Books, Inc., 1976), p. 50.

8. See Ricardo García, *Teaching in a Pluralistic Society: Concepts, Models, Strategies* (New York: Harper & Row, 1982), pp. 37–57; and Charles R. Foster, "Double Messages: Ethnocentrism in the Education of the Church" (Nashville: Scarritt Graduate School, 1986).

9. Richard H. de Lone, *Small Futures: Children, Inequality and the Limits of Liberal Reform* (New York: Harcourt Brace Jovanovich, 1979), pp. 153–160.

10. *Teaching in a Pluralistic Society,* pp. 37–45.

11. Ian Malcolm, "The Christian Teacher in the Multicultural Classroom," *Journal of Christian Education,* papers 74 (July 1982): pp. 48–60.

12. "Double Messages," pp. 457–458.

13. *Teaching in a Pluralistic Society,* pp. 8, 105.

14. Marina Herrera, "The Hispanic Challenge," *Religious Education* 74 (September–October 1979), p. 458.

Glossary

A

a fuerza: by force, the hard way

a sus órdenes: at your service

abuela: grandmother

abuelito: grandpa

actos: one-act plays

aguardiente: brandy, liquor

alabados: Spanish hymns of praise

alba: dawn; also a morning prayer or song of praise

altarcitos: little altars; family altars in the home honoring saints or departed family
    members

amigos: friends

ánimo: spirit, energy

año nuevo: new year

artista: artist

así lo quiere Dios: it is God's will

autos sacramentales: medieval Spanish morality plays

B

bacalao: codfish

bailamos: shall we dance

bananales: banana plantations, groves

bandoneón: large concertina, used in Argentina

barrio: neighborhood, usually a Latino neighborhood

bendito: blessed

bochinche: gossip

bodega: grocery store

bodeguero: grocery store owner

bolita: small ball or marble; here it refers to a numbers racket

bomba: Afro-Puerto Rican dance

boricua: Puerto Rican

Borinquen: Puerto Rico

botánica: a type of drug store where healing herbs and religious articles are sold

bracero: agricultural laborer, usually Mexican, admitted to do seasonal labor in the
    bracero program, 1942–1964

brujería: witchcraft

bueno: good, well

buey: ox

burro/a: donkey

C

cacica: chief (female)

cafetales: coffee plantations, groves

caja: box

californios: Californians

calzones: underwear

cambios de humor: mood swings

campesinos: farmers, people from the countryside

canario: canary

cantinas: taverns, bars

cantos, cánticos: songs

caporal: overseer; boss

caribeña: Caribbean; someone from the Caribbean

carne: meat

carreta: cart

casa cualquiera: an ordinary house

casas: houses

casitas: little houses, cultural centers in New York Puerto Rican communities

causa: the cause

centavo: cent

chambelán: male attendant at a *quinceañera* or wedding

cherife: sheriff

chica: girl

chicano: one who is of Mexican descent and living in the United States, political term for Mexican American that gained popularity in the 1960s

chicharrones: fried pork rinds

chicos: boys, kids

chiflor: chimney (New Mexico)

chile verde: green chile

cholo: derogatory term for Mexican American, slang for gang member

cinco de mayo: May 5, commemorates the Mexican victory over the French at Puebla in 1862

cofradías: brotherhoods

cojón: usually in the plural, "cojones," "balls," testicles

colonias: neighborhoods, usually refers to poor communities

colonos: residents of colonias

colquets: coffee (New Mexico)

comadre: best friend (female), someone who is like a family member and can be counted on for financial or emotional assistance

comité de apoyo: support group

compadrazgo: system of ritual kinship based on friendship rather than blood lines

compadre: best friend (male). See definition for "comadre."

comunidades de base: base communities, groups of Christians who meet to study the Bible and apply it to their lives, often to promote social change

con mucho gusto: my pleasure

con pie derecho: on the right foot

¡con safos!: Same to you! (usually an insult)

concientizado: to have raised consciousness; to have been made politically aware

concientizar: to raise awareness

congrio: eel

constancias; proof, official papers

consultas: counsel, advice

contratista: contractor, foreman

conversi: Spanish Jews and Muslims who were forcibly converted to Christianity at the time of the expulsion of non-Christians in 1492

coplas: couplets; verses; short, lyrical stanzas

corrido: Mexican and lower Río Grande popular ballad form, dates from mid-nineteenth century

coyote: coyote; someone who, for a fee, illegally transports immigrants across the Mexico–U.S. border

cuartel: military headquarters

cuarteros: field workers who keep plow animals moving and who clear stones from the path of the plow; so called because they work in groups of four

cubano: Cuban; someone from Cuba

cuchifritos: Puerto Rican fried dish, usually made with pork

cueca: Chilean folk dance

cultura: culture

curandera/o: healer (male or female), female may also be a midwife

cursillo: intense weekend experiences intended to promote religious renewal. Cursillos provide a personal and relational, rather than an institutional, sense of one's faith; usually, but not always Catholic.

D

dama: lady; in this case, a female attendant

danza: dance, also a musical form expressing lyrical and sentimental themes, but sometimes given a narrative form

de ninguna manera: no way

décima: Cuban country ballad, also a folk form of ten-line stanzas

despegados: alienated, detached

destacar a nuestra gente: highlight or emphasize our people; make our people stand out

día de los muertos: Day of the Dead

discutir: discuss, argue

dominicano: Dominican; from the Dominican Republic

doña: title of respect for women

dramaturga: playwright; dramatist (female)
dulces: sweets

E

echar la casa por la ventana: literally, throw the house out the window; "go for broke," spare no expense
educación: education; also refers to one's upbringing
ejido: common land; land grant to a community
el Cristo Español: the Spanish Christ, meaning the Spanish understanding of Christ
el día del pavo: Thanksgiving; literally, Turkey Day
el 2 de noviembre: November 2, All Soul's Day, the Day of the Dead
el eje: the axis, the hub
el niño: the child; here, the Christ child
el norte: the north; commonly used to refer to the United States
él que manda: the one in charge; the decision-maker
el viejo barrio: the old neighborhood
empacadoras: packing plants
empanadas: turnovers, usually filled with meat and vegetables
en buenas condiciones; in good condition
En el nombre del Padre, del Hijo, y el Espíritu Santo: in the name of the Father, the Son, and the Holy Spirit
en la calle: in the street
enchilada; a casserole made of tortillas filled with cheese or meat and baked with a sauce
entiendes: you understand
era naranjero: I was an orange picker
eclavos: slaves
es tuya, Mamá: she's yours; it's yours
está muerto: he's dead
estaba el mero frío: it was freezing cold
eventuales: those who would be hired eventually, later on
excúsame: excuse me
Explícamelo bien: Explain it to me well

F

fábrica: factory, plant
factorías: factories (coll)
fakerías: fake stuff, cheap imitations (coll)
familias: families
fiestas: parties, festivals
fíjate, era pura poesía: I mean to tell you, it was pure poetry
flecha: arrow
flores para los muertos: flowers for the dead
fogón: stove; hearth (New Mexico)

fracasado/a: failure

fricasé de pollo: chicken fricassee

frijol: bean

frontera: frontier, hinterland, border

fue una buena compañera: she was a good companion, a good friend

G

gabacha: Chicano term for a white woman

ganados: livestock

gandul: bean

genta obrera: working people

gente humilde: common people, poor people

gente rica: rich people

gentrificación: gentrification

gran: great

gringa total: total gringo

gringos: North Americans

guacamaya: macaw

guaguancó: Caribbean rhythm

guajiro/a: a rustic, or "hillbilly"; also refers to a Puerto Rican musical style

guardia: national guard of former Nicaraguan dictator Anastasio Somoza

güero: fair, blond (Mexican)

guerrilleros: guerrillas, rebels

guineo verde: green banana

güiro: a bottle gourd, played as a musical instrument

guitarreros: guitarrists

gusto: pleasure

guyabera: popular style of men's shirt worn especially in Mexico, Central America and the Caribbean

H

hablas mucha mierda, mi pana: you talk a lot of shit, my friend

hacendados: owners of large landed estates

hermana: sister

hermandad: sisterhood; brotherhood

hermanos penitentes: penitent brothers, members of a lay religious brotherhood in New Mexico, known for its secrecy, acts of penance, and community service

hidalgo: nobleman

hijitas: little daughters (an endearment); here refers to Las Hijas de María, the Daughters of Mary, a Catholic lay organization for women

hispanos: Hispanics

hongos: mushrooms

hornos: ovens

huaraches: Mexican style leather sandals

huelga: labor strike
huipil: type of loose fitting blouse popular in Mexico and Guatemala
humitas: sweet tamales, corn cakes; popular in South America

I

indio: Indian, Native American
inditas: a type of music in which Native American steps are set to European music

J

jefa de producción: production manager (fem)
jíbaro: country "hillbilly"; also refers to a type of popular Puerto Rican music
jugo de piña: pineapple juice
junkerías: junk stores (coll)

L

la caballona: "horsey"(coll)
La Gran Pascua Florida: Easter celebration
la isla: the island
la liberación femenina: women's liberation
La Lluvia de Oro: Rain of Gold
las mujeres no predican: women do not preach
la vida: life
la vida es más fuerte: life is harder
la Virgen: the Virgin
libre comercio: free trade
licenciado: a lawyer; sometimes used to refer to any professional person with a
    college degree
llano: plain, flatlands
lo corrieron: they ran him out
loro: parrot
los ingleses: the English, people from England
los tiempos cambian: times change
los tiempos de antes: the old days

M

machismo: exaltation of masculinity and of male dominance
machista/macho: someone displaying characteristics of machismo
madrina: godmother
mal de ojo: evil eye
mamá: mom
maquila/maquiladora: factory, assembly plant on the U.S.-Mexican border
marcha: march
mariachis: musicians who play mariachi music, a typical Mexican style of music

marielitos: Cubans who emigrated to the United States in 1980 from the port of Mariel in Cuba

maroma: stunt

más chiquito: smaller

mataquino: matachine, masked dancer

mate: a type of bitter tea popular in parts of Uruguay, Argentina, Chile, and southern Brazil

me portaba como una india: I was acting like an Indian (derogatory usage)

medio ambiente: the environment

mercado: market

mestizaje: racial mixture; miscegenation; most often refers to mixture of European and Native American blood

mestizo: someone of mixed blood; typically part European and part Native American

mexicanos: Mexicans; people from Mexico

mi hija, ahi es donde se aprende: my daughter, there is where you learn

mica: green card, working papers

migra: immigration officials; specifically, from the United States Immigration and Naturalization Service (INS)

mija . . . ¿quieres café?: my darling, would you like coffee?

m'ija: from "mi hija," my daughter (term of endearment); equivalent to darling, dear

milagro: miracle; an offering given in thanksgiving for a miracle, often for a cure or a successful operation

mira, nomás: look here (Mexico)

misterioso: mysterious

mitote: Native American dance

moradas: abodes, houses of worship

morral: deep canvas shoulder bag

muchachas: girls, young women

mucho café: a lot of coffee

mulata/o: mulatto

murre de bien (New Mexico); *muy bien*: very well

música ranchera: "country" music (Mexico)

muy: very

muy católico: very Catholic

muy mexicano: very Mexican

muy poco: very little

N

nada: nothing

nalgas: ass, butt

no deja de ser prisión: it's still prison

no entiendes: you don't understand

no entiendo nada: I don't understand anything

novelas: novels, soap operas

noviazgo: courtship, engagement

novio: boyfriend, fiancé

nuecerías: pecan processing plants

nuestra santa voz indígena: our holy Indian voice (word)

Nuyorican: term for Puerto Ricans living in New York or for something New York Puerto Rican in style

O

ojalá que haiga: would that, I wish that (New Mexico)

orejas: ears, slang for spies

orixás: African gods

oye m'ijito: listen, my child, my son

P

padrino: godfather

pa'fuera: outside

pandereta: a hand-held drum, tambourine

panga: a big plastic boat

papá: dad

partera: midwife

pastorelas, pastores: shepherds' plays

patero: someone who crosses illegal immigrants over the Río Grande into the U.S.

patrón: boss

penitente: a penitent

perdidos: lost

perdón, tícher: pardon me, teacher

personalismo: an approach to life that emphasizes the importance of close, intimate personal relationships

peso: dollar; specifically, the currency in Mexico

petate: straw sleeping mat

piña: pineapple

plena: Afro-Puerto music that is improvised, often has call and response structure, and treats social issues of the day

pobrecito: poor thing

poderosos: powerful ones

politécnico: polytechnic

pollero: one who crosses illegal immigrants over land borders into the United States

Ponceños: people from Ponce, Puerto Rico

por la pura fianza: just for the bail

¿por qué no?: why not?

por si acaso: just in case

porquería: a mess

posadas: inn; lodging; a play about the story of the birth of Christ

preparatoria/prepa: secondary school, preparatory school

promotores: organizers, promoters

pueblo: the people, small town

puertorriqueños: Puerto Ricans; people from Puerto Rico

pura naranja: just oranges

puro caminar: just walking

puro campo: pure coutryside

Q

¡Qué alegría!: what happiness!

¡Qué barbaridad! : how horrible!

¿Qué cosa es eso?: what's that?

¿Qué dices?: what are you saying?

¿Qué es lo que pasa?: what's going on?

querida: beloved, dear (term of endearment)

quinceañera: a girl's fifteenth birthday celebration, somewhat similar to sweet sixteen

R

radio-grabadora: radio/tape recorder

rajetas: split; having betrayed your word

ranchero: rancher, farmer

ranchos: small, humble, rural dwellings, usually in Mexico

retablo: altarpiece, tableau, religious icon, series of wood carvings or of paintings, often on tin, representing an event or story

Reyes: kings, the Three Kings' Day

ricos: rich people

río: river

romance: historical ballad; Spanish ballad form brought to Río Grande area by first settlers in 1749

romances fronterizos: ballads from the United States-Mexico border area

romerías: pilgrimages

ropa vieja: old clothes; refers to a dish made with shredded pork, onions, tomatoes, and garlic

S

sabes: you know

salmos: psalms

salvadoreño: Salvadoran; someone from El Salvador

santería: religion based in both Catholicism and African religions

santero: a saint intercessor, a santería priest, also one who makes figures of saints *santiguador*: a healer

santísimo: most holy

se hinca sobre la fe católica: he prostrates himself before the Catholic faith

se murió la Kika anoche: Kika died last night

seis: Puerto Rican folk dance and its music

señor/a: man/woman; sir/ madam

señor obispo: bishop (coll)

señores: sirs, gentlemen, men

Sí, cómo no: Yes, why not?

sin fronteras: without borders

sindicatos: syndicates, unions

sinvergüenza: one who is shameless, brazen

sociodramas: role playing activities by which Mexican women maquila workers practice defending their rights in the workplace

sofrito: lightly fried; a fried mixture of oil, vegetables, and spices used as a flavor base for cooking

sola mi abuela: only my grandmother

soy: I am

suerte: luck, fortune

susto: bad fright

T

tabaqueros: tobacco workers

taíno: name of extinct Indian people and their language; Caribbean, specifically Puerto Rican

tamales: Mexican dish of minced or shredded meat and red peppers rolled in corn meal, wrapped in a corn husk and steamed

tata/tatita Dios: Daddy, our father God, affectionate indigenous term

te di'te gusto nena: did you enjoy yourself, child?

tejanos: Texans of Mexican descent

tejer: to weave

telenovelas: soap operas

temaskal: bath house, sweat lodge

tertulias: social gatherings, often including poetry and song

tía: aunt

todo: all, everything

trabajitos: little jobs, odd jobs

trigueño: wheat-colored; refers to skin color, mainly a Puerto Rican term

U

un espectáculo: a show

un poco mocho: a little cropped, blunted; refers here to speaking broken Spanish

un saludo a la bandera: a salute to the flag

una brocha: a brush

Una dama. Una verdadera dama: A lady. A real lady.

una india pendeja: an ignorant, backward Indian

V

valorarnos: to value ourselves

vámonos: let's go

varsoviana: a type of New Mexican music brought by Polish immigrants from Warsaw

vasija: pitcher, vessel

vaso: drinking glass

verdadera bosa: real boss (coll)

vieja: old woman, slang for wife

viejitos: old people

vino: wine

virgencita: little virgin

virtuoso: virtuous

vitral: colored glass

Y

y: and

ya no manda: is no longer in charge, no longer calls the shots

yo sebo (New Mexico); *yo soy*: I am

yo traiba (New Mexico); *yo traía*: I brought

Z

zempoalxochitles: marigolds

zócalo: town square, central plaza

Index

Permissions

Part 1   The Ties That Bind—*La Familia*

Excerpts from *Rain of Gold* are reprinted with permission from the publisher of *Rain of Gold* (Houston: Arte Público Press-University of Houston, 1992).

Rolando Hinojosa Smith, "Sweet Fifteen," reprinted with permission from the publisher of *Texas Monthly,* vol. 16, 1988.

Sandra Cisneros, from *The House on Mango Street.* Copyright © 1985 by Sandra Cisneros. Published in the United States by Vintage Books, a division of Random House, Inc., New York, and distributed in Canada by Random House of Canada Limited, Toronto. Reprinted by permission of Susan Bergholz Literary Services, New York.

Family Installments: Memories of Growing Up Hispanic. Copyright © 1982 by Edward Rivera. By permission of William Morrow & Company, Inc.

Famous All Over Town. Copyright © 1983 by Danny Santiago. Reprinted by permission of Simon & Schuster, Inc.

"After Calling," by Carlos Cumpián, is reprinted with permission of the publisher of *Coyote Sun*, MARCH/Abrazo Press, P.O. Box 2890, Chicago, IL 60690.

"Raining Backwards," by Roberto Fernández is reprinted with permission from the publisher of *Raining Backwards* (Houston: Arte Público Press-University of Houston, 1988).

Part 2   *"Buenos Días, Mi Dios"—La Religión*

"Filomena," by Roberta Fernández is reprinted with permission from the publisher of *Intaglio: A Novel in Six Stories* (Houston: Arte Público Press-University of Houston, 1990).

"Coyote Sun," by Carlos Cumpián, is reprinted with permission from the publisher of *Coyote Sun*, MARCH/Abrazo Press, P.O. Box 2890, Chicago, IL 60690.

Song, "Alarru, Chiquito," © 1987, Arsenio Córdova. Published by OCP Publications, 5536 NE Hassalo, Portland, OR 97213. All rights reserved. Used with permission.

Song, "Buenos Días, Mi Dios," © 1982, OCP Publications, 5536 NE Hassalo, Portland, OR 97213. All rights reserved. Used with permission.

"First Communion" and ". . . Before people left," by Tomás Rivera translated by Evangelina Vigil-Piñón are reprinted with permission from the publisher of *Y no se lo tragó la tierra . . . And the Earth Did Not Devour Him* (Houston: Arte Público Press-University of Houston, 1987).

"The Future of the Hispanic Church," by Moisés Sandoval, is reprinted with permission from the publisher of *On the Move, A History of the Hispanic Church in the United States* (Maryknoll, N.Y.: Orbis Books, 1990).

Part 3   All for One and One for All—*La Comunidad*

Part 4   We Come Bearing Gifts—*Las Artes*

Part 5   In the Belly of the Beast—(Im)migration and Exile

Badikian, Cisneros, Cortéz, Cumpián, Gallaher, López-Castro, Niño, *Emergency Tacos*, MARCH/Abrazo Press, P.O. Box 2890, Chicago, IL 60690.

"Garage Sale People," by Juan Armando Epple edited by Fernando Algría and Jorge Rufinelli, is reprinted with permission from the publisher of *Paradise Lost or Gained? The Literature of Hispanic Exile* (Houston: Arte Público Press-University of Houston, 1990).

"Sugarcane," by Achy Obejas edited by Evangelina Vigil-Piñon, is reprinted with permission from the publisher of *Woman of Her Word: Hispanic Women Write* (Houston: Arte Público Press-University of Houston, 1983).

"Dear Tía," by Carolina Hospital, in *Cuban American Writers, Los Atrevidos,* ed. Carolina Hospital (Princeton: Ediciones Ellas/Linden Lane Press, 1988) is reprinted with permission from the publisher.

"Elena," by Pat Mora is reprinted with permission from the publisher of *Chants* (Houston: Arte Público Press-University of Houston, 1985).

Part 6   "My Roots Are Not Mine Alone"—*La Identidad Cultural*

"Dedication," by Gustavo Pérez Firmat, is reprinted with permission of the editor of *Triple Crown: Chicano, Puerto Rican, and Cuban American Poetry* (Arizona State University, Tempe, Ariz.: Bilingual Press/Editorial Bilingüe, 1987).

Excerpt from Rudolfo A. Anaya's *Bless Me, Ultima* is reprinted with permission from the author. Copyright © 1972 Rudolfo A. Anaya. For more information on the novel *Bless Me, Ultima* contact the author.

"Señora X No More" and "A Voice," by Pat Mora are reprinted with permission from the publisher of *Communion* (Houston: Arte Público Press-University of Houston, 1991).

Recipes from Viviana Carballo's "Kitchen Tropicale" column are reprinted with permission from *The Miami Herald*.

"Finding Home," by Carolina Hospital edited by Fernando Alegría and Jorge Ruffinelli, is reprinted with permission from the publisher of *Paradise Lost or Gained? The Literature of Hispanic Exile* (Houston: Arte Público Press-University of Houston, 1990).

"To live in the Borderlands means you . . ." is reprinted from *Borderlands/La Frontera, The New Mestiza* ©1987 by Gloria Anzaldúa. Reprinted with permission from Aunt Lute Books, San Francisco, (415) 558-8116.

Excerpt from *"With His Pistol in His Hand": A Border Ballad and Its Hero*, by Américo Paredes, copyright © 1958. By permission of the author and the University of Texas Press.

"Double Dutch: Reflections of an Hispanic North American on Multicultural Religious Education," by Robert Pazmiño, in *Voces/Voices from the Hispanic Church*, ed. Justo González (Nashville: Abingdon Press, 1992), reprinted with permission from Robert Pazmiño.

Virgil P. Elizondo's excerpt from *The Future Is Mestizo: Life Where Cultures Meet* (Bloomington: Meyer Stone Books, 1988) is reprinted with permission from the publisher.

Photo Credits

All photos by Denis Lynn Daly Heyck except as follows:

Street Festival, San Antonio, Texas, p. 16, Shannon Daly Heyck; Good Friday in Pilsen Neighborhood, Chicago, p. 92, John Prokos; the island of Janitzio, p. 105, María Guadalupe Acosta Zepeda; Adam and Eve, p. 118, Arsenio Córdova; Matachín Dancer, p. 119, Arsenio Córdova; Los Pastores, p. 121, Arsenio Córdova; Abuelos, p. 125, Arsenio Córdova; Street Festival, San Antonio, Texas, pp. 160, 161, Shannon Daly Heyck; Los Pleneros, p. 252, New York Times Pictures; Taos Mountain, p. 317, Arsenio Córdova; Abuelo, p. 370, Arsenio Córdova; Celia Cruz, p. 371, Adam Scher, New York Times Pictures.